IN PURSUIT OF JUSTICE:

The Jurisprudence of Human Rights in Islam

ALSO BY MAHER HATHOUT

Jihad vs. Terrorism

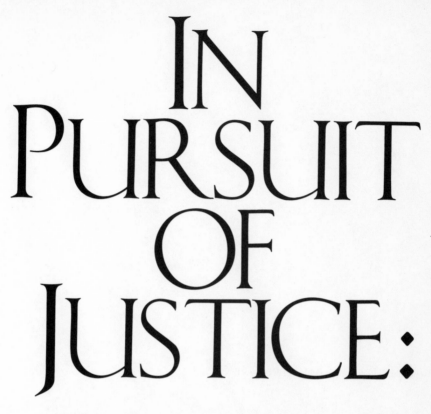

IN PURSUIT OF JUSTICE:

The Jurisprudence of Human Rights in Islam

MAHER HATHOUT
with Uzma Jamil, Gasser Hathout & Nayyer Ali

A Publication of the Muslim Public Affairs Council

Muslim Public Affairs Council
3010 Wilshire Boulevard, # 217
Los Angeles, California 90010
Phone (213) 383-3443 • Fax (213) 383-9674

ISBN 0-9774404-051295 Paperback

Cover and Book Design: Ozman Trad
Cover Photograph: Getty Images

Printed in the United States of America

First Edition

10 9 8 7 6 5 4 3 2 1

Acknowledgements

his book was made possible by the commitment of the Muslim Public Affairs Council. Its financial support and intellectual resources were critical from the start. The essential principles developed here on the vast range of issues tackled have been enunciated by Maher Hathout for over thirty years as one of the leading members of the Muslim-American community. In that sense his thinking lies at the heart of the book. Uzma Jamil did the bulk of the research and writing, and made major analytical and intellectual contributions. Gasser Hathout wrote the two appendices on methodology, and his thinking influenced many aspects of this work. Nayyer Ali wrote several sections, and acted as editor and coordinator for the project. Laila Al-Marayati, as a member of the Research committee of the Muslim Public Affairs Council helped shape the book in its initial stages. Hedab Eltarifi shared her industrious attention to detail in the production process as well. This work would not have been possible without the appreciated efforts of Edina Lekovic, who serves as MPAC's Communications Director. Using her editorial skills, Edina relentlessly pushed this project from the early draft all the way through the final stages of production.

Table of Contents

Historical Synopsis

rabia in the late 6th century of the Common Era (CE) was a backwater of the Middle East. Rome had fallen over a century earlier, collapsing the Roman Empire in Western Europe and ushering in the Dark Ages of the West. The eastern half of the Roman Empire, known as the Byzantine Roman Empire, or Byzantium, continued to thrive. It was Greek-speaking, centered at Constantinople, and controlled most of the Eastern Mediterranean including Egypt, Palestine, and Syria. Further to the east lay the Persian empire. The Arabian Peninsula was a sparsely populated land of independent towns and villages, and nomadic tribes, but with no history of a large-scale central government. Small groups of Christians and Jews lived throughout the region, but the vast majority of the Arabic-speaking inhabitants engaged in a polytheistic religion that centered around pilgrimage to a shrine in Mecca which housed hundreds of idols. This shrine was the cubic-shaped Kaaba, whose exact origin was unknown to the Meccans. According to Meccan tradition, they traced their origin as a people to Abraham (Ibrahim) through Ishmael (Ismail), and believed that the Kaaba had been built by Abraham. The Meccans acknowledged the one God, but believed that he had "daughters" and helpers that were represented by the idols.

Mecca was a small town located mid-way down the west side of the Arabian Peninsula, and it lay along important trade routes. The people of the town also derived significant wealth from the pilgrimage business to the idols in the Kaaba. Most of the inhabitants were members of the tribe of Quraysh, and were divided into clans and families. The social system was abysmal, with all manners of human degradation and suffering. Women were chattel, while slaves were treated with severe harshness. Among the most gruesome of the social aberrations was the practice of female infanticide, carried out by burying alive newborn girls. This came from the overwhelming preference for male children.

Muhammad (peace be upon him, hereafter abbreviated as pbuh), was born an orphan in 570 CE, as his father died before his birth. His mother passed away when he was five, and the boy was raised by his grandfather and subsequently by an uncle. Muhammad (pbuh) married a widow named Khadija at the age of 26 who was 15 years his senior. She had been impressed by the honesty and quality of his service when he led a caravan on behalf of her business.

Over the years, Muhammad (pbuh), who did not share in the idolatry of his people, would spend time in a cave on a hill called Hira where he would meditate. At the age of 40, in the year 610 CE, the Angel Gabriel (Jibril) revealed himself to Muhammad (pbuh) in the cave on Hira, and brought the first revelation of the Quran to him. Muhammad (pbuh) was now the prophet of Islam. He was to convey the two basic points of Islam, monotheism and social justice. Over the next 23 years, Gabriel would bring portions of the Quran to Muhammad (pbuh), often in response to specific circumstances or as an answer to certain questions. Knowing those circumstances can shed much light on the meanings of the text.

For the first three years, the Prophet (pbuh) preached in secret, only to his family and friends. He gradually acquired a few adherents, the first being his wife and the second his cousin Ali.

After the third year, he received the command to preach in public, and began to do so. This public preaching, especially his clear rejection of idolatry, and his critique of the pervasive social injustice, threatened the Meccan social order. In particular, it threatened the lucrative pilgrimage business. Meccan society turned against him, and the next ten years would be spent under varying levels of persecution.

In 623 CE, the thirteenth year of his Prophethood, he had convinced the people of Yathrib, a town to the north of Mecca, to accept his message and to provide him and his followers a new home. Preparations were made for the migration to the new city, but the Meccans feared what might become of Muhammad (pbuh) outside of their control. They attempted to murder him but the Prophet (pbuh) avoided the trap and made his way to Yathrib, henceforth known as Medina. This migration, known as the *hijra*, is the seminal moment in the history of the Muslims, and the Islamic calendar dates from that year.

In Medina, which was now a mixed city of Muslims, several Jewish tribes, and pagans, a Compact was drawn up that acknowledged the political authority of the Prophet (pbuh) and the rights and duties of all the components of this pluralistic society.

Two years after arriving in Medina, a Meccan army of about 1000 moved north to confront the Prophet (pbuh). With about 300 men he engaged the Meccans at the wells of Badr. This was the first time the Prophet (pbuh) took up arms in a conflict. The battle of Badr ended in a Muslim victory.

The Meccans returned the next year with 3,000 men intending to obtain revenge. Muhammad (pbuh) set out with 1000 and fought the battle of Uhud. Early in the battle, the Muslims appeared to be on the verge of another victory, but this turned to defeat as archers left to guard the rear deserted their posts in search of war booty, and a Meccan cavalry force took advantage. However, although the Meccans won the day's battle, they were too bloodied and exhausted to march on Medina and instead returned home.

Two years after Uhud, the Meccans decided to obliterate the Muslims entirely, and gathered all their desert allies in a grand force of 10,000 men. The Muslims had no strength to match them in the field, and adopted the tactic of digging a trench around Medina as a defensive line. The Meccans invested the city and laid siege. To further add to the desperate situation, one of the Jewish tribes of Medina, the Bani Qurayzah, broke the Compact and joined the Meccans.

But the besieging army then was assaulted by the weather as a terrible storm blew in for three days. This greatly affected the Meccan allies who had been anticipating an easy victory and not a siege in difficult conditions. The Quraysh too were unwilling to bear the conditions, and one of their leaders gave the order to retire. The siege collapsed. For Bani Qurayzah, the consequences were worse. They retired to their forts but were reduced in a siege by the Muslims. What happened next is a historical mystery. The Quran only refers to the events in a very vague manner. But Ibn Ishaq, the first man to write a biography of the Prophet (pbuh) roughly 90 years after the Hijra, claims that the Bani Qurayzah asked that judgment on them for breach of the Compact be pronounced by a Muslim who was related to them and who they felt would be lenient. This was agreed to. He supposedly declared that all adult males (700 men) be killed and the rest of the tribe sold into slavery. There are no contemporary records or Quranic verses that support this story, and even major scholars who were contemporaries of Ibn Ishaq (such as Ibn Malik[1]) declared the story to be false. Given that in all of the battles that the Prophet (pbuh) fought the combined death toll was less than 1000, it is unlikely that the Quran would have been silent on such a major episode.

In 629 CE, the Prophet (pbuh) set out with 1,400 followers to perform the first *Hajj*, or pilgrimage to the Kaaba in Mecca. For Muslims, the Kaaba was the first House of God, built by Abraham and dedicated to the worship of the true God. They intended to return it to its rightful purpose. The Meccans had no intention of allowing Muhammad (pbuh) to enter the city, and blocked him. A negotiation ensued, which resulted in the treaty of Hudaybiyah. This treaty called for a ten-year truce between the Muslims and their pagan allies, and the Meccans and their allies. In addition, the Muslims would be allowed to carry out the Haj each year starting the following year.

In 631, the Meccans attacked and massacred a clan from a pagan ally of the Muslims, a direct and deliberate breach of the treaty. In the intervening two years, Muslim power had grown tremendously as a result of large-scale conversions in Arabia. The Prophet (pbuh) as a result was able to march on Mecca with an army of 12,000. The Meccans could not stand in face of such a force, and surrendered. The Prophet's response was a blanket amnesty for all the Meccans, with a handful of exceptions for a few war criminals. He then, along with Ali, cleansed the Kaaba of idols.

The next year, the Prophet (pbuh) consolidated his position in the Arabian Peninsula. From all over, the desert tribes and small towns announced their allegiance to the new religion. The next year, 633 CE, was the end of his Prophethood, and he passed away at the age of 63, leaving behind a single daughter as his only biological heir.

The fledgling Muslim community now had a quandary. There were no instructions on how to order the newly formed state or who should have political power. The institution of the caliphate was created, and the first caliph was Abu Bakr, followed by Umar, Othman, and finally Ali, the Prophet's cousin and son-in-law, and the father of his two grandchildren Hassan and Hussain. Each of these caliphs came into the office through a different mechanism.

The time of the first four caliphs, all of whom were close friends and companions (*sahaba*) of the Prophet (pbuh), was tumultuous. There was civil war, conflicts with Byzantium, expansion into Egypt, Syria, and Iraq, and state-building. Three of the four caliphs died from political assassination. Those who felt that the Prophet's family, through Ali and his sons, should rule, became a separate movement in Islam and this political division led to the Shi'a/Sunni split. The Shi'a were the party of Ali. All Muslims still view this period as a "golden age" morally, as the four caliphs are referred to as "rightly-guided".

After Ali's assassination, the caliphate was moved to Damascus in Syria, and fell into the hands of Muawiyah, a member of the Quraysh. After his death, his son Yazid succeeded him, and a dynastic system was born. Yazid saw Hussain, Ali's son, as his chief rival, and had his army kill him and his entourage at Karbala in modern Iraq. This massacre is marked in the calendar as the day of Ashura.

The new dynastic model owed much to the imperial systems of the Near East, and this first Muslim dynasty, known as the Ummayyads, ruled for over a century. During their time, Arab armies conquered all of North Africa and Spain, and most of Anatolia. They also overwhelmed the Persian Empire and reached what is now southern Pakistan (Sindh). They were stopped at the gates of Constantinople in the Balkans, and in Western Europe at the battle of Tours by the Franks about a hundred miles south of Paris.

In the 8th century, the Ummayyads were overthrown by the Abbasids, except in Spain, where an Ummayyad remained on the throne.

The Ummayyad/Abbasid period was a time of cultural and scientific achievement of the highest order. Over the next centuries Muslims would make great contributions to medicine, philosophy, chemistry, mathematics, optics, astronomy, poetry, the birth of the first universities and hospitals, and many other fields.

In the religious realm there were also major developments. Shortly after the Prophet's death, the Quran was compiled and written down in a complete format that remains unchanged to this day. It is an article of faith that the Quran is the literal word of God, and that it is a completely accurate and unchanged rendition of what was revealed to Muhammad (pbuh). But to understand the Quran, Muslims often turned to oral stories about what he did and said during his life. About a century after his death these stories were collected into the "*Hadiths*". Several scholars made their collections. One, Bukhari, collected over 600,000 such stories, of which all but 6,000 he dismissed as not meeting his criteria for accuracy. Of the remaining, how to interpret them or assess their authenticity has been a major occupation of Islamic religious thought.

Also during these first few centuries, Muslim thinkers and judges began to interpret Quranic principles and *hadiths* in specific matters of law. Out of this interaction was born Islamic jurisprudence. It organized itself into four major Sunni schools of interpretation and the several Shi'a schools. The jurists applied the principle of *ijtihad,* or reasoning, to derive laws.

In the thirteenth century, for complex reasons, the gates of *ijtihad* were "closed" meaning that the four Sunni schools became fixed, and it was by a trend of most jurists that no further change of this heritage was allowed. What is commonly referred to as *sharia* by many Muslims is these schools of Islamic law, or *fiqh*.

By the 11th century, the Abbasids had weakened, and much of the Middle East again lacked a central authority. Meanwhile, Turks from Central Asia had passed through the Muslim lands, converted to Islam, and began to settle in Anatolia, where they were gradually pushing back the Byzantine Greeks. In this unsettled environment came the First Crusade out of Western Europe. The Crusaders marched unmolested all the way to Jerusalem, and captured the town in 1099, a victory they capped by then putting to death every Muslim and Jew inside.

Over the next hundred years, the Crusaders were gradually worn down, and Jerusalem was retaken in 1187. Far to the west, Muslim Spain was undergoing a gradual decline as well, as the Christian Reconquista was pushing south down the Iberian Peninsula.

In the 13th century, the Muslim world suffered its greatest calamity as the Mongols swept down and overran all of the Middle East until being stopped at Ain Jalut in Sinai by an Egyptian army. The Mongols left an unbelievable trail of devastation in their wake.

Out of this debris, three new empires rose. The Ottoman Turks in the West, the Persians in the center, and the Moghuls in India. These empires dominated the Muslim world into the 18th century and based their power on gunpowder technology. The Ottomans were the largest, and at their height in the 16th century they controlled all of North Africa, Arabia, Iraq, Syria, Anatolia, and the Balkans up to the gates of Vienna. In addition to these empires, Islam had been carried by traders to sub-Saharan Africa, and to the islands and coasts of southeast Asia. In addition, large-scale conversion in South Asia shifted the demographic center of the Muslim world out of the Middle East.

But despite this numerical and military expansion, the Muslim lands had lost their intellectual and economic vitality. They had gradually slipped further and further behind the West. By the 19th century, the Muslim lands lay wide open for colonization. By 1920, only the Turks and Persians among all the Muslim peoples were not living in a European colony.

After the Second World War, decolonization freed the Muslims to once again seek their own destinies. At first, there was jubilation over the end of colonialism, but eventually the lack of rapid development, and the persistent weakness of the Muslims in international relations, led to deep disillusionment. For some Muslims, the problem was diagnosed as "not enough Islam", while others felt that much less Islam would allow Muslims to advance. The fundamental questions were now being asked. What is the relationship of Islam to the modern state? What is the value of the ancient *fiqh* created eight centuries ago? How do we develop our nations? Some Muslims formed violent groups to seize power and impose their version of "Islamic law", while others created justifications for a strong role for jurists to rule in the state (Ayatollah Khomeini among the most prominent). In state after state, many Muslims saw not Islam, but injustice and oppression. Where does the Muslim world go from here?

Islam is not a monolithic faith, nor one that has been monolithically experienced in all parts of the world. There is significant variation in how it is lived and practiced in different countries, from Indonesia to Iran to the United States. What seems unfortunately prominent in the Muslim world is the abuse of religion by those in authority, whether it be religious or political, such that the outcome is an intolerant version of Islam that is disproportionately preoccupied with punishments and restrictions on human rights. We have seen the application of this under the Taliban in Afghanistan, in Sudan, Egypt and Saudi Arabia, to name a few countries. There is also a lack of human rights in Muslim countries which are not theocratic but claim to be Islamic, i.e. Pakistan.

Why are we writing this book? What question are we trying to formulate an answer too? The answer is convoluted and complex, but fundamentally cuts to the very heart of the real challenge confronting the Islamic tradition of civilization.

The first spark that began this project was a visit by Ibrahim Yazdi, the noted independent Iranian thinker and politician, who gave the keynote address at the Muslim Public Affairs Council first convention in Los Angeles in December 2001. He challenged us to create a Muslim human rights organization, to champion the cause of human rights in the Muslim world. Our response was limited by our meager resources, both financial and human. However, we resolved to begin to monitor human rights in major Muslim countries and start a process of "country reports" to grade major Muslim nations on their policies. But we quickly ran into a major methodological issue, namely on what basis can we critique the policies of nations who claim to be acting in the name of Islam? A secular critique, one that relies on American or European legal and ethical traditions, would not be an Islamic critique, and these nations would simply ignore our reports as irrelevant at best, and utterly derivative of secular Western human rights organizations at worst. Clearly we needed to base our critique on fundamental values, and these values must be derived from the Quran, backed up and supported by *hadith* and juristic opinion.

As we approached this issue more closely, we saw that Islamic civilization is in fact grappling with a very fundamental question. How is the power of the modern state to be controlled, and to what purpose should it be directed? The immense power of the modern nation-state is far beyond any other polity in human history. The modern state is virtually indestructible, except in the setting of prolonged civil war (Afghanistan, Somalia). It can engage in mass vaccination effective enough to eliminate entire diseases, and it can engage in mechanized slaughter of its own citizens. It can create secure spaces for artistic and intellectual expression and it can trample on the rights of its citizens leaving no private space even for the family or the mind.

The modern state system now encompasses the entire globe, but the first peoples to experience it were the English and the French. The

English put forward two great political philosophers who attempted to understand this new phenomenon, Thomas Hobbes in the 17th century, and John Locke in the 18th century. Hobbes recognized the monstrous power of the state, and aptly referred to it as a "Leviathan". His basic view was that the security provided by the state was of such importance, that it outweighed and justified any tyranny that may result as a by-product. This notion has an echo in the Arab proverb that one hundred years of tyranny is preferable to one day of anarchy.

Locke offered a different perspective. For him the state existed as a voluntary compact of free men. Its purpose was not simply physical security of its citizens, but the preservation of their liberty. It could only exercise as much power and authority as necessary to protect the liberty of its citizens. While George Washington is considered by Americans to be the father of the country, in an intellectual sense John Locke is the father of the United States.

For Muslims, the issue of how religion should interact with the state is a profound one. Muslims believe that the Quran is a divine text, containing eternal truths not just about how to achieve salvation in the hereafter, but also how to create the just society today. For Muslims, the key question is how does that message intersect with the modern nation-state. Is it a "Leviathan" to be accepted without criticism, or is there some duty on the part of the state to be virtuous and not trample on God-given human rights?

This project therefore seeks to answer these fundamental questions. What is the purpose of the state? How can Islamic values be incorporated without creating tyranny? What constitutes justice? How are Muslims to integrate the eternal message of the Quran and the reality of the modern nation-state? How would human rights as defined by contemporary international standards fit within Islamic applications? We cannot criticize states that are self-described as "Islamic" on Islamic grounds without formulating a coherent and comprehensive response.

To tackle this problem, we had to start with the basics. We had to decide what is the critical test on which we will approach this question.

It only makes sense that this should first and foremost be grounded in the Quran itself. Quranic values are the bedrock on which we build our analysis. Anything else in the Islamic tradition and heritage that conflicts with the Quran has to be downgraded. This means that the particular ruling of jurists in the distant past is not necessarily binding on us today. These jurists were part of a living intellectual tradition, one in which debate and discussion and disagreement was a constant. It is not intellectually valid to simply pick one or more of these jurists and try to squeeze modern society and its legal needs into the rulings they made in their own time and place. It is valid though to look at the Quran itself for eternal guidance, and that is what we have done.

Let us now touch on the *hadith*, which are the recorded sayings and actions of the Prophet (pbuh). Far too often, *hadith* is used highly selectively, with little knowledge of its limitations. There are only a handful of *hadith* which are considered to be almost certainly true, the so-called *mutawattir hadith*, and in one juristic opinion, there is only one *hadith* that is so classified, and that *hadith* of course says "deeds are judged by their intentions." Sahih Bukhari, collected over 600,000 *hadith* when he put together his definitive collection, and he discarded 99% of them as not meeting his criteria of scrutiny, and the remaining several thousand vary in their strength and authority. Our approach is to be very aware of the limitations of the *hadiths*, and measure them up to Quranic principle. The book itself consists of 18 chapters. After the introduction, we will delve into specific issues. These include justice, women, non-Muslims, democracy, life, freedom of religion, of speech, children's rights, property rights, and several others. We end with a call for "neo-jurism". By this we mean a return to intellectual vitality in Muslim civilization. What we want to see is the return of debate and discussion of these major issues throughout the Muslim world, a debate led by our best scholars, but accessible to the average educated Muslim. This active living juristic debate will help shape the interpretation of Islam that people believe is correct. There is no Pope in Islam to control interpretation. Ultimately, it must come down to superior rational argument and discussion. Let the best and most convincing approach win, knowing that tomorrow a new critique or new circumstances may force us to change our opinion. What we want to see is that Islam be a living religion for the thinking Muslim.

Our book is a comprehensive attempt to bring the Quran into our context. We claim no special superiority to other such trial attempts. But we do claim that ours is the most convincing approach to these questions, and we would require those with an opposing argument to develop and put forth a better one. We hope that this book will help in the development of the religious life of the Muslim American community. This work comes out of a need to address this situation by offering an alternative interpretation of the values and ideals of Islam in the context of a human rights framework, one that supports a progressive outlook and stands up against a curtailing of any aspect of human dignity and freedom. We stress that this is an interpretive effort, and does not represent an "absolute Islam," any more than that which is professed by the Islamic scholars and religious authorities in other parts of the world. The Quran is divine in origin but humans are limited in their understanding by their own particular factors. Outside of the Prophet (pbuh) himself, none of us can ever know what is "absolute Islam".

We believe that there is a need for Muslim Americans to experience and explain Islam for themselves, intellectually and spiritually, and not rely solely on the traditional interpretations of those in religious authority. Drawing specifically on issues that have relevance to the contemporary lives of Muslim Americans, we offer an Islamic perspective that aims to fulfill this task. Furthermore, as a component of MPAC's goals in promoting a vibrant Muslim American community, this project reflects a textual and scriptural basis for MPAC's platform.

Beyond the Muslim American community, this work is also relevant to a larger audience of both Muslims and non-Muslims. It provides a benchmark to assess and critique the human rights practices of other Muslim countries, one which is grounded in principles that move beyond just a traditional religious perspective.

Methodology

We view this work as being an attempt to articulate our understanding, emphasizing human reason and critical thought as a component of interpretation. This applies in particular to issues that have not been dealt with directly in the text of the Quran or that were not relevant in the early centuries of Islam when the *hadith* were recorded and compiled. While it is beyond the scope of this book to engage in a lengthy discussion on the merits and significance of *ijtihad* as a concept in Islamic juristic thought, nevertheless, we believe that it is vital, and indeed, incumbent upon us to engage in it in the contemporary context of our lives in North America.

The methodological basis for this work lies primarily in textual and scriptural analysis from the Quran and the *hadith*. As the final word of God, the Quran is clearly the most significant source of guidance for Muslims. It presents a framework for moral, ethical and religious behavior for its followers. However, the text is open to interpretation, and in many cases, there are conflicting interpretations by Quranic commentators and scholars. Our emphasis here is on the fact that understanding Quranic text involves an interpretive process.[2]

The *hadith* form the second part of the primary source materials we are using, after the Quran. They refer to the sayings and actions of the Prophet, as narrated by a particular chain of individuals, and then compiled by scholars in the early centuries of Islam. We have drawn primarily from the six major books of *hadith*, and have tried to make a distinction where possible between *hadith* that refer to manners and those that refer to law. We rely on non-controversial *hadith*, and take into account where relevant the likely authenticity of *hadith*. Where *hadith* contradict Quranic principle, we view with skepticism the likelihood that the *hadith* is authentic.

Classical Islamic jurisprudence and episodes from early Islamic history are relied on to a more limited degree as supporting evidence for our arguments. There are three reasons for this. One is that juristic principles are the product of human effort and never claimed to be absolutely binding. Second, for many issues in this project, there is little or no existing discussion by jurists, so that we are compelled to develop our argument from primary sources. Third, where there is previous discussion, part of the purpose of this project is to construct an argument that challenges the intolerant attitude that has characterized some areas of fiqh in more recent history.

In conclusion, this project reflects intellectual and scholarly rigor in constructing a framework for our arguments. We hope it will serve as a starting point for advocating a more progressive Islamic perspective on human rights issues.

Definitions

Islam   The fundamental belief of Islam is that there is One God and that Prophet Muhammad is His Messenger. The fundamental text is the Quran, the direct revelation of God's message through the Angel Gabriel to the Prophet (pbuh).

Quran   The Quran serves as the primary source of guidance for Muslims, as the literal and final word of God, and is therefore, given paramount importance and authority. However, this does not take away from the fact that, as a text, the Quran is open to interpretation by its readers, and that there often exist conflicting interpretations of the same text.

Hadith   This refers to the sayings and teachings of the Prophet, transmitted by a chain of narrators. The authenticity of the chain of transmission and the context within which a particular *hadith* is relevant are issues of concern in using *hadith* as a reference. After the Quran, the *hadith* are the second source of supporting evidence in this work.

Sharia Literally "the way", it is the ideal application of the Islamic message in real life. All attempts at interpreting the Quran and developing a system of law and government on the basis of Islamic principles can be seen as a search for the sharia. To many Muslims, the sharia is incorrectly confused with fiqh (described below). We clearly distinguish between the two.

Ijtihad Literally, the term means "maximum effort". In the juristic sense, it refers to the exercise of independent human reasoning to elaborate and explain juristic principles from the sources of sharia, on issues that have not been discussed clearly in the Quranic text. While some believe that the gates of *ijtihad* were closed after the classical era, we do not subscribe to this assumption, and believe that *ijtihad* is necessary to further our understanding of Islam in the context of our contemporary lives.

Ijma' The consensus of opinion among jurists. There are questions though about the binding nature of *ijma'*, the requirements and conditions for it and whether or not, it is limited by time and place.

Fiqh The body of legal judgments, opinions, rulings, and other works that make up a school of Islamic jurisprudence. There are four major schools in the Sunni tradition and several in the Shi'a tradition. Taking a body of *fiqh* from centuries ago, and using that as the basis of law in the modern state is what many Muslims see as the correct way to return to governance by the sharia.

Ra'y A considered opinion on a matter that has not been regulated by the Quran or the example of the Prophet (*sunna*), but which is arrived at by introspection and investigation of the available knowledge on a particular subject. It can be coexistent with *ijtihad* or not, although it contains an element of arbitrariness, in the sense that it is a personal opinion, and does not necessarily have to coincide with *ijma'* (consensus of opinion) on an issue.

Footnotes

1 W. N. ARAFAT, Journal of the Royal Asiatic Society of Great Britain and Ireland, (1976),pp. 100-107.
2 Khaled Abou El Fadl discusses the power dynamic of the relationship between Quranic text, the reader and the interpretation in his book, *And God Knows the Soldiers: The Authoritative and Authoritarian in Islamic Discourse* (Lanham, MD: University Press of America, 2001).

CHAPTER ONE

Justice

he *American Heritage Dictionary* gives two main definitions for the word "justice": "the principle of moral rightness, equity" and "the upholding of what is just, especially fair treatment and due reward in accordance to honor, standards, or law; fairness." From here we can see that justice encompasses both moral and legal components, and is key both in creating and in implementing laws. Philosophers from Plato and Aristotle to Immanuel Kant and John Stuart Mill have written key treatises that deal with the theme of justice exclusively. What are the central notions of justice that should be upheld by a society, how should they be codified into laws, and how should these laws then be justly implemented?

In his edited anthology entitled *Justice*, author Jonathan Westphal points out "a significant ambiguity in the word 'justice.'" The first meaning of the word that Westphal examines is that of "the application of law to society." When a person is found guilty of a crime and sent to prison, then that is an application of justice. When an innocent person is falsely accused and subsequently sent to prison, then that is a miscarriage of justice. "So," as Westphal surmises, in this case 'justice being done' means the impartial, equal, fair, and successful application of the law." Sending a guilty person to jail is a just action; sending an innocent one is not.[1]

But then, as Westphal points out, there is another manifestation of justice. Is it just that some people in society have many resources, whereas others have few? Here an attempt to carry out justice is not as simple as applying a law, but rather requires a particular ideologically driven and somewhat complex framework. This is a social or distributive aspect of justice, based on the condition of the various elements of society, as well as that of the society as a whole.

This differentiation is also apparent in the Quran. Absolute justice, meaning equality before the law and a possession of equal rights, is often referred to as 'adl in the Quran. 'Adl in classical Arabic denotes "a combination of moral and social values denoting fairness, balance, temperance, and straightforwardness."[2] Distributive justice, on the other hand, is relative, and its application is heavily dependent on the make-up of a particular society. In the Quran, the term often used in this context is qist, with words such as nasib (share), mizan (scale), and taqwim (straightening) also frequently used in this context.[3] These terms concern human social interaction, and emphasize the notion of fairness in dealing with others.

This study will examine these two expressions of justice. The first, which will be termed legal justice, is an expression of justice within the law. The second, which will be termed distributive justice, is the manifestation of social justice within the different groups in society. The chapter will argue that the Quran holds strong procedural imperatives for each of these two expressions of justice, but that historically, it was crucial to practice ijtihad in order to arrive at how to apply these injunctions in a way that was best suited to their particular time and place. In order to contextualize the argument, the chapter will begin with an examination of justice in pre-Islamic times, will continue to a basic explanation of justice in Islam, before examining each application of justice in detail. While it draws on Quranic verses, hadith, historical examples and legal procedures to make its argument, clearly a cursory discussion of justice such as this cannot possibly use the countless illustrations found in Islamic texts and practice. Rather, the purpose of this chapter is to paint a broad picture of the principles of justice in Islam, with a discussion of the earliest applications of these principles and a call for an open-minded examination of priority in similar applications today.

Justice in pre-Islamic Times

The Quran was revealed in a specific historical context, where ensuring public security was a challenge, in the midst of inter-clan rivalries and feuds. Pre-Islamic Arabia was a society that was politically unstable, rife with such feuding and alliances (often of unequal power) that were built in that context of that instability. Mecca, a city ruled by an oligarchy, possessed no codified laws, but rather operated under certain mutual "understandings" between parties. Medina, before the advent of the Prophet and the Muslim community, was a society that had been exhausted by a lengthy war between its two main tribes, and was completely lacking in any sort of social structure or legal framework.

Survival in pre-Islamic Arabic was a primary concern, and the most prized characteristics of a person were epitomized in the word *muruwwa. Muruwwa*, meaning "manliness," embodied a set of knightly characteristics such as courage and a sense of honor. But honor and courage often led to brutality and oppression, and particularly at the expense of the underdog. In the absence of codified laws, justice was often executed in the form of retribution against an individual and his family or clan, rather than through attempts at fairness, balance, and temperance. At times a dispute between two parties would be referred to a third, more neutral party, whose wisdom was well-established, and who could be relied upon to give a ruling that all parties would deem equitable. This informal judge had no reference point for his ruling other than prevailing customs and his own astuteness at arriving at a suitable solution.

Furthermore, in the sixth century, Mecca – and to a lesser extent Medina – was in a state of social transition. The old clan system was weakening in favor of an economically driven system. As Mecca had become a flourishing trade center, more and more allegiances were created across trade lines, with the foremost goal of economic prosperity. The poor and needy were thus falling out from under the auspices of clan protection. Orphans, widows, and other disadvantaged members of society were left without financial or social care. People would sometimes bury their baby girls alive soon after birth, presumably because these girls were less likely to later provide economically for the family, and thus were seen as an unnecessary expense. The disparity within the social structure and the frequent warfare and feuding also meant that there was a sizable slave population in both Mecca and Medina.

It is important to understand these circumstances when examining the concept of justice in the Quran. The Quran came to a society that was suffering legally, socially, and in many cases economically. In order to reform the society, the Quran spoke directly to many of these issues, providing procedural directives for transformation. These directives were then applied in the appropriate context by the Prophet Muhammad, his Companions, and subsequent jurists, scholars, and rulers.

Islamic Views on Justice

In order to position justice in the Islamic framework, it is important to understand the nature of Islam's public order. God is the Sovereign, the ultimate Ruler and Legislator. But the role of the human being in interpretation is also crucial. According to the Quran, every human being is the vicegerent (*khalifa*) of God on earth: *"And Lo! Thy Sustainer said unto the angels: 'Behold, I am about to establish upon earth one who shall inherit it.' They said: 'Wilt Thou place on it such as will spread corruption thereon and shed blood – whereas it is we who extol Thy limitless glory, and praise Thee, and hallow Thy name?' [God] answered: 'Verily, I know that which you do not know'"* (Surah al-Baqara – The Cow, 2:30). God commanded the Prophet David (Dawud), *"[And We said:] 'O David! Behold, We have made thee a [prophet and, thus, Our] vicegerent on earth: judge, then, between men with justice, and do not follow vain desire, lest it lead thee astray from the path of God"* (Surah Sad - Sad, 38:26).

In the Islamic context, justice is ultimately God's will. Human beings take the commands that God gave them, and then attempt to apply them using their human reasoning. Thus there is divine justice, which is perfect, and human justice, which is fallible. The ultimate expression of Divine Justice is God's justice to the human being on the Day of Judgment. In this world, the fallible human being can only do what is within his/her abilities, and he/she is rewarded for these attempts.

Justice is mentioned in general terms throughout the Quran numerous times. Below are just a few examples:

"[Before Him] prostrate themselves and stars and the trees. And the skies has He raised high, and has devised [for all things] a measure, so that you [too, O men,] might never transgress the measure [of what is right]: weigh, therefore, [your deeds] with equity, and cut not the measure short!" (Surah ar-Rahman – The Most Gracious, 55:6-9).

"Indeed, [even aforetime] did We send forth Our apostles with all evidence of [this] truth; and through them We bestowed revelation from on high, and [thus gave you] a balance [wherewith to weight right and wrong], so that men might behave with equity" (Surah al-Hadid - Iron, 57:25).

"O you who have attained to faith! Be ever steadfast in your devotion to God, bearing witness to the truth in all equity; and never let hatred of anyone lead you into the sin of deviating from justice. Be just: this is closest to being God-conscious. And remain conscious of God: verily, God is aware of all that you do" (Surah al-Maida – The Repast, 5:9).

"O you have attained to faith! Be ever steadfast in upholding equity, bearing witness to the truth for the sake of God, even though it be against your own selves or your parents and kinsfolk. Whether the person concerned be rich or poor, God's claim takes precedence over [the claims of] either of them. Do not, then, follow your own desires, lest you swerve from justice: for if you distort [the truth], behold, God is indeed aware of all that you do!" (Surah an-Nisa - Women, 4:135).

From here we can see that divine and human justice are interconnected. God has established justice, and the human being should operate within that framework. While God lays out the moral imperative for distinguishing justice from injustice, it is up to individuals to understand this and put human justice into practice. The emphasis on human comprehension and thinking is noted throughout the Quran: *"...will you not, then, use your reason?"* (Surah al-Muminun – The Believers, 23:80); *"...in this, behold, there are messages indeed for people who think!"* (Surah ar-Rum – The Byzantines, 30:21); *"for in this, behold, there are messages indeed for all who are possessed of [innate] knowledge!"* (Surah ar-Rum – The Byzantines, 30:22); *"...will they not, then, use their reason?"* (Surah Ya Sin – O Thou Human Being, 36:68); *"In [all] this, behold, there are messages indeed for people who think!"* (Surah az-Zumar – The Throngs, 39:42).

In Islam, justice is encapsulated in three elements. First are the Divine laws prescribed in the Quran, and second is the example of the Prophet Muhammad in applying these laws, as can be read in the *hadith*. These two bodies of material are then interpreted through *ijtihad* (human reasoning), via a variety of tools such as *qiyas* (analogy). Historically, numerous scholars and jurists used these tools to develop and codify their own interpretations of the Divine Laws, leading to distinct legal schools such as the Hanafi, Maliki, Shafi'i, Hanbali and Jafari schools, each with their own methodologies and conclusions on legal issues. The multiplicity of these methodologies and conclusions exemplify the plurality of human interpretation according to each individual's personal and societal circumstances, a topic that will be explored at greater depth below.

Legal Justice

Legal justice entails equality before the law and a possession of equal rights. It calls for each person's entitlement to his/her legal rights, and the obligation to pay the penalty for injustices he/she may commit. These rights and obligations are absolute in nature, although the form in which they are carried out can vary depending on the context. This section highlights seven key procedural principles of the application of legal justice in society. These are: fairness in trial, fairness in judgment, proportionate punishment, importance of intention, individual judgment and punishment, equality, and mercy.

Fairness in Trial

Fairness in trial is based on the general principle that the accused has the right to be treated fairly and humanely. It is similar in its components to what is usually referred to as "due process." This includes the rights of the accused while under investigation, such as right to counsel, right to know the evidence and charges against him/her, right to refuse questioning and/or remain silent, and access to exonerating evidence as part of one's defense.

From the outset, a person cannot be arrested without sufficient evidence. In one instance, "the Prophet (pbuh) was delivering a lecture in his mosque, when a man got up and asked, 'O Prophet of God! For what crime have my neighbors been arrested?' The Prophet didn't answer him and continued with his speech. The man asked the same question twice more and received no response. The third time, the Prophet (pbuh) commanded that the man's neighbors be released. The reason is because the Prophet (pbuh) knew that the man who arrested them was also present in the congregation, and if there was a good reason for their arrest, he would have spoken up. Since he didn't give any reason for the arrest openly, it was sufficient grounds for the Prophet (pbuh) to call for their release."[4]

Once a person is arrested and is undergoing a trial, the most basic type of fairness (and therefore justice) that is key to the trial process is the opportunity to grant each party in a case equal time. A *hadith* narrated by Ali ibn Abi Talib stresses this:

"The Apostle of God (pbuh) sent me to the Yemen as judge, and I asked, 'Apostle of God, are you sending me when I am young and have no knowledge of the duties of a judge?' He replied, 'God will guide your heart and keep your tongue true. When two litigants sit in front of you, do not decide till you hear what the other has to say as you heard what the first had to say; for it is best that you should have a clear idea of the best decision.'"[5]

The Quran includes an example of a case when this did not take place. It involves the case of the Prophet David (Dawud), who was asked to render judgment on a dispute between two men. The first had 99 ewes, while the second had only one, and the former was insisting that the latter owes him that lone ewe also. The second man complained to David, who hastily rushed to his defense without hearing from the first man, saying, *"He has certainly wrong thee by demanding that thy ewe be added to his ewes!..."* (Surah Sad - Sad, 38:22).

Immediately, David realized the hastiness of his judgment, and asked God for forgiveness: *"And [suddenly] David understood that We had tried him: and so he asked his Lord to forgive him his sin, and fell down in prostration, and turned unto Him in repentance"* (Surah Sad - Sad, 38:24). In response, God reminds him of his duty to uphold justice: *" 'O David! Behold, We have made thee a [prophet and, thus, Our] vicegerent on earth: judge, then, between men with justice, and do not follow vain desire, lest it lead thee astray from the path of God: verily, for those who go astray from the path of God there is suffering severe in store for having forgotten the Day of Reckoning!' "* (Surah Sad, 38:26).

The individual also has the right to refuse questioning or to remain silent in interrogation, without the silence being used as incriminating evidence against him. Any confession that has been obtained through coercion is legally invalid and inadmissible as evidence. Caliph Umar is reported to have said, "A man would not be secure from incriminating himself if you made him hungry, frightened him, or confined him."[6] In another incident, Mohammed ibn Ishaq reports that a man accused of theft was arrested and beaten. He confessed his guilt. The governor of the region sent him to Abdullah ibn Umar, a renowned scholar, asking what should be done about his punishment. Ibn Umar said not to cut off his hand, since he had confessed after being beaten and therefore his confession was unlawful.[7]

The individual has the additional right of initiating a complaint to the administration or the courts in self-defense. He/she can defend his/her case in court even by attacking those that launched the initial accusations. This is one of the few instances where a person is allowed to denounce others in public: *"God does not like any evil to be mentioned openly, unless it be by him who has been wronged [thereby]. And God is indeed all-hearing, all-knowing"* (Surah an-Nisa - Women, 4:148).

This comprehensive approach to trial is witnessed in the ultimate distribution of justice: the afterlife. In this context, every human being will be treated to a complete and overt record of all the deeds he/she carried out: *"And every human being's destiny have We tied to his neck; and on the Day of Resurrection We shall bring forth for him a record which he will find wide open; [and he will be told:] 'Read this thy record! Sufficient is thine own self today to make out thine account!'"* (Surah al Isra – The Night Journey, 17:13-14).

The human being will then have the opportunity to respond to the charges against him/her: *"For, on that Day He will call unto them, and will ask: 'Where, now, are those [beings or powers] whom you imagined to have a share in My divinity?' – [whereupon] they against whom the word [of truth] shall thus stand revealed will exclaim: 'O our Sustainer! Those whom we caused to err so grievously , we but caused to err as we ourselves had been erring. We [now] disavow them before Thee: it was not us that they worshiped!' And [they] will be told: 'Call [now] unto those [beings or powers] to whom you were wont to ascribe a share in God's divinity! – and they will call unto them [for help], but those [false objects of worship] will not respond to them: whereupon they will see the suffering [that awaits them – the suffering which could have been avoided] if only they had allowed themselves to be guided! And on that Day He will call unto them, and will ask: 'How did you respond to My message-bearers?' – but all arguments and excuses will by then have been erased from their minds, and they will not [be able to] obtain any [helpful] answer from one another. But as against this – anyone who repents and attains to faith and does righteous deeds may well [hope to] find himself among those who achieve a happy state [in the life to come]"* (Surah al-Qasas – The Story, 28:62-67).

Fairness in Judgment

Judges are required to discharge their responsibilities with the utmost accountability. The Quran enjoins *"And whenever you judge between people, to judge with justice. Verily, most excellent is what God exhorts you to do: verily, God is all-hearing, all-seeing!"* (Surah an-Nisaa - Women, 4:58). Likewise, the Prophet emphasized the importance of the role of the judge, distinguishing between "three types, one of whom will go to Paradise, and two to Hell. The one who will go to Paradise is a man who knows what is right and gives judgment accordingly; but a man who knows what is right and acts tyrannically in his judgment will go to Hell; and a man who gives judgment for people when he is ignorant will go to Hell."[8]

Presumption of innocence until the defendant is proven guilty is key. That the benefit of the doubt must be given to the accused is evident in God's disapproval of those who engage in slander or false accusations against another's reputation. The onus is on the accuser to present four supporting witnesses to substantiate his allegation. If he/she is unable to do so, he/she is subject to punishment: *"And as for those who accuse chaste women [of adultery], and then are unable to produce four witnesses [in support of their accusation], flog them with eighty stripes; and ever after refuse to accept from them any testimony – since it is they, they are truly depraved!"* (Surah an-Nur – The Light, 24:4).

The Quran goes on to stress the presumption of innocence in the context of an actual specific event where rumors had flown about the acts of women: *"Why do not the believing men and women, whenever such [a rumor] is heard, think the best of one another and say, 'This is an obvious falsehood'? Why do they not [demand of the accusers that they] produce four witnesses to prove their allegation? – for, if they do not produce such witnesses, it is those [accusers] who, in the sight of God, are liars indeed! "* (Surah an-Nur – The Light, 24:12-13). The verse clearly brands those who dispense with the presumption of innocence as liars, regardless of whether the original charge was or was not actually true.

Likewise, the Prophet's treatment of prisoners exemplifies a presumption of innocence in human justice. In one case, a man accused of theft was brought before him. The Prophet addressed him gently and asked, "I don't think you stole. Did you?"[9] The Prophet demonstrated that the man was innocent until proven guilty, by questioning him and giving him an opportunity to defend himself against the charge.

In order to ensure that judges can function fairly and impartially, it is important to ensure that the judiciary as a branch of government is free from political pressure and bias. The Prophet's injunction that "The best fighting (*jihad*) in the path of God is a word of justice against an oppressive ruler'" highlights the responsibility of upholding justice independent of the political ruler.[10] Historically, the early Islamic Caliphate upheld a division whereby the judiciary was a separate – although not entirely removed – branch of the government; Caliph Umar was the first ruler to delegate his judicial duties to others, by appointing judges to the various cities of the Muslim realm. These judges were paid monthly salaries by the state, and provided with necessities so that they were not susceptible to corruption or bribes.

Fairness in judgment is apparent in the Divine Justice of the Day of Judgment. God, the Just, judges people according to their circumstances. This includes the idea that a person will only be judged according to his/her knowledge of God and His message. A person that was never exposed to this cannot be judged based on its framework. Thus, *"Whoever chooses to follow the right path, follows it but for his own good; and whoever goes astray, goes but astray to his own hurt; and no bearer of burdens shall be made to bear another's burden. Moreover, We would never chastise [any community for the wrong they may do] ere We have sent an apostle [to them] "* (Surah al-Isra – The Night Journey, 17:15); *"And never would We destroy a community unless its people are wont to do wrong [to one another]"* (Surah al-Qasas – The Story, 28:59).

Proportional Punishment

In executing justice, the judge has to ensure that the punishment is proportional to the crime. For example, theft is punished according to the value of the item stolen.[11] In a case where the two Prophets David and Solomon differed on their judgments on an issue, Solomon's verdict was deemed preferable since it was proportionate to the magnitude of the initial wrongdoing, whereas David's pronouncement was considered too harsh (see below for more on this).

In the same way, on the Day of Judgment, every punishment and reward given by God will be proportional to the deed: *"On that Day will all men come forward, cut off from one another, to be shown their [past] deeds. And so, he who shall have done an atom's weight of good, shall behold it; and he who shall have done an atom's weight of evil, shall behold it"* (Surah al Zalzala – The Earthquake, 99:6-8). But God tilts the balance well in favor of the good each person does: *"Whoever shall come [before God] with a good deed will gain ten times the like thereof; but whoever shall come with an evil deed will be requited with no more than the like thereof; and none shall be wronged"* (Surah al Anam - Cattle, 6:160).

Intention

Central to the idea of proportional punishment is the concept of intention. Murder and manslaughter both involve the taking of a life, but whereas the former includes intention, the latter is an accident in which the perpetrator did not intend to kill his/her victim. Both of them are different from self-defense, in which the perpetrator often has no choice but to kill, in order to save his/her own life. The Quran sharply differentiates between the three (Surah an-Nisa – Women, 4:92-3), emphasizing the significance of the circumstances behind each in great detail.

Emphasis throughout the Quran is on the fact that only God knows the true intention within a person's heart, and it is this intention that will be key on the Day of Judgment. God warns people against false oaths: *"And do not allow your oaths in the name of God to become an obstacle to virtue and God-consciousness and the promotion of peace between men: for God is all-hearing, all-knowing. God will not take you to task for oaths which you may have uttered without thought, but will take you to task [only] for what your hearts have conceived [in*

earnest]: *for God is much-forgiving, forbearing"* (Surah al-Baqara –
The Cow, 2:224-225). The Quran emphasizes this point again: *"It is
We who have created man, and We know what his innermost self whispers within him: for We are closer to him than his neck-vein"* (Surah
Qaf - Qaf, 50:16).

In the *hadith*, there is consensus about the Prophet's statement that
"deeds are judged by their intention." This *hadith* is ubiquitous in the
collection of Bukhari, and appears also in that of Muslim and other
transmitters, thus pointing to the importance of intention in all aspects
of life. In fact, the very first *hadith* quoted in Bukhari begins, "Umar
bin Al-Khattab narrated: I heard God's Apostle saying, 'The reward of
deeds depends upon the intentions and every person will get the reward
according to what he has intended.'"

Individual Judgment

Individualization of judgment calls for punishment of the culpable
person only, and not of his/her family or friends just by virtue of their
association with the guilty party. The Quran details the importance of
individual responsibility for one's actions, and the reward/punishment
for deeds being determined solely on an individual basis and in proportion to the deed. But individual judgment also entails taking into
account the individual's circumstances, both personal and societal. The
above-mentioned differentiation between murder and self-defense is
pertinent here.

This individualization of judgment is emphasized in many verses
throughout the Quran. Prophet Joseph (Yusuf) stressed this when he
was requested by his half-brothers to capture one of them as a substitute for their brother who was accused of theft: "He answered: *'May
God preserve us from [the sin of] detaining any other than him with
whom we have found our property – for then, behold, we would indeed
be evildoers!'"* (Surah Yusuf - Joseph, 12:79).[12] In general, a person can
only carry his/her own burden: *"That no bearer of burdens shall be
made to bear another's burden; and that nought shall be accounted unto
man but what he is striving for"* (Surah al-Najm – The Unfolding,

53:38-39). *"And no bearer of burdens shall be made to bear another's burden; and if one weighed down by his load calls upon [another] to help him carry it, nothing thereof may be carried [by that other], even if it be one's near of kin. Hence, thou canst [truly] warn only those who stand in awe of their Sustainer although He is beyond the reach of their perception, and are constant in prayer, and [know that] whoever grows in purity, attains to purity but for the good of his own self, and [that] with God is all journeys' end"* (Surah al Fatir – The Originator, 35:18; see also Surah al-Anam – Cattle, 6:164; Surah Fusilat – Clearly Spelled Out, 41:46; Sural an-Nisaa - Women 4:111, 123). In other words, not even one's closest relative, a parent, sibling or child, can bear the burden of one's own moral choices before God.

Yet at the same time, there is emphasis on the fact that God does not burden a person with more than he/she can bear. Responsibility can only be within a person's abilities, as witnessed by the following verse: *"'God does not burden any human being with more than he is well able to bear: in his favor shall be whatever good he does, and against him whatever evil he does. 'O our Sustainer! Take us not to task if we forget or unwittingly do wrong! 'O our Sustainer! Lay not upon us a burden such as Thou didst lay upon those who lived before us! O our Sustainer! Make us not bear burdens which we have no strength to bear! 'And efface Thou our sins, and grant us forgiveness, and bestow Thy mercy upon us! Thou art our Lord Supreme: succor us, then, against people who deny the truth!'"* (Surah al-Baqara – The Cow, 2:286). People are not responsible for what they cannot control, and this includes issues about which they may have forgotten, or even simple mistakes that they may have made.

Equality

The precept of justice in the Quran calls for equal legal rights. It does not distinguish between rich and poor, as can be seen in a tradition where the Prophet pronounced, "The people before you were destroyed because they used to inflict the legal punishments on the poor and forgive the rich. By Him in Whose Hand is my soul! If Fatima (the daughter of the Prophet) did that (i.e. stole), I would cut off her hand."[13] Equality also does not differentiate in religion. A Muslim and a non-Muslim are to be treated equally. In a case when a Muslim and a Jew came disputing to 'Umar ibn al-Khattab, the Caliph decided the case in favor of the Jew.[14]

The Quran consistently stresses humanity's unity of origin: *"O mankind! We created you from a single (pair) of a male and a female, and made you into nations and tribes, that ye may know each other (not that ye despise each other)."* As a result of this unity of origin, the only real difference between individuals is that which is based on conduct: *"Verily, the noblest of you in the sight of God is the one who is most deeply conscious of Him. Behold, God is all-knowing, all-aware"* (Surah al-Hujurat – The Private Apartments, 49:13). Differences based on gender, race, and ethnicity, among others, exist merely to allow for greater cooperation and harmony between individuals, rather than to create any sort of hierarchy. The only valid distinctions arise from the degree of righteousness that an individual achieves.

This equality is dissected into its specific parts in other verses. Verses such as *"And [as for] the believers, both men and women – they are close unto one another: they [all] enjoin the doing of what is right and forbid the doing of what is wrong, and are constant in prayer, and render the purifying dues"* (Surah at-Tawbah - Repentance, 9:71) emphasize equality between the sexes (see also Surah al-Ahzab – The Confederates, 33:35; Surah an-Nahl – The Bee, 16:97; Surah al-Imran – The House of Imran, 3:195; Surah an-Nisa - Women, 4:124). The same emphasis on equality is noted in the Quran with regard to religious identity. The universality of God's message is such that it is not the exclusive spiritual domain of any one religious community. It is not limited to Muslims over Christians or Jews, for example. The Quran emphasizes that *"Unto every one of you have We appointed a [different] law and way of life. And if God had so willed, He could surely have made you all one single community: but [He willed it otherwise] in order to test you by means of what He has vouchsafed unto you. Vie, then, with one another in doing good works! Unto God you all must return; and then He will make you truly understand all that on which you were wont to differ"* (Surah al-Maida – The Repast, 5:48). Here we see that religious differences are a part of God's plans for humanity, whereby all people are equally enjoined to turn towards virtuous action, regardless of the "law" or the "way" that they follow (see also Surah al-Baqara – The Cow, 2:62, 213, 256).

Mercy

So far, we have outlined some clear principles to be followed in the execution of justice. Some of these are definite and unambiguous, such as allowing both sides to present their cases. Other points require more individual extrapolation, as in the case of attempting to establish intention. But they are all universal principles that together form a straightforward coherent framework.

But contrary to common misperceptions, the Islamic criminal justice system is not a rigid framework. Justice in Islam includes another crucial element, that of mercy. We saw this in the Quran's description of how God weighs deeds, where a good deed is weighed ten-fold, whereas a bad deed is weighed only once. Similarly, when it comes to human application, justice is tempered with mercy and thus humanity.

The Quran clearly and continuously emphasizes mercy and forgiveness as central to the application of justice. In the case of theft, for example, *"as for him who repents after having done wrong, and makes amends, behold, God will accept his repentance: verily, God is much-forgiving, a dispenser of grace"* (Surah al-Maida – The Repast, 5:39). If God can forgive a thief for his/her crime, then a judge can also impose a lesser sentence or pardon that offender altogether.

In many of the examples of equal treatment that were discussed above, mercy and forgiveness are provided as alternative (or sometimes even preferred) methods of dealing with the situation. For example, in the previously-mentioned case of a defendant who has the right to self-defense in court, this defendant is encouraged to forgive those who falsely accused him/her. After laying out the person's right to overt self-defense (Surah al-Nisaa, 4:148), the next verse reads, *"Whether you do good openly or in secret, or, pardon others for evil [done unto you]: for, behold, God is indeed an absolver of sins, infinite in His power"* (Surah an-Nisaa - Women, 4:149).

In the above two examples, the emphasis is on the mercy and forgiveness by God. This is highlighted in the context of other previously mentioned verses, such as the continuation of the verse explaining that God does not burden a human being with more than he/she can bear (Surah al-Baqara – The Cow, 2:286). This verse continues with the words, *"And efface Thou our sins, and grant us forgiveness, and bestow Thy mercy upon us!"*

Mercy is key in references to the Day of Judgment: *"With My chastisement do I afflict whom I will – but My grace overspreads everything: and so I shall confer it on those who are conscious of Me and spend in charity, and who believe in Our messages"* (Surah al-Araf – The Faculty of Discernment, 7:156; see also Surah al-Ahzab – The Confederates, 33:43-44; Surah al Anam – Cattle, 6:12).

Distributive Justice

In addition to laying out the procedural injunctions of legal justice, the Quran also addresses similar precepts with regard to distributive justice. One of the main messages of Islam to the early Arabs was to repair the cracks of social injustice in their society. The principle of equality mentioned in the legal justice system above is key to the application of distributive justice.

Just as Islam affirmed belief in the One God, so it called for the unity of humanity, as mentioned above. This oneness meant that the society was to function as a whole: "The Prophet said, 'A believer to another believer is like a building whose different parts enforce each other.' The Prophet then clasped his hands with the fingers interlaced (while saying that)."[15] The pillars of Islam all focus on personal faith but are also communally oriented, from the declaration of faith that is a personal statement but made in the presence of witnesses during the conversion process, to prayer five times a day that is encouraged to be communal, to the highly collective and universal pilgrimage process. Almsgiving is of course the ultimate expression of the unity of the community and its need to care for all its members.

As opposed to legal justice that calls for equal rights for all, distributive justice is by definition relative and highly contextual. Thus a discussion of distributive justice is best outlined with regard to the main groups towards whom this practice is directed. Accepting Islam meant accepting a social code that called for assuming responsibilities the poor, in general, and orphans in particular. Verses calling for distributive justice speak to these two groups is some detail.

The Poor and Needy

Spending on the poor is prescribed in both general and specific terms. Giving and spending on the needy is highlighted in such verses as *"This divine writ – let there be no doubt about it – is [meant to be] a guidance for all the God-conscious who believe in [the existence of] that which is beyond the reach of human perception, and are constant in prayer, and spend on others out of what We provide for them as sustenance"* (Surah al-Baqara – The Cow, 2:2-3; see also 2:195, 261-274; Surah al Imran – The House of Imran, 3:92; Surah an-Nisaa - Women 4:38; 14:31; 16:71; 76:8-9).

There are certain institutions within Islam that support distributive justice. The most obvious of these is of course the institution of almsgiving, or *zakat*, the third pillar of Islam. In addition to this, a person can give further voluntary charity contributions: *"The offerings given for the sake of God are [meant] only for the poor and the needy, and those who are in charge thereof, and those whose hearts are to be won over, and for the freeing of human beings from bondage, and [for] those who are overburdened with debts, and [for every struggle] in God's cause, and [for] the wayfarer: [this is] an ordinance from God – and God is all-knowing, wise"* (Surah at-Tawbah - Repentance, 9:60). Throughout time, various charitable institutions have been established with specific purposes: for example, the *Awqaf* (religious endowments) is an institution that endows schools, hospitals, wayfarers, and the poor.

Charity can complement and supplement socio-economic justice, but by itself it serves only as a "quick-fix solution" to a perpetual and profound problem that is deep within the framework of society. The Quran therefore provides other institutions that seek to temper inequality among the various elements of society. Among these elements of distributive justice is the prohibition against *riba* or usury (Surah al-Baqara – The Cow, 2:275-276, 278-81), a system by which a person makes money effortlessly through the exploitation of another.

Giving to the poor and needy is not maintained through material sustenance only. When he came to Medina, the Prophet instituted a brothering system, whereby the local Medinan population shared what they had with the Meccan immigrants who had had to give up much of their material possessions upon migration. Each Meccan was brothered with a Medinan, a system that provided the Meccan not only with material resources, but also with a moral and psychological support system. This was particularly crucial since many of the Meccans had also had to leave family members behind upon migration, and therefore were in need of psychological as well as material sustenance.

Orphans

In addition to mandating distributive justice with regard to the poor and needy in general, the Quran specifically highlights orphans as a group that is in need of such attention. At a time of high mortality due to disease and warfare, and at a juncture when tribal ties were weakening, many orphans were in a situation where they completely lacked a support system to provide them with any material resources. The Prophet himself was also of course an orphan, having lost both his parents at a young age. He was supported during his formative years by his uncle Abu Talib, but upon Abu Talib's death, the Prophet himself lacked a strong support system within his immediate family.

The emphasis on orphans is addressed generally in verses such as *"Therefore, the orphan shalt thou never wrong, and him that seeks [thy] help shalt thou never chide, and of thy Sustainer's blessings shalt thou [ever] speak"* (Surah ad-Duha – The Bright Morning Hours, 93:9-11; see also Surah al-Maun – Assistance, 107:1-7). The importance of distributive justice, especially with regard to orphans, is so paramount that those who *"you are not generous towards the orphan, and you do not urge one another to feed the needy, and you devour the inheritance [of others] with devouring greed, and you love wealth with boundless love!"* (Surah al-Fajr – The Daybreak, 89:17-20) are immediately warned about their fate on the Day of Judgment (Surah al-Fajr – The Daybreak, 89:21-25).

Orphans are consistently singled out from among other needy groups for charity: *"And when [other] near of kin and orphans and needy persons are present at the distribution [of inheritance], give them something thereof for their sustenance, and speak unto them in a kindly way"* (Surah an-Nisa – Women, 4:8). Here the orphans and other needy people are such part of the system of distributive justice that their lot is equated with that of the near of kin of the deceased, highlighting again the image of the society as one cohesive whole.

Importance of Ijtihad

The above sections outline some key elements in the application of legal and distributive justice. However, they also outline a certain flexibility in the application. While discussing fairness in trial and judgment, we mentioned several cases in which the defendant was exonerated due to various circumstances. The inclusion of the concepts of proportional punishment, intention, and individual responsibility all point to the importance of the individual circumstances outlining a crime, rather than some generalities that are just to be applied blindly to every instance. The emphasis on mercy and distributive justice highlight that justice can be achieved through openness and forgiveness, rather than negativity and consistent punishment.

All these elements reiterate that while the Quran embodies the laws of Divine Justice, it is up to the human being – fallible as he/she is – to determine the method of application of these laws. Any error in such attempts is still seen as a positive step: "Amr b. al-'As reported that he heard God's

Messenger (pbuh) as saying, 'When a judge gives a decision, having tried his best to decide correctly and is right, there are two rewards for him; and if he gave a judgment after having tried his best (to arrive at a correct decision) but erred, there is one reward for him.'"[16]

The Prophet himself pointed out his fallibility in judgment. In a *hadith* he said, "I am a human being and the claimants bring to me for (the dispute), and perhaps some of them are more eloquent than the others. I judge him to be on the right, and thus decide in his favor. So he whom I, by my judgment, (give the undue share) out of the right of a Muslim, I give him a portion of Fire; he may burden himself with it or abandon it."[17]

Even individual differences between people that can result in divergent decisions can still both be seen to be valid. After all, in a dispute both parties usually believe that theirs is the just claim. An interesting example of this is with regard to the two Prophets David and Solomon (Dawud and Sulayman): *"And [remember] David and Solomon – [how it was] when both of them gave judgment concerning the field into which some people's sheep had strayed by night and pastured therein, and [how] We bore witness to their judgment: for, [though] We made Solomon understand the case [more profoundly], yet We vouchsafed unto both of them sound judgment and knowledge [of right and wrong]. And we caused the mountains to join David in extolling Our limitless glory, and likewise the birds: for We are able to do [all things]"* (Surah al-Anbiya – The Prophets, 21:78-79).

In this account, a farm owner complained to King David that some sheep had strayed into his land and destroyed his tillage. David ruled that the sheep be given to the farmer as compensation. But upon hearing of this, David's son Solomon commented that the ruling was too harsh, since now the original owner of the sheep had lost all his belongings, whereas the other farmer still had his land. Solomon instead suggested giving the farmer of the land temporary rights over the other's sheep, and the sheep farmer a mandate to take care of the other's land until it reached its former state of tillage. David was convinced by this suggestion and changed his previous ruling, showing the importance of ijtihad in assessing and at times overturning previous rulings.[18]

What is interesting to note here is not only that David and Solomon practiced *ijtihad* to reach their individual decisions, but that they arrived at different results. While Solomon's decision (a more merciful one, as pointed out previously) was deemed the more appropriate *"We vouchsafed unto both of them sound judgment and knowledge [of right and wrong]"* showing that the differing verdicts reached by the two Prophets are a simple and enriching effect of the application of *ijtihad*. While the two men were Prophets, they are fallible like any other people (as can be seen by the previously-mentioned example of David's hasty judgment in the case of the two men with the ewes), yet the process by which they reached their final decision is lauded.

Human viewpoints are by definition subject to adaptation and refinement. Just as David was willing to adapt and adjust his point of view after hearing that of his son, which was deemed to be more fitting to the circumstances of that particular case, so human beings should in general be able to adapt and refine their perspectives and thoughts in light of new information and diverging circumstances. These changes may span a particular case like the one above, or they may be more generally relevant to changing conditions and the growing needs of the community. For example, life circumstances of a person in twenty-first century America are very different from those of his/her predecessor in ninth-century Baghdad. It would therefore be highly unlikely that the former would have the same perspective, logic, and way of reasoning as the latter, however much he/she tried to approximate the predecessor's thinking. Also, the issues that were crucial to the life of the Baghdadi predecessor may no longer be important or even relevant to the twenty-first century American, while the contemporary American may be grappling with some issues that the Baghdadi may never have encountered. The political model adopted by the Muslims after the Prophet's death was devised quickly. Just laws had to be devised, but they were devised not only on the basic of what ought to be, but on what had to happen post facto in the Muslim community.

While the Quran is the divine origin of laws and thus of justice, the translation of Quranic principles is carried out within a particular human context. The result of this has been considerable debate on the application of justice in law. The *sharia*, which is usually identified as "Islamic law," is characterized as the vehicle for applying the Quranic imperative of justice. But, we need to examine this term and its meaning very closely, since it is often used in popular or media discourse to allude to a variety of meanings. Generally, *sharia* is used to refer to a rigid, detailed body of law that is in contrast to Western, legal codes. It is conceived of as being purely of divine origin, and adherence to it is often deemed to be synonymous with observation of religious practice and faith in Islam. Within the popular imagination, it is held responsible for sanctioning diverse practices, from polygamy to criminal penalties such as limb amputation or stoning.

Often, complex legal injunctions in Islam are seen to be the norm. Let us take the case of inheritance, for example. The Quran is often quoted in its very detailed commands regarding inheritance, in which it specifies the proportions that each relative would receive under varying sets of circumstances (Surah an-Nisaa – Women, 4:11-14). While these rules for inheritance are very complex, they actually only serve as a "stop-gap" measure. The existence of a will not only would supersede them all, but is actually required: *"It is ordained for you, when death approaches any of you and he is leaving behind much wealth, to make bequests in favor of his parents and [other] near of kin in accordance with what is fair: this is binding on all who are conscious of God"* (Surah al-Baqara – The Cow, 2:180). Thus, the inheritance laws can be applied when necessary, but they are by no means the preferred way of dealing with an issue. The will, designed with the distributive goal of "what is fair," is ultimately the "obligation on all who are conscious of God."

Thus, the individual's prerogative may be preferable in the case of inheritance. The individual human being is granted with the due to take the procedural elements of distributive justice and apply them in the way that he/she sees as most appropriate under the circumstances. We know that classical jurists may disagree, yet we feel that a fresh debate is needed and should be initiated. Likewise, the individual is encouraged to weigh each criminal case based on its own set of conditions, considering intention and individual circumstances in each case, and weighing mercy and forgiveness as key options that often surpass other considerations.

Let us apply this to criminal law, in particular with regard to *hudud*. *Hudud* crimes are a category of crimes that are distinguished by the fact that the Quran declares a specific penalty for them. Among commonly cited *hudud* crimes are theft, slander, and public lewdness. But clearly the application of these *hudud* was not always uniform. We have seen previously the fact that the *hudud* for theft was not practiced in all cases during the time of the Prophet. In other words, if the literal application of *hudud* is inappropriate or unmerciful in a particular case, it was not applied. How about if it is unmerciful to a given society? The standard of mercy and punishment varies through history. In the present day, lifetime confinement, with the provisioning of food, clothing, shelter, and medical care, is considered a severe punishment. Such a sentence would have been considered something far different in the medieval era.

In assessing the central Divine Laws in Islam, one must distinguish between the Quran, the *sharia*, and *fiqh*. The Quran is the primary source of guidance for Muslims, as a book of moral and religious instruction. It is the only religious source of divine origin, as the literal word of God, and therefore the text cannot be changed or amended in any way without giving rise to charges of heresy.[19] The sharia is an ideal translation of Quranic principles into human law for the specific time, place, and circumstances of society. Lastly, *fiqh* refers to the body of Islamic jurisprudence, which is an attempt by Muslims of the classical period to develop *sharia*. *Fiqh* is a product of human efforts, and is not of divine origin.

Many current day Muslims believe that a resurrection and imposition of a body of *fiqh* from 10 centuries ago is the most appropriate way to translate Quranic principles into current reality. But this implies that *fiqh* is the sole component of *sharia* that needs to be considered when applying justice, by extension suggesting that man-made law is necessary for the existence of justice. This goes against the idea of God as the Originator and Ruler, from whom all principles originate. Justice exists first, as a Quranic principle. Human beings then elaborate upon it and create laws that uphold justice as the end goal. These laws can change over time, as the circumstances of the individual and society evolve. Therefore, *sharia* exists wherever there is justice, regardless of the specific laws in question.

The Quran's use of the term *sharia* supports this argument. It refers to *sharia* as "a path" or "a way" to apply what is "good" or "right." This can be seen in the usage of the word in contexts such as *"We have set thee on a way by which the purpose [of faith] may be fulfilled: so follow thou this [way], and follow not the likes and dislikes of those who do not know [the truth]"* (Surat al-Jathiyah – Kneeling Down, 45:18). The verse does not refer to a specific legal standard. Instead, the abstract definition emphasizes the fact that humans need to exercise their own judgment and reasoning to interpret and apply the term with regard to a legal framework. The resulting legal framework, or *fiqh*, is not a fixed legal blueprint that we merely need to apply without reflection. It is a body of work, including both juristic opinion and religious text, which constitutes a framework for realizing justice in human affairs. The Quranic component of it is immutable, although the human being's ability to understand those verses may change; the rest of it is of human origin and therefore subject to amendment. The decision of the second caliph, Umar ibn al-Khattab, to suspend the punishment for theft due to poor economic conditions is a direct example of where suspending the law due to extenuating circumstances can be applied in the modern era.

In other words, the human being is encouraged to perform *ijtihad*, the independent practice of human reasoning and judgment to determine a legal position, as opposed to strict adherence to the rulings of previous jurists. The encouragement to practice *ijtihad* can be seen in the account of a conversation between the Prophet and Mu'adh ibn Jabal, when the former was sending the latter to Yemen. The Prophet asked Mu'adh, "'How will you judge when the occasion of deciding a case arises?' He replied, 'I shall judge in accordance with God's Book.' He [the Prophet] asked, 'And if you do not find any guidance in God's Book?' He replied, '(I shall act) in accordance with the Sunna of the Messenger of God (pbuh).' He [the Prophet] asked, 'And if you do not find any guidance in the Sunna of the Messenger of God and in God's Book?' He replied, 'I shall do my best to form an opinion and I shall spare no effort.' The Messenger of God (pbuh) then patted him on the breast and said, 'Praise be to God Who has helped the messenger of the Messenger of God to find something that pleases the Messenger of God.'[20]

This *hadith* distinguishes between the Quran, the *sunna*, and *ijtihad*, in decreasing importance, as tools for adjudication. It alludes to the possibility that not all legal issues will necessarily be covered in religious sources. Therefore, the need to tailor the framework to specific circumstances allows for flexibility in the development of legal institutions over time, and the application of the Quranic ideal of justice. This point is of particular importance in the framework for justice. While there is a significant body of juristic writing on the procedural details of a justice system, some of this work is restrictive in its interpretation of the Quran. Therefore, it has the potential of being contrary, in practice, to certain Quranic ideals that have been emphasized in this discussion: namely the importance of individual liberty and freedom, equality of all individuals, and justice for all.

Conclusion

An examination of the Quranic text and subsequent applications of its precepts reveals an emphasis on both legal and distributive justice. Legal justice can be detailed in seven key elements: fairness in trial, fairness in judgment, proportionate punishment, importance of intention, individual judgment and punishment, equality, and mercy. Distributive justice constitutes general exhortations towards helping the poor and needy, with emphasis on the orphans. Both underscore the importance of applying these elements of justice according to the human being's humanly fallible but divinely recognized sense of fairness and wisdom.

There is no doubt that the Quran serves as the basis for the establishment of justice as a moral principle, as a religious duty and as a legal system. It gives rise to the *sharia*, which seeks to apply God's Law to human affairs in a variety of areas, with the goal of upholding justice and equality. But, the interpretation and application of *sharia* has become fixed over time, such that justice is deemed to exist only where revealed laws exist, and that individuals can apply justice as long as they study these laws. Justice exists a priori as a Quranic ideal. It exists independent of jurisprudence and other sources within the *sharia*, and its application has historically and textually been pursued by the human being according to his/her own sense of justice and mercy.

We call upon legal experts and jurists to shape a fresh, modern and practical reading of applying the sharia in a way that will realize its goals in modern times.

Secondary References

Mohammad Hashim Kamali. *Freedom, Equality and Justice in Islam.* Cambridge, UK: Islamic Texts Society, 2002.

Majid Khadduri. *The Islamic Conception of Justice.* Baltimore & London: The Johns Hopkins University Press, 1984.

Fathi Osman. *Concepts of the Quran: A Topical Reading.* Second Edition. Los Angeles, CA: MVI Publications, 1999.

Osman Abd al Malek al-Saleh. "The Right of the Individual to Personal Security in Islam." *The Islamic Criminal Justice System,* ed. Cherif Bassiouni. New York: Oceana Publications, 1982.

Jonathan Westphal (ed.). *Justice.* Hackett Readings in Philosophy. is, IN: Hackett Publishing Company, 1996.

Footnotes

1   Jonathan Westphal (ed.). *Justice.* Hackett Readings in Philosophy (Indianapolis, IN: Hackett Publishing Company, 1996), xi.
2   Majid Khadduri, *The Islamic Conception of Justice* (Baltimore & London: The Johns Hopkins University Press, 1984), 8.
3   See Khedduri, Justice, 7, for more on this.
4   Abu Dawud, Kitab al-Aqdiyah, 3566.
5   Abu Dawud, Kitab al-Aqdiyah, 3575.

6   Abu Yusef, cited in Osman Abd al Malek al-Saleh, "The Right of the Individual to Personal Security in Islam," *The Islamic Criminal Justice System*, ed. Cherif Bassiouni, (New York: Oceana Publications, 1982), 73.

7   Ibid.

8   Abu Dawud, *Kitab al-Aqdiyah*, 3566.

9   Abu Yusef in al-Saleh, "Right," 72.

10 See inter alia Abu Dawud, 4330. This of course brings up the issue of political justice, or the justice of the ruler towards his people. For a detailed examination of this, see Khadduri, *Justice*, 13-38.

11 See inter alia Muslim, Kitab al-Hudud, 4175-4186.

12 See Fathi Osman, *Concepts of the Quran: A Topical Reading*. Second Edition (Los Angeles, CA: MVI Publications, 1999), 939 for more on this.

13 Muslim, Kitab al-Hudud, 778.

14 Malik, Muwatta' Kitab al-Aqdiyah 430:1394; see Mohammad Hasan Kamali, *Freedom, Equality and Justice in Islam*, (Cambridge, UK: Islamic Texts Society, 2002), 83, 89, 116, for more examples.

15 Bukhari, 626.

16 Muslim, *Kitab al-Aqdiyyah*, 4261-4263.

17 Ibid., 4247-4250, with slight variations.

18 Osman, *Concepts*, 933.

19 This has not prevented some Muslims from imposing a similar rigidity on the interpretation of the text.

20 Abu Dawud, *Kitab al-Aqdiyah*, 3585.

Chapter Two

Constitutionalism

Islamic history, certainly after the death of the last of the "rightly-guided" caliphs, has been dominated by caliphates and empires based on dynastic, hereditary rule. These political models were not bounded by written constitutional limits in practice, although in theory the ruler might claim to be applying the Sharia and upholding Islamic practices. The only exception is the nascent city-state of Medina, which the Prophet (pbuh) founded in 622. The Constitution of Medina is the closest viable model we have for an Islamic constitution that recognizes and preserves the importance of the rule of law, religious freedom and plurality and equality of all members of the community. It also upholds the separation of religious authority from political authority (in the form of the Prophet's (pbuh) role as the leader of the community), and the issue of popular sovereignty. These serve as key points in our theoretical framework.

How do we conceptualize an Islamic constitutional framework? The foundational principles of the Constitution can easily be drawn from the Quran, with supplementary support from historical practice. The full text of the Constitution of Medina and an analysis of its contents is the subject of a significant portion of this chapter. The section following details the gap between Islamic political theory and history. The political community of Medina did not have a far-reaching impact on the evolution of Islamic political theory and history. The Caliphate played a more significant role in that respect, although there remain gaps between the actual and the ideal form of political leadership represented by the caliph. In particular, what seems to have been lost in practice is the notion of a government limited by the rule of law and one that is not subject to manipulation by absolute executive power.

The question remains as to who will interpret Quranic principles in a constitutional framework, and who will apply them. The last section of this chapter examines these questions. With regard to interpretation, we place this power within the polity itself, to emerge as a negotiated consensus and then codified into the Constitution. It is the responsibility of the judiciary to interpret and apply the Constitution.

Definition

In general, we use the term "constitutionalism" in this chapter, to refer to a conception of a state that includes limited government, adherence to the rule of law and the protection of fundamental rights.[1] These ideas may be codified in a single written document or implicitly identified in a collection of texts, both of which serve the same purpose of identifying the guiding principles of the state.

A more formal definition describes the constitution as the "organic and fundamental law of a nation or a state. [It] establish[es] the character and conception of its government; organizing such government, and regulating, distributing, and limiting the functions of its different department, and prescribing the extent and manner of the exercise of sovereign powers."[2] It sets out a framework, based on a "government of law, and not of men."[3] In other words, the constitution transcends the authority of rulers, and holds them accountable to a fixed standard, rendered in law.

Nevertheless, a constitution is more than just the collection of laws and institutions. It is an expression of fundamental values and principles, which the constituent community has collectively agreed upon as the standard by which they shall be governed.[4] It provides the normative framework within which the political order is articulated, in addition to the operational one. For example, the Bill of Rights in the United States is an expression of American political values.

A constitutional model of a state may bear striking similarities to a liberal, democratic system, particularly with regard to the three characteristics noted above, limited government, adherence to the rule of law and protection of individual rights.[5] But the two are not necessarily synonymous, since a constitution may lay the framework for any kind of political system. There are over 150 countries in the world today that have constitutions, and all of them are certainly not liberal democracies.[6]

Nation-State and Constitutionalism

The concept of a sovereign nation-state is tied integrally to a constitutional model, but both are products of fairly recent historical developments. It is only by the end of the eighteenth century that the principle of national sovereignty was firmly established in Europe, and deemed to be a legitimate source of political power.[7] In the following century, the state developed into a "service-rendering organization independent of dynastic kingship," one which promoted the economic and social rights of its citizens. But the parameters of this sovereign state were not codified. The stage was set then for a written constitution as a way to fill this gap, to limit state authority by insisting on its adherence to certain standards.[8]

The Americans were the first to put this principle into practice, although the English had already argued for the idea of "fundamental laws" that did not derive their validity from the king's will. In the English case, these remained unwritten, but nevertheless retained their power as transcendental standards of the political order. In contrast, the founding fathers in Virginia not only "established a procedure for the creation of written constitutions by a collective representative body,... [but also] established the procedure for the ratification of draft constitutions by popular vote."[9]

How does the development of the nation-state and a written constitution relate to Islamic theories of constitutionalism? The political units that dominated Islamic history were the Caliphate and empires based on dynastic, hereditary rule. Neither of these political models were bound by written constitutional limits in practice, although in theory the ruler might claim to be applying the *sharia* and upholding Islamic practices.

The nation-state is a relative newcomer to Islamic political history. Most have been created only within the last century, and in many cases, in the aftermath of colonialism. Among Muslim states that have written constitutions, there is no evidence that they are particularly Islamic in substance (drawn from Quran or other sources), beyond the fact that they pay lip service adherence to "Islam and the *sharia*". This leaves us with a relatively clean slate for developing an Islamic constitutional model today. The prevalence of the nation-state means that it is the only template upon which a framework can be fashioned. We have assumed the existence of the nation-state as the context within which an Islamic constitutional model is developed.

The Quran and Constitutionalism

There are certain similarities between the purpose of the Quran and a constitution. Both refer to the individual as the intended subject. Both seek to institute order within a pluralistic society. The Quran establishes equity and justice as the guiding principles for relations between social groups, and aims to protect the rights of the weaker segments of society against the power of the stronger. We see this in the concern for the poor, orphans, refugees, slaves, and women, all of whom were historically disadvantaged members of Arabian society. Similarly, "constitutionalism is a man-made attempt at closing the gap between the strong and the weak, between the influential and the non-descript."[10]

But, there are also key differences. While the Quran offers a moral and ethical blueprint for accomplishing this task, the constitution provides a uniquely political one. A constitution is only concerned with achieving order in this world. The Quran's mandate, in contrast, covers both the temporal world and the Afterlife. Although both are concerned with the individual, they are addressed to vastly different kinds of communities. The Quran is a message to the *umma* made up of Muslims, although other faiths are not excluded from learning from it if they so choose. The constitution is addressed to all those with loyalty to the state regardless of religious belief, and does not draw religious distinctions. These differences point to a vital distinction between a religious community privileging Muslims and a political community made up of various faiths, and in general, to a religious/moral framework for organizing human affairs versus a political one.[11]

Nevertheless, the Quran is still useful for giving us basic values within which to shape a constitutional model for an Islamic state. It serves as a Divine source, out of which the guiding principles and the law of the state can be fashioned. This is in contrast to man-made natural law, that came to be the basis of much of Western political thought.[12] In addition to the Quran, we also selectively consider other Islamic sources, such as the *sunna* and the *fiqh*, as complementary sources for developing the constitution of an Islamic state.

An Islamic Constitutional Model

By far the most important precedent for an Islamic constitution is set by the Medinan document negotiated by the Prophet (pbuh) with the residents soon after his arrival in Medina in 622. Alternately referred to as the Constitution of Medina, or the Pact of Medina, it is notable in that it gives us concrete, basic principles for governing the nascent city-state of Yathrib (later known as Medina). It creates the reality of a religiously pluralistic state. It grants moral and religious autonomy to the Jews and other non-Muslims, while stressing the mutual obligations of all of the communities in matters of security.

There is evidence that the document was not written entirely at one time, but that the clauses were determined piecemeal and edited together later. In general though, the document dates from the early Medinan period.[13] We also know that the first half of the document referring to the relations between the *Ansar* and the *Muhajirun* was written in the first year after the Prophet's (pbuh) arrival in Medina, and the second half added later. But there is dispute as to whether that was before or after the Battle of Badr in 624.[14]

The Prophet (pbuh) did not seek to establish the absolute rule of the Muslims over the inhabitants of Medina. The Constitution represents the social consensus of the diverse groups that made up the residents of the city. A population census ordered by the Prophet (pbuh) revealed that of the 10, 000 people who lived there, only 1,500 were Muslims, 4,000 were Jews and 4,500 were polytheist Arabs.[15] The Muslims were therefore in the minority, and it was imperative to create a political arrangement through which the Muslims could live in Medina in safety. This would only be possible to achieve by working in tandem with the Jewish and Arab tribes, as equal parties.[16]

The Prophet's (pbuh) first priority upon his arrival was to arrange for the resettlement of the Meccan refugees, also known as the *muhajirun* (emigrants). For this, he needed the aid of the Medinan Muslims, or the *ansar* (helpers). One of the goals of the constitution was therefore to define the mutual rights and duties of these two groups, and establish harmonious relations among them. Beyond this immediate concern, other priorities revolved around making political arrangements with the non-Muslim inhabitants, and ensuring the political and military security of the city.[17]

The translated text of the document is below.[18] An analysis of the main principles and themes follows.

CONSTITUTION OF MEDINA

In the name of God, the Most Merciful, the Compassionate

1. This is a prescript (*kitab*) of Muhammad, the Prophet on behalf of the believers and Muslims of Quraysh and Yathrib, and those who follow them and are attached to them who crusade along with them. They are a single community (*umma*) distinct from (other) people.

2. The Emigrants of Quraysh, according to their former condition, pay jointly the blood-money between them, and they (as a group) ransom their captive(s), (doing so) with uprightness and justness between the believers.

3. Banu 'Awf, according to their former condition, pay jointly their blood money, and each sub clan ransoms its captive(s), (doing so) with uprightness and justness between the believers.

4. Banu'l-Harith, according to their former condition, ... (same as #3).

5. Banu Sa'idah.... (same as #3).

6. Banu Jusham.... (same as #3).

7. Banu'n-Najjar.... (same as #3).

8. Banu'Amr b.'Awf.... (same as #3).

9. Banu'n-Nabit.... (same as #3).

10. Banu'l-Aws.... (same as #3).

11. The believers do not forsake a debtor among them, but give him (help), according to what is fair, for ransom or blood money.

12. A believer does not take as a confederate the client of a believer without his (the latter's) consent.

13. The God-fearing believers are against whoever of them acts wrongfully or plans an act that is unjust or treacherous or hostile or corrupt among the believers; their hands are all against him, even if he is the son of one of them.

14. A believer does not kill a believer because of an unbeliever, and does not help an unbeliever against a believer.

15. The security (*dhimma*) of God is one: the granting of "neighborly protection" (*yujir*) by the least of them (the believers) is binding on them; the believers are patrons of one another to the exclusion of (other) people.

16. Whoever of the Jews follows us has the (same) help and support (as the believers), so as long as they are not wronged (by him) and he does not help (others) against them.

17. The peace (*silm*) of the believers is one; no believer makes peace apart from another believer, where there is fighting in the way of God, unless this peace be the same and equally binding on all.

18. In every expedition made with us the parties take turns with one another *[everyone takes equal part in military action]*.

19. The believers exact vengeance for one another where a man gives his blood in way of God. The God-fearing believers are under the best and most correct guidance.

20. No idolater (*mushrik*) gives "neighborly protection" (*yujir*) for good or property of the Quraysh, nor intervenes in his (a Qurayshi's) favor against a believer.

21. When anyone wrongfully kills a believer, the evidence being clear against him, then he is liable to be killed in retaliation for him, unless a representative of the murdered man is satisfied (with a payment). The believers are against him (the murderer) entirely; nothing is permissible for them except to oppose him.

22. It is not permissible for a believer who has agreed to what is in this document (*sahifa*) and believed in God the Last Day to help a wrong-doer or give him lodging. If anyone helps him or gives him lodging, then upon this man is the curse of God and His wrath on the Day of Resurrection, and from him nothing will be accepted to make up for it or take its place.

23. Where ever there is anything about which you differ, it is to be referred to God and to Muhammad (pbuh).

24. The Jews bear expenses along with the believers so long as they continue at war.

25. The Jews of Banu' Awf are a community (*umma*) along with the believers. To the Jews their religion and to the Muslims their religion. (This applies) both to their clients and to themselves, with the exception of anyone who has done wrong or acted treacherously; he brings evil only on himself and on his household.

26. For the Jews of Banu'n Najjar the like of what is for the Jews of Banu'Awf.

27. For the Jews of Banu'l-Harith the like of what is for the Jews of Banu'Awf.

28. For the Jews of Banu Sa'idah the like of what is for the Jews of Banu'Awf.

29. For the Jews of Banu Jusham the like of what is for the Jews of Banu'Awf.

30. For the Jews of Banu'l-Aws the like of what is for the Jews of Banu'Awf.

31. For the Jews of Banu Tha'labah the like of what is for the Jews of Banu'Awf, with the exception of anyone who has done wrong or acted treacherously; he brings evil only on himself and his household.

32. Jafnah, a subdivision (*batn*) of Tha'labah, are like them.

33. For Banu 'ah-Shutaybah the like of what is for the Jews of Banu 'Awf; honorable dealing (comes before treachery).

34. The clients of Tha'labah are like them.

35. The sub branches (*bitana*) *[referring to alliances not necessarily based on blood ties]* of the Jews shall have the same rights as themselves [the principal members].

36. No one of them (those belonging to the *umma*) may go out (to war) without the permission of Muhammad (peace be upon him), but he is

not restricted from taking vengeance for wounds *[retaliation]*. Whoever acts rashly, it involves only himself and his household except where a man has been wronged. God is the truest (fulfiller) of this (document).

37. It is for the Jews to bear their expenses and for the Muslims to bear their expenses. Between them (that is, to one another) there is help (*nasr*) against whoever wars against the people of this document. Between them is sincere friendship (*nash wa nasiha*), and honorable dealing, not treachery. A man is not guilty of treachery through (the act of) his confederate *[not guilty by association]*. There is help for (or, help is to be given to) the person wronged.

38. The Jews bear expenses along with the believers so long as they continue at war.

39. The valley of Yathrib is sacred for the people of this document.

40. The "protected neighbor" (*jar*) is as the man himself so long as he does no harm and does not act treacherously.

41. No refuge will be given (by the protected person to others) without the permission of the original people of the place. [Watt's translation cites this clause as "No woman is given "neighborly protection" without the consent of her people.]

42. Whenever among the people of this document there occurs any incident (disturbance) of quarrel from which disaster for it (the people) is to be feared, it is to be referred to God and to Muhammad, the Messenger of God (God bless and preserve him). God is the most scrupulous and truest (fulfiller) of what is in this document.

43. No "neighborly protection" is given to Quraysh and those who help them.

44. Between them (the people of this document) is help against whoever suddenly attacks Yathrib.

45. If the Jews are invited to a peace to participate in and adhere to it, they shall participate in and adhere to it; and if they invite likewise, the same shall be incumbent upon the believers in their favor, excepting whoever wars against religion; for (incumbent upon) each man is his share from their side which is towards them *[meaning obscure, might mean that each person is responsible for contributing to expenses for the part of the city he lives in]*.

46. The Jews of al-Aws, both their clients and themselves, are in the same position as belongs to the people of this document while they are thoroughly honorable in their dealings with the people of this document. Honorable dealing (comes) before treachery.

47. A person acquiring (guilt) acquires it only against himself. God is the

most upright and truest (fulfiller) of what is in this document. This pre-script (*kitab*) shall not protect any oppressor or violator of pledge; and whoever goes out (on a military expedition) shall have security, and whoever stays in Medina shall have security; except one who commits oppression and violation of the pledge.; God is the protector of those who fulfill and observe the pledge scrupulously, even as Muhammad, the Messenger of God – may God bless and protect him – is (the protector).

Analysis

The introductory statements of the Constitution of Medina define the parties involved in its construction and administration: the emigrant Muslims of the Quraysh, the Muslims of Yathrib, the Jews, and the client tribes that are attached to all of these parties through military/political alliances. It is a distinctly pluralistic community made up of autonomous social groups. This implies the equal participation of all in the political community that the document proposes, without regard to religious identity. It is worth underscoring precisely for its departure from the notion of a homogeneous Islamic state that privileges Muslims over other citizens.

We also see the mutual co-existence of multiple *ummas*, or communities, based on religion, kinship and patron-client ties in the city-state of Medina. Along religious lines, there is the *umma* of Muslims, and existing alongside them, the *umma* of the Jews (Article 25). But more pertinent is the citizenry that constitutes the political *umma*. It includes the principal parties to the Pact and their *mawla*, the client tribes, who are also given protection. The political community subsumes the religious communities, which also include the polytheist Arabs, or the *mushrik* (Article 20).

Also noteworthy is the fact that the religious communities are not regulated by political authority and individual freedom of religion is left unfettered. Neither is there official recognition of the dominance of one religious group over another, nor pressure for others to convert to Islam. In fact, Article 25 distinctly states, "To the Jews their religion and to the Muslims their religion." The only cause for distinction between believers and nonbelievers is if one party threatens to disrupt the peace or violates the treaty, and is therefore punished or expelled by the community. If a polytheist is to be shunned, it is because he has sided with the Meccan Quraysh against the Muslims of Medina (Art. 20).[19]

In addition, other markers are used to refer to the communities, instead of religion. For example, the Jews and Arabs are referred to through their tribal affiliations, and their clients, likewise (Art. 3-10 and 25-35). Since the Jews acceded to the Constitution by clans, and not as one religious community, when one tribe broke the pact, only it was expelled from Medina, and not the entire Jewish community (Art. 16).[20] The Muslims are identified as being either the emigrants from Mecca, or the helpers from Medina (preamble), or in other instances, as simply "believers." All of these details illustrate the fact religious identity is not the basis for membership within the political community of Medina.

Security is the pivotal concern of the Constitution of Medina. "The security of God is one" (Article 15). The protection granted by God to the community encompasses all of its members. The borders of the city-state of Medina are demarcated and the security of all of the inhabitants is ensured in Article 39: "The valley of Yathrib is sacred for the purpose of this document." All those who threaten this security from outside these borders face the collective military strength of the Medinans (Art. 44). In conjunction with Articles 17 and 18, which deal with equal rights to make peace and compulsory military service for all, respectively, all of these articles point to the regulation of war and peace and the paramount goal of maintaining the security of the political community. Political security takes precedence over any and all individual social and religious concerns.

Equality is another main theme of these constitutional articles. It refers to both individual rights and group rights. Equality of crime and punishment for individuals is noted in Articles 13, 21, 22 and 47. All the members of the pact are bound together, and no group or individual can make a separate peace or other treaty with an enemy of Medina (Articles 17 and 40). Every person has the right to take grievances to the Prophet (pbuh) and ask for a just settlement of differences, according to Article 23. A victim is entitled to help or compensation. "There is help for the person wronged" (Article 37).

The equality of social groups is more prominent in the Constitution, however. First, the individual tribes are equally responsible for ransoming their captives and paying the blood money of their members. Second, each tribe contributes to military security, both financially and through active duty. Article 18 states that every party will take equal turns in military combat, and Articles 37 and 38 reiterate that the Jews and Muslims will independently bear military expenses as long as war continues. Third, financial autonomy is also delineated by tribe and district, so that the members of each locality pay towards the upkeep of their district.21 "Incumbent upon each man is his share from their side which is towards them" (Article 45). Fourth, religious groups are given autonomy and freedom of practice and belief, as noted earlier. We can also see a nascent system of social welfare, wherein a debtor is to be helped by the members of his religious group or tribe, and is not to be forsaken (Article 11).

Adherence to the rule of law and the equality of all before the law is another component of this city-state vision, and particularly relevant for this discussion on constitutionalism. The rule of a law is a key characteristic of a constitutional system, because it provides a normative standard by which the community is governed, and its members held accountable. Although behaving with justice is generally emphasized throughout, Article 13 explicitly states that anyone who engages in criminal behavior, i.e. "acts wrongfully" broadly defined, will be ostracized from his group and held accountable before the law, administered by God and the Prophet (pbuh). The individual is not protected by membership in his particular tribe/community. The intervention of the individual's tribe in his defense will be futile, even if he is the son of one of them. In addition, individual criminal responsibility is upheld, so that only the person guilty may be punished. "A man is not guilty of treachery through his confederate" (Article 37). "A person acquiring guilt only acquires it against himself" (Article 47).

Article 21 applies these legal principles specifically towards the murder of a Muslim, and prescribes retaliation or the payment of compensation when the guilt of the murderer is proven.[22] It also states, "The believers are against him (the murderer) entirely; nothing is permissible for them except to oppose him." The subsequent article, Article 22, condemns anyone who has agreed to the terms of the pact to give protection to a wrongdoer. Therefore, membership in the political community, while all-encompassing with regard to social and religious identity, is severely restrictive against those who threaten its foundational security. We can also argue that justice is a primary principle of the city-state created by the Prophet (pbuh).

The Constitution appears to contradict itself by allowing two levels of justice to exist simultaneously. On one hand, each tribe is responsible for payment of blood money of its members, and is allowed to extract retaliation against the perpetrator if one of their members is killed. On the other hand, it also establishes certain legal principles regarding criminal justice, and a higher authority, presided over by the Prophet (pbuh) to rule on evidence against an individual accused of murder, or to settle differences or quarrels among people. One can see in this a process of transition from tribal authority to centralized authority. If there is a center of power that is willing and able to enforce the law against all, then guilt and punishment can and should be individualized. If the central authority is non-existent or weak, then tribal or clan-based systems of justice come into play.

How can we understand this dichotomy and apply it towards a contemporary constitutional model? Certainly, in the present-day context, individuals or groups are not allowed to take the law into their own hands and to retaliate for the death of their kin. This was a historical practice, specific to the society in which the Prophet (pbuh) lived, and it would have been difficult to outlaw it altogether. Retaliation, or the law of talion, is also mentioned in the Quran, although forgiveness for the killer or the payment of *diyya* (compensation) are recommended alternatives. But talion is applied by the state, not by individuals acting on their own.

More important from our perspective is the role of a higher judicial authority in the form of God and the Prophet (pbuh) (Art. 23,42,47). Certainly, God's guidance to Prophet (pbuh) is undisputed, but His Will was conveyed through His Messenger, a human being. Medina was not directly ruled by God. In terms of the actual, physical presence of judicial authority, the Prophet (pbuh) occupied that role as the political leader. While it is evident that the Muslims would accept the Prophet's (pbuh) authority, it is a little less obvious why the Jews and other non-Muslim inhabitants of Medina would do the same. For example, there is evidence that Jews asked the Prophet (pbuh) to settle disputes among them as well, and that he ruled according to their biblical law.[23] One explanation is that the Prophet (pbuh) did not render justice as a prophet, since not all the parties involved were Muslims, but that he did so as a political leader, to whom obedience and loyalty were given in return for the security that he guaranteed. Acts of the Prophet (pbuh) as a ruler do not have the status of divinely inspired or mandated acts. The secular, political aspect of the Prophet's rule is particularly important as a standard of a constitutional model today. It underlines the role of delivering true justice as the overarching standard that guarantees equality of all citizens, regardless of religious identity.

An analysis of the Constitution of Medina shows that the early Islamic state distinguished between religious and political authority, but also included an element of popular sovereignty. This state is in contrast to the Western conception of a secular state. The latter explicitly excludes divine Revelation as a constitutional basis, and also subscribes to a formal separation of religious and political authority.[24] In applying the Medinan model to an Islamic constitutional framework, we are locating the source of it in the Divine, i.e. the Quran as revealed by God to His Messenger.

We now approach the crux of the matter. What ultimately is the basis of the law? Where are the first principles drawn from? Do they come out of thin air? Are they an expression of popular choice? We find the basic principles of human law to be sourced in Divine revelation, specifically in the Quran. God provides an absolute standard by which we can erect a society. Without it, what prevents society from legalizing acts that are morally reprehensible by even the most liberal Western standard, i.e. racial discrimination? Western political theory has not answered this question very well. Appeals to "natural law" on the one hand, or to Biblical sources on the other, are problematic for a secular and rational approach. If we take the Western notion of separation of church and state to its logical conclusion, we abandon any source of moral certainty in drafting the law.

However, we do accept and support a formal separation of mosque and state, which *is* part of the traditional, Western definition of "secularism." We do not include formal religious institutions as part of the *structure* of an Islamic state, nor do we *institutionalize* a religious body charged with maintaining the moral and ideological conformity with "Islamic standards". In this sense, we subscribe to the absence of Islam as the official religion, as interpreted and administered by the state. Religious pluralism and freedom are not to be restricted by state authority. In addition, to the extent that religious interpretation of Quranic principles is necessary with regard to legislation, it is carried out through social consensus as expressed through the constitution and not imposed from above.

As a related point to secularism, we need to discuss, briefly, the difference between the Quran and *sharia* as divine Law. The Quran is the Book of God. It is primarily a moral and ethical blueprint, out of which we can draw out certain principles as the basis for more concrete legislation. It informs the process of constitution-building as a normative standard. When we use the term "*sharia*-based" in this chapter, we are referring to a body of work, composed primarily of extra-Quranic sources, but not exclusively so. This body of law developed as a part of several schools of thought in the classical age of Islam. Traditional supporters of an "Islamic state" desire mostly to resurrect and install this ancient legal system. In contrast, we present a definition of *sharia* as an evolving body of ethical norms and legal rulings, which is open to interpretation in keeping with social and historical changes. Our definition de-emphasizes the binding power of previous *fiqh* and narrow interpretations of the Quran in favor of a more inclusive, tolerant perspective that stresses key universal, Quranic principles (such as freedom, justice and equality), and supplements them through other religious sources.

The second point of comparison between the Medinan model and Western constitutionalism is that of popular sovereignty. Popular sovereignty refers to the presence of the people's political will as demonstrated through voting and other mechanisms. It places limits on governmental authority by making it accountable to the people it governs. An Islamic understanding of government is compatible with this perspective. Despite the fact that God is accepted as the Absolute Sovereign, this does not preclude the idea of human political sovereignty. We see this illustrated in Medina by the fact that although God is deemed the protector of the community, it was the negotiations carried out by the Prophet (pbuh) and the Medinan tribes which resulted in the creation of the city-state. We have no way to know the will of God directly, and given that, the will of the people as a whole is the only understandable representation of God's will. Investing the right to declare God's will in one person, no matter how pious he or she may appear to others, is irrational and the height of folly.

In conclusion, the Constitution of Medina serves as the basis for a constitutional framework in an Islamic context because it applies Quranic principles of individual freedom, equality and justice for all. It also incorporates pluralism and diversity into the normative standard for government by recognizing the autonomy of social and religious groups. We note that it is highly significant that the Medinan constitution limited the political authority of the Prophet (pbuh) himself. He was bound by it to the same extent that everyone else was bound to it. But, the city-state was ruled by the Prophet (pbuh) for only a short time period. His death, ten years later, put an end to this political vision. The remainder of Islamic political history did not live up to the constitutional ideals that the Prophet (pbuh) had put into place during his lifetime. The following section will explore the gap between Islamic political history and theory in light of the model provided by the Medinan Constitution.

Political Theory vs. History

There is a gap between the ideals of an Islamic constitutional model that the Constitution of Medina represents and the direction in which political history evolved in the centuries following the Prophet's (pbuh) death. For one thing, his death symbolized the beginning of the schism between the political and the religious leadership of the Muslim *umma*, since the Prophet (pbuh) had embodied both roles in his lifetime. In addition, the lack of a clear political successor to the Prophet (pbuh) meant that there arose competing notions of the basis for political leadership of the Muslim community. Eventually, Abu Bakr was elected by the consensus of the Companions of the Prophet (pbuh), and designated the "Successor (caliph/*khalifa*) of the Prophet of God."

This event had far-reaching ramifications. First, it laid the foundation for the Caliphate[25] as the predominant political institution in later Islamic thought. It was the ideal which later historians, jurists and scholars referred to in order ground their own work. The later dynastic kingship/sultanate systems in Islamic political history share the quality of individualistic rule that the caliphate model embodied. (Although, we can also argue that these empires had no intrinsically "Islamic" quality to them, but were more strongly influenced by Byzantine and Persian political models of kingship and hereditary rule.) Second, the introduction of the caliphate represented the collision of Islamic history with constitutional theory. The designation of the caliph and the political institutions that developed within the caliphate system historically became part of the theoretical justification for adherence to the *sharia* as the basis for political leadership.[26]

To elaborate further on these two points, we need to consider the transition from the Prophet's (pbuh) model of leadership to that of the Caliphs. The Prophet (pbuh) was the only Muslim ruler with uncontested claim to political and religious legitimacy and authority in the eyes of Muslims. He embodied the executive, legislative and judicial roles, as a sovereign, although we should note that at critical junctures, such as tactics used at the Battle of Uhud, he would abide by the majority view. After him, the nature of the rule of the four Rightly-Guided Caliphs changed fundamentally. Although the caliphate was still based on a theory of personalistic rule, the individuals having been chosen, in theory, on the basis of their moral integrity and other leadership qualities, the four caliphs did not embody ultimate sovereignty in the way the Prophet (pbuh) had done. They did not claim to be prophets, or to legislate on the basis of direct divine command. Their role was limited to executing and implementing the Prophet's (pbuh) teachings, what later came to be codified as part of the *sharia*. Application of the *sharia* became a standard component of political leadership in Islamic political theory.

But, other aspects of the caliph's leadership were also incorporated into Islamic political theory and history. In theory, the caliph's right to rule was based on his moral integrity and faithfulness to the teachings of the Prophet (pbuh). In practice, though, there was no way of evaluating this on a frequent basis by the community. Once the caliph was initially appointed and confirmed, an oath of allegiance (*baya*) was made, and that was the limit of a formal mechanism for ensuring the accountability of the ruler to the law or to the ruled. Although the caliph's authority was ostensibly based on popular support, in practice there was no way for that popular support to be freely given or withdrawn at any stage after his appointment. This disconnect is what has historically been a fundamental institutional weakness in Islamic political history.[27] Even the "rightly-guided" Caliph Othman was the victim of a sort of violent impeachment that ended in his assassination.

In addition, although in theory the caliph followed the Prophet's (pbuh) example of leadership in implementing Revelation, in practice, he was the ultimate decision-maker on applying the *sharia*, at least usually and according to his understanding of it. On the one hand, he was bound by the limits of the *sharia*, but on the other, he was the supreme authority on what rule, and what interpretation of it would be applied in a given case. Caliph Umar, for example, is known for having made innovations in the distribution of *fey*, or conquered lands. In essence then, he was still the ultimate legislative and executive authority.[28] Even though the *ulama* and other members of society functioned in an advisory role, which he did take into account, their advice was not necessarily binding upon the caliph. The limitation of the *sharia* on executive political authority was therefore, in practice, not very effective.

The ramifications of this political tradition for a constitutional model of government today are profound for the gap they demonstrate between Islamic political theory and political history. First, in addition to the individualistic nature of political rule, the caliphate symbolized the concentration of power within the executive branch, with the judiciary and legislative usually occupying more supplementary roles. Second, although theoretically, the caliph's authority was bound by the limits of Revelation and the Prophet's (pbuh) example, in practice, those boundaries were not absolute, and it was mostly a self-regulated boundary. In other words, it was only the fear of God that provided the limits on governmental authority. This moral/ethical imperative was not translated into an effective institutional mechanism.

In contrast to the limitations of the caliphate model, we are presenting a constitutional theory that recognizes and applies more explicitly the characteristics of limited government, a system of checks and balances among the executive, legislative and judicial branches, and the rule of law. This is in addition to the ideals of protection of individual and groups rights on the basis of equality and justice that the Constitution of Medina articulated. Combining aspects of both the

Medinan model and the Caliphate, we are offering an Islamic constitutional framework that prevents the arbitrary exercise of power by the executive by institutionalizing legal limitations on government. The role of the judiciary is vital in accomplishing this goal. The following section details this aspect more fully.

The Judiciary: Interpreting an Islamic Constitution

It is the judiciary's responsibility to decide on specific cases both civil and criminal. In addition, the highest court in the land is granted the role of deciding whether specific laws are permissible within the framework of the constitution. This is essentially the power to interpret the constitution of the state. In a broader sense, the latter represents the boundaries of the rule of law, which is a key characteristic of a constitutional state.

A vital issue in a constitutional Islamic state is that of the boundaries of interpretation and application of an Islamic constitution. If the judiciary is responsible for upholding the rule of law, as enshrined in constitutional principles, how do we choose the judiciary? How do they determine whether or not a particular piece of legislation is in conformity with the constitution? Whose interpretation of the Quran is to be the authoritative basis for it?

Traditionally, the interpretive role was appropriated by the *ulama*, those who are learned in Islamic jurisprudence, and they served as a moral check on the legislative and executive authority of the government. But, they did not hold political authority, and they were not necessarily accountable to anyone. Muslim jurists living under Abbasid rule were notable in their insistence on independence from imperial, political authority. Abu Hanifa (d. 767), al Shafi (d. 820) and Ahmad b. Hanbal (d. 855), all of whom were founders of Sunni legal schools, and scholars Abu Yusuf (d. 795) and al-Shaybani (d. 805), are all examples of classical Muslim jurists who resisted attempts of co-optation into the administrative structure of government.[29] This basic judicial independence from the political control exercised by the executive needs to be institutionalized in the constitution of contemporary Islamic state.

But, while we subscribe to the idea of the independence of the judiciary, we do not grant them a monopoly on religious and moral authority similar to that the members of the *ulama* have enjoyed historically. We do not create a special or privileged class that interprets the Quran. The creation of an autonomous body of jurists with the unique power to interpret the Quran and hence develop the *sharia*, and to determine the degree of conformity of all laws with the *sharia*, without any limitations whatsoever, risks potential abuse of power by that body.[30] It also raises the question as to how people are selected to join such a body, and on what criteria can they be removed from it. From our perspective, the role of Supreme Court judges is to exercise their reasoning based on the principles of governance that the community has already collectively decided as key, as derived from the Quran and other sources, and enshrined in the constitution. The values of the Quranic message are translated into the constitution by the polity as a whole. This is accomplished through the democratic process only. It is the nation as a whole that interprets the Quran and translates that interpretation into the written constitution. The judiciary does not interpret the Quran; it only interprets the constitution. A change in the interpretation of the Quranic message of the constitution would require a legal amendment, not a Supreme Court ruling. Membership in the Supreme Court should ultimately derive from a democratic process, although we believe that there are multiple ways to achieve that.

How should an Islamic democratic state write and amend the constitution? What kind of mechanisms and processes should be put into place, and how will they be determined? The answers to these questions need to come about through pluralistic and democratic debate, discussion and negotiation within the polity. The discussion needs to be as inclusive as possible, so that outcomes can reflect the views of a substantial majority and not just those of a minority group. We reject a monopoly over Quranic interpretation by any one group in society. People must use their own reason to determine their views on particular interpretations. There are and will be competing views of what constitutes a "right" or "wrong" interpretation of various Quranic verses. With the recognition that only God is the ultimate judge, we can nevertheless engage with others in discussing these interpretations, and allow a negotiated consensus to emerge. Also, we should stress that everyone should have access to this political process. In particular, women and non-Muslims should be treated on equal footing with others. We have already established in other chapters the basis for granting them equal rights, so we will merely reiterate here, the imperative to uphold these before the law.

Another important point is the need to include mechanisms for amendments to the constitution in the future. The interpretation of the Quran is limited by our human understanding, and is often determined by the contemporary contexts in which we live and how we see the world. In order for these principles to be relevant to later generations, they need to be enshrined in such a way that the constitution can be open to amendment later on in a clear, institutional process. This is not the same as amending the Quran, since that is a text that remains immutable as God's Word. But, the constitution does not have divine stature. It is a product of human efforts, and therefore may have flaws and limitations that will need to be addressed at a later date. A clear and defined constitutional amendment process is therefore very important in maintaining a viable Islamic constitutional, democratic state. It is at this level that we grant a role to religious leaders. They can mobilize political support for their views and be shapers of public opinion. They can even be heads of political parties as long as they respect the rights of others who disagree with them to compete in the political arena on an equal basis.

Conclusion

To recapitulate, how do we conceptualize an Islamic constitutional framework? First, the foundational principles of the Constitution are drawn from the Quran. These include freedom, justice, rule of law, and equality before the law, among others. Our specific interpretations of these principles are elaborated upon in the course of this book, in their own individual chapters. Second, the example of the Constitution of Medina gives us a concrete idea of how these principles can be applied in an Islamic context, one which preserves the importance of the rule of law, religious freedom and plurality and equality of all citizens. It provides concrete precedent for writing a constitution that limits the power of the state and guarantees fundamental rights. But, the political community of Medina did not have a far-reaching impact on the evolution of Islamic political theory and history. The Caliphate played a more significant role in that respect, although there remain gaps between the actual and the ideal form of political leadership represented by the caliph. In particular, what seems to have been lost in practice is the notion of a government limited by the rule of law and one that is not subject to manipulation by absolute executive power. Pulling all of these elements together, our argument is built upon the positive aspects of the nascent constitutional model of Medina and later political systems in Islamic history, while learning from the negative ones.

Most importantly, we stress the need to keep in mind an expansive definition of public good as the basis of an Islamic state. Such a conception allows for a state in which security and order are privileged, and individual citizens are free to live their lives in accordance with their own moral/religious/social beliefs as long as they do not threaten public security. A constitution that preserves citizens' rights, advocates the rule of law and limited political power of the government is necessary for creating this kind of community. The key is for each society to balance the means and the ends of constitutionalism, so that a proper balance between complete individual liberty and total social justice is achieved, while also achieving public good.[31]

Lastly, we comment upon the role of the *sharia* in an Islamic constitution. As Nathan Brown argues, "If constitutionalism is defined as a set of ideologies and institutions predicated on the idea of the limitation and regulations of government authority by law, then the Islamic *sharia* would seem to lend itself to constitutionalist interpretations fairly naturally."[32] The underlying theme is that the boundaries on government rule are set by the *sharia* as based on the Quran, and governments are accountable to this Law. This concept is not new in Islamic political theory, and classical Muslim scholars, in addition to more recent ones, have stressed these themes.[33]

But the manner in which these goals are to be achieved are subject to differing interpretations. The *sharia* is not a political manual that lays out specific procedures and institutions of government.[34] This flexibility in determining the best vehicle (in terms of procedures and institutions) to achieve the goals of the *sharia* is precisely what makes it so attractive to Muslim political thinkers today, and furthers its compatibility with a constitutional form of government. Most importantly, it furthers discussion and consensus among the community, to develop the *sharia* according to their own use of reason and intellect, and to apply it towards political organization in the way they see fit. Again, to emphasize, we are speaking of the *sharia* as an ideal legal framework based on Divine revelation, and not the specific rulings of jurists and schools of *fiqh* (jurisprudence) developed in the classical era. As such, all humans can do is to try to find *sharia* ("the way") knowing that ultimately we can only approximate it, but never fully realize it.

Footnotes

1   Michel Rosenfeld, "Modern Constitutionalism as Interplay Between Identity and Diversity," in *Constitutionalism, Identity, Difference and Legitimacy: Theoretical Perspectives*, ed. Michel Rosenfeld (Durham: Duke University Press, 1994), p. 3.
2   Henry C. Black, *Black's Law Dictionary*, 5th ed, cited in An-Na'im, p. 70.
3   G.A. Forrest, "Constitution and Constitutional Law," *Encyclopedia Britannica*, vol. 6 (1967), p. 398.
4   An'-Na'im, p. 71.
5   More on liberal democracy from an Islamic perspective in its own separate chapter.
6   Said Amir Arjomand, "Religion and Constitutionalism in Western History and Iran and Pakistan," The Political Dimensions of Religion, (Albany: SUNY Press, 1993), p. 76.
7   Arjomand, "Religion and Constitionalism", p. 76.
8   Said Amir Arjomand, "Constitutions and the Struggle for Political Order," *Archives Europeens de Sociologie* 33(1992): 45(39-82).
9   Arjomand, "Constitutions and the Struggle for Political Order," p. 45.
10 Lawrence Ziring, "Constitutionalism and the Quran in the Final Decades of the 20th Century," *Journal Institute of Muslim Minority Affairs*, Vol. 9:2(1988), p. 225.
11 This is in keeping with our broader argument in this work. We have repeatedly emphasized the separation between religious

and political membership within society, and the need to de-link morality from law in the political responsibilities of the state.

12 Arjomand does a historical survey of the development of natural law and sacred law in the West in his article, "Constitutions and the Struggle for Political Order," cited above.

13 Noted Muslim historian Ibn Ishaq preserved the entire document in his Sirah. Frederick M. Denny, "Ummah in the Constitution of Medina," *Journal of Near East Studies*, 36:1(1977), p. 39.

14 Muhammad Hamidullah, *The First Written-Constitution in the World*, (Lahore: Sh. Mohammad Ashraf, 1968), p. 23.

15 This census is noted by Bukhari, in Ali Bulaç, "The Medina Document," *Liberal Islam*, ed. Charles Kurzman, (New York: Oxford University Press, 1998), p. 170.

16 Bulaç, p. 173.

17 Hamidullah, p. 15.

18 The translation is drawn from both Muhammad Hamidullah, *The First Written Constitution in the World*, and Frederick Denny's translated citation from Montgomery Watt's *Muhammad at Medina* (Oxford: Oxford University Press, 1956), p. 226. Arabic terms and parenthetical notes are from the original translation. Italicized comments are author's.

19 Quraysh is the name of the Prophet's (pbuh) tribe. In the earlier portions of the Constitution, the term refers to the Muslims who migrated with the Prophet (pbuh), in contrast to the Medinan Ansar. In later portions, the term is used exclusively to refer to the non-Muslim, Meccan Quraysh who used to torment the Prophet (pbuh) while he was still living in Mecca. They were therefore the enemies of the Muslims who undertook the hijra. One of the Prophet's (pbuh) concerns was that the non-Muslims of Medina might collude with Meccan Quraysh against the Emigrant Muslims. Articles 20 and 43 expressly prohibit this.

20 Hamidullah, p. 33.

21 Hamidullah, p. 26.

22 Murder falls under the category of *qisas* crimes. See more on this in chapters on justice and sanctity of life, respectively.

23 Hamidullah, p. 35; Bulaç, pp. 174-175.

24 Arjomand, "Constitutions and the Struggle for Political Order," p.42.

25 The Caliphate refers exclusively to the reign of the four caliphs, Abu Bakr, Umar, Uthman and Ali, from 632 to 660. They are called the Rashidun, or the Rightly-Guided Caliphs because of their authority to implement the revealed law of God. After Ali, the religious component of the title of Caliph, was contested vigorously and eventually came to be a merely symbolic title that later rulers took on purely for political expediency.

26 H.A.R.Gibb, "Constitutional Organization," *Law in the Middle East*, v. 1, eds. Majid Khadduri and Herbert Liebesny, (Washington, D.C.:Middle East Institute, 1955), p. 4.

27 An-Na'im, pp. 76-77.

28 An-Na'im, p. 80.

29 Kemal A. Faruki, *The Evolution of Islamic Constitutional Theory and Practice* (Karachi: National Publishing House, 1971), p. 33. For more on the historical development of the Sharia, see chapter on justice.

30 For example, the Iranian Supreme Council of Guardians has overturned laws passed by the Majles, which guarantee freedom of press, on the grounds of being "un-Islamic". This is in contrast to the freedom of speech and expression that we have argued, in another chapter, are Quranically mandated. Nevertheless, their interpretation holds because there are no constitutional principles that would prevent such a restrictive interpretation from being applied in the first place.

31 An-Na'im, p. 71.

32 Nathan J. Brown, "Islamic Constitutionalism in Theory and Practice," *Democracy, the Rule of Law and Islam*, ed. Eugene Cotran and Adel Omar Sherif, (Cambridge: Kluwer Law International, 1999), p. 491.

33 See also the individual chapters on democracy and justice systems for more on this theme.

34 Brown, p. 492.

Democracy

he central political challenge for modern Muslim thinkers is to develop a coherent understanding of how to create democratic institutions within the Muslim religious and historical heritage.   On both counts we face some challenges, but they are not insurmountable. First, the Quran does not give us concrete details of an ideal system of governance. But it does develop universal principles for organizing public affairs. Some of these are outlined individually in other chapters; for example, protection of individual freedoms, adherence to justice, and equality of all citizens before the law. But these principles, though divinely ordained, are mere signposts for the guidance of humankind. In and of themselves, they do not proclaim the supremacy of one kind of political system over another. Hence, there is a need for human interpretation and application of these principles towards political life. It is at this point of intersection between the divine text and society where we place our argument for an Islamic perspective on democracy, and conclude that it is the best form of political governance for our urban, industrial society, and in this time period.

This leads us to the second point. We are faced with the historical Muslim political experience, in which democracy has been notably absent as an institutional framework. Instead, the predominant trend since the end of the Rightly Guided Caliphs has been of absolute political rulers, legitimized through the combination of the theory of kingship and the sanction granted by Muslim jurists through the various *fiqh* that support political absolutism. This is the popular understanding of what a caliph was, and certainly some Muslims today see it as a desirable model of governance. The outcome is that we do not have a classical, historical example of a pluralistic, participatory, and representative form of government, upon which we can base current attempts at defining an Islamic framework for democracy. There are however ways to approach the issue. The political community founded by the Prophet (pbuh) at Medina in 622[1] and the rule of the four Rightly-Guided Caliphs (632-661) offer us certain principles of governance conducive to democracy, such as a social contract between ruler and ruled, protection of individual rights, and representative political participation.

This chapter will draw out these principles, among others, from both the Quran and historical examples, and demonstrate the synthesis between democracy as a representative, political system and Islamic values of the relationship between the ruler and the ruled. The chapter begins by offering a definition of democracy as the basis for the rest of this discussion. It continues by examining two common arguments against the compatibility of Islam and democracy, and refuting them by arguing that the concepts of popular sovereignty and separation of religious authority and the state can be supported within an Islamic framework. The following section details Islamic political theory and history to demonstrate what these models of governance offer us today for building a democratic model of an Islamic state. Subsequent portions of this chapter are organized according to key concepts that are part of a democratic system: a contractual relationship between the ruler and the ruled and *shura*, the mutual consultation between the two.

Definition

Underpinning the idea of democracy is a political contract between the ruler and the ruled, such that government derives its authority to rule from the express political will of the people. At a minimum, it refers to a political system in which sovereignty resides in the citizens, and is manifest through their direct and indirect participation in the workings of the political system. In the American context, it includes the right to choose elected representatives, both to the legislative and executive branches of government. Democratic procedure allows policy-making and laws to be shaped by majority rule, while at the same time maintaining the rights and input of those in the minority. Democracy also includes respect for the rule of law among citizens and their representatives and constitutional guarantees of freedom of assembly and expression and other civil and political liberties.[2] These issues will be addressed in the course of this chapter.

Sovereignty of the People vs. Sovereignty of God

The first issue is that of sovereignty of the people, which is one of the hallmarks of a democratic system. Sovereignty, in this case, refers to the highest authority. In a political context, sovereignty of the people means that citizens have the ultimate power to determine law and to express their political will by electing representatives who uphold that law.

A common argument against the compatibility of democracy and Islam is the idea that a political system that emphasizes people's sovereignty does so at the expense of the sovereignty of God as Lawmaker. According to the Quranic worldview, absolute sovereignty is associated only with God, and humans are designated as His vicegerents on earth. From this perspective, the duty of an Islamic state is to apply God's law, as revealed in the Quran and fleshed out by the historical *fiqh* (juristic tradition) as a manifestation of the ideal *sharia*. This eliminates absolute, political sovereignty as vested in a temporal ruler or the people who elect that ruler. Power flows one way, top down, from God to humankind, via the political ruler who applies His Law. However, this is a simplistic view of ordering political affairs, and one that excludes the role of human agency in the interpretive and political processes.

While it is certainly indisputable that God is the Ultimate

Sovereign, this does not preclude the concept of popular sovereignty vested in the people[3] and in the political ruler. God denotes humans as His Vicegerents in Surah al Baqara – The Cow, 2:30. *"And lo! Thy Sustainer said unto the angels: 'Behold, I am about to establish upon earth one who shall inherit it.' They said: 'Wilt Thou place on it such as will spread corruption thereon and shed blood – whereas it is we who extol Thy limitless glory, and praise Thee, and hallow Thy name?' [God] answered: 'Verily, I know that which you do not know'."* He empowers them with the free will to think and to make decisions on how to live their lives in accordance with Quranic values and ideals. *"In this way God makes clear His messages unto you, so that you might take thought"* (Surah al Baqara –The Cow, 2:266).

On the same basis, the decision about the best way to apply Islamic principles in political affairs is also left to humans. This autonomy implies that God does accept differences in how the ultimate end is achieved: to realize a spiritual, social and political order that is in harmony with Quranic principles of freedom, equality and justice. With regards to democracy, a representative system that allows for popular will to choose the political leader that is best suited for achieving this goal is also compatible with the notion of God as Absolute Sovereign. The person or persons most capable of steering the state toward justice, freedom, and equality, are the persons best suited to being in power. The public as a whole should decide who that person or persons are. This would allow both Muslim and non-Muslim, male and female, to hold elective office in an Islamic democracy.

Separation of Clergy and State = Democratic State?

In addition to the sovereignty issue, the separation of religion and state as a requirement of democracy is commonly perceived as an obstacle to an Islamic democratic framework. This line of argument states that there is no separation of religion and politics in Islam.[4] This precludes the rise of an inherently Islamic, democratic system, comparable to a Western notion of democracy. This position combines political and religious elements together by making the sole purpose of political power in an Islamic state to be the implementation of religious teachings. While there is some degree of truth to the unity of religion and politics argument, it needs to be considered in a broader fashion.

On a superficial level, we can refute this argument on a number of grounds. It is based on certain simplistic assumptions about the nature of Islam as a religion and as a means for ordering social and political affairs in society. First, this perspective assumes that Islam is a self-evident, comprehensive, and highly detailed blueprint for society. It combines Islam as a religion with Islamic jurisprudence as an all-encompassing and timeless law. By this we mean that while it is theologically correct for a Muslim to view Islam as giving definitive answers about the nature of God or the Hereafter, it is not correct to assume that Islam has granted a definitive answer about the specific detailed laws or political institutions that a society should have on Earth. Also, it overlooks the complexity that makes up both the religion and the changing society, and denies the role of human interpretation of religious text. There is no single "Islamic" set of government institutions and systems of power in a society. Multiple variations could all be Islamic, if they adhered to the values of Islam as laid out in the rest of this work.

Second, in creating a monolithic version of Islam as a religion, it fails to appreciate the dynamic nature of the human society to whom Revelation is addressed. We are not living in seventh-century Arabia, and therefore our understanding of the Quran and of other religious sources are, of necessity, informed by our experiences as members of contemporary society. A system of governance that is appropriate to a nomadic illiterate society in the distant past is inappropriate to a literate industrial society of today. Both societies can construct Islamically valid forms of governance, but they could be quite different from each other. One could speculate that in the far future, representative democracy may be superseded by another mode of governance made possible by technological and social change.

Third, this perspective confuses the Quran, as a moral text, with *fiqh* (Islamic jurisprudence), and gives both equal standing in determining religious, moral and legal affairs. In fact, while the Quran is Divine Revelation, the *fiqh* component of *sharia* is not. It is a product of human efforts. The Quran is primarily a moral text that offers a basis for legislation. It is the primary source for drawing out general values, guidance and principles which inform how people will organize a political system. But it does not generally offer specific statutes pertaining to every legal situation. The latter need to be determined by individual societies themselves, keeping in mind general Quranic principles. Therefore, it is necessary to refute claims that the Quran is synonymous with Islamic law, that there exists a monolithic fixed body of Islamic law known as the *sharia*[5] and that all of these are requirements of an Islamic state. This does not mean, however, that the rule of law is not an important priority in a democratic state.[6] But, state-made law is merely a reflection of human interpretation of Quranic text. It is not synonymous with the Quran itself.

As an illustration of this idea, there are four types of states, from a Muslim perspective, that we can place along a spectrum regarding the separation/inclusion of religion and state. On one end of the spectrum, there is an atheistic state, such as the Soviet Union under Stalin, which not only does not acknowledge the existence of religion at all, but is actively hostile to it and therefore prevents any expression of it, in any form, in the public sphere. It wouldn't protect freedom of religion, as a legal right, for example.

Next, there is a secular state, which does acknowledge the existence of religion, but limits its expression primarily to the private sphere, and not the public. Current France would be a reasonable example, as would the United States, although the U.S. is more tolerant of public expressions of religion. It would protect freedom of religion for all citizens, but would limit its overt manifestation in the public sphere.

Then, we have two types of Islamic states: "progressive" and "rigid." Both of these would acknowledge the existence of Islam specifically, as opposed to any other religion, but codify its influence in different ways.

A "progressive Islamic state" would be based on a democratic consensus of Quranic values, interpreted and enshrined in the constitution. The Islamic identity of the state would be derived from this constitution, and not the individual religious identity of its leader, or that person's religious beliefs. The elected government would be tasked with ruling in accordance with the constitution, but would otherwise be free to write law and set policy as it sees fit to realize the benefits and interests of all its people. There would be no explicit need for the officers of the state, as long as they are acting in accordance with the constitution, to interpret and enforce the Quran or any other Islamic religious text. Therefore, both non-Muslims and Muslims would be eligible for holding elected offices, including the executive office. The state would not interfere with private religious worship, although it would protect freedom of religion as a right for all groups. Unfortunately, there is no current example of such a state.

In contrast, a "rigid Islamic state" would apply its interpretation of the Quran as the only legitimate expression, without allowing room for disagreement or for amendment in the interpretation. It would regulate all aspects of religious worship, public and private, as a coercive moral authority. And it would limit access to political power to a privileged few based on their having the correct credentials and adhering to the "correct interpretation" of Islam. There are several examples of such a state. In Sunni Islam, we have the Saudi government. In Shi'a Islam, there is the Iranian state. There is a significant difference between the two, in that the particular Shi'a version introduced by Ayatollah Khomeini is based on the explicit notion that religious scholars are the only people who should exercise political authority. This was the contribution of the Ayatollah Khomeini who developed the notion of the "rule of the jurist" or *"Welayet-el-Faqih"*. This system creates a privileged class of scholars who are presumed to know better than the rest of the Muslim *umma* how to interpret the meaning of the Quran. We reject this theory as having no basis in the Quranic revelation itself. In addition, it should be seen for the modern innovation that it is. There is no prior history of such a state, and the juristic community, even in the classical period, never held direct political power.

The rigid Islamic state is often perceived of as being the only possible type of "Islamic state" that can exist today. However, we disagree with this idea. In arguing for an "Islamic democratic state" in this chapter, we conceive of it as being fundamentally open to discussion and negotiation in the interpretation of Quranic principles and how they are to be implemented in practical matters.

Coming back to the theory regarding the separation of religion and state as the basis of an Islamic democratic state, we need to consider what it is that should be separated and the purpose of it. If the issue is the formal separation of the spheres of religious and political authority, then we adhere to that in our democratic framework. We do not include formal religious institutions as part of the structure of an Islamic state, nor do we institutionalize a religious body charged with maintaining moral and ideological conformity with "Islamic standards." We should note that throughout Islamic history, temporal political power was separated from the religious scholars. In this sense, there was a separation of state authority and religious authority. But we do believe that the fundamental values that a society holds, such as all men being equal, can and should be derived from God himself, who is the ultimate source of moral principle.

Islamic Political Theory vs. History: Models of Governance

Medina

This brings us to the issue of Islamic political theory and the history that have shaped the creation of certain forms of political governance. The Prophet's (pbuh) example is the natural starting point for this survey. In addition to his religious role, the Prophet (pbuh) also established a political community in Medina, which is often described as the first Islamic polity. Although a more detailed analysis of the constitutional nature of Medina is available in the chapter on constitutionalism, a few points are noteworthy here as well.

Medina was a distinctly pluralistic community made up of autonomous social groups, including the Muslims, Jews and polytheist Arabs. All of these groups participated equally in the political community, without regard to religious identity. Their loyalty to the Prophet (pbuh) as the leader was based solely on his ability to provide protection and security to all of the inhabitants. For Muslims, of course, he was recognized as a prophet. But more significantly, his duty to uphold justice and equality before the law distinguished him and secured the obedience of all citizens to his political authority.

But the Prophet's (pbuh) example is also unique because he occupied a singular role as both religious and political leader. One could also argue that his primary role was to establish the existence of the *umma* of Muslims, a community founded on common faith instead of tribal or kinship affiliations. Engaging in statecraft was therefore a secondary concern, one which came out of the need to provide a secure political and social environment for the Muslim community to thrive in. But his example as the leader of Medina was not long-lived. The Prophet (pbuh) died in 632 AD, without leaving clear instructions on how to choose a political successor or who that successor might be. This absence opened the door to competing theories of political governance, and the historical example of the Caliphate as a particularly noteworthy Islamic political institution.

The Caliphate

The role of the Caliphate as a political institution deserves deeper examination by virtue of its association with the first four Rightly-Guided Caliphs, who were the successors to political leadership of the Muslim community after the Prophet's (pbuh) death in 632. Before continuing further, we should draw a distinction in how the term is used in this work. Caliphate, spelled with an uppercase letter "c," refers to the rule of the four Rightly-Guided Caliphs (632-661). When spelled with a lowercase letter "c", it refers to the general concept of the caliphate. The term "Caliph" was also used as a symbolic religious title by many

Muslim rulers who came after the Rightly-Guided Caliphs as a way to bolster their legitimacy.

The Prophet (pbuh) was the only Muslim ruler with uncontested claim to political and religious legitimacy and authority. His death symbolized the beginning of the schism between the political and the religious leadership of the Muslim *umma*, since the Prophet (pbuh) had embodied both roles in his lifetime. In addition, the lack of a clear political successor to the Prophet (pbuh) meant that there arose competing notions of the basis for political leadership of the Muslim community. Eventually, Abu Bakr was elected by the consensus of the Companions of the Prophet (pbuh), and designated the "Successor (caliph/*khalifa*) of the Prophet of God."

Abu Bakr was first of the four Caliphs, followed by Umar, Uthman, and Ali. The Caliphs were holders of political and not religious authority. They did not claim to be prophets, or to have religious standing that competed with that of the Prophet (pbuh). Their religious authority was merely symbolic in nature, as in the title "Commander of the Believers," or the "Rightly Guided Caliphs."[7] They were charged with implementing Islamic teachings, instead of being responsible for conveying them from God.

Nevertheless, the early Caliphate (referring to the specific rule of the first four Caliphs) retained importance far beyond its initial existence. It became the predominant political institution under discussion in classical Islamic political thought. It was "the ideal" upon which later Muslim historians, jurists and scholar based their own theory-making. Classical jurists devoted considerable effort to discussing the necessity of the institution, the requirements for choosing a caliph and the grounds for obedience to him.[8] In general, both the Sunni and the Shi'a agreed that the caliphate was necessary for the survival of the community, and for applying God's Law, as manifest in Divine Revelation. They also believed that the ruler should have a certain degree of seniority as well as personal, moral qualities considered important for him to be able to fulfill his duties.[9] The main difference among the two, however, was the Shi'a emphasis on Ali as the rightful heir to political leadership, by virtue of his membership in the Prophet's (pbuh) family, versus the Sunni idea that the Caliph should be chosen from among the Quraysh, the Prophet's (pbuh) tribe. This difference eventually led to a schism between the sects in both theory and practice, one that exists today as well.

In theory, the caliph's right to rule was based on his moral integrity and faithfulness to the teachings of the Prophet (pbuh), but in practice, there was no way of evaluating this on a frequent basis by the community. Although theoretically it was the consensus of the community that brought him to power, once the caliph was initially appointed and confirmed, and an oath of allegiance (*baya*) was sworn to him, there was no further formal mechanism for ensuring the accountability of the ruler to the law or to the ruled.[10] The "popular" element of the caliph's political legitimacy was in contrast to the fact that his authority and power did not fundamentally derive from the people; he owed only his appointment to them.[11] This disconnect is what has historically been a fundamental weakness in Islamic political theory and facilitated the abuse of power by the ruler in political history.

In addition, although in theory the caliph followed the Prophet's (pbuh) example of leadership in implementing Revelation, in practice, he was the ultimate decision-maker on applying the *sharia*. On one hand, he was bounded by the limits of the *sharia*. But, on the other, he was the supreme authority on what rule, and what interpretation of it, would be applied in a given case. Caliph Umar, for example, is known for having made innovations in the distribution of fey, or conquered lands. In essence then, theoretically, the caliph was still the ultimate legislative and executive authority.[12] Even though the *ulama* and other members of society functioned in an advisory role, which he did take into account, their advice was not necessarily binding upon him. The limitation of the *sharia* on executive political authority was therefore, in practice, not very effective.

The ramifications of this political tradition for a constitutional model of government today are profound for the gap they demonstrate between what is called Islamic political theory and actual political history. First, in addition to the individualistic nature of political rule, the caliphate symbolized the concentration of power within the executive branch. Second, although theoretically, the caliph's authority was bounded by the limits of Revelation and the Prophet's (pbuh) example, in practice, those boundaries were not absolute, and it was mostly a self-regulated boundary, although the jurists exerted a moral restraint and ultimately the people could revolt. But for the most part, it was only the fear of God that provided the limits on governmental authority. This humility did inform the practices of the Caliphs, as numerous examples have detailed in this work, but this moral/ethical imperative was not translated into an effective and enduring institutional mechanism politically. It is this gap that needs to be remedied through the political framework of a constitutional democracy.

Kingship

The later dynastic kingship/sultanate systems in Islamic political history share the qualities of individualistic rule and the concentration of power in the executive that the caliphate model represented.

The classical Muslim scholar, Ibn Khaldun discusses the differences between the caliphate and kingship in his political text, the *Muqaddimah* (Introduction). He is notable in his critique of how the caliphate became divorced from royal authority, and gave way to a cyclical pattern of dynastic rule. Both the caliphate and kingship are based on feelings of *'asabiyya* (group solidarity) and depend on military strength to secure their power. But, royal authority is distinguished by the fact that it corrupts men by habituating them to luxury and indulgences and has no end greater than itself. In contrast, the caliphate, in theory, has a religious purpose, in that it is employed as a means to apply divine commands.[13] It has both a mundane and sacred purpose: to rule the people, but to do so within the restraining influence of the Prophet's (pbuh) teachings.[14]

Eventually, the caliphate lost its religious element and was replaced altogether by royal authority. Royal authority demands that power and glory be concentrated within one person, the king, and lends itself to sanctioning the theory of divine right of kings. This transformation took place through the course of the Ummayyad and Abbasid dynasties.[15] The Abbasids, in particular, borrowed from the royal practices of Persia and created an imperial court which centered around the glorification of the ruler.[16] "Then the characteristic traits of the caliphate disappeared, and only its name remained. The form of government came to be royal authority pure and simple. Superiority attained the limits of its nature and was employed for particular (worthless) purposes, such as the use of force and the arbitrary gratification of desires and for pleasure."[17]

But, superiority achieved through use of force was limited to a finite territory, usually the urban centers where the court was established and the ruler could extend his dominion over his subjects. The periphery was left outside the royal orbit, and it was from this area where challengers to the central political authority arose and eventually replaced the ruling dynasty by force. This process repeated itself generally every 100 years, or three generations.[18]

Ibn Khaldun's paradigm is important for its demonstration of the divergence between Islamic political theory and political history over time. In contrast to the leadership of the Prophet (pbuh) and the first four caliphs, Persian and Byzantine influences ultimately resulted in an Islamic empire, with the ruler as king, imposing his authority by force upon his subjects. This model was then perpetuated down to the early 1900s, when the Ottoman empire was finally dissolved.

Where does this leave us with regard to an Islamic democratic model today? For one, it highlights the need to place constitutional limits on the authority of the ruler. The "restraining influence" that Ibn Khaldun mentions with regard to the caliphate needs to be revived, but in this case institutionalized through political mechanisms. Two, this process needs to happen in the context of a nation-state, which is the dominant actor in the international system today. The caliphate in its classical form is extinct for all intents and purposes, but some of its principles can still be applied today, within a democratic framework. Three, a democratic model needs to be predicated upon political and social contract between the ruler and the ruled. The glaring absence of this principle in the kingship models of much of Islamic history is in singular contrast to the Prophet's (pbuh) leadership in Medina.

Contract Theory

Thomas Hobbes and John Locke (Hobbes and Locke were Englishmen living in the 17th century) are held up as political theorists whose ideas on the social contract between the ruler and the ruled have influenced the American democratic experiment. Both of these writers essentially conducted "thought experiments" where they speculated what human life was like in the "state of nature" prior to the formation of any government, and what was the motivation for these free men joining together to form government. We will briefly outline the ideas of each with regard to the state of nature, the role of government and the details of the contract between the people and government in this section. The following section will then compare these theories with Islamic political theories on the same issue.

Hobbes

Hobbes characterizes the state of nature as synonymous with a state of war, one of constant struggle and conflict. Full-scale conflict is inevitable because there is a power struggle among individuals, as they each strive to satisfy their desires and appetites. In the famous phrase, Hobbes describes the life of man in a state of nature as "solitary, poor, nasty, brutish and short".[19]

How does man survive in this state of nature? One solution is by following the "laws of nature", or the rules of self-preservation.[20] Since the state of nature is intolerable precisely because its lacks security, then these laws of nature are designed to ensure survival by encouraging individuals to observe certain limits and refrain from attacking others. Thus, the first law of nature is that every person should try to seek peace, as far as possible. This also includes being willing to give up some of their rights for the sake of peace. But, if it is not possible to achieve peace otherwise, then "he may seek and use all helps and advantages of War."[21]

The willingness to give up certain rights in a state of nature in order to achieve survival and peace is key for the creation of a political society. It also leads us into a discussion of the role of government according to Hobbes. Although the laws of nature, if followed, would be sufficient to put an end to the brutish state of nature, the absence of political authority, one which would compel people to obey these rules, prevents this end from coming about. A government is therefore necessary to enforce obedience to the laws of nature, and to create a state of security, for which individuals are willing to give up their "right to all things."[22] This is the nature of the "contract" between government and the people, a trade-off between the security which is so severely lacking in the state of nature, and the right of man to do as he wishes to satisfy his own desires.

On the surface, this appears to be in keeping with contract theory, as it is generally understood. The contract entails a mutual transfer of rights and obligations between the people and their ruler. The people agree to obey the ruler, as long as he provides a state of security. Thus, his tenure is conditional, upon adherence to certain requirements and roles.

But, Hobbes is notable among liberal political theorists, in that he is calling for a political authority with unlimited power, with the exception of capital punishment. This is in response to his conception of the undesirable state of nature, which is so lacking in security. Although he emphasizes a contract, it entails obedience to a political power that provides all-encompassing security. Examined in more detail, this contract does not imply an equal exchange of rights and obligations between the ruler and the ruled. It is, in fact, skewed, disproportionately in favor of the ruler's authority, since according to Hobbes, the contract is not binding upon the ruler. The ruler can gain power through force or through institutional means, neither of which detract from his right to be obeyed by the people. Clearly, this does not, in practice, conform to the usual dictates of contract theory, which includes the people's voluntary consent to be governed as a condition of political obedience.[23]

Locke

John Locke, in contrast to Hobbes, is more of a traditional contract theorist. Starting with his idea of the state of nature, first of all, he does not deem it to be synonymous with a state of war. While man in Hobbes' state of nature lives in a hierarchical society, and is engaged in power struggles and competition with his fellow human beings, his Lockean counterpart lives as an equal in harmony with other individuals. He is also free, but he exists in a state of liberty, and not of license.[24]

The limits placed on individual behavior are also derived from "laws of nature", but Locke uses the term in a very different way than Hobbes. The law of nature depends on God, as the Creator of Man. It is by virtue of this Creation that man acquires certain "natural rights" and must obey certain moral "laws." In the state of nature, human beings are all equal enforcers of this natural law. They treat themselves and others with a certain degree of respect and do not cause harm to themselves or to others because all are equally God's creatures. Locke's view is focused on moral equality, such that everyone mutually enforces natural, moral laws, and everyone mutually submits to it as well.[25]

Given this utopian state of nature, how does Locke explain the transition to a political society and the creation of government? Hobbes posited its need because of the need for security in the tumultuous state of nature. Locke envisions the transition to political society as a voluntary act. First, people must agree to form a community by giving up their natural freedom, and the right to enforce natural law by themselves. They cede this power to the community. But in effect, it is handed to certain individuals designated to act on behalf of the community, subject to majority rule. This is in the form of a legislature, which has the power to enforce the law of nature. Locke attaches significant importance to the role of the legislative branch of government, in contrast to the executive.[26]

The contract between the legislature and the people is significant as part of the overall political structure that Locke envisions. The legislature carries out its functions as part of the trust the people grant it. It has the power to make laws, but people have the right to judge its performance. In other words, the people still retain ultimate power to elect or remove individuals from office.[27] The legislative also has the power to appoint the executive, to enforce the laws it makes. If it deems that the executive is not doing its job properly, then it can withdraw power from this body.

The conditional nature of government is very important to Locke because of his dislike of arbitrary, monarchical rule. Thus, to avoid the possibility of it, he emphasizes the contractual nature of the relationship between the people and the legislature, the legislature and the executive, and the people and government, in general. The underlying theme is that the ability to hold office being conditional upon fulfilling certain requirements. If and when the government violates the terms of this contract, it loses its power over its subjects, and they no longer have to obey it. The people then have the right to withdraw power from it and place it in new hands.[28]

Separation of powers among the legislative and executive is also another way to avoid the specter of despotic rule. However, Locke deems the executive to be subordinate to the legislative, which in turn is subordinate to the will of the people.[29]

What constitutes consent? If a person enjoys the benefits of being ruled by the government, then he consents to it. Locke draws a distinction between tacit and explicit consent. For example, owning property in a country denotes tacit consent, in that it requires obedience to the country's laws regarding ownership. Express consent would be signified more through citizenship, or membership in the political community, with all its rights and obligations.[30] In contrast to Hobbes, Locke's views on the consent of the people to be governed is an integral component of his contract theory.

In conclusion, there are several common themes that emerge from this brief survey of contract theory: the nature of political authority, the terms of consent (to be governed), and the tension between individual freedom and state authority. All of these issues were also of concern to classical Muslim jurists, but were not discussed in the same context. The following section explores this topic in more detail.

Contract Theory in Islam

The preoccupation with delineating the nature and purpose of political authority is also reflected by classical Muslim jurists, but it is discussed in the context of a caliphate-style of government which focuses more on the individual leader than the political system as a whole. This gap has already been commented upon earlier in this chapter.

One of the imperatives for a Muslim ruler is to apply the Sharia, broadly defined, and to uphold justice. The debate about how justice is to be achieved is illustrated by two divergent views, which share similarities with Hobbes' and Locke's state of nature discourse. The first perspective, advanced by Ibn Khaldun and al-Ghazali, holds that by their nature, human beings are prone to conflict and are not inclined to mutual cooperation. Therefore, government is required in order to force people to cooperate with each other, and to promote justice through safeguarding the general public good. The second view, whose proponents include al Mawardi and Ibn Abi al-Rabi, states that human beings, by nature, desire justice and will cooperate with each other to achieve it. This is because God has created them weak, so that if left to their own devices in a state of nature, they will be unable to achieve moral fulfillment by themselves and will naturally seek out others to help them. Though people may be willing to work with each other for a common good, the ruler is important as a way to further the cooperation of the people and to achieve a just society. He comes to power only by virtue of this contract with the people he aims to govern.[31] By extension, this underscores the importance of accountability of the ruler to the ruled, and the people's sovereignty in choosing or removing their elected representative.

These two perspectives highlight certain characteristics of the ideal contract between the ruler and the ruled. Fundamentally, the idea of a contract presumes a mutual exchange of rights and responsibilities between the people and their leader. It predicates the consent of the governed and their obedience to the political authority on the latter's adequate discharge of duties. This includes upholding justice, among other Quranic principles, as the basis for governance.

This paradigm has been applied to the caliphate model in juristic literature. Most Sunni jurists agree that the caliph remains a legitimate ruler as long as he implements God's mandate. He cannot be removed from power unless he commits a sin, and is deemed morally unfit for the office. This denotes the contract, if any, to be between the ruler and God.[32] But, there is also a contract between the caliph and the *ahl al-hall wa al-'aqd* ("those who loose and bind")[33] who pledge their allegiance to the caliph in return for his promise to uphold the contract. The terms of this contract are not elaborated in particular, but in general, jurists have referred to the obligation to apply the *sharia* as the core of it.[34] Historically, this strengthened the moral power of jurists, to bestow and withdraw legitimacy from the caliph, by being the sole interpreters of *sharia*, which in turn was the standard component of the political contract. In effect then, though contract theory aimed to create a balanced relationship between the ruler and the ruled, it did not accomplish this in a very democratic or representative fashion.

In contrast, our emphasis here is on contract theory as a way to delegitimize the absolute authority of the ruler, or the absolute authority of an exclusive group who monopolize the standard for judging the ruler. This theme is present in the Quran, which condemns tyranny as contrary to the absolute authority of God and because it undermines the freedom given by God to people. The Quran is resistant to the idea of concentration of political power within one person, or one ruling party, or group of individuals, on the grounds that it leads to arrogance, which is contrary to Islam, or "submission to God's Will."

The Pharaoh is the most prominent example in the Quran of a tyrannical ruler. He is described in Surah Yunus and Surah al Qasas as an unjust and arrogant ruler because he rules through fear and violence. *"But none save a few of his people declared faith in Moses, [while others held back] for fear of Pharaoh and their great ones, lest they persecute them: for, verily, Pharaoh was mighty on earth and was, verily, of those who are given to excesses"* (Surah Yunus – Jonah, 10:83). *"Behold, Pharaoh exalted himself in the land and divided its people into castes. One group of them he deemed utterly low; he would slaughter their sons and spare [only] their women: for, behold, he was one of those who spread corruption [on earth]"* (Surah al Qasas – The Story, 28:4).

An encounter between Musa (Moses, pbuh) and the Pharaoh illustrates the duty to challenge tyranny. Musa (pbuh) speaks up against the tyranny of the ruler, despite the fact that the Pharaoh provided shelter to and raised Musa. *"[But when Moses had delivered his message, Pharaoh] said: 'Did we not bring thee up among us when thou wert a child? And didst thou not spend among us years of thy [later] life? And yet thou didst commit that [heinous] deed of thine, and [hast thus shown that] thou art one of the ingrate!' Replied [Moses]: 'I committed it while I was still going astray; and I fled from you because I feared you. But [since] then my Sustainer has endowed me with the ability to judge [between right and wrong], and has made me one of [His] message-bearers. And [as for] that favor of which thou so tauntingly remindest me – [was it not] due to they having enslaved the children of Israel?'"* (Surah ash Shuara – The Poets, 26:18-22). Musa is not deterred from his commitment to speak freely and to challenge injustice, even at the expense of a personal relationship. It demonstrates the evil of tyranny and the need to prevent it at all costs.

In another example, an exchange between Ibrahim (Abraham) and a Babylonian ruler[35] also illustrates the negative attitude towards one who claims to have power equal to that of God. *"Art thou not aware of that [king] who argued with Abraham about his Sustainer, [simply] because God had granted him kingship? Lo! Abraham said: 'My Sustainer is He who grants life and deals death.' [The king] replied: 'I [too] grant life and deal death!' Said Abraham: 'Verily, God causes the sun to rise in the east; cause it, then, to rise in the west!' Thereupon he who has bent on denying the truth remained dumbfounded: for God does not guide people who [deliberately] do wrong"* (Surah al Baqara – The Cow, 2:258).

All three of these Quranic examples highlight God's condemnation of concentration of absolute political authority in any one person. Although Surah an Nisaa (Women) is used to justify obedience to political leaders, we stress that it does not sanction absolute obedience. *"O you who have attained to faith! Pay heed unto God, and pay heed unto the Apostle and unto those from among you who [represent you and you] have entrusted with authority"* (Surah an Nisaa - Women, 4:59). Human freedom, granted by God, cannot be arbitrarily suppressed by a political leader. They lend support to the juristic concerns of the need for a contract between the ruler and the ruled as a way to avoid injustice in governance.

Along the same theme, various *hadith* stress the responsibility of the ruler to be just, and to protect his people as a moral duty. All of these qualities are also relevant as terms of the contract. "A ruler who, having obtained control over the affairs of the Muslims, does not strive for their betterment and does not serve them sincerely shall not enter Paradise with them."[36] "The worst of guardians is the cruel ruler. Beware of being one of them."[37]

An oft-repeated *hadith* states that "There is no obedience in sin. Obedience is enjoined only in righteousness."[38] Similarly, "it is obligatory upon a Muslim that he should listen (to the ruler appointed over him) and obey him whether he likes it or not, except that he is ordered to do a sinful thing. If he is ordered to do a sinful act, a Muslim should neither listen to him nor should he obey his orders."[39] This *hadith* has been interpreted to justify absolute obedience to the ruler as long as he does not interfere with private religious worship. In fact, this has led to abuse of power by many Muslim rulers. We disagree with this misinterpretation, and point to another *hadith* in which the Prophet (pbuh) is reported to have said, "When you see my community afraid of telling a tyrant, 'O tyrant', then it is not worth belonging to it anymore."[40] The latter stresses the moral duty to criticize the ruler and to counter tyrannical behavior, if necessary by withdrawing political obedience. But, political obedience should be viewed as part of the political contract between the ruler and his people. The ruler is not entitled to absolute obedience, on par with that which is granted to God.

The importance of an informal contract between the ruler to the ruled is also demonstrated in the leadership of the Rightly-Guided Caliphs. The first person to hold the office of the Caliph after the death of the Prophet (pbuh) in 632 AD., Abu Bakr, declared in his inaugural address, "O people, I have been entrusted with authority over you, but I am not the best of you. Help me if I am right, and rectify me when I am wrong."[41] Similarly, Caliph Umar also asked the people to aid him and correct him when they felt he was wrong. When one man responded by saying that they would correct him even by use of force, the Caliph's supporters criticized the man for threatening the Caliph. However, Caliph Umar allowed him to be, saying that it was his right to express his opinions and that it would behoove him as the ruler to deny him that right.[42] In another example, the third caliph, Caliph Uthman sent a proclamation to his governors stating that leaders should act as guardians of the people and not as tax collectors. They bear responsibility to ensure the overall welfare of those they rule, and not simply to burden them by extracting taxes to further the power of the state.[43]

Of course, the most notable example of a social contract is the Prophet's (pbuh) negotiation with the inhabitants of Medina upon his arrival there to take up leadership of the community. The Pact of Medina, which is the outcome of this negotiation, is evidence of the primacy of the political sovereignty of the tribes, who agreed to surrender their individual tribal rights for the collective gain of security provided by the

Prophet (pbuh). Obedience to political authority was not absolute, but conditional, and could be withdrawn at a later date.

Baya

Baya refers to an oath or pledge of allegiance and support between the ruler and the ruled. It is a manifestation of the contractual relationship between the ruler and the ruled and can be mutually negotiated. Also, if the ruler violates the social contract and does not adequately fulfill his duties, he can be replaced.

The symbolic importance of the *baya* come from the Prophet's (pbuh) time. Shortly before undertaking the *hijra* (migration) to Medina, the Prophet (pbuh) received the oath of allegiance from 73 men and 2 women of Medina, who accepted Islam, at Aqabah.[44] Later, it was codified as a political symbol in the constitution of Medina. During the Caliphate, it served to confirm the caliph's role as leader, as determined by the consensus of the Companions. But, it was not conditional and could not be withdrawn at a later point if the people disagreed with the ruler.

We are arguing for the principle of *baya* to be institutionalized, to refer to allegiance or support gained through a frequent election process. If the ruler's conduct is acceptable to the electorate, then they have the option of renewing his mandate as leader by re-election. However, if it is not, or another candidate is deemed more suitable for the job, then the voters have the option to elect him/her.

In conclusion, this section has aimed to demonstrate evidence supporting the desirability of contract theory, both directly and indirectly, by examining the Quran, Islamic political theory and *hadith* literature, while also highlighting its limitations in practice. There are two key issues that define the political contract between the ruler and the people – obedience to authority and legitimacy of the ruler. Both are intertwined, since the ruler's legitimacy is what ensures obedience from the people. Jurists were cognizant of the danger of a tyrannical ruler, but failed to prevent it from arising in practice. The kingship model noted earlier is proof of the divergence between Islamic classical political theory and history in safeguarding the rights of the ruled in the context of a political contract with the ruler. In sum, while the elements conducive to a representative and democratic form of governance, as evidence through contract theory, are there in Islamic history, they have not been translated effectively into practice.

Shura

Shura is not exclusively an Islamic concept, since it also existed in pre-Islamic Arab society.[45] It has become part of the discourse on Islamic political theory over time, though, and the textual basis for it drawn from the Quran. It is described as the underpinning of a participatory and representative form of government.

The term itself comes from the Quran, noted in two verses. The first verse is Surah ash Shura - Consultation, 42:38: *"And who respond to [the call of] their Sustainer and are constant in prayer; and whose rule [in all matters of concern] is consultation among themselves; and who spend on others out of what We provide for them as sustenance."* The fact that this verse refers to *shura* in between the duties of prayer and charity-giving is noteworthy and underscores the obligatory nature of it, since prayer and charity-giving are two of the five pillars of Islam.

The second verse, Surah al Imran – The House of Imran, 3:159, is addressed to the Prophet (pbuh) and states, *"Pardon them, then, and pray that they be forgiven. And take counsel with them in all matters of public concern; then, when thou hast decided upon a course of action, place thy trust in God: for, verily, God loves those who place their trust in Him."* This verse refers to *shura* in general terms, as a way of arriving at a decision through collective deliberation. What is remarkable here is that the Quran instructs the Prophet (pbuh) to consult his fellow Muslims. If the Prophet himself is instructed to consult with his people, then no political system is valid that does not include that element at its core. And it does not necessarily exclusively apply to political affairs. But, since we are discussing a political framework in this chapter, we will focus on the political ramifications of *shura* as a Quranic principle and its manifestation in practice.

In interpreting this verse, Al Qurtubi (d. 1273), a noted Muslim jurist, viewed *shura* as the responsibility of the ruler to consult with men of knowledge and jurists, failure of which would mean removal from office.[46] Other jurists, such as al Basri, al Hasan bin Yassar (642-728) and al Dahhak bin Muzahim,(d. 723), had interpreted the instruction to the Prophet (pbuh) to consult the Muslims as setting an example for future political tradition, since he was not necessarily solely dependent upon their opinions (given that he was receiving Divine Revelation and his authority was based on this prophetic role).[47] Nevertheless, the Prophet (pbuh) consulted with his Companions and took their counsel in preparation for the battles of Badr (623 AD) and Uhud (624 AD), and also with regards to freeing captured prisoners of war.[48] Al Qurtubi notes that the Prophet (pbuh) did not consult with his people on religious and legal matters, since the Quran laid those out, but did do so on issues of war, peace and administration.[49]

Shura was also extended to the time of the Caliphs, with the use of *ijtihad* (religious reasoning) as an acceptable tool for exercising judgment on some legal issues as well. For example, Caliph Umar consulted with the people in organizing a social security system, appointing local governors, establishing the Al-Hijri calendar, limiting the absence of soldiers from their families to a maximum of four months, and regulating punishments for civil servants and officials.[50] Also, shortly before his death, he appointed a consultative committee of seven Companions to elect one of themselves as Caliph. Some authors have identified this as the equivalent of an electoral college.[51]

In other instances as well, Caliph Umar was known to consult with the prominent early Meccan Companions, on numerous political and legal issues.[52] On a trip to Syria, Caliph Umar and his escort reached Sargh, where they were met by the commanders of the Muslim armies in Syria and urged to turn back because of the seriousness of the plague in the region. Umar ordered Ibn al Abbas to assemble the *muhajirun* (emigrants) for consultation as to whether to continue on or to turn back for Medina. When they could not reach an agreement on the issue, Umar ordered the *ansar* (helpers) to be assembled for their opinion. They also failed to reach an agreement. Finally, the Caliph ordered the leaders of the Quraysh who converted after the conquest of Mecca, to be gathered together and consulted. They unanimously recommended a return to Medina, and the Caliph followed their advice.[53]

One could argue that these examples indicate that *shura* was not necessarily representative or broad-based consultation, as one might see in a democratic government today. Also, the Caliph had discretionary powers, to some degree, on whether or not to follow the rulings, since there were not any formal political mechanisms to remove him from office, if he were not to comply. Political authority was still firmly concentrated in the executive, the ruler. However, the example of Caliph Umar does indicate that the operating principle behind it is valid, and can be found in Islamic political history. In current conditions, we argue that *shura* should be broadly based and involve all elements of society. It should apply systematically and in both local and national affairs. The best way to ensure that the concerns of the people are being heard is to subject the holders of political power to the judgment of the people on a regular basis through election.

Sadek Sulaiman, a contemporary Arab former diplomat and intellectual, argues that *shura* is relevant today as a principle compatible with democracy. It was not a fixed system of governance during the Prophet's (pbuh) time, and is not today either. But to the extent that any political system that fulfills the principle of *shura*, "constitutionally, institutionally and practically", the more "Islamic" it becomes.[54] As a concept, it implies that a decision reached through "collective deliberation is more likely to lead to a fair and sound result for the social good than individual preference."[55] According to Sulaiman, *shura* shares certain elements with a democracy in that it accepts the idea of the equality of people in their rights and responsibilities as citizens, and the application of their will through majority rule and rule of law, instead of through autocratic decree by the executive.[56]

As a Quranic and moral principle, *shura* signifies a resistance to tyranny of the ruler. In contrast to the classical juristic interpretation of it, we interpret it to mean broad-based, binding consultation between the ruler and the ruled, as mediated through elected representatives. This excludes an emphasis on jurists or other scholars as being the sole legitimate heirs to this tradition. In addition, we render the rulings of this body to be binding legislation, not just advisory proclamations.

Conclusion

We are faced with the historical Muslim political experience, in which democracy has been notably absent as an institutional framework. Instead, the predominant trend has been of absolute political rulers, legitimized through the combination of the theory of kingship and the sanction of a *sharia*-based rule of law as defined by Muslim jurists. This is popular understanding of what a caliph means, and certainly some Muslims today see it as a desirable model of governance. The outcome is that we do not have a classical, historical example of a pluralistic, participatory, and representative form of government, upon which we can base current attempts at defining an Islamic framework for democracy. This chapter seeks to fill that gap, and has outlined a theoretical argument for the synthesis between a democratic political system and Islamic values of the ideal ruler-ruled relationship.

The Quran recognizes pluralism as inherent within Creation. It affirms religious pluralism, pointing out the variety of spiritual paths that lead towards Truth. Political pluralism, then, is not at odds with an Islamic perspective on ordering social and political affairs, although the historical tendency has leaned towards authoritarian, absolute rule by the head of state. The power dynamic had been strictly vertical, with the ruler at the top, disconnected from his subjects below. A pluralist, democratic political system does not necessarily do away with this power hierarchy, but it diffuses power within multiple institutions of the state and places limits on political authority.

The issue of *baya*, or sworn loyalty to the ruler, is often used by those who wish to invest political authority in a single individual, a Muslim "philosopher-king" to use the Greek model. This claim is based on *hadith* that state that Muslims are required to give *baya* to their legitimate ruler. We broaden the concept and definition to mean that *baya* is given to the legitimate executive authority, in the sense that we are all committed to obeying the law. We would interpret the historical concept of the caliphate in today's terms as being the executive branch of the government. Loyalty is then owed to that branch, as long as it is acting to uphold and advance justice. Loyalty is not required if it slips into tyranny.

The Islamic nature of the democratic framework we have outlined here begs the question of what exactly constitutes "Islamic" and "un-Islamic" legislation or rule? Pushing this further, what if the majority decides that they no longer want to be governed by an Islamically-based democratic system? The answer to this question forces us to examine the boundaries of the political system, and to what extent it can stretch the interpretation of Islam in response to democratic decisions while still be legitimately "Islamic" in its character. Ultimately, the people themselves must choose whether they want to live in a state that conforms to Quranic principles or not. If they choose not to, that is a choice that is answerable to God. In fact, as none of us can know with certainty whether our interpretation of the core values of the Quran are correct, we cannot know for certain whether the state we have created is actually "Islamic" or "un-Islamic" in God's judgment. The answer to that question lies with God only. We as humans can only do our best to interpret the Quran in a fair-minded fashion.

Islam's compatibility with democracy is based on its recognition of four elements. These are the contractual relationship between the ruler and the ruled, *shura*, the limitation of power (which is seen as early as the Compact of Medina), and the freedom of religion and speech as endorsed by the Quran. Putting these elements together in the modern context leads to the reasonable conclusion that representative democracy is the form of government that is most in compliance with these principles (Several of these principles will be further developed in their own chapters). Hence the logical conclusion of this argument is that Islam is not merely compatible with democracy; it demands democracy.

Footnotes

1 See constitutionalism chapter for detailed analysis of the foundational document of this polity, the Pact of Medina.

2 John Keane, "Power-Sharing Islam?" *Power-Sharing Islam*, ed. Azzam Tamimi, (London: Liberty for Muslim World Publications, 1993), p. 27.

3 One might conceivably argue that "the people" should be limited to the umma, and therefore only Muslims have the right to interpret God's Will, as it is embodied in the Quran and *sharia*. Our response is that God does not prohibit anyone from exercising their interpretive and analytical faculties. He has endowed intellect on all mankind. Therefore, it is an artificial and man-made "rule" to limit authority or sovereignty only to Muslims in a polity.

4 What Leonard Binder refers to as the "unity of politics and religion in Islam" in his book, *Religion and Politics in Pakistan* (Berkeley: University of California Press, 1961).

5 Ther e are four legal schools in Sunni Islam, with their body of opinions, all of which are accepted as legitimate and orthodox.

6 See also justice chapter for more on the *sharia* and constitutionalism chapter on the rule of law.

7 The Caliphate refers exclusively to the reign of the four caliphs, Abu Bakr, Umar, Uthman and Ali, from 632 to 660. They are called the Rashidun, or the Rightly-Guided Caliphs because of their authority to implement the revealed law of God. This authority is deemed to be on par with that of the Prophet's (pbuh) to receive Revelation. After Ali, the religious component of the title of Caliph, was contested vigorously and eventually came to be a merely symbolic title that later rulers took on purely for political expediency.

8 H.A.R. Gibb, "Constitutional Organization," *Law in the Middle East*, ed. Majid Khadduri and Herbert Liebesny, eds. (Washington,D.C.: Middle East Institute, 1955), pp.7-11.

9 Khadduri, p. 16.

10 An Naim, pp. 76-77.

11 Khadduri, p. 19.

12 An Naim, p. 80.

13 Ibn Khaldun's preoccupation with the application of God's Law as a purpose of political governance is in keeping with that of most Muslim jurists and scholars throughout history. It has been revived in current discussions of what constitutes an Islamic constitutional state. See also the constitutionalism and justice chapters for more on *sharia*.

14 Ibn Khaldun, *Muqaddimah*, transl. Franz Rosenthal, ed. N. J. Dawood, (Princeton: Princeton University Press, 1989), p. 161.

15 Ibn Khaldun details the various Ummayyad and Abbasid rulers. *Muqaddimah* pp. 164-165.

16 Faruki, p. 32.

17 Ibn Khaldun, p. 166.

18 Ibn Khaldun, pp. 128-138.

19 Hobbes, *Leviathan*, Ch. 13, cited in George Klosko, History of Political Theory: An Introduction, v. 2, (Belmont: Wadsworth/Thomson Learning, 1995), p. 46.

20 Hobbes does not use the term "laws of nature" as they are traditionally understood to be derived from God, by other philosophers. He means general rules that should be followed by people, and which are arrived through the use of their reason. Klosko, p. 49.

21 Hobbes, *Leviathan*, ch. 14, cited in Klosko, p. 49.

22 Klosko, pp. 51-55.

23 Klosko, pp. 61-63.

24 Locke, Second Treatise, cited in Klosko, p. 98.

25 Locke, Second Treatise, cited in Klosko, pp. 98-103.

26 Locke, Second Treatise, cited in Klosko, p. 107.

27 Locke, Second Treatise, cited in Klosko, p. 108.

28 Klosko, p. 127.

29 Klosko, p. 124.

30 Locke, Second Treatise, cited in Klosko, p. 111.

31 Khaled Abou el Fadl, "Islam and the Challenge of Democracy," *Boston Review*, April/May 2003, p. 9.

32 Abou el Fadl, "Islam and the Challenge of Democracy," p. 5.

33 Abou el Fadl describes them as "the people who have the power of contract", p. 5. It implies a group of representatives who

choose a ruler. They may or may not be popularly elected.

34 Abou el Fadl, "Islam and the Challenge of Democracy," p. 5.

35 The text does not name the ruler, but Yusuf Ali's commentary suggests that it might Nimrod, or another Babylonian ruler, equally condemned for his tyrannical ways.

36 Sahih Muslim, Book 20, *Kitab al Imara (Book of Government)*, No. 4502.

37 Sahih Muslim, Book 20, No. 4504.

38 Cited in Kamali, *Freedom, Equality and Justice in Islam*, p. 23.

39 Sahih Muslim, Book 20, No. 4533.

40 Cited in Kamali, *Freedom, Equality and Justice in Islam*, p. 24.

41 Kamali, *Freedom, Equality and Justice in Islam*, p. 24.

42 Kamali, *Freedom, Equality and Justice in Islam*, p. 24.

43 H. Munawir Sjadzali, *Islam and Governmental System*, (Jakarta: INIS, 1991), p. 22.

44 Ibrahim A. Al Marzouqi, "Political Rights and Democracy in Islamic Law," *Democracy, the Rule of Law and Islam*, ed. Eugene Cotran and Adel Omar Sharif, (London: Kluwer Law International, 1999), p. 462.

45 Ronald L. Nettler, "Islam, Politics and Democracy: Mohamed Talbi and Islamic Modernism," *Religion and Democracy*, ed. David Marquand and Ronald L. Nettler, (Oxford: Blackwell Publishers, 2000), p. 55.

46 al Qurtubi, Tafsir, Vol 4, pp. 249-253, cited in Al Marzouqi, p. 458.

47 Al Marzouqi, p. 458.

48 Ibn Hisham, cited in al Marzouqi, pp. 458-459.

49 Al Marzouqi, p. 459.

50 Al Marzouqi, p. 460.

51 Al Marzouqi, p. 460.

52 Wilferd Madelung, *The Succession to Muhammad*, (Cambridge: Cambridge University Press, 1997), p. 59.

53 Tabari, cited in Madelung, *The Succession to Muhammad*, p. 59.

54 Sadek J. Sulaiman, "Democracy and Shura," in *Liberal Islam: A Sourcebook*, ed. Charles Kurzman, (New York: Oxford University Press, 1998), p.98.(96-98)

55 Sulaiman, p. 98.

56 Sulaiman, p. 98.

CHAPTER FOUR

Sanctity of Life

 ife is a divinely-granted trust that humans are under obligation to treat with the utmost sanctity. What does it mean for a person to take another human life? Is it a question of impinging on Divine Will? Is it ever justified to take a human life?

This chapter will examine answers to these questions by focusing on the moral and legal aspects of several specific issues: abortion, suicide, euthanasia, and the role of law in punishing murder and in imposing the death penalty. The first section of the chapter explores Quranic references to the sacred quality of life, and notes the insistence on "just cause" as the only justification for taking a life. The subsequent sections apply the Quranic framework towards these contemporary issues that challenge the application of the sanctity of life principle, including abortion rights, suicide, euthanasia and physician-assisted suicide.

Quranic Perspective on Life

By virtue of being the Creation of God, humans are granted life, with the admonition that they live it as moral beings. They are given free will and the independence to be able to make choices, and to take responsibility for the consequences of their choices and actions. Religion serves as a source of moral guidance for people, even as they exercise their free will.

The Prophet's (pbuh) role was to make people aware of God and of His Presence in their lives, so that they may make moral choices. *"Say [O Muhammad]: 'O mankind! Verily, I am an apostle of God to all of you, [sent by Him] unto whom the dominion over the heavens and the earth belongs! There is no deity save Him; He [alone] grants life and deals death!' Believe, then, in God and His Apostle – the unlettered Prophet who believes in God and His words – and follow him, so that you might find guidance!"* (Surah al Araf – The Faculty of Discernment, 7:158).

Belief in God requires a belief in His Power over all aspects of life and death, from the process of creation to the duration of each individual's life. He grants life and death as He wishes. *"There is no deity save Him: He grants life and deals death: He is your Sustainer as well as the Sustainer of your forebears of old"* (Surah ad Dukhan – Smoke, 44:8). *"And God has created you, and in time will cause you to die"* (Surah an Nahl – The Bee, 16:70). Referring to the process of creation, the Quran states *"And [remember:] God creates [every one of] you out of dust, then out of a drop of sperm; and then He fashions you into either of the two sexes. And no female conceives or gives birth unless it be with His knowledge"* (Surah Fatir – The Originator, 35:11). God has control over both the original creation of mankind, as a race, and the conception of individual human beings. Once given life, the duration of that life is also divinely ordained. *"And none that if long-lived has his days lengthened – and neither is aught lessened of his days – unless it be thus laid down in [God's] decree: for, behold, all this is easy for God"* (Surah Fatir – The Originator, 35:11).

God upholds the sanctity of life as a universal principle. *"And do not destroy one another: for, behold, God is indeed a dispenser of grace unto you!"* (Surah an Nisaa – Women, 4:29). This can be interpreted as a prohibition on suicide, as well as murder: Do not kill your individual self, and do not kill other humans, who are like yourselves.

The parable of Cain and Abel illustrates God's negative attitude towards those who transgress this principle. Both offer a sacrifice to God, but the sacrifice of the righteous, God-fearing brother is accepted while his brother's is rejected. The rejected brother flies into a rage and threatens to kill his brother out of jealousy. *"And convey unto them, setting forth the truth, the story of the two sons of Adam – how each offered a sacrifice, and it was accepted from one of them whereas it was not accepted from the other. [And Cain] said: 'I will surely slay thee!' [Abel] replied: 'Behold, God accepts only from those who are conscious of Him. Even if thou lay thy hand on me to slay me, I shall not lay my hand on thee to slay thee: behold, I fear God, the Sustainer of all the worlds"* (Surah al Maida – The Repast, 5:27-28).

But the rejected brother refuses to listen to him and ultimately murders his brother. *"But the other's passion drove him t o slaying his brother; and he slew him: and thus he became one of the lost"* (Surah al Maida – The Repast, 5:30). One who kills another ensures that he will be "lost" to God's guidance in this life, and denied entry to Paradise in the Afterlife. Eventually, Cain realizes the enormity of his deed, and he is stricken by remorse. *"Thereupon God sent forth a raven which scratched the earth, to show him how he might conceal the nakedness of his brother's body. [And Cain] cried out: 'Oh, woe is me! Am I then too weak to do what this raven did, and to conceal then nakedness of my brother's body?' – and was thereupon smitten with remorse"* (Surah al Maida – The Repast, 5:31).

In sum, the Cain and Abel example underscores the sanctity and value of human life in Islam. As the moral of the story, God states, *"Because of this did We ordain unto the children of Israel that if anyone slays a human being – unless it be [in punishment] for murder or for spreading corruption on earth – it shall be as though he had slain all mankind; whereas, if anyone saves a life, it shall be as though he had saved the lives of all mankind"* (Surah al Maida – The Repast, 5:32). The value of merely one life is such that it is worth the lives of an entire nation. To murder another person is to murder one's own brother, since all human beings are the progeny of Adam.

God views murder as a major sin, condemning the offender in the Afterlife. This theme is mentioned, for example, in the following two *hadiths.* "One of the evil deeds with bad consequence from which there is no escape for the one who is involved in it is to kill someone unlawfully."[1] "The Prophet said, "The first cases to be decided among the people (on the Day of Resurrection) will be those of blood-shed."[2]

The following three verses elaborate on the value of life, but also introduce the role of law to deal with murder as a crime, and not just as a sin. Surah al Furqan equates the sanctity of life with belief in a monotheistic God, illustrating the high value that life holds in Islam. *"And who never invoke any [imaginary] deity side by side with God, and do not take any human being's life – [the life] which God has willed to be sacred – otherwise than in [the pursuit of] justice, and do not commit adultery. And [know that] he who commits aught thereof shall [not only] meet with a full requital"* (Surah al Furqan – The Standard of True and False, 25:68). If life has to be taken, it should only be through the due process of law, or "just cause." *"Be they open or secret; and do not take any human being's life – [the life] which God has declared to be sacred – otherwise than in [the pursuit of] justice: this has He enjoined upon you so that you might use your reason"* (Surah al Anam – Cattle, 6:151).

"And do not take any human being's life – [the life] which God has willed to be sacred – otherwise than in [the pursuit of] justice. Hence, if anyone has been slain wrongfully, We have empowered the defender of his rights [to exact a just retribution]; but even so, let him not exceed the bounds of equity in [retributive] killing. [And as for him who has been slain wrongfully -] behold, he is indeed succored [by God]!" (Surah al Isra – The Night Journey, 17:33). This verse echoes the reference to "just cause" noted in the other two verses, but then goes to discuss the role of law in the determining how punishment is to be regulated. Wrongful death (death due to negligence or accident) falls under the category of qisas crimes, for which the deceased's heirs can either demand retribution, compensation or forgive the killer. All of these verses point out that the due process of law is key in regulating how to punish a killer for taking a life.

Examining the themes of these three verses, we can summarize several conclusions. One is that all life is valuable, regardless of the identity of the individual. Two, the value of life is indicated by equating it with the unity of God (*tawhid*), which is central to the theological underpinnings of Islam. Third, in cases where taking a life is justified, the only permissible reason is by "just cause", which refers to the rule of law. Despite the fact that murder is a sin, in this world, the punishment for it as a crime has to be determined on the basis of law. In short, preserving life and stressing the value of it are key to Islamic teachings.

Due Process of Law: Murder and Capital Punishment

Murder

The debate on when taking a life is justifiable centers on defining the parameters of "just cause," which directs us to consider the rule of law. One of the fundamental interests of the *sharia* is to preserve and protect human life. Thus, killing someone, whether intentionally or unintentionally, carries with it legal punishment.

Homicide falls under the category of *qisas* crimes, those that are punished by the principle of equivalence. *Qisas* has been erroneously translated as retaliation, which implies revenge, and is contrary to the meaning of *qisas* as "redress[ing] a wrong by equalizing the harm [suffered by the victim and/or his family]."[3] This makes qisas best translated as punishment that is proportional to the crime. As a general principle, it is noted in the Quran, although it is more rigorously explicated in the juristic legal texts.

There are five *qisas* crimes: 1) murder; 2) voluntary killing (voluntary manslaughter); 3) involuntary killing (involuntary manslaughter); 4)intentional physical injury or maiming; and 5) unintentional physical injury or maiming.[4] For our purposes in this section, we will focus primarily on the first three categories.

The allowed sanctions for these crimes include forgiveness, "equivalent infliction of physical or bodily harm against the person who committed the act", or the payment of *diyya* (compensation).[5] We are interpreting the principle of equivalent punishment outlined in the following verses to also refer to a prison sentence of appropriate duration, determined by the nature of the crime.

Surah al Isra (17:33) and Surah al Maida (5:45) are two verses which relate to *qisas*. *"And do not take any human being's life – [the life] which God has willed to be sacred – otherwise than in [the pursuit of] justice. Hence, if anyone has been slain wrongfully, We have empowered the defender of his rights [to exact a just retribution]; but even so, let him not exceed the bounds of equity in [retributive] killing. [And as for him who has been slain wrongfully -] behold, he is indeed succored [by God]!* (Surah al Isra – The Night Journey, 17:33). *"And We ordained for them in that [Torah]: A life for a life, and an eye for an eye, and a nose for a nose, and an ear for an ear, and a tooth for a tooth, and a [similar] retribution for wounds; but he who shall forgo it out of charity will atone thereby for some of his past sins. And they who do not judge in accordance with what God has revealed – they, they are the evildoers!"* (Surah al Maida – The Repast, 5:45). This verse establishes talion,[6] which is also noted in Judeo-Christian teachings, but then stresses that it is more charitable to forego its practice.

The following verse elaborates on this theme. *"O you who have attained to faith! Just retribution is ordained for you in cases of killing: the free for the free, and the slave for the slave, and the woman for the woman. And if something [of his guilt] is remitted to a guilty person by his brother, this [remission] shall be adhered to with fairness, and restitution to his fellow-man shall be made in a goodly manner. This is an alleviation from your Sustainer, and an act of His grace. And for him who, none the less, willfully transgresses the bounds of what is right, there is grievous suffering in store: for, in [the law of] just retribution, O you who are endowed with insight, there is life for you, so that you might remain conscious of God!"* (Surah al Baqara – The Cow, 2:178-179). This lengthy verse was revealed to limit the practice of retaliation and blood-feuds common in Arab tribal societies. The principles here are for a more lawless environment, and do not directly apply to a more civilized context in which the only punishment would fall on the wrongdoer himself, and not be exacted from some other member of his or her family. We can interpret this verse as emphasizing the need to maintain equivalence in redress. The value of the life lost, be it of a free person, a slave, or a woman, is to be compensated for by the forfeit of the equivalent from the criminal's tribe. But, if the victim's family chooses not to follow this practice, and asks for some other form of compensation, then they are also entitled to receive it.

In all of the verses discussed above, the application of the "law of equality" should be viewed in light of the pre-Islamic historical context when they were revealed. In keeping with the practices of that time period, when there was no organized criminal justice system to punish offenders, families often engaged in violent, bloody feuds to settle disputes or to punish murders. What these verses did was to place conditions around this kind of behavior, so as to limit the violence. Thus, in theory, the victim's family was allowed to inflict the same degree of harm upon the perpetrator. The limitation was that it had to be the equivalent, so as to prohibit spawning a cycle of retribution between the two sides. For example, if a woman had been killed, the victim's family had the right to seek retaliation by asking for the life of a woman from the criminal's family.[7]

In contemporary practice though, with the creation of a criminal justice system, and legal codes, the provisions of *qisas* have been interpreted differently. In general, Islamic jurisprudence limits it to particular categories of crimes, and to a manner that is least likely to cause pain.[8] The literal application of "a life for a life" is no longer carried out as readily. The Quran itself calls for this interpretation; verse 179 of Surah al Baqara – The Cow, highlights this restraining spirit by noting that the law of equality was revealed precisely to *"you who are endowed with insight, there is life for you, so that you might remain conscious of God!"*

If there is a choice between retaliation and compensation, the Quran prefers the latter in line with a spirit of mercy and forgiveness for the perpetrator. The principle of *diyya* is established in Surah an Nisaa – Women, 4:92. *"And it is not conceivable that a believer should slay another believer, unless it be by mistake. And upon him who has slain a believer by mistake there is the duty of freeing a believing soul from bondage and paying an indemnity to the victim's relations, unless they forgo it by way of charity. Now, if the slain, while himself a believer, belonged to a people who are at war with you, [the penance shall be confined to] the freeing of a believing soul from bondage; whereas, if he belonged to a people to whom you are bound by a covenant, [it shall consist of] an indemnity to be paid to his relations in addition to the freeing of a believing soul from bondage. And he who does not have the wherewithal shall fast [instead] for two consecutive months. [This is] the atonement ordained by God: and God is indeed all-knowing, wise"* (Surah an Nisaa – Women, 4:92). Thus, there are a number of options, other than retaliation, available to redress the harm caused by a killing, namely, to free a slave and/or to pay compensation, or to fast for two months.

Several schools of jurisprudence limit the penalty of *talion* to intentional killings and/or intentionally inflicted serious bodily harm, and apply *diyya* to less serious crimes, such as unintentional killings or bodily harm.[9] In general, the purport of Quranic discussion of qisas crimes is as "a general deterrence policy which recognizes the victim's sense of vindictiveness against the aggressor, while limiting the consequences of the penalty to the harm done and establishing the alternative remedies of victim compensation or outright forgiveness."[10] We suggest interpreting these verses and the primary principle behind qisas sanctions to be that of equivalence of the punishment to the crime. It is in society's best interest to punish murder as a serious crime, in order to maintain an overall level of security for the community. In certain cases, victim compensation may not be adequate for achieving this purpose. Therefore, the justice system can determine a prison sentence as a relevant and equivalent penalty for murder and remain within the spirit of *qisas* sanctions. Although the Quran discusses forgiveness for the criminal as a virtuous and charitable act, it does not serve the public interest to leave criminals unpunished for as serious a crime as murder.

The interests of justice and of public safety must be taken into account when allowing compensation for crime. The state has an interest in public safety that requires that crime be punished even if the victim's family is satisfied with a monetary payment. There is also the injustice that occurs in several Muslim countries where murders, particularly so-called honor killings which have nothing to do with Islam, within the family result in tremendous familial pressure to accept compensation or forgive the killer, which results in these crimes being encouraged rather than deterred.

Capital Punishment

People tend to take for granted the fact that the death penalty is sometimes applied as punishment for murder. However, there is no direct basis for it in the Quran. In fact, the Quran emphasizes the sanctity of life as a general principle and does not require the death penalty for any crime. As described in the previous section, even in cases of murder, where *qisas* would be applicable, it counsels forgiveness or payment of compensation as the preferred actions. In addition, there is no specific method of capital punishment endorsed in the Quran.

Nevertheless, the death penalty has been applied as a form of legal punishment for certain crimes, such as apostasy and adultery. But, the sanction for this comes primarily from juristic rulings and not from the Quran. While apostasy has been discussed more fully in the chapter on Freedom of Religion, we will briefly explore the topic of capital punishment for adultery here. The purpose is to re-evaluate its classification as a crime punishable by death.[11]

Adultery

The Quran does not prescribe stoning as the punishment for adultery. It is very specific as to the procedure that is to be used to adjudicate in adultery cases, and mentions flogging. *"As for the adulteress and the adulterer – flog each of them with a hundred stripes"* (Surah an Nur – The Light, 24:2). In order to prosecute sexual misconduct as a crime, four witnesses, who can testify to the actual act of penetration during sexual intercourse, must come forward. Furthermore, their witnessing must have been obtained without violating the defendant's privacy.[14]

If this condition cannot be satisfied – and the likelihood of four witnesses to the act is very small – then flogging is prescribed for the accuser, and his/her testimony is inadmissible for all other legal cases as well. *"And as for those who accuse chaste women [of adultery], and then are unable to produce four witnesses [in support of their accusation], flog them with eighty strips; and even after refuse to accept from them any testimony – since it is they, they that are truly depraved!"* (Surah an Nur – The Light, 24:4).

The basis for stoning as the punishment for adultery is drawn instead from a *hadith* on the matter. "When an unmarried male commits adultery with an unmarried female (they should receive) one hundred lashes and banishment for one year. And in case of married male committing adultery with a married female, they shall receive one hundred lashes and be stoned to death."[12]

A *hadith* narrated by Abu Hurayra highlights the gravity of adultery as an issue. According to the report, a man came up to the Prophet (pbuh) and tried to confess to adultery four times. All four times the Prophet (pbuh) turned away from him and pretended not to hear, so as to avoid having to pronounce judgment on the issue. Ultimately, when the man continued to persist, he asked him if he was insane. The man responded negatively. He asked him then if he was married, to which the man replied in the affirmative. The Prophet (pbuh) then indicated that stoning was the punishment for him.[13] It is debatable as to whether this is an accurate account of what happened, and what the significance of the incidence should be to Islamic jurisprudence. Even if the Prophet (pbuh) called for stoning in this particular case, it does not follow that the punishment for adultery, or any other crime, should be controlled by this example. To shed blood based on a *hadith* that is inconsistent with the Quran is to overstep. We do not find such a conclusion warranted.

The import of this discussion on adultery is to emphasize the gravity of accusations of sexual misconduct against an individual. The accuser must meet a heavy burden of proof, or face punishment him/herself. *"Why do they not [demand of the accusers that they] produce four witnesses to prove their allegation? – for, if they do not produce such witnesses, it is those [accusers] who, in the sight of God, are liars indeed! And were it not for God's favor upon you, [O men,] and His grace in this world and in the life to come, awesome suffering would indeed have afflicted you in result of all [the calumny] in which you indulge"* (Surah an Nur – The Light, 24:13-14).

With such a heavy burden of proof, our suggested interpretation of these verses is that the crime is realistically only punishable if the two parties were to commit the act in public, which is unlikely to be the case. Therefore, the crime is in fact public indecency, and not sex.[15] Sexual misconduct is a private affair between the two individuals, and is not a crime, even though it is a sin. Even if it were to be prosecuted, stoning is not the prescribed punishment according to the Quran.

This section underlines the fact that the Quran does not require capital punishment as the sole punishment for any crime. In fact, the emphasis on the sacred nature of life refutes any such interpretation. The Quran clearly states, *"If anyone slays a human being unless it be [in punishment] for murder or for spreading corruption on earth – it shall be as though he had slain all mankind; whereas, if anyone saves a life, it shall be as though he had saved the lives of all mankind"* (Surah al Maida – The Repast, 5:32). Interpreting this principle then, prohibits the deliberate application of the death penalty. Even in homicide cases, the Quran restricts the literal use of "a life for a life" rule and stresses the virtues of mercy and forgiveness, allowing for lesser, equivalent penalties, such as jail time, to be meted out instead of capital punishment.

Abortion

From a moral perspective, abortion raises the issue of taking a life, and the circumstances under which it can be done. From a legal perspective, it is controversial as to what point in its gestation the fetus becomes a person, with certain legal rights. Some Muslim jurists denote abortion as reprehensible (*makruh*), while others deem it forbidden (*haram*).[16] But there is a range of legal opinions between these two points, all of which are deemed equally legitimate from the legal perspective. The main source of disagreement arises from when to consider the fetus as a living soul, as opposed to a living organism. Those that place this transformation at some point in the first trimester of pregnancy allow an abortion to be carried out within that time period (Hanafis, Hanbalis and some Shafi'is). Others disagree and consider abortion to be tampering with Divine Will at any point in the pregnancy and therefore prohibited (Malikis, some Shafi'is) In all cases though, if the mother's life is endangered, saving her life takes precedence and a medically-necessary abortion is permissible as "the lesser evil" (as opposed to the greater one of letting the mother die).[17] We will outline both perspectives, for and against abortion, using the Quran and *hadith* literature, in addition to the juristic rulings of the main legal schools.

The Quran describes the process of fetal development in a number of stages, from a sperm drop, to a clot, to a morsel of flesh/lump, to a human being with a soul. *"And then We create out of the drop of sperms a germ-cell, and then We create out of the germ-cell an embryonic lump, and then We create within the embryonic lump bones, and then We clothe the bones with flesh – and then We bring [all] this into being as a new creation: hallowed, therefore, is God, the best of artisans!"* (Surah al Muminun – The Believers, 23:14). The following verse also mentions dust as the first step, referring to the creation of Adam and mankind by God, but the rest of the verse describes the same human gestation process. *"O men! If you are in doubt as to the [truth of] resurrection, [remember that,] verily, We have created [every one of] you out of dust, then out of a drop of sperm, then out of a germ-cell, then out of an embryonic lump complete [in itself] and yet incomplete, so that We might make [your origin]clear unto you. And whatever We will [to be born] We cause to rest in the [mothers'] wombs for a term set [by Us], and then We bring you forth as infants and [allow you to live] so that [some of] you might attain to maturity"* (Surah al Hajj – Pilgrimage, 22:5). Only after the first three stages have passed does the fetus become "ensouled."[18] In other words, it becomes a human being, instead of just a living organism.

But how does one determine when the first three stages are over? Within the descriptive, biological markers noted in these verses, this question is answered in a *hadith* that introduces the element of time to this process. The Prophet (pbuh) is reported to have said that each stage lasted forty days. "The constituents of one of you are collected for forty days in his mother's womb in the form of blood, after which it becomes a clot of blood in another period of forty days. Then it becomes a lump of flesh and forty days later God sends His angel to it with instructions concerning four things, so the angel writes down his livelihood, his death, his deeds, his fortune and misfortune."[19] Notwithstanding the precise biological accuracy of the description, the *hadith* nevertheless defines each of the three stages as lasting roughly 40 days.

Another *hadith*, narrated by Bukhari, echoes the same process, but without specifying the time component. "The Prophet said, 'At every womb God appoints an angel who says, 'O Lord! A drop of semen, O Lord! A clot. O Lord! A little lump of flesh.' Then if God wishes (to complete) its creation, the angel asks, '(O Lord!) Will it be a male or female, a wretched or a blessed, and how much will his provision be? And what will his age be?' So all that is written while the child is still in the mother's womb."[20] Therefore, relying on *hadith* evidence, jurists agree that after 120 days, the fetus is considered to be a person.[21]

The proponents of abortion argue that it is permissible before the 120 days are up, because since the fetus is not a person, abortion does not constitute a criminal act, i.e. murder.[22] However, there are juristic differences on the time period up to which abortion is allowed. The majority of Hanafi and some Shafi'i scholars allow abortions to be performed up to 120 days. The Hanbali allow it up till 40 days. Some Shafi'i place the cut off date at 80 days,[23] while some Maliki jurists do so at day 40.[24]

Despite the flexibility for determining the time period in which an abortion is permissible, there is still the need to have a good reason for doing it. In general, the mother's health is a primary concern. Juristic texts cite the risk of a difficult labor potentially endangering the mother's life, a disease, or the mother's young age (under fifteen years) as potential reasons for an abortion.[25] One recognized rationale is if a woman becomes pregnant while nursing a baby. Since lactation sometimes ceases following a new pregnancy, a wet nurse would need to be hired to replace the mother, which might be an undue financial burden on the family. Alternately, the mother might continue to nurse the baby as long as possible, but at the risk of depriving the fetus of necessary nutrition.[26] In more contemporary contexts, if the child is conceived as a result of rape or if prenatal diagnosis results reveal it has a severe genetic disorder or deformity that would limit its chances of leading a healthy, normal life, abortion is also possible.[27]

The Maliki jurists who prohibit abortion under all circumstances share the stance of the Hanafi and Hanbali scholars who allow it, in that all agree killing a living soul is reprehensible and constitutes murder. But while the proponents of abortion give some leeway as to when that point of ensoulment occurs, those who argue against abortion do not believe that there is any flexibility in determining this. They posit that from the moment of conception onwards, the fetus is a potential human being and its life is in the hands of God. Abortion amounts to interfering with Divine Will, and an act of murder. All life is sacred, even life that is still within the womb.[28]

The moral import of the Quranic passages on infanticide are used to support this line of argument. *"Say: 'Come, let me convey unto you what God has [really] forbidden to you: 'Do not ascribe divinity, in any way, to aught beside Him; and [do not offend against but, rather,] do good unto your parents; and do not kill your children for fear of poverty – [for] it is We who shall provide sustenance for you as well as for them; and do not commit any shameful deeds"* (Surah al Anam - Cattle,

6:151). Also in the same surah, *"Lost, indeed, are they who, in their weak-minded ignorance, slay their children and declare as forbidden that which God has provided for them as sustenance, falsely ascribing [such prohibitions] to God: they have gone astray and have not found the right path"* (Surah al Anam – Cattle, 6:140). God unequivocally condemns infanticide, especially if it is done for fear of economic or financial difficulties caused by having a child to feed. Even though one could argue that a fetus is not the same as a newborn child, for those who condemn abortion, this distinction does not take away from the fact that both are human beings. Therefore, killing one or the other is still a matter of killing a living soul, and condemned by God.

The discussion so far has focused on the pivotal issues of the time period within which abortion is permissible, and distinguishing between the fetus as a solely biological being and as a person, with a soul.[29] However, it is necessary to stress that *all* legal schools permit an abortion if the mother's life is endangered at any point in the pregnancy. Since the mother is the source of life for the fetus, her well-being takes priority. The doctrine that applies is "necessity knows no laws", in this case, the mother's health being the necessity.[30]

In conclusion, one could argue that even among the legal schools that condemn abortion, it is still tolerated as a lesser evil in certain circumstances. Some jurists place very high restrictions on it, and rule it out unless the mother's life is specifically endangered. Others are more flexible and allow an abortion within the first 120 days, in addition to a medically-necessary abortion at a later point in the pregnancy. All schools require justifiable reasons for having one, though these are subject to debate. The abortion issue illustrates that upholding the sanctity of life principle involves gray areas in its application.

Biology, the Soul, and Abortion

The key question in abortion is whether the fetus is a "human" and worthy of the law's protection to the same extent as a newborn baby, or if it is not yet truly "human" and therefore does not merit that protection. From a religious perspective shared by Islam, Christianity, and

Judaism, this question quickly turns into a spiritual question of whether the fetus contains a soul. The reason for this is fairly straightforward. Death or loss of human tissue constantly occurs without it being considered murdered. A person who accidentally cuts himself shaving loses some blood, and the cells in that blood die, but he has not committed murder. A person who is involved in an auto accident and loses a limb has not murdered that limb. When a surgeon removes a diseased organ, she does not "murder" the organ. Murder involves more than the loss of human tissue. What constitutes murder is the death of the brain. If all the organs in a body die with the exception of the brain, we still consider the person to be alive. Conversely if all the organs in the body are healthy but the brain is dead, we consider the person to have died. A patient who is brain dead and who donates his heart, lungs, intestines, liver, kidney, pancreas, skin, bone, and corneas to other human beings is not alive, even though all these elements remain very much alive in other bodies.

Islam understands the soul to be immortal. But once the brain dies and the patient is considered dead, the soul is no longer in the body. The matter-spirit link between body and soul has been broken, and the soul departs the physical body, which then decays. Given that the key organ remains the brain, we are forced to conclude that the brain is the necessary physical home for the soul. Without the brain, all we have is tissue and organs, which do not have the standing of being a "human". Murder, in any context, can then be defined as deliberately killing the physical home of the soul, forcing it to depart the material body.

This has significant implications for the issue of abortion. Opponents of abortion base their objection on the grounds of abortion being morally the equal of murder. To kill an embryo is the same as killing a live baby. But from a spiritual standpoint, it cannot be murder unless the tissue in question contains a soul. This is the source of the discussion about "ensoulment," or the divine act of investing the developing embryo with a soul. For a soul to no longer inhabit an adult body, the brain must be dead, and for a soul to enter the body there must be a brain that accepts it. This leads to the conclusion that ensoulment cannot occur until at least the simplest brain has developed at a minimum.

The developing embryo creates two neural buds at the seventh week of gestation that are the source of the two halves of the brain. These buds of nerve cells constitute the earliest moment at which a rudimentary brain can be said to exist. There is a rare but well described birth defect in which these two buds never form. In that case the baby is born without a brain entirely, and the skull is empty. This condition is known as anencephaly. An anencephalic baby, a baby with no brain whatsoever, is mere tissue but cannot logically be said to have ever been a "human". In fact since it never had even the potential for consciousness or rational thought, it cannot be said to have ever had a soul. To claim that such a baby has a soul or had a soul at some point is equivalent to claiming that an arm or leg can possess a soul. These babies, when found by prenatal ultrasound, are often aborted. We find no argument that suggests this would be murder, as these babies cannot be said to have ever possessed a soul.

These biological facts have significant implications for the issue of abortion. Even if we accept the ensoulment paradigm as a useful way to think about the morality of abortion, it does create a rational basis for allowing abortion in the first six weeks of pregnancy. Abortion before the earliest brain tissue even exists would not be the moral equivalent of murder, as the soul cannot link to a mass of tissue without the brain being involved and present. If there is no home for the soul, the soul cannot be present. If murder is killing the physical home of the soul and forcing it to depart the body, this would not prevent abortion at a time when the soul has not yet entered the embryo precisely because there does not exist the necessary home for it, the brain.

There are some who would object to this rationale by claiming that ensoulment begins with conception, when sperm and egg first meet. Although the brain eventually becomes the physical home of the soul, for those first 6 weeks of embryonic development, the soul adheres in some spiritual way to the embryo as a whole. After the 7th week, the soul somehow adheres only to the brain itself. Therefore, even the earliest abortions constitute murder. This paradigm, of conception and ensoulment being simultaneous, has no recognized basis in the Quran, the *hadith*, or the juristic tradition. It is in fact a borrowing from the Catholic Church and conservative Protestant churches who have embraced this doctrine. It has no authentic Islamic root. Even more importantly in the light of modern medical knowledge, this position leads to an absurd conclusion.

Medical investigation has shown that conception occurs in many if not nearly all months of a healthy married couple's life, if the wife is still in her fertile years. But clearly viable pregnancies do not occur quite that often or easily. The reason is that most of the products of conception suffer from genetic defects. These defects prevent normal growth, and the early embryo fails to implant in the wall of the uterus and is simply passed out to its death. A large fraction of these fertilized eggs do implant, but the uterus and the embryo fail to interact properly and the pregnancy fails to develop. This process probably explains the occasional delay in menstrual flow in a given month, as a very early pregnancy fails after 5 or 10 days, but does disrupt the normal monthly pattern. Even if the embryo implants and survives a few days, first trimester miscarriages are very common, affecting 15-20% of confirmed pregnancies. There is no evidence that the Prophet (pbuh) would offer funeral prayers for the product of early (or for that matter, late) miscarriages. If these miscarried babies had souls, the Prophet (pbuh) would have prayed for them.

Modern obstetrical knowledge leads to the conclusion that over 70% of conceptions fail to develop into a live birth. If ensoulment were to occur with conception, and yet 70% of such conceptions live no more than a few hours, days, or weeks in the womb naturally, then it would seem that the progeny of Adam consists mostly of these kinds of "humans" rather than the world we know and inhabit. On the Day of Judgment, most souls who stand before God will be these sorts of souls, and on what basis would God judge them, and to what purpose were they created? This conclusion has no basis in the Quran and appears to be highly problematical from a theological standpoint. The argument that ensoulment occurs with conception is therefore fundamentally flawed.

Suicide, Physician-Assisted Suicide and Euthanasia[31]

If life is divinely-granted, and its duration only determined by God, do individuals have the right to end it voluntarily? Suicide, physician-assisted suicide and euthanasia are issues which challenge the idea of the sanctity of life. If all life is equally valuable, then who can decide in what circumstances it loses its value, enough so that it should be terminated?

The theological and spiritual relationship between humans and God is based on faith and man's acceptance of God's all-encompassing Power over all of Creation. To take a life, one's own or someone else's, is therefore deemed to be a sin. Societies translate this moral principle into law by creating a criminal justice system that punishes such behavior, which we have described above. Currently, in most parts of the world, suicide is not prosecuted, for obvious reasons, as a legal crime, but it is still noted as a crime. With regards to physician-assisted suicide and euthanasia, from both a moral and legal perspective, doctors who intentionally facilitate the death of their patients, whether directly or indirectly, commit an immoral, as well as an illegal, act.[32]

Suicide

The prohibition against suicide is derived from the Quranic emphasis on faith in God as Creator. *"There is no deity save Him: He grants life and deals death"* (Surah al Dukhan – Smoke, 44:8). *"And none that is long-lived has his days lengthened – and neither is aught lessened of his days – unless it be thus laid down in [God's] decree: for, behold, all this is easy for God"* (Surah al Fatir – The Originator, 35:11). Suicide is considered to be a violation of that faith, because it imposes the individual's own (limited, human) understanding of the value of his/her life against the value that God has placed on that life in creating it in the first place. Suicide contradicts the value of life, as a general principle, and in the specific case of the person involved. It also contradicts the message of the Quran as one of hope for people. *"God does not burden any human being with more than he has given him – [and it may well be that] God will grant, after hardship, ease"* (Surah al Talaq – Divorce, 65:7).

In terms of specific verses condemning suicide, Surah al Baqara – The Cow, 2:195, notes *"And let not your own hands throw you into destruction; and persevere in doing good: behold, God loves the doers of good"* In other words, taking one's own life is the opposite of doing good, and does not invite God's favor. Surah an Nisaa – Women, 4:97 elaborates further on the negative view of suicide. Suicide is considered a moral transgression, and the individual is subject to punishment in the Afterlife. *"Behold, those whom the angels gather in death while they are still sinning against themselves, [the angels] will ask, 'What was wrong with you?' They will answer: 'We were too weak on earth.' [The angels] will say: 'Was, then, God's earth not wide enough for you to forsake the domain of evil?' For such, then, the goal is hell – and how evil a journey's end!"* (Surah an Nisaa – Women, 4:97). We interpret "those who die in sin against their souls" as reference to those who commit suicide. They do so because of feelings of oppression and powerlessness. But God condemns these people, who do not take steps to consciously move away from these feelings, and who give in to "the evil" of taking their own lives.

There are also two *hadith*, which elaborate on the negative moral implications of suicide. "And whoever commits suicide with piece of iron will be punished with the same piece of iron in the Hell Fire." Narrated Jundab the Prophet said, "A man was inflicted with wounds and he committed suicide, and so God said: My slave has caused death on himself hurriedly, so I forbid Paradise for him."[33]

"Narrated Sa'd bin Sahl As-Sa'idi: The Prophet looked at a man fighting against the pagans and he was one of the most competent persons fighting on behalf of the Muslims. The Prophet said, "Let him who wants to look at a man from the dwellers of the (Hell) Fire, look at this (man)." Another man followed him and kept on following him until he (the fighter) was injured and, seeking to die quickly, he placed the blade tip of his sword between his breasts and leaned over it till it passed through his shoulders (i.e., committed suicide)." The Prophet added, "A person may do deeds that seem to the people as the deeds of the people of Paradise while in fact, he is from the dwellers of the (Hell) Fire: and similarly a person may do deeds that seem to the people as the deeds of the people of the (Hell) Fire while in fact, he is from the dwellers of Paradise. Verily, the (results of) deeds done, depend upon the last actions."[34] This *hadith* illustrates that it is a person's final actions which determine whether the individual will be saved in the Afterlife. Even if the person had done good deeds, such as fighting on the side of the Muslims in the context of this *hadith*, the final act of taking one's own life has its own deleterious consequences and assigns the person to Hell.

Although it may be evident that suicide is not morally or spiritually acceptable, physician-assisted suicide and euthanasia can also be similarly condemned. Spiritually, the end result of someone who chooses to commit suicide is the same, whether he/she commits the act himself or has the assistance of a physician.

Euthanasia/Physician-Assisted Suicide

Part of the argument advocating euthanasia is for ending the suffering of the patient, who may be in extreme physical pain. Hence, we see the popular use of the term "mercy killing" to describe euthanasia. In prohibiting these acts, though, we argue that God does not lack mercy or awareness of human suffering and ailments.

For example, the pain of childbirth is mentioned in Surahs al Ahqaf and Luqman, with the admonition for obedience to one's mother as a result. *"We have enjoined upon man goodness towards his parents: his mother bore him by bearing strain upon strain, and his utter dependence on her lasted two years: [hence, O man,] be grateful towards Me* and towards thy parents, [and remember that] with Me is all journeys' end" (Surah Luqman – Luqman, 31:14). "In pain did his mother bear him, and in pain did she give him birth" (Surah al Ahqaf – The Sand-Dunes, 46:15). Similarly, the pangs of death are noted in Surah al Qiyamah – Resurrection. "The while he [himself] knows that this is the parting, and is enwrapped in the pangs of death -: at that time towards thy Sustainer does he feel impelled to turn!" (Surah al Qiyamah – Resurrection, 75:28-30).

Even with the awareness of suffering, God reminds humans that He has answered their calls for help when they have turned to Him. "Misfortune and hardship befell them, and so shaken were they that the apostle, and the believers with him, would exclaim, 'When will God's succor come?' Oh, verily, God's succor is [always] near!" (Surah al Baqara – The Cow, 2:214).

"God wants to lighten your burdens: for man has been created weak" (Surah an Nisaa – Women, 4:28). Physical pain and suffering are part of the travails of being human, and God is aware of that, and is inclined to show His Mercy to those who suffer.

"Nay – who is it that responds to the distressed when he calls out to Him, and who removes the ill [that caused the distress], and has made you inherit the earth? Could there be any divine power besides God? How seldom do you keep this in mind!" (Surah al Naml – The Ants, 27:62).

"And be not faint of heart when you seek out the [enemy] host. If you happen to suffer pain, behold, they suffer pain even as you suffer it: but you are hoping [to receive] from God what they cannot hope for. And God is indeed all-knowing, wise" (Surah an Nisaa - Women, 4:104).

The purport of these verses is that despite suffering and hardship, human beings are asked to maintain their faith in the mercy and wisdom of God.[35] On a more temporal level, patients are entitled to compassion and support from their family, friends and community, in addition to their doctor, during their time of hardship. The physician's responsibility in such a case is to alleviate the pain through medical treatment, not to kill him/her to end the suffering.

Yet, there is the matter of the limits to which the doctor can help the patient, given the degree of the illness and the extent to which the patient may reasonably expect to be cured. It is evident that the doctor must make the strongest effort to save the patient's life. However, he/she is also obligated to remember that God determines life and death, and if it appears that death is imminent, then heroic means to preserve the patient's life must be tempered by a realistic assessment of the situation. In cases where death is inevitable however, the physician's intention clearly matters, since he/she has to tread the fine line between fully relieving any suffering (through pain relief, or sedation, for example) and actively killing the patient outright.

In conclusion, we can rule out the moral permissibility of all three acts, suicide, physician-assisted suicide and euthanasia. The last two in particular call upon the doctor to make a judgment on the duration and value of life, which is contrary to an awareness of God's role as a life-giving and life-affirming Power. The doctor's role is to save life, and to allow individuals to live healthier lives by treating their illnesses. It also includes providing relief when death is inevitable through the means available. From a legal perspective, this aspect of a physician's role ties in with one of the primary goals of the sharia: to preserve life. Thus, physicians do not have the moral or legal authority to transgress those boundaries, from an Islamic perspective.

Conclusion

This chapter has explored the relationship between the moral principle of the sanctity of life, as described in the Quran, and its practice in society. The role of law is especially important in upholding this principle, by regulating legal punishment for murder and placing boundaries on the circumstances in which life may be taken, in the case of the death penalty. Even in extreme cases, however, human life does not lose its value. Thus, abortion, although permissible, is subject to certain restrictions. Similarly, suicide, physician-assisted and euthanasia are all equally condemned in Islam as actions that impinge on the Divine role of God. Life is a gift, bestowed upon humans by God. An awareness of one's humanity and role in this world requires an attitude of faith that one's life always has value, despite difficult circumstances, and moments of pain and suffering.

Footnotes

1   Sahih Bukhari, Volume 9, Book 83, Number 3.

2   Sahih Bukhari, Volume 9, Book 83, Number 4.

3   M. Cherif Bassiuoni, "Quesas Crimes," *The Islamic Criminal Justice System*, ed. Cherif Bassiouni (New York: Oceana Publications, 1982), p. 203.

4   Bassiouni, p. 203.

5   Bassiouni, p. 204.

6   Defined as the law of an eye for an eye, and a tooth for a tooth.

7   Bassiouni, p. 204.

8   Bassiouni, p. 205.

9   Bassiouni, pp. 205-206.

10 Bassiouni, p. 205.

11 See chapter on the justice system for more on the definition and types of hudud crimes.

12 Sahih Muslim, Book 17, No. 4191.

13 Sahih Muslim, Book 17, No. 4196.

14 Quraishi, p. 4.

15 Salama, cited in Quraishi, p.4.

16 Vardit Rispler-Chaim, "The Right Not to be Born: Abortion of the Disadvantaged Fetus in Contemporary Fatwas" *The Muslim World*, 89:2, April 1999 (Hartford, CT: Hartford Seminary), p. 133; Donna Lee Bowen, "Abortion, Islam and the 1994 Cairo Population Conference," *International Journal of Middle East Studies*, 29:2 (1997):165; Bassim Musallam, *Sex and Society in Islam: The Sanction and Medieval Techniques of Birth Control*, Diss., Harvard University, 1973, p. 124.

17 Bowen, p. 164.

18 Fazlur Rahman, "Birth and Abortion in Islam," Abortion: A Reader, ed. Lloyd Steffen (Cleveland, OH: Pilgrim Press, 1996), p. 204.

19 Sahih Muslim, *Kitab al Qadr*, Book 33, Number 6390. The same *hadith* is noted in various forms in No. 6391-6397 of the same source.

20 Sahih Bukhari, Volume 1, Book 6, Number 315.

21 According to some accounts, the fetus has inheritance rights, and if it is killed after 120 days, (the mother miscarries as a result of injury by someone else) punishment includes the payment of compensation, similar to qesas crimes for adult individuals. The difference is that retaliation is not an option.

22 Whether or not it is still a sin is debated among the legal schools. Therisa Rogers, "The Islamic Ethics of Abortion in the Traditional Islamic Sources" *The Muslim World*, 89:2, (April 1999), p. 122.

23 Bowen, p. 164. See also Musallam, p. 128, n. 11 for complete citation of juristic texts.

24 Al-Dasuqi, *Hashiyat*, vol. 2, p. 267, cited in Musallam, p. 129, n. 16.

25 Ibn Sina, *Qanun*, cited in Bowen, p. 165.

26 Bowen, p. 165.

27 See Vardit Rispler-Chaim, "The Right Not to be Born: Abortion of the Disadvantaged Fetus in Contemporary Fatwas", *The Muslim World*, 89:2, April 1999 (Hartford, CT: Hartford Seminary) pp. 130-143 for more on this subject.

28 Bowen, p. 164.

29 Rogers, p. 123.

30 Bowen, p. 164.

31 The difference between physician-assisted suicide and euthanasia depends on who performs the last causal step that brings about the individual's death. If it is the patient him/herself, then it is the former. If the doctor carries out the act (gives the fatal

injection, etc.), then it is termed euthanasia.

32 The only legal exception is in the state of Oregon and the country of Holland, where euthanasia is legally permissible.

33 Sahih Bukhari, *Kitab al Janaa'iz*, Vol. 2, Book 23, Number 445.

34 Sahih Bukhari, Vol. 8, Book 76, Number 500.

35 Jalaluddin Umri, "Suicide or Termination of Life," transl. S.A.H. Rizvi, *Islamic and Comparative Law Quarterly*, Vol. 7:2 (June 1987), pp. 138-139.

Freedom of Speech

reedom refers to a state of being in which an individual is able to make a choice in thought, behavior or speech, as he or she wishes, or to avoid doing so, without violating similar freedom on the part of others and within the restraints imposed by society. This freedom is often regulated by law in society, i.e. enshrined in a constitution.

From this general definition, we can extrapolate three main ideas. First, freedom has both positive and negative aspects. It includes the freedom to do something, as well as the freedom not to do it. Second, there are limits or restraints on individual freedom, such that it cannot impinge upon another person's freedom. Third, because it is a choice, the individual is then accountable for his/her actions and the consequences deriving from his/her choices. All three of these qualities need to be kept in mind as we consider the role of freedom of speech in Islam.

This chapter will define free speech from a legal perspective, relying primarily on Quranic evidence, non-controversial *hadith*, and to a more limited degree, on Islamic juristic principles. While normative moral imperatives are also relevant to the discussion, we make a distinction between speech which is immoral and that which is illegal. It is the latter type that we are concerned with here, since we are focusing on behavior that can be regulated by law. The purpose of this work is to indicate the broadest parameters available, from an Islamic perspective, for defining freedom of speech within a socio-political context, particularly given the experience of political repression that has been justified in the name of Islam within the *umma* (global Muslim community).

This chapter has three sections. The first section explores the philosophical argument in the Quran for freedom as a natural human state. From this concept derives the importance of freedom of expression as a principle, which is discussed in the second section. Textual, allegorical and juristic evidence are offered in support of this argument. The third part outlines the broad scope of free speech as a legal right, with the exception of when it poses a clear threat to public safety.

Freedom: A Philosophical Perspective

This section will establish a theoretical framework for our argument, and briefly outline the concept of freedom as a natural and necessary factor in human existence, as indicated in the Quran.

The idea of freedom relates to two aspects of human existence: it can be articulated in terms of individual liberty, and in terms of free will. Individual liberty has to do with the position of human beings as members of society, in a socio-political sense. Free will has to do with the relationship between human beings and God, and is a more philosophical/theological issue. Free will is a vital component of individual liberty. Both of these concepts will be discussed here.

The issue of human freedom in Islam has three aspects, and is similar to the definition given in the introduction. First is the notion that humans are born free from original sin. Adam and Eve were forgiven for their sins by God, although their human descendents would have to live on earth, which would serve as a test to their faith *"But Satan caused them both to stumble therein, and thus brought about the loss of their erstwhile state. And so We said: 'Down with you, [and be henceforth] enemies unto one another; and on earth you shall have your abode and your livelihood for a while! Thereupon Adam received words [of guidance] from his Sustainer, and he accepted his repentance: for, verily, He alone is the Acceptor of Repentance, the Dispenser of Grace.*

[For although] We did say, 'Down with you all from this [state],' there shall, none the less, most certainly come unto you guidance from Me: and those who follow My guidance need have no fear, and neither shall they grieve" (Surah al-Baqara – The Cow, 2:36-38).

Second, given this test, we believe that humans are free to choose their actions. God has created humans such that they have an innate ability to know the difference between good and evil, and in doing so, have the freedom to choose good. *"Consider the human self, and how it is formed in accordance with what it is meant to be, and how it is imbued with moral failings as well as with consciousness of God! To a happy state shall indeed attain he who causes his [self] to grow in purity, and truly lost is he who buries it [in darkness]"* (Surah ash Shams – The Sun, 91:7-10). It is only by having this freedom that choosing to obey God becomes a meaningful process. This point is noted in Surah al-Kahf – The Cave, 18:29, *"And say: 'The truth [has now come] from your Sustainer: let, then, him who wills, believe in it, and let him who wills, reject it'"*, and also in Surah al-Insan – Man, 76:3, *"Verily, We have shown him the way: [and it rests with him to prove himself] either grateful or ungrateful."*

Third, to be able to choose one's actions then implies that one has to deal with the consequences of them as well. Humans are accountable to God on the Day of Judgment, and will be rewarded or punished by Divine Will accordingly, as evidenced in Surah al-Isra – The Night Journey, 17:13: *"And every human being's destiny have We tied to his neck; and on the Day of Resurrection We shall bring forth for him a record which he will find wide open."*

This brief discussion illustrates that the natural state for human beings, as indicated in the Quran, is that of freedom, granted by God. This position is also agreed upon by jurists. Given that the juristic principle that what is not expressly forbidden is permissible, it follows that freedom is therefore the natural condition.[1]

This point is important because it contrasts the idea of human fallibility with divine infallibility and omniscience on moral issues. As a matter of principle then, no human authority has the right to take away that moral freedom, nor to stand in moral judgment over others for their actions. This serves as a strong injunction for any governmental authority against regulating or policing the moral behavior of society.

Surah al-Baqara – The Cow, 2:256, summarizes this idea: *"There shall be no coercion in matters of faith. Distinct has now become the right way from [the way of] error."* Although a number of meanings may be drawn from this verse, the most basic one, which concerns us here, is the fact that coercion is to be eschewed as a component of religion, or faith. Freedom is an absolute principle, and is not qualified in any way as an element of Islamic teaching.

This does not mean, however, that there is no check on human behavior. Even if final accountability for one's actions is only to God, these actions do have consequences here on earth. As members of society, we are of course responsible for our actions, such that they are not at the expense of the safety or rights of others. This is where legal restrictions regulating behavior are important, and where we draw the distinction between immoral versus criminal behavior. This temporal aspect of freedom will be addressed further in the third section.

Freedom of Expression as a Principle

Freedom of expression derives logically from the general idea of freedom as a natural human state. Thus, we move from the philosophical/moral sphere towards a more temporal understanding relating to man's position in society, rather than his individual relationship to God. While there is no direct reference to freedom of expression in the Quran, we can infer, however, its existence as a positive principle, textually and allegorically.

If humans are free to choose their actions, then it follows that they are also free to think and express their choices, since without the latter, the choice becomes meaningless. The Quran supports this idea in Surah al Baqara – The Cow, 2:266, which states, *"God makes clear His messages unto you, so that you might take thought."*

Encouraging rational enquiry would be futile without the freedom to express one's thoughts.

Free speech is an aspect of human dignity. It is an essential part of individual growth and development, and to place restrictions on it then also curtails one's dignity as a human being. The Quran declares dignity as a natural right in Surah al-Isra – The Night Journey, 17:70, *"Now, indeed, We have conferred dignity on the children of Adam."* There is no evidence that this absolute declaration is qualified anywhere in the Quran, and therefore can be considered to be a normative principle of Islam.[2]

Freedom of expression is also related to matters of faith. Religion cannot be a meaningful experience without equal ability to express doubt or faith. Even prophets are not immune from expressing doubt; they are still given the leeway to question God. For example, *"And, lo, Abraham said: 'O my Sustainer! Show me how Thou givest life unto the dead!' Said He: 'Hast thou, then, no faith?' [Abraham] answered: 'Yea, but [let me see it] so that my heart may be set fully at rest.' Said He: 'Take, then, four birds and teach them to obey thee; then place them separately on every hill [around thee]; then summon them: they will come flying to thee. And know that God is almighty, wise'"* (Surah al Baqara – The Cow, 2:260).

If religion can be questioned, then conversely, religious claims made by individuals must also be supported by evidence. Since God is the only omniscient authority, people cannot limit others from expressing their ideas by judging the value of them beforehand. *"And they claim, 'None shall ever enter paradise unless he be a Jew' – or, 'a Christian'. Such are their wishful beliefs! Say: 'Produce an evidence for what you are claiming, if what you say is true!'"* (Surah al Baqara – The Cow, 2:111). Two other verses on this theme are: Surah al Anbiya – The Prophets, 21:24, *"And yet, they choose to worship [imaginary] deities instead of Him! Say [O Prophet]: 'Produce an evidence for what you are claiming: this is a reminder [unceasingly voiced] by those who are with me, just as it was a reminder [voiced] by those who came before me' But nay, most of them do not know the truth, and so they stubbornly turn away [from it]"*; and Surah al Qasas – The Story, 28:75, *"And [they will remain silent: for by then] We will have called forth witnesses from within every community, and will have said [unto the sinners]: 'Produce an evidence for what you have been claiming!' And so they will come to understand that all truth is God's [alone]; and all their false imagery will have forsaken them."*

Though God judges individuals on their intentions, He also judges them on their actions and their speech. In fact, it is a moral obligation for people to articulate Truth,[3] when they know what it is. *"And do not overlay the truth with falsehood, and do not knowingly suppress the truth"* (Surah al Baqara – The Cow, 2:42). Also, *"They unto whom We have vouchsafed revelation aforetime know it as they know their own children: but behold, some of them knowingly suppress the truth"* (Surah al Baqara – The Cow, 2:146).

Other verses that express the necessity of freedom of expression as a component of religion are:

"At that, a believing man of Pharaoh's family, who [until then] had concealed his faith, exclaimed: 'Would you slay a man because he says, 'God is my Sustainer' – seeing, withal, that he has brought you all evidence of this truth from your Sustainer? Now if he be a liar, his lie will fall back on him; but if he is a man of truth, something [of the punishment] whereof he warns you is bound to befall you: for, verily, God would not grace with His guidance one who has wasted his own self by lying [about Him]" (Surah Ghafir - Forgiving, 40:28).

" 'Do you claim that Abraham and Ishmael and Isaac and Jacob and their descendants were 'Jews' or 'Christians'?' Say: 'Do you know more than God does? And who could be more wicked than he who suppresses a testimony given to him by God? Yet God is not unmindful of what you do" (Surah al Baqara – The Cow, 2:140).

"And do not conceal what you have witnessed – for, verily, he who conceals it is sinful at heart; and God has full knowledge of all that you do. Unto God belongs all that is in the heavens and all that is on earth.

And whether you bring into the open what is in your minds or conceal it, God will call you to account for it; and then He will forgive whom He wills, and will chastise whom He wills: for God has the power to will anything" (Surah al Baqara – The Cow, 2:283-284).

All of these verses imply that belief, or faith, goes hand in hand with the freedom to express doubt or support, and that upholding religion requires a commitment to critically examining and affirming its components, to the best of an individual's ability. God is the only authority to ultimately judge the veracity or falsity of a religious claim. No other authority can punish individuals for expressing their ideas, regardless of whether they are true or false. This is illustrated in Surah Ghafir - Forgiving, 40:28, above, and also in the following verses in which the threat of stoning is levied against those who brought Islam to nonbelievers.

In an encounter between Abraham and his father in Surah Maryam – Mary, 19:46-47, *"He answered: 'Dost thou dislike my gods, O Abraham? Indeed, if thou desist not, I shall most certainly cause thee to be stoned to death! Now begone from me for good!' [Abraham] replied: 'Peace be upon thee! I shall ask my Sustainer to forgive thee: for, behold, He has always been kind unto me'"*

Another example is in Surah Yasin – O Thou Human Being, 36:18-19, *"Said [the others]: 'Truly, we augur evil from you! Indeed, if you desist not, we will surely stone you, and grievous suffering is bound to befall you at your hands!' [The apostles] replied: 'Your destiny, good or evil, is [bound up] with yourselves! [Does it seem evil to you] if you are told to take [the truth] to heart? Nay, but you are people of who have wasted their own selves!'"* Both of these examples express a negative view of authorities which try to restrict the freedom to express religious ideas because they are contrary to their own beliefs. This theme will be addressed again later on in this chapter, and in more detail in the chapter on religious freedom.

Turning to allegorical evidence supporting freedom of expression, there are three examples that are noteworthy. The first is that of Iblis'

(Satan) refusal to bow down before Adam when God commands all the angels to do so, mentioned in Surah al-Baqara – The Cow, 2:34. *"And when We told the angels, 'Prostrate yourselves before Adam! – they all prostrated themselves, save Iblis, who refused and gloried in his arrogance: and thus he became one of those who deny the truth."* Although the angels also question God on His decision to place Adam on earth as vicegerent, ultimately they do obey. *"And lo! Thy Sustainer said unto the angels: 'Behold, I am about to establish upon earth one who shall inherit it.' They said: 'Wilt Thou place on it such as will spread corruption thereon and shed blood – whereas it is we who extol Thy limitless glory, and praise Thee, and hallow Thy name?' [God] answered: 'Verily, I know that which you do not know"* (Surah al-Baqara – The Cow, 2:30). When Iblis refuses, however, he is cursed for his disobedience, but not punished by God. Instead, he is allowed to continue in his rebellion, and to carry out his role in tempting humans towards evil until the Day of Judgment. *"Said He: 'Go forth, then, from this [angelic state]: for, behold, thou art [henceforth] accursed, and [My] rejection shall be thy due until the Day of Judgment!'"* (Surah al Hijr – Al Hijr, 15:34-35). If this freedom to question and criticize is granted to Iblis by God, then it is no less than that which is granted to humans. Furthermore, no restriction is placed by God on the spirit of questioning, either by the angels or by Iblis.

The second example that supports the argument for protection of the spirit of criticism and questioning, even when it is hurtful, is that of Abu Lahab, the Prophet's Uncle, who is known to have openly criticized and persecuted the Prophet frequently. His wife is said to have placed thorns on the path outside the Prophet's house so that he may trip over them in the dark. Surah al-Lahhab, 111, refers to this and states that the punishment for these actions will be in the Hereafter, by God, and not in the temporal realm. *"Doomed are the hands of him of the glowing countenance, and doomed is he! What will his wealth avail him, and all that he has gained? [In th life to come] he shall have to endure a fire fiercely glowing, together with his wife, that carrier of evil* tales, [who bears] around her neck a rope of twisted strands!" (Surah al Masad – The Twisted Strands, 111:1-5). The connecting theme in these two examples is that of support for the principle of freedom of expression, even when it is rude, harmful or outright disobedient. Both Iblis and Abu Lahab are held liable for their actions, but the punishment for it is not adjudicated by human authority.

The third example is that of the encounter between Moses and the Pharaoh, in which Moses speaks up against the tyranny of the ruler, despite the fact that the Pharaoh provided shelter to and raised Moses. *"[But when Moses had delivered his message, Pharaoh] said: 'Did we not bring thee up among us when thou wert a child? And didst thou not spend among us years of thy [later] life? And yet thou didst commit that [heinous] deed of thine, and [hast thus shown that] thou art one of the ingrate!' Replied [Moses]: 'I committed it while I was still going astray; and I fled from you because I feared you. But [since] then my Sustainer has endowed me with the ability to judge [between right and wrong], and has made me one of [His] message-bearers. And [as for] that favour of which thou so tauntingly remindst me – [was it not] due to thy having enslaved the children of Israel?'"* (Surah ash Shuara – The Poets, 26:18-22). Moses is not deterred from his commitment to speak freely and to challenge injustice, even at the expense of a personal relationship. This example illustrates the importance of political expression and freedom granted to individuals by God.

The Prophet (pbuh) is also known to have consulted with his companions, and debated with them on political and military issues. For example, during the Battle of Uhud (624), the Prophet (pbuh) commanded his followers to fight against the enemy in Medina. They asked him whether that order stemmed from divine guidance or if it was his own personal opinion. He replied that it was the latter, in which case they expressed their disagreement, and said that the battle should be fought instead on the grounds of Uhud. The Prophet (pbuh) agreed with their suggestion.[4] He also consulted with them and took their counsel in preparation for the battle of Badr (623).[5]

Moving from Quranic support for freedom of expression to Islamic scholastic tradition, even though there is no specific work on this issue, the closest is the discussion of *hurriyyah al-ra'y* (freedom of opinion), as the term is used, to refer to freedom of speech (instead of *hurriyyah al-qawl*, which would be the more precise equivalent).[6] It indicates the importance given to *ra'y*, or personal opinion, as the paramount aspect of this freedom.[7] *Ra'y* is defined as a considered opinion on a matter that has not been regulated by the Quran or the *sunna*, but which is arrived at by introspection and investigation of the available knowledge on a particular subject. It can be coexistent with *ijtihad* or not. It contains an element of arbitrariness, in the sense that it is a personal opinion, and does not necessarily have to coincide with *ijma'* (consensus of opinion) on an issue.[8]

In the context of early juristic thought, *ra'y* came to be associated with liberality and extrapolation in personal preferences, giving rise to a rift between two groups of scholars, the partisans of *Hadith (Ahl al-Hadith)* and the partisans of opinion *(Ahl al-Ra'y)*. The former preferred a more methodologically rigorous basis for exercising *ra'y*, in contrast to the *Ahl al-Ra'y*. This does not take away from the fact, though, that the disagreement between the two schools was more a matter of orientation rather than a total rejection of *ra'y* as a principle.[9]

This is merely one example of the diversity of opinion that constitutes the *fiqh*, or Islamic jurisprudence. It took nearly 200 years for the content of Islamic jurisprudence to be debated, developed and codified, as the cumulative effort of numerous scholars and jurists.[10] Today, it is dominated in Sunni Islam by four legal schools: Hanafi, Maliki, Shafi' and Hanbali, and a Shi'a school of jurisprudence, each of which have their own methodologies and conclusions on legal issues. The historical importance of *ra'y* as a component of *fiqh* indicates that the spirit of freedom of expression which is enshrined in the Quran is also reflected in juristic tradition.

The discussion so far has presented supporting evidence for the general principle of freedom of expression, from textual, allegorical and juristic perspectives in Islam. To summarize, free speech derives from freedom as a natural human state. It is not restricted as a principle, even when it is rude, disobedient, or reflects evil behavior. Evil speech, though it may be sinful, cannot be punished by human authority.

Freedom of Speech as a Legal Right

The general definition of free speech as a legal right refers to freedom of expression in public speech, or other forms of public media such as books, newspapers, photos, films, plays and TV, which are subject to legal regulation. It can be divided into political, artistic or commercial expression.

In a socio-political context, freedom of speech has two aspects. One is that it is a morally-based right, and therefore stems from and is used to advocate a particular moral perspective.[11] This book has demonstrated so far that an Islamic viewpoint embraces this idea to the extent that the *principle* of free speech is supported, as a natural extension of human freedom, dignity and moral autonomy. But, the moral or immoral content of the speech is not an issue that can be regulated by human authority.

The other aspect, one that concerns us more in this section of the paper, relates to free speech as an instrumentalist-based right. In this case, it is justified as a means necessary to achieve another goal. This can also be a utilitarian argument, used to justify a greater public good. For our purposes, we define free speech as a means to allow various ideas to compete against each other in the public sphere, without judging the moral value or content of those ideas. To the extent that a larger goal, of ascertaining "truth" for example, is a component of free speech, that is left to individuals to determine for themselves, without governmental interference.[12] Given this flexibility in defining the objective of free speech, the only restriction that is placed on it is that it does not directly endanger public safety. This point will be developed further in the discussion on seditious speech.

Examining Islamic sources in more detail, there is no specific definition of free speech as a legal and political right in the sharia, nor any discussion of criminal penalties for violations of freedom of speech.[13] Freedom of expression is referred to in the Quran primarily in the context of moral injunctions, such that good speech is preferred over evil speech, as in *"God does not like any evil to be mentioned openly, unless it be by him who has been wronged [thereby]. And God is indeed all-hearing, all-knowing"* (Surah an-Nisaa – Women, 4:148). Lying and backbiting are strongly discouraged, for example, in Surah al-Hujurat – The Private Apartments, 49:11-12: *"And neither shall you defame one another, nor insult one another by [opprobrious] epithets: evil is all imputation of iniquity after [one has attained to] faith; and they who [become guilty thereof and] do not repent – it is they, they who are evil-doers! O you who have attained to faith! Avoid most guesswork [about one another] – for, behold, some of [such] guesswork is [in itself] a sin; and do not spy upon another, and neither allow yourselves to speak ill of one another behind your backs. Would any of you like to eat the flesh of his dead brother? Nay, you would loathe it!"* Furthermore, the punishment for this type of evil speech is left to God, as illustrated by the Quranic examples of Iblis and Abu Lahab.

The only context in which temporal implications are mentioned for violations of freedom of speech is for slander and libel, which are forbidden according to Surah an-Nur – The Light, 24:19: *"Verily, as for those who like [to hear] foul slander spread against [any of] those who have attained to faith – grievous suffering awaits them in this world and in the life to come: for God knows [the full truth], whereas you know [it] not"* In the Quran, slander refers to a specific accusation of sexual misconduct, which has serious implications for the honor of a law-abiding individual. In contrast, libel is a more general category, meaning a knowingly false and malicious accusation regarding another person. In the case of slander, the onus is on the accuser to present four supporting witnesses to support the charge of adultery. *"Why do they not [demand of the accusers that they] produce four witnesses to prove their allegation? – for, if they do not produce such witnesses, it is those [accusers] who, in the sight of God, are liars indeed!"* (Surah an Nur – The Light, 24:13). If this is not possible, the accuser is subject to punishment himself. *"And as for those who accuse chaste women [of adultery], and then are unable to produce four witnesses [in support of their accusation], flog them with eighty stripes; and ever after refuse to accept from them any testimony – since it is they, they that are truly depraved! "* (Surah an Nur – The Light, 24:4).

Verse 19 of Surah an Nur (above) is noteworthy only because it refers to punishment in this life, in addition to the Hereafter. But again, it does not specify what exactly the penalty should be, nor does it expressly portray accusations of adultery as a crime. In general, these verses can be taken to indicate the seriousness with which intentionally false accusations against others' reputations are taken, even if they do not embody legal prescription.

There is a considerable gap between discouraging evil speech and allowing human authority to enforce and regulate legal restrictions on free speech, based on moral grounds. What is immoral speech is not necessarily also illegal speech. To make this distinction would require that human authority know the true nature and value of the speech in question, which is impossible because any human authority is inherently fallible in its judgment. Omniscience and infallibility lie only with Divine Authority. Furthermore, to regulate "good speech" would imply the enforcement of a single standard of morality for everyone, thereby condemning all other forms of speech that might differ from or be critical of the standard set by the government, but that may still have "good" content. This could potentially lead to an abuse of power by the government to stifle all public dissent or criticism.

This argument then leads us to minimize the morality-based component of freedom of speech and emphasize the instrumentalist aspect in delineating the legal boundaries. The lack of a clear legal definition of free speech in the *sharia*, in conjunction with the juristic principle that all behavior is permissible (*halal*) in principle unless expressly forbidden,[14] supports a flexible approach, so that free speech is given broad protection unless it is directly harmful to public security.

Freedom to express political opinions is one kind of free speech that is protected according to this approach. The *hadith* literature discusses the importance of citizens' freedom to monitor and criticize governmental policies and/or the government leaders. One *hadith* indicates that "the best form of *jihad* is to tell a word of truth to a tyrannical ruler."[15] It implies that one should be willing to go as far as risking one's life in order to speak the truth. In a related *hadith*, the Prophet (pbuh) is reported to have said, "When you see my community afraid of telling a tyrant, 'O tyrant', then it is not worth belonging to it anymore."[16]

The importance of exercising free speech as a positive political right, one that derives from a contractual relationship between the ruler and the ruled, is also illustrated in the inaugural speeches of the Caliphs Abu Bakr and Umar. The first person to hold the office of the Caliph after the death of the Prophet (pbuh) in 632 AD., Abu Bakr, declared, "O people, I have been entrusted with authority over you, but I am not the best of you. Help me if I am right, and rectify me when I am wrong."[17] Similarly, Caliph Umar also asked the people to aid him and correct him when they felt he was wrong. When one man responded by saying that they would correct him even by use of force, the Caliph's supporters criticized the man for threatening the ruler. However, Caliph Umar allowed him to be, saying that it was the man's right to express his opinions and that it would behoove him (Umar) as the ruler to deny him that right. [18]

There are two other instances relating to Caliph Umar which also illustrate his protection of the right to free speech. In the first one, while on a journey to Syria, Caliph Umar addressed a public gathering in which he recounted his reasons for dismissing Khalid bin Waleed. A man got up and criticized the Caliph, saying that he had been unjust and had taken such a step out of envy of Khalid bin Waleed. The Caliph only responded with "You have felt indignant because of loyalty to your brother." Most importantly, he did not punish the man for expressing his criticism.[19] The second one also recounts public criticism of the Caliph. In a public gathering, an individual stood up and addressed Caliph Umar, "O Umar! Fear God!" Another person restrained him, but the Caliph said, "Let him say it. If these people do not say so, they are of no use; and if we do not listen to them, we are of no use."[20]

Caliph Ali's treatment of the Kharijites, a group which opposed his political authority, is another example of the protection of free speech. The Kharijites were known to abuse the Caliph openly and threatened to murder him. "Whenever they were arrested for these offenses, [the Caliph] would set them free and tell his officers: 'As long as they do not actually perpetrate offenses against the state, the mere use of abusive language or the threat of the use of force are not such offenses for which they can be imprisoned.'"[21] This incident exemplifies the freedom of speech, given to the Kharijites even when it was deemed offensive, and clearly oppositional to the political authority in question. All of these examples underscore our argument for the broad protection that should be given to freedom of speech.

The freedom to criticize the government does not include the right to advocate violence against it though. As noted earlier, the only restriction on free speech is when it poses a direct threat to public security. Seditious speech, which incites civil disorder (*fitna*) and calls for violence against the government, is an example of this.[22]

Fitna and Free Speech

Fitna has a number of different meanings in the Quran, *hadith* and juridicial literature, depending on the context in which it is used. The Quran refers to *fitna* primarily in a moral context, as enticement or temptation: *"And know that your worldly goods and your children are but a trial and a temptation, and with God there is a tremendous reward"* (Surah al Anfal – Spoils of War, 8:28); *"Your worldly goods and your children are but a trial and a temptation, whereas with God there is a tremendous reward"* (Surah at-Taghabun – Loss and Gain, 64: 15). It is also referred to in contrast to the truth in Surah at-Tawbah

– Repentance, 9:48, *"Indeed, even before this time have they tried to stir up discord and devised all manner of plots against thee, [O Prophet,] until the truth was revealed and God's will became manifest, however hateful this may have been to them."*

The *hadith* literature, on the other hand, refers to *fitna* in a political sense, as war and civil disorder.[23] It originates in the chaos and insecurity arising from challenges to the ruler's authority, which historically was the case when Caliph Abu Bakr initially came to power, and again when Caliph Ali was assassinated. The negative implications of this kind of civil conflict were so profound that classical jurists placed significant normative emphasis on maintaining order and obedience to political authority, as a way of countering this potential threat.

Applying this definition of *fitna* to the discussion here, seditious speech is restricted on a legal basis to the extent that it causes civil disorder. But the links between the speech in question and the potential outcome need to be supported by clear evidence. The mere probability or suspicion of a link is not sufficient for denoting certain speech as seditious and criminal behavior. For example, even when Caliph Ali knew that the Kharijites were a potential threat to him, he did not punish them or limit their freedom of speech, simply because they disagreed with him and spoke of violence against his rule. He was later assassinated by a Kharijite.

Blasphemy and Free Speech

The notoriety surrounding Salman Rushdie's publication of *The Satanic Verses* and the subsequent death fatwa issued against him by Ayatollah Khomeini of Iran in the early 1990s first brought to world attention the issues of blasphemy and apostasy as offenses in Islam. Blasphemous speech is dealt with here as a particular type of restriction on freedom of expression in the minds of some Muslims, and is treated as a crime in some Muslim countries.[24]

Blasphemy and apostasy are not necessarily synonymous, but they are usually linked together as similar offenses concerning faith.

Blasphemy can be defined as a deliberate expression of contempt or insult towards God, the Prophet or the fundamentals of the religion,[25] and considered as either a transgression of freedom of religion or freedom of speech. It is distinct from apostasy in that the latter is an unequivocal renunciation of Islam altogether, regardless of whether or not it is an outcome of blasphemy.

To the extent that blasphemy is derived from faith/religious belief (or the lack thereof), it comes under freedom of religion and cannot be subject to legal regulation, as noted in Surah al Baqara – The Cow, 2: 256: "*There shall be no coercion in matters of faith*"[26] Faith is an individual and internal choice, which only God has true knowledge of and can pass judgment on. We strongly oppose the state's use of coercion in regulating the content or degree of an individual's religious belief, through prescribing punishments for blasphemy.

However, with regard to free speech, blasphemy is only proscribed if it is combined with a clear intent to violate public safety. The instrumentalist definition of free speech that was introduced earlier comes into play here. Blasphemy is not restricted simply because it reflects disagreement with Islamic belief, no matter how forcefully expressed. It may be a sin against God, but it cannot be considered criminal behavior. As the example of Abu Lahab illustrates, the punishment for it will come in the Hereafter and will be meted out by God, not human beings.

The underlying theoretical issue in discussing punishment for blasphemy is that of rights: the right of God versus the right of man. The error is made when men presume to act as the injured party in an offense against God. Some jurists argue that because the role of *sharia* is to apply God's Will in organizing the affairs of the Muslim community, then a sin against God is also a transgression against the rights of the community (*umma*) and therefore carries legal punishment as a crime. This perspective superimposes the boundaries defining the religious community on the boundaries defining the political community. It is illustrated in *hadith* used by jurists in support of capital punishment for apostasy, where severing ties to Islam coincides with severing ties to the political community of Muslims.[27] There is some historical basis for this perspective, in the "ridda wars" that faced Abu Bakr when he became the Caliph. Certain tribes revolted against their pacts with the Prophet (pbuh) and refused to pay their dues. Their political disloyalty was also viewed as disloyalty to the religious community, headed by the Caliph. Abu Bakr was obliged to fight them militarily and eventually managed to subdue the revolt.

The problem with this argument is that it cannot be applied in a contemporary Islamic state without giving rise to the potential for abuse by the state itself. The desire to impose morality through the power of the state has led to the political repression that we see in Islamic countries today.[28] We must separate the right of God from that of man in defining freedom of speech as a legal right. The right of God refers only to the moral obligations of Muslims towards God, and is adjudicated by God. The state cannot act as a coercive moral authority, in effect representing God's Will on earth, because it does not have the right to do so. In the context of freedom of speech, the state's responsibility is to uphold and protect it as the right of all humans, as granted by God, without exercising moral judgment on the content and/or manner of the speech.

Coming back to the issue of *The Satanic Verses*, we would apply our interpretation of freedom of speech to allow Rushdie the leeway to profess or renounce Islam as he wishes, without enforcing capital punishment. However, we must make a distinction between blasphemy and apostasy here, one which was lost in the controversy over the book. Blasphemy does not automatically entail apostasy. Blasphemy is intentionally offensive behavior or speech that contravenes fundamental principles of Islam and therefore is offensive to Muslims. Apostasy is a clear renunciation of Islam altogether. Blasphemous actions may not necessarily imply renunciation, since non-Muslims can also commit blasphemy. Regardless of the definition though, the state does not have the legal right to punish individuals for either offense, which are both offenses against the right of God and not of man. The action recommended is to fight speech with speech.

Proselytizing

Given the freedom to choose one's faith, as granted by God, the state cannot enforce religious indoctrination, nor limit proselytizing of Islam or any other religion. As noted earlier, there is a clear injunction that persuasion is to be the only method for inviting others to Islam, which requires a commitment to the protection of free speech. With regard to other religions, the same argument applies, with the understanding that it is an individual's moral responsibility what religion he chooses to follow. The state must grant citizens of other religious groups equal opportunity to proselytize, although foreign missionaries have no particular right to proselytize, and their actions and behavior are subject to government permission and oversight. The government can limit the circumstances or places where proselytizing may occur without infringing on the integral right of religious freedom. For example, it can limit proselytization that aims to attract followers in exchange for material rewards, or that targets children without obtaining parental consent.

Conclusion

Freedom of expression is a part of the mandate of the umma to uphold the Quranic principle of *hisba*, "enjoining what is good and forbidding what is evil." The "good" in this case is the free exchange of ideas and opinions in society. The balance between affirming free speech and delineating its boundaries is one that is determined by each society on its own. For example, in the American case, it is noted in a 1969 U.S. Supreme Court ruling in Brandenburg vs. Ohio which states, "the constitutional guarantees of free speech and free press do not permit a state to forbid or proscribe advocacy of the use of force or of law violation except where such advocacy is directed to inciting or producing imminent lawless action, and is likely to incite or produce such action."[29]

However, we believe, based on the evidence cited in this chapter, that an Islamic perspective necessitates the broadest possible protection for freedom of speech as a legal right, without placing moral restrictions on the content of the speech. The law cannot be used to enforce one standard of morality over another, because moral judgment lies in the hands of God and not of humans. Even in the case of Iblis' disobedience to God, we see that God does not prevent him from expressing evil speech. The only restriction we can place on free speech, then, is based on a concern for public safety, so that any speech that poses a direct and explicit threat to it is prohibited.

Furthermore, the experience of autocracy and political repression in Muslim countries has shown us quite explicitly how easy it is to abuse the spirit of questioning and criticism allowed in Islam, in the name of enforcing "Islamic standards" on political speech and behavior. Therefore, given what we have learned about the benefits of freedom and the ills of repression, we conclude with a strong insistence that, in the contemporary context, any society which does not guarantee full protection of freedom of speech as a legal and political right has betrayed Islam.

Footnotes

1   Kamali, *Freedom, Equality and Justice in Islam*, p. 31. See also Muhammad Asad's The Message of the Quran, Surah Yunus - Jonah, 10:59, n. 81, p. 300; Surah an Nahl – The Bee, 16:114-115; Surah al Hajj – The Pilgrimage, 22:30,n. 4, p. 510; Surah al Baqara – The Cow, 2:168-169, n.137, p. 34.

2   Mohammad Hashim Kamali, *Freedom of Expression in Islam* (Kuala Lumpur: Berita Publishing, 1994) p. 12.

3   This encompasses both meanings of the word: 1) Truth as synonymous with Religion(Islam); 2) truth as generally distinct from falsehood. In both cases, the obligation to express truth remains integral to free speech.

4   Hassan, p. 51.

5   Ibn Hisham, cited in al Marzouqi, pp. 458-459.

6   Kamali, *Freedom of Expression*, p. 61.

7   Kamali, *Freedom of Expression*, p. 62.

8   Kamal, *Freedom of Expression*, p. 62.

9   Kamali, *Freedom of Expression*, p. 63.

10 Hasan, p. 125.

11 James Weinstein, *Hate Speech, Pornography and the Radical Attack on Free Speech Doctrine* (Boulder: Westview Press, 1999), pp.13-14.

12 Also described as the "truth discovery rationale" for free speech. "The only way for any truth to be tested is for it to compete with other truths in the marketplace of ideas." Weinstein, p. 13.

13 The sharia prescribes clear legal directives for criminal behavior in very few cases, such as that for murder or theft. See Abdullahi Ahmed An-Na'im, *Toward an Islamic Reformation*, (Syracuse: Syracuse University Press, 1990) p.32.

14 A Quranic verse often cited in support this juristic principle is Surah al Araf – Faculty of Discernment, 7:32, *"Say: 'Who hath forbidden the beautiful (gifts) of God, which He hath produced for His servants, and the things, clean and pure, (which He*

hath provided) for sustenance?' Say: 'They are, in the life of this world, for those who believe, (and) purely for them on the Day of Judgment.' Thus do We explain the signs in detail for those who understand." See also Muhammad Asad's *The Message of the Quran*, Surah Yunus - Jonah, 10:59, n. 81, p. 300; Surah al Nahl – The Bee, 16:114-115; Surah al Hajj – The Pilgrimage, 22:30,n. 4, p. 510; Surah al Baqara – The Cow, 2:168-169, n.137, p. 34.

15 Abu Dawd, cited in Kamali, *Freedom of Expression in Islam*, p. 12.

16 Cited in Kamali, FEJ, p. 24.

17 Kamali, FEJ, p. 24.

18 Kamali, FEJ, p. 24.

19 Hassan, p. 52.

20 Kitab al Kharj, p. 125, cited in Hassan, p. 52.

21 Shaikh Shaukat Hussein, *Human Rights in Islam* (New Delhi: Kitab Bhavan, 1990), p. 48.

22 Kamali, *Freedom of Expression in Islam*, p. 183.

23 Kamali, *Freedom of Expression in Islam*, p. 185.

24 Blasphemy laws also exist in some non-Muslim countries, such as Great Britain, for example. However, the British law considers blasphemy as a civil offense and not a criminal one, and it only gives protection to Christianity and the Church of England, not to any other religions.

25 Kamali, *Freedom of Expression in Islam*, p. 207.

26 See also chapter on Freedom of Religion.

27 These *hadith* are recounted in detail in the discussion on apostasy in the Freedom of Religion chapter.

28 See also Khalid Abou El Fadl's works, *The Place of Tolerance in Islam*, and *And God Knows the Soldiers* for more on the negative implications of this kind of restrictive interpretation of Islamic law.

29 Brandenberg v. Ohio, 395 U.S. 444, 447-48 (1969).

CHAPTER SIX

Freedom of Religion

reedom of religion includes both freedom of belief and freedom of worship, including religious practice in all its forms. From a legal perspective, the state cannot enforce religious belief since that is a component of the individual moral freedom granted to all humans by God. The state cannot presume to intervene in the spiritual relationship between humans and God, nor stand in moral judgment on their religious beliefs or actions because it does not have the ability to determine internal faith or religiosity. More importantly, the meaning of life from an Islamic standpoint is that it stands as an individual test of each soul and its willingness to have faith in God and do good works. For the state to interfere in that free choice is an illegitimate interference with the very purpose of our existence. Only God has true knowledge of an individual's inner religious conscience. Therefore, the state must allow the broadest legal protection to all citizens, Muslim and non-Muslim, to believe in and practice a religion of their choice.

This chapter will draw from the Quran, the Sunna, juristic and historical precedents for Muslim-non-Muslim relations, as part of its argument for freedom of religion. In the first section, we offer a philosophical and theological framework for understanding freedom of religion in the Quran. This includes a discussion of the principles of tolerance and respect for religious pluralism as applied to the state's Islamic duty to uphold justice for all of its citizens, regardless of their religious identity. The second section outlines historical and juristic examples supporting a flexible interpretation of religious freedom as political right. The last section applies our argument towards several contemporary examples of religious freedom, including the issue of apostasy.

Quranic Perspective

Establishing a philosophical/theological framework will facilitate our understanding of religious freedom as a political right. On one side is the human agent as a component of God's Creation and as a recipient of God's Message. On the other is God and the Message that He makes available to all mankind, using the Quran as the primary vehicle for relaying it. Freedom of religion involves protecting the individual moral autonomy of the human recipient, as well as prohibiting any restrictive interpretation on the fundamental universality of the message of Islam itself. The following discussion will illustrate why human political authority (the state) cannot limit either of these two aspects, both of which have been granted by God.

Freedom of Belief

In line with the argument for free will developed in other chapters,[1] God has created all human beings with equal capacity to make moral choices between good and evil, and to achieve faith. Everyone has equal moral responsibility and accountability for their actions in front of God. In fact, it is a moral obligation for people to articulate Truth,[2] when they know what it is. *"And do not overlay the truth with falsehood, and do not knowingly suppress the truth"* (Surah al Baqara – The Cow, 2:42). Also, *"They unto whom We have vouchsafed revelation aforetime know it as they know their own children: but, behold, some of them knowingly suppress the truth"* (Surah al Baqara – The Cow 2:146).

Freedom of belief comes out of this concept of individual autonomy, and is available to all mankind, not just to Muslims. *"And [thus it is:] had thy Sustainer so willed, all those who live on earth would surely have attained to faith, all of them: dost thou, then, think that thou couldst compel people to believe"* (Surah Yunus – Jonah, 10:99).

Furthermore, submission to God's Will, which is the essence of faith (*iman*) and synonymous with the meaning of the word "Islam," is meaningless if it is not done voluntarily. The Quran unequivocally eschews any form of coercion or duress in faith. Surah al Baqara – The Cow, 2:256 states *"There shall be no coercion in matters of faith. Distinct has now become the right way from [the way of] error: hence he who rejects the powers of evil and believes in God has indeed taken hold of a support most unfailing, which shall never give way: for God is all-hearing, all-knowing."*

This verse was revealed on the occasion when the Prophet had given orders for the Jewish tribe of Banu Nadir to leave Medina, in response to clashes between them and the Muslims. Some Companions of the Prophet (pbuh) asked him for permission to compel their relatives who were members of Banu Nadir to become Muslim, which would have resulted in their remaining in Medina. Surah 2:256 was revealed and the Prophet (pbuh) denied permission, saying instead that they were to be given the choice to decide which religion they wished to follow.[3]

Religion cannot be a meaningful experience without equal ability to express doubt or faith. Even prophets are not immune from expressing doubt; they are still given the leeway to question God. For example, *"And, lo, Abraham said: 'O my Sustainer! Show me how Thou givest life unto the dead!' Said He: 'Hast thou, then, no faith?' [Abraham] answered: 'Yea, but [let me see it] so that my heart may be set fully at rest.' Said He: 'Take, then, four birds and teach them to obey thee; then place them separately on every hill [around thee]; then summon them: they will come flying to thee. And know that God is almighty, wise'"* (Surah al Baqara – The Cow, 2:260).

If God does not restrict His prophets' freedom of conscience, then neither does He allow Prophet Muhammad (pbuh) the right to infringe on anyone else's freedom of belief. The Quran refers to him frequently as a Messenger and a Guide; for example, in Surah al Gashiyah – The Overshadowing Event, 88:21, *"And so, [O Prophet,] exhort them; thy task is only to exhort:"* Surah Yunus - Jonah, 10:108, states *"Say [O Prophet]:*

'O mankind! The truth from your Sustainer has now come unto you. Whoever, therefore, chooses to follow the right path, follows it but for his own good; and whoever chooses to go astray, goes but astray to his own hurt. And I am not responsible for your conduct.'" Since the Prophet (pbuh) did not exercise moral coercive authority in matters of religion, then the state certainly does not have the right to do so.

Several more Quranic verses supporting this line of argument are:

"[And as for thee,] O Prophet – behold, We have sent thee as a witness [to the truth], and as a herald of glad tidings and a warner, and as one who summons [all men] to God by His leave, and as a light-giving beacon" (Surah al-Ahzab – The Confederates, 33:45-46).

"But if they turn away [from thee, O Prophet, know that] We have not sent thee to be their keeper: thou art not bound to do more than deliver the message [entrusted to thee]" (Surah Ash-Shura – Consultation 42:48).

"Thus, [O Prophet,] if they argue with thee, say, 'I have surrendered my whole being unto God, and [so have] all who follow me!' – and ask those who have been vouchsafed revelation aforetime, as well as all unlettered people, 'Have you [too] surrendered yourselves unto Him?' And if they surrender themselves unto Him, they are on the right path; but if they turn away – behold, thy duty is no more than to deliver the message: for God sees all that is in [the hearts of] His creatures" (Surah al Imran – The House of Imran, 3:20).

"Say: " Pay heed unto God, and pay heed unto the Apostle. And if you turn away [from the Apostle, know that] he will have to answer only for whatever he has been charged with, and you, for what you have been charged with; but if you pay heed unto him, you will be on the right way. Withal, the Apostle is not bound to do more than clearly deliver the message [entrusted to him]" (Surah An-Nur – The Light, 24:54).

"Fully aware are We of what they [who deny resurrection] do say; and thou canst by no means force them [to believe in it]. Yet none the less, remind, through this Quran, all such as may fear My warning" (Surah Qaf – Qaf 50:45).

The preceding verses repeatedly lay out the concept of the Prophet as a warner, not an enforcer of religion. If Muhammad (pbuh) was not given authority to enforce religious belief or observance, even though he was armed with the best understanding of the true meaning of the religion, then it is illogical to claim that any Muslim, whether in or out of government, could presume to do so.

The Quran is uncompromising about the fact that only God has the right to judge in matters of belief. *"Unto God belongs all that is in the heavens and all that is on earth. And whether you bring into the open what is in your minds or conceal it, God will call you to account for it; and then He will forgive whom He wills, and will chastise whom He wills: for God has the power to will anything."* (Surah al Baqara – The Cow, 2:284). *"And if there be some among you who have come to believe in the message which I bear, the while the others do not believe, then have patience in adversity till God shall judge between us [and them]: for He is the best of all judges!"* (Surah al Araf – The Faculty of Discernment, 7:87).

Even among those who call themselves Muslims, God knows who has true faith and who only appears to have it. *"For, [many are] they [who] say, 'We believe in God and in the Apostle, and we pay heed!' –but then, some of them turn away after this [assertion]: and these are by no means [true] believers"* (Surah An-Nur – The Light, 24:47). In another instance, *"The Bedouin say, 'We have attained to faith.' Say [unto them, O Muhammad]: 'You have not [yet] attained to faith; you should [rather] say, 'We have [outwardly] surrendered – for [true] faith has not yet entered your hearts. But if you [truly] pay heed unto God and His Apostle, He will not let the least of your deeds go to waste: for, behold, God is much-forgiving, a dispenser of grace'"* (Surah al Hujurat – The Private Apartments, 49:14).

Since God is the only omniscient authority, people cannot be the judge of who is worthy of His favor and who is not. *"And they claim, 'None shall ever enter paradise unless he be a Jew' – or, 'a Christian'. Such are their wishful beliefs! Say: 'Produce an evidence for what you are claiming, if what you say is true!"*(Surah al Baqara – The Cow, 2:111). In other words, only God is able to judge the truth of a person's faith, not others. *"And yet, they choose to worship [imaginary] deities instead of Him! Say [O Prophet]: 'Produce an evidence for what you are claiming: this is a reminder [unceasingly voiced] by those who are with me, just as it was a reminder [voiced] by those who came before me'"* (Surah al Anbiya – The Prophets, 21:24-25).

All of these verses imply that belief, or faith, goes hand in hand with the freedom to express doubt or support, and that upholding religion requires a commitment to critically examining and affirming its components, to the best of an individual's ability. God is the only authority to ultimately judge the veracity or falsity of a religious claim. No other human authority can punish individuals for expressing their religious beliefs. This is also illustrated in Surah al Ghafir – Forgiving, 40:28, *"At that, a believing man of Pharaoh's family, who [until then] had concealed his faith, exclaimed: 'Would you slay a man because he says, 'God is my Sustainer' – seeing, withal, that he has brought you all evidence of this truth from your Sustainer? Now if he be a liar, his lie will fall back on him; but if he is a man of truth, something [of the punishment] whereof he warns you is bound to befall you: for, verily, God would not grace with His guidance one who has wasted his own self by lying [about Him]."* The speaker is referring to Moses, who was subject to persecution by the Pharaoh. He warns the Pharaoh that it is better to leave it up to God to decide on the authenticity of Moses' claims. If Moses' message is a lie, God will punish Moses; but if his message is the truth, then God will punish the Pharaoh for persecuting Moses. Since there is no way for the Pharaoh to know with certainty whether or not Moses is lying, then he is better off not restricting his freedom of belief at all. In sum, the verse emphasizes the fact that human authority must protect freedom of religious belief, since it cannot judge its veracity or falsehood. Only God can do that.

This section of the chapter has indicated why freedom of belief needs to be protected to the fullest degree possible by the state, since no one, not even the Prophet (pbuh) has the right to take it away from human beings. God grants all mankind equal opportunity to achieve faith, and does not limit it to Muslims. He is the only Judge of who has faith and who does not, and the consequences of it are only adjudicated by God. The state cannot restrict individual human agency in choosing a faith.

The next section will discuss the second component of freedom of religion: the universality of God's message for people of all faiths, and the state's need to protect freedom of religion as the right of all religious communities, not just of Muslims.

Religious Pluralism

According to one interpretation of the Quran, there is often a distinction drawn between Muslims and People of the Book (Jews and Christians primarily)[4], by virtue of which the latter are considered to be spiritually inferior to Muslims. This erroneous line of thinking is used to justify the treatment of non-Muslims as second-class citizens in a number of Muslim countries, and has allowed governments to discriminate against their own citizens in the name of "upholding Islam."[5] The principle behind this is that the unequal relationship of these two groups before God allows non-Muslims to be treated unequally before the (temporal) law as well.

We rigorously critique this interpretation in this section. While reiterating again that God is the only judge of moral and spiritual matters, we argue that tolerance and religious pluralism are necessary components for the state's relationship with Muslim and non-Muslim communities on earth.

Islam presents itself as part of the continuous process of the Revelation of Truth from God, exemplified in all the Prophets and their Books that were sent by Him. For example, Surah al-Imran – The House of Imran, 3:84 states *"Say: 'We believe in God, and in that which has been bestowed from on high upon us, and that which has been bestowed upon Abraham and Ishmael and Isaac and Jacob and their descendants, and that which has been vouchsafed by their Sustainer unto Moses and*

Jesus and all the [other] prophets: we make no distinction between any of them. And unto Him do we surrender ourselves.'" Surah al Nisaa – Women (4:136) further affirms this precept: "O you who have attained to faith! Hold fast unto your belief in God and His Apostle, and in the divine write which He has bestowed from on high upon His Apostle, step by step, as well as in the revelation which He sent down aforetime: for he who denies God, and His angels, and His revelations, and His apostles, and the Last Day, has indeed gone far astray."

The Quran moves beyond a narrow definition of religion and emphasizes submission to God's Will as the universal hallmark of faith, one that transcends man-made boundaries among religious communities. Thus, Abraham (pbuh) is described as the first Muslim, one who submits to God, in Surah al Imran – House of Imran, 3:67. "Abraham was neither a 'Jew' nor a 'Christian', but was one who turned away from all that is false, having surrendered himself unto God; and he was not of those who ascribe divinity to aught beside Him." A distinction between a Muslim (with a capital M), one who submits to God and observes the tenets of Islam, and a muslim (lowercase m) any individual who submits to God's Will, regardless of religious identity, is necessary to point out here. In this case, Abraham is being described as the latter, and part of the line of monotheistic believers.

Also, God's command to change the direction of the Qibla from Jerusalem towards the Holy Kaaba in Mecca can be viewed as indicative of the emphasis on Abraham (pbuh, Abraham according to Muslim tradition built the original Kaaba) as an example for all believers, and not just for the followers of any one monotheistic faith. "And when Abraham and Ishmael were raising the foundations of the Temple, [they prayed:] 'O our Sustainer! Accept Thou this from us: for, verily, Thou alone art all-hearing, all-knowing!'" (Surah al Baqara – The Cow, 2:127).

The need to transcend the boundaries of formal religion to encompass faith as a universal concept is also described in the Quran. "For, never will the Jews be pleased with thee, nor yet the Christians, unless *thou follow their own creeds. Say: 'Behold, God's guidance is the only true guidance.' And, indeed, if though shouldst follow their errant views after all the knowledge that come unto thee, thou wouldst have none to protect thee from God, and none to bring thee succor. Those unto whom We have vouchsafed the divine writ [and who] follow it as it ought to be followed – it is they who [truly] believe in it; whereas all who choose to deny its truth – it is they, they who are the loser!"* (Surah al Baqara – The Cow, 2:120-121).

As the reference to Abraham illustrates, God does not accept any religious community staking exclusive moral and spiritual claim to truth or faith, when God Himself has not limited anyone from it.[6] Surah al Baqara – The Cow, 2:111 states: *"And they claim, 'None shall ever enter paradise unless he be a Jew' – or, 'a Christian'. Such are their wishful beliefs! Say: 'Produce an evidence for what you are claiming, if what you say is true!"* This point is reiterated again in verse 113 of the same Surah. *"Furthermore, the Jews assert, 'The Christians have no valid ground for their beliefs,' while the Christians assert, 'The Jews have no valid ground for their beliefs' – and both quote the divine writ! Even thus, like unto what they say, have [always] spoken those who were devoid of knowledge; God's response to this bickering is, "Yea, indeed: everyone who surrenders his whole being unto God, and is a doer of good withal, shall have his reward with his Sustainer; and all such need have no fear, and neither shall they grieve"* (Surah al Baqara – The Cow 2:112). In reference to the dispute between Christians and Jews, *"but it is God who will judge between them on Resurrection Day with regard to all on which they were wont to differ"* (Surah Al Baqara – The Cow 2:113). The reference to doing good as a virtue on par with submission to God is notable because it reflects the accessibility of moral standing for everyone.

Faith, therefore, means more than just membership in a formal religious community or practice of a formal religion. In a universal sense, a muslim is a person who submits to God's Will, and lives life as a moral human being, striving to achieve good, in all ways. We can argue that one needs to be a muslim, according to this definition, in order to be a Muslim (with a capital M), an individual who belongs to the formal religious community, the umma. But the two can also exist separately, since there are many non-Muslims who accept and submit to God and strive to do good in their own religions. This would also apply to those who never heard the message of the Quran due to geography or other historical factors. It would also apply to those who may have heard a portion of the Islamic message, but due to cultural or family factors, the person was not able to assess the truth Islam in an objective manner, and this prevented him or her from embracing the religion. Salvation is open to all who believe in a single God and do good works.

In short, we emphasize the definition of faith in the Quran to be inclusive, and extend the meaning of these Quranic verses to be generally supportive of religious tolerance and pluralism on earth. The universality of God's message is such that it is not the exclusive spiritual domain of any one religious community. It is not limited to Muslims over Christians or Jews, nor vice versa. Only God knows who has true faith and who does not since only He is capable of gauging an individual's moral and spiritual conscience. Therefore, in order to apply Islamic teaching in an authentic and genuine manner, the state must exercise tolerance and respect for religious diversity, which is a component of God's creation. It cannot legally differentiate in protecting the religious freedom of Muslims over non-Muslims, because human authority cannot limit either God's message or God's authority as the only Judge of true faith.

Religious tolerance is discussed as an ethical norm in the following three verses of the Quran. We begin with Surah al Hujurat – The Private Apartments, 49:13, which stresses the diversity that is part of God's Creation. *"O men! Behold, We have created you all out of a male and a female, and have made you into nations and tribes, so that you might come to know one another. Verily, the noblest of you in the sight of God is the one who is most deeply conscious of Him. Behold, God is all-knowing, all-aware."* It calls for an active engagement among various communities in a manner that leads to peaceful relations, and greater knowledge of their differences.

The second verse, Surah al Maida – The Repast, 5:48, introduces the concept of religious pluralism to the idea of human diversity. *"And unto thee [O Prophet] have We vouchsafed this divine writ, setting forth the truth, confirming the truth of whatever there still remains of earlier revelations and determining what is true therein. Judge, then, between the followers of earlier revelation in accordance with what God has bestowed from on high, and do not follow their errant views, forsaking the truth that has come unto thee. Unto every one of you have We appointed a [different] law and way of life. And if God had so willed, He could surely have made you all one single community: but [He willed it otherwise] in order to test you by means of what He has vouchsafed unto you. Vie, then, with one another in doing good works! Unto God you all must return; and then He will make you truly understand all that on which you were wont to differ."*

The same theme is also developed in Surah al Baqara – The Cow, 2:148, *"for, every community faces a direction of its own, of which He is the focal point. Vie, therefore, with one another in doing good works. Wherever you may be, God will gather you all unto Himself: for, verily, God has the power to will anything."*

God readily admits that religious differences are a part of His Plan for humankind. Adherents of all religions should compete to do good. Everyone is equally enjoined to turn towards virtuous action, regardless of the "law" or the "way" they follow. This point reiterates our definition of faith as a universal concept above. The reference is similar to the one in Surah al Baqara – The Cow, 2:62, *"Verily, those who have attained to faith [in this divine writ], as well as those who follow the Jewish faith, and the Christians, and the Sabians – all who believe in God and the Last Day and do righteous deeds – shall have their reward with their Sustainer; and no fear need they have, and neither shall they grieve"* and also in Surah al Baqara, 2:112, discussed above, where a believer is also described as a "doer of good." Again, religious differences between people are not treated as an obstacle to harmonious co-existence and moral and spiritual orientation towards God.

The third verse, Surah al Baqara, 2:213, continues this line of argument: *"All mankind were once one single community; [then they began to differ -]whereupon God raised up the prophets as heralds of glad tidings and as warners, and through them bestowed revelations from on high, setting forth the truth, so that it might decide between people with regard to all on which they had come to hold divergent views. Yet none other than the self-same people who had been granted this [revelation] began, out of mutual jealousy, to disagree about its meaning after all evidence of the truth had come unto them. But God guided the believers unto the truth about which, by His leave, they had disagreed: for God guides onto a straight way him that wills [to be guided]."* Abdulaziz Sachedina argues that this verse serves as a cornerstone for understanding the universality of the Quranic conception of religious pluralism. It affirms the unity of mankind as part of God's Creation, but also enumerates the specific instances of Prophets who brought revelation (a Book) to their people as a means of resolving differences among them. Most notably, this verse does not imply that these religious differences need to be eradicated in any way.[7]

Freedom of Worship

Applying the spirit of religious tolerance, the state must provide equal protection to all citizens in their right to exercise freedom of worship. We can use Surah al Kafirun – Those Who Deny the Truth, 109 to support this contention. It distinctly illustrates the harmonious co-existence of differing religions and forms of worship. It states " '*I do not worship that which you worship, and neither do you worship that which I worship. And I will not worship that which you have [ever] worshiped, and neither will you [ever] worship that which I worship. Unto you, your moral law, and unto me, mine!'*" (Surah al Kafirun – Those Who Deny the Truth, 109:2-6). This verse extends its injunction both to the past and to the future, indicating that humans cannot judge other peoples' religious practices and must allow them all to exist. Again, there is to be no compulsion on anyone to follow any faith.

The same injunction is noted in Surah al Baqara – The Cow, 2:145. The verse describes the change in the direction of the *Qibla*, which was moved from Jerusalem to Mecca by the Prophet (pbuh), upon God's command. The verse stresses that the different religious groups are entitled to worship in the direction of their own *qibla*, without any compulsion for everyone to follow the same. *"And yet, even if thou wert to place all evidence before those who have been vouchsafed earlier revelation, they would not follow thy direction of prayer; and neither mayest thou follow their direction of prayer, nor even do they follow one another's direction. And if thou shouldst follow their errant views after all the knowledge that has come unto thee, thou wouldst surely be among the evildoers"* (Surah al Baqara – The Cow, 2:145).

Surah al Baqara, 2:114 also refers to the need to protect freedom of worship in all places that celebrate God's name. *"Hence, who could be more wicked than those who bar the mentions of God's name from [any of] His houses of worship and strive for their ruin, [although] they have no right to enter them save in fear [of God]? For them, in this world, there is ignominy in store; and for them, in their life to come, awesome suffering."*

Freedom of Religion as a Legal Right

A recurring, although subliminal, theme in the argument so far has been the importance of justice in the treatment of Muslims and non-Muslims with regards to freedom of religion. Keeping in mind that it is God's responsibility to mete out justice to humans in light of their moral behavior, the state is responsible for ensuring justice and equity for all its citizens, as derived from their legal rights and duties. *"those who eagerly listen to any falsehood, greedily swallowing all that is evil! Hence, if they come to thee [for judgement], thou mayest either judge between them or leave them alone: for, if thou leave them alone, they cannot harm thee in any way. But if thou dost judge, judge between them with equity: verily, God knows those who act equitably"* (Surah al Maida – The Repast, 5:42). Justice is an Islamic duty, indicated in Surah al Nahl – The Bee, 16:90 *"Behold, God enjoins justice, and the doing of good, and generosity towards [one's] fellow-men; and He forbids all that is shameful and all that runs counter to reason, as well as envy; [and] He exhorts you [repeatedly] so that you might beat [all this] in mind."* Furthermore, it applies towards all mankind, without distinction, Surah al Nisaa – The Women 4:135, states, *"O you who have attained to faith! Be ever steadfast in upholding equity, bearing witness to the truth for the sake of God, even though it be against your own selves or your parents and kinsfolk. Whether the person concerned be rich or poor, God's claim takes precedence over [the claims of] either of them. Do not, then, follow your own desires, lest you swerve from justice: for if you distort [the truth], behold, God is indeed aware of all that you do!"*

The state must treat all of its citizens, Muslims and non-Muslims, as equal before the law. This equality derives from the equality of all human beings, with their moral freedom and human dignity, as created by God. It does not depend on the idea of spiritual equality of all individuals before God, because the state cannot take on that role of moral authority. Therefore, applying the Quranic concepts of tolerance and respect for religious pluralism noted earlier to the legal realm means protecting the religious freedom of all citizens on the basis of equality and justice. In theory, the *sharia* already recognizes protection of religion among its five primary goals: protection of life, religion, intellect, family and property. But, we are expanding this definition to include all religions, and not just Islam, in addition to giving equal protection to groups espousing different interpretations of Islam.

The discussion so far dispels the notion that any authority other than God has a right to limit freedom of religion. To summarize our argument, the state needs to uphold both components of the philosophical framework introduced at the beginning of this chapter. First, it must protect freedom of religion of all citizens, because it is part of the moral autonomy granted to all individuals by God. Therefore, it cannot limit human agency. Second, it cannot place restrictions on what defines Faith in Islam by favoring Muslims over non-Muslims, since God is the only Judge of what is true Faith. Thus, it cannot limit the universality of Islam as Message of Faith. The state's duty includes exercising tolerance and respect for religious differences, since these differences are also a part of God's Creation, and ensuring these are protected in the law, without judging on the moral or spiritual authenticity of any other religion, or among differing interpretations of Islam.

Historical and Juristic Perspectives on Religious Liberty

The argument so far has articulated the philosophical and doctrinal reasons for why the state needs to uphold a broad definition of religious freedom for all citizens, regardless of whether they are Muslims or non-Muslims. This section will examine historical and juristic perspectives on the relationship between these two communities in order to add to the strength of the argument for religious freedom. While there were certainly historical periods in which these principles were violated, they represent the exception and not the rule and are by no means binding.

The first point has to do with the freedom of religious belief as articulated in the Quran. In line with the restriction on the use of compulsion in religion, Muslims are required to make efforts to spread Islam through explanation and persuasion, not by force. For example, Ibn Qudamah, a Hanbali jurist/theologian, has commented on the impermissibility of obtaining a confession of faith from a non-Muslim (a *dhimmi* or a *musta'man*, person of protected status) under any kind of duress.[8]

The primary example of this approach is when the Prophet (pbuh) first started preaching in Mecca to the hostile inhabitants. He suffered abuse and criticism, but nevertheless persisted, and succeeded, in setting a positive example through his words and actions as a Muslim in order to attract followers. As one author has suggested, "Since Islam itself began by inviting and persuading people to embrace it on the merit of its rationality and truth... it can only be expected to validate freedom of belief if it were to remain true to its own beginnings."[9]

This Quranic norm served to guide the practice of the Caliphs as well. One incident is cited by Abu Zahrah, where an elderly Christian woman came to request an audience with the Caliph Umar b. al-Khattab. He responded to her request favorably, and afterwards invited her to embrace Islam, but she refused. At this, the Caliph became anxious that his invitation might be construed as compulsion by the woman, and expressed his remorse, "O my Lord, I have not intended to compel her as I know that there must be no compulsion in religion,...righteousness has been explained and distinguished from misguidance."[10]

The legal category of *dhimmi* in the early history of Islam is the most obvious blueprint for looking at the treatment of non-Muslims in an Islamic state.[11] Early jurists recognized that non-Muslims who entered into a peace treaty with Muslims were allowed religious freedom, in belief and in worship, and equal protection under the law, with regard to personal safety and property. The first such pact we can examine is the Constitution of Medina, or the Medina Charter, which was established by the Prophet (pbuh) in Medina soon after the migration from Mecca to Medina.[12] The Charter was negotiated between the Muslims, led by the Prophet (pbuh), and the Jewish communities and (non-Muslim) Arab tribes who already resided in Medina. The overall purpose of the pact was to maintain peace and security by protecting the life and property of the inhabitants and fighting injustice and aggression regardless of tribal or religious affiliations.[13] The Charter is notable in that it does not declare the state religion to be Islam and protects freedom of religion for the whole community, regardless of religious identity. It states, in Article 16, "Whoever of the Jews follows us has the (same) help and support (as the believers), so as long as they are not wronged (by him) and he does not help (others) against them." Article 25 continues "The Jews of Banu 'Awf are a community (umma) along with the believers. To the Jews their religion and to the Muslims their religion. (This applies) both to their clients and to themselves, with the exception of anyone who has done wrong or acted treacherously; he brings evil only on himself and on his household."[14] Although these articles refer specifically to the Jews, polytheists were also considered to be part of the polity, and granted equal protection by the Prophet by virtue of being client tribes.

Another foundational document that guarantees a similar freedom of religion is the Charter of Rights, issued by Caliph Umar in 638, upon the surrender of Jerusalem. The charter states, "In the name of God, the Merciful, the Compassionate. This is the security which Umar, the Servant of God, the Commander of the Faithful, grants to the people of Aylia. He grants to all, whether sick or sound, security for their lives, their possessions, their churches, and their crosses, and for all that concerns their religion. Their churches shall neither be changed into dwelling places, nor destroyed, neither shall they, nor their appurtenances, nor any of their possessions, be in any way diminished; nor shall any constraint be put upon them in the matter of their faith; nor shall any one of them be harmed."[15]

Classical jurists applied the spirit of these charters and clearly recognized the moral autonomy of non-Muslim communities, and their right to practice their own religions without interference by the state. For example, all the various schools of jurisprudence agreed that non-Muslims were to be ruled according to their own laws instead of by Islamic law. They recognized their right to hold public office, including positions of judges and minister. The only difference among jurists was whether the positions held by non-Muslims as judges or ministers, were to be characterized as judicial or political in nature.[16]

The Prophet (pbuh) advocated respect in the treatment of non-Muslims living under Muslim rule. The *hadith* states "Beware that I myself shall be the opponent, on the Day of Judgment, of anyone who is unjust to a covenanted person, or burdens him with something he cannot bear, or takes something from him, or makes him suffer a loss without his valid consent."[17] Although this *hadith* does not refer explicitly to freedom of religion as a legal right, we can infer from it the need to uphold justice and treat non-Muslims as equals (to Muslims) before the law, and therefore extend the same protection of religious freedom to them as well.

Beginning with the early Caliphate, the kind and just treatment of non-Muslims is emphasized by Caliphs Abu Bakr, Umar and Ali. For example, under the rule of Abu Bakr, a treaty made by Khalid Bin Waleed on the conquest of Hira stated that if an elderly non-Muslim person became incapable of working, or fell sick, or became destitute, such that his co-religionists had to start giving him money, then his *jizya* would be remitted. He and his children would be allowed to receive a maintenance allowance from the public treasury as long as he lived in Muslim country. If he left, then the Muslims would not be under obligation to maintain his family.[18]

Caliph Umar ibn al Khattab advised his successors to fulfill their covenant and be good to non-Muslims, to defend them against aggression and not to cause them hardship.[19] He also lived up to this ideal during his own reign. An ordinance to his army commanders in Iraq stated "Take services from whichever mounted soldiers you feel the need and remit their *jizya*."[20] In one incident, a [non-Muslim] Syrian cultivator claimed that the army had trampled his crops. Caliph Umar ordered the payment of 10,000 dirhams to him as compensation out of the public treasury.[21] In another example similar to the one under Abu Bakr's rule, the Caliph saw an old man begging, in order to pay his *jizya*. He brought him back to his house, gave him some cash, and sent word to the treasury officer that the elderly, who could not earn their living, should be given stipends from the public treasury. He said, "It is not just that we derive benefit from men while they are young and drive them out when they are old."[22]

The Caliph Ali is similarly noted as saying that "they [non-Muslims] only entered the covenant so that their lives and properties would be [protected] like our lives and properties."[23] The equality with which all are to be treated before the law is illustrated when the Caliph lost his armor in the battle of Siffin. A few days later, he noticed a Christian wearing that armor. He referred the case to a judge, and both he and the Christian appeared before the judge, each arguing that it was his armor, but the Christian stated that his possession of it was proof of his ownership. Caliph Ali could not produce any witnesses to support his own claim to it. When the judge hesitated in pronouncing a verdict, given the Caliph's status, he exhorted the judge to disregard any such considerations. The judgment was in the Christian's favor, and the Caliph accepted it.[24]

All of these examples from the rule of various Caliphs demonstrate the importance of justice and equality in the treatment of non-Muslims. They also illustrate the fact that they are not inferior to Muslims in essential dignity and rights.

However, in the following centuries of Islamic rule, jurists developed a notably more restrictive body of juristic rules regarding the civil and religious rights of non-Muslims, and the example set by the Prophet (pbuh) for co-existence among differing religious communities came to be disregarded. Starting in the eighth century, under the Abbasids, these juristic rules treated non-Muslims living under Islamic political rule as second-class citizens, inferior to Muslims in civil, political and social rights. An agreement between the Caliph Umar and the Syrian Christians is held up as emblematic of this shift, even though its historical authenticity is subject to debate. Its intention appears to be to humiliate Christians by prohibiting them from manifesting their religion publicly, because it would be considered offensive to Muslims.[25]

This limitation on the freedom of religion for non-Muslims comes out of historical practice, and not from Islamic teaching. The Quranic evidence noted in the previous two sections stands in striking contrast to this restrictive definition. In addition, the precedent set by the Medina Constitution for harmonious co-existence with all religious groups, monotheists and polytheists, is important to note. The principle of tolerance and the affirmation of religious diversity are components of Islamic teaching, as indicated in the Quran. Therefore, the state must emphasize them over historical practice as components of the legal right to freedom of religion for all its citizens.

Applying Religious Freedom

This section will highlight a few examples illustrating the application of freedom of religion, as it has been defined in the discussion above. In principle, the state must allow the broadest protection on the legal right to freedom of religion, and in particular, the exercising of religious practice. It cannot discriminate against citizens on the basis of religious identity, in general with regards to their civil and political rights, and more specifically in their right to exercise their religious beliefs. Therefore, all public places of worship and religious institutions of all faiths are protected and to be equally accessible to all.

The only limitation is that the state has the right to restrict an individual's right to religious freedom where it is directly harmful to public security. For example, religious practice that calls for human sacrifice is not permissible, since deliberately taking human life is a crime. Another instance would be religious belief that advocates violence against other citizens or the state. However, gray areas exist on where to draw the line on state involvement in less extreme cases, and these must be negotiated by the collective community in light of the Quranic principles cited earlier.

Regarding education, the government cannot enforce religious indoctrination of any kind in schools. But that does not mean it cannot allow moral instruction. A Islamic government can make available basic Islamic/religious education in public schools, so that Muslim students can learn basic Arabic and gain familiarity with basic principles of Islam and Islamic history. Participation in these classes should not be required of non-Muslims though.

Another example of non-coercive moral instruction is an advertising campaign encouraging Muslims to pay *zakat*, or observe other religious practices. But the state cannot legally enforce religious behavior, and in the case of *zakat*, prescribe criminal punishment for those who do not pay it.[26]

Proselytizing

Given the freedom to choose one's faith, as granted by God, the state cannot enforce religious indoctrination, nor limit proselytizing of Islam or any other religion. As noted earlier, there is a clear Quranic injunction that persuasion is to be the only method for inviting others to Islam. With regard to other religions, the same argument applies, with the understanding that it is individual moral responsibility what religion an individual chooses to follow. The state must grant all religious groups that are residents of the state equal opportunity to proselytize. It may extend permission for foreign missionaries to enter the country for the same purpose, but has the right to regulate their entry as well. The government can limit the circumstances or places where proselytizing may occur without infringing on the integral right of religious freedom. For example, it can limit proselytization that aims to attract followers in exchange for material rewards. The state can also regulate proselytizing to children in schools. The primary duty for religious upbringing of children falls to their parents, however, and not to the schools.

Apostasy

The notoriety surrounding Salman Rushdie's publication of *The Satanic Verses* and the subsequent death fatwa issued against him by Ayatollah Khomeini of Iran first brought to world attention the issues of blasphemy and apostasy as offenses in Islam. However, this was merely the most publicized example, and does not obscure the fact that a number of Muslim countries have apostasy as a capital offense in their criminal legal codes. Therefore, this issue warrants closer examination in light of our argument for freedom of religion.

We strongly oppose the state's use of coercion in regulating Islamic belief in such a manner, since faith is a matter of individual choice on which only God can adjudicate. While apostasy may be a sin in the eyes of God, we do not consider it to be criminal behavior. This section will briefly examine the evidence for capital punishment for apostasy and then indicate its ineffectualness in light of other *hadith* that support our argument for freedom of religion.

Despite the fact that the Quran does not once mention the death penalty for apostasy,[27] jurists have relied on two *hadith* texts for their argument. The first one states "whoever changes his religion shall be killed."[28] The second is "It is not lawful to kill a man who is a Muslim except for one of the three reasons: *Kufr* (disbelief) after accepting Islam, fornication after marriage, or wrongfully killing someone, for which he may be killed."[29] Notwithstanding the fact that the chain of transmission on the first *hadith* has been found to be weak,[30] both of them contradict the Quran and other instances in which the Prophet (pbuh) did not compel anyone to embrace Islam, nor punish them if they recanted. The general rule is that a single chain *hadith* cannot be used to justify capital punishment.

In one incident, the Prophet (pbuh) pardoned Abdullah bin Sa'd, after he renounced Islam. Abdullah bin Sa'd was one of the people chosen by the Prophet (pbuh) as a scribe, to write down Quranic text as it was revealed to the Prophet (pbuh). After spending some time with the Muslims in Medina, he recanted and returned to the religion of the Quraysh. When he was brought before the Prophet (pbuh), Osman bin Affan pleaded on his behalf, and the Prophet (pbuh) subsequently pardoned Abdullah bin Sa'd.[31]

A second *hadith* states, "The Prophet said, 'Whoever swears by a religion other than Islam, is, as he says'; and …cursing a believer is like murdering him; and whoever accuses a believer of disbelief, then it is as if he had killed him."[32] The gravity of mere accusations of disbelief is so great that it is inconceivable that the Prophet (pbuh) would sanction the actual killing of an individual merely on those grounds.

Another *hadith* recorded by both Bukhari and Muslim also supports this point. A Bedouin Arab came to the Prophet (pbuh) and accepted Islam. Then, he became ill with a fever and the next day asked the Prophet (pbuh) if he could take back his pledge. He asked three times and was refused each time. The Prophet (pbuh) said "Medina is like bellows which rejects its dross and retains its purity." The Bedouin was allowed to leave unharmed. [33] The refusal to allow the Bedouin to take back his pledge indicates that a profession of faith is made between the individual and God, and the Prophet (pbuh) does not retain any right to mediate on behalf of God in that respect. This includes the fact that no temporal punishment is prescribed for an apostate.

Surah al Nisaa – The Women, 4:137 affirms this principle, because it allows room for both belief and disbelief. *"Behold, as far those who came to believe, and then deny the truth, and again come to believe, and again deny the truth, and thereafter grow stubborn in their denial of the truth – God will not forgive them, nor will He guide them in any way."* The reference to repeated acceptances and rejections of faith indicates that God gives individuals that freedom of conscience in the first place, and therefore applying the death penalty at the first instance of disbelief is contrary to God's Will. Furthermore, the only punishment for rejection of faith is not of a temporal nature, but comes in the guise of God's displeasure, with all its moral implications. The state has no role in this because it cannot know who professes internal belief or disbelief. Only God has that knowledge.

The same principle is stressed in the following Quranic verses as well. *"How would God bestow His guidance upon people who have resolved to deny the truth after having attained to faith, and having borne witness that this Apostle is true, and [after] all evidence of the truth has come unto them? For, God does not guide such evildoing folk. Their requital shall be rejection by God, and by the angels, and by all [righteous] men. In this state shall they abide: [and] neither will their suffering be lightened,, nor will they be granted respite. But excepted shall be they that afterwards repent and put themselves to rights: for, behold, God is much-forgiving, a dispenser of grace. Verily, as for those who are bent on denying the truth after having attained to faith, and then grow [even more stubborn] in their refusal to acknowledge the truth, their repentance [of other sins] shall not be accepted:*

for it is they who have truly gone astray. Verily, as for those who are bent on denying the truth and die as deniers of the truth – not all the gold on earth could ever be their ransom. It is they for whom grievous suffering is in store; and they shall have none to succor them" (Surah al Imran – The House of Imran, 3:86-91).

"Verily, as for those who will not believe in God's messages, God does not guide them aright; and grievous suffering will be their lot [in the life to come]. It is but they who will not believe in God's messages that invent his falsehood; and it is they, they who are lying! As for anyone who denies God after having once attained to faith – and this, to be sure, does not apply to one who does it under duress, the while his heart remains true to his faith, but [only to] him who willingly opens up his heart to a denial of the truth -: upon all such [falls] God's condemnation, and tremendous suffering awaits them: and all this, because they hold this world's life in greater esteem than the life to come, and because God does not bestow His guidance upon people who deny the truth. They whose hearts and whose hearing and whose sight God has sealed – it is they, they who are heedless! Truly it is they, they who in the life to come shall be the losers!" (Surah al Nahl – The Bee, 16:104-109).

"God has promised those of you who have attained to faith and do righteous deeds that, of a certainty, He will cause them to accede to power on earth, even as He cause [some of] those who lived before them to accede to it; and that, of a certainty, He will firmly establish for them religion which He has been pleased to bestow on them; and that, of a certainty, He will cause their erstwhile state of fear to be replaced by a sense of security – [seeing that] they worship Me [alone], not ascribing divine powers to aught beside Me. But all who, after [having under-stood] this, choose to deny the truth- it is they, they who are truly iniq-uitous!" (Surah An Nur – The Light, 24:55).

"For, [many are] they [who]say, 'We believe in God and in the Apostle, and we pay heed!' – but then, some of them turn away after this [assertion]: and these are by no means [true] believers." (Surah An Nur

– The Light, 24:47). Those who choose not to have faith do injustice only to themselves, and are not punishable by temporal law. *"Is there disease in their hearts? Or have they begun to doubt [that this is a divine write]? Or do they fear that God and His Apostle might deal unjustly with them?"* (Surah An Nur – The Light, 24:50). *"Verily, those who turn their backs [on this message] after guidance has been vouchsafed to them, [do it because] Satan has embellished their fancies and filled them with false hopes"* (Surah Muhammad – Muhammad, 47:25).

All of these verses point out that only God can determine one's level of faith, and not other human beings. Yet, there are proponents of capital punishment for apostasy who base their argument on the juristic view that since the role of sharia is to apply God's Will in organizing the affairs of the Muslim community, then a sin against God is also a transgression against the rights of the community (*umma*). The sin therefore carries legal punishment as a crime. This perspective erroneously superimposes the boundaries defining the religious community upon the boundaries defining the political community. It is illustrated in the second *hadith* used by jurists in support of capital punishment for apostasy, where severing ties to Islam coincides with severing ties to the political community of Muslims.

The problem with the argument for punishment for apostasy is that it cannot be applied in any Islamic state without giving rise to the potential for abuse by the state itself. Erroneously equating moral with political power in the determination of law has led to the political repression that we see in Islamic countries today.[34] We must separate the right of God from that of man in defining freedom of religion as a legal right. The right of God refers only to the moral obligations of Muslims towards God, and is adjudicated by God. The state cannot act as a coercive moral authority, in effect representing God's Will on earth, because it does not have the right to do so. In the context of freedom of religion, the state's responsibility is to uphold and protect it as the right of all humans, as granted by God, without exercising moral judgment on the content and/or manner of exercising those religious beliefs.

Coming back to the issue of *The Satanic Verses*, we would apply our interpretation of freedom of religion to allow Rushdie the leeway to profess or renounce Islam as he wishes, without enforcing capital punishment. However, as detailed in the chapter on "Freedom of Speech", we must make a distinction between blasphemy and apostasy here, one which was lost in the controversy over the book. Blasphemy does not automatically entail apostasy. Blasphemy is intentionally offensive behavior or speech that contravenes fundamental principles of Islam and therefore is offensive to Muslims.[35] Apostasy is a clear renunciation of Islam altogether. Blasphemous actions may not necessarily imply renunciation, since non-Muslims can also commit blasphemy. Regardless of the definition though, the state does not have the legal right to punish individuals for either offense, which are both offenses against the right of God and not of man.

As a closing point in this discussion of apostasy, we should also note our position on minorities, such as the Ahmadis and the Bahais, who have challenged Islamic tenets in the development of their own doctrinal beliefs. Both communities trace their origins to Islam, but also accept the messianic role of their respective founders.

To give some background, in 1888 in India, Mirza Ghulam Ahmad, the founder of the Ahmadiyya community, announced his claim to be the Promised Messiah, Mahdi, and a prophet. Similarly, in the 1840s in Iran, the founder of the Baha'is, proclaimed himself as the *Bab* (gate), the *Mahdi* (the Guided One) and the *Qaim* (He Who Will Arise).[36] This contravenes orthodox Muslim understanding of Prophet Muhammad's (pbuh) role as the Seal of the Prophets. In addition, for the Shi'a, Bahaullah's claim is also controversial because it elevates him to the status of the "Hidden Imam", who, according to Shi'a theology, is given all authority over human affairs.[37]

According to the self-definition of both minorities, both state that, while they accept the Finality of Prophethood doctrine, it does not prohibit the emergence of mujaddids, or reformers in Islam, nor does it negate the continuation of the process of prophetic revelation as a whole. Ahmadis claim that unlike the Prophet (pbuh), the founder of the Ahmadiyya sect is "a prophet without a law and without a book."[38] In contrast, the Baha'is state that while their founder did bring a new law and new book to his people, it does not take away from their understanding of Baha'ism as stemming from the Revelation of Islam. While Ahmadis consider themselves to be a sect of Sunni Islam, Bahais claim to belong to a religion separate from Islam altogether.

In line with our argument for freedom of belief and worship that has been detailed in this chapter, it is necessary for the state to allow religious minorities such as these two groups the right to practice their faith, as they choose to believe it. It is not for the state to judge anyone else's authenticity of faith. All beliefs are subject to debate, and while we disagree with the dogmas mentioned, God will make that decision on the Day of Judgment. Furthermore, differences in doctrinal beliefs do not constitute a basis for differentiation in citizenship rights. All citizens, regardless of individual faith or belief, have equal civil, political and legal rights in an Islamic state.

Conclusion

The state cannot function as a coercive religious authority and cannot legally adjudicate on the content of religious belief of its citizens, nor prevent them from practicing their religion as they wish. All citizens have the same right to freedom of belief and worship, regardless of the actual faith they follow.

Governments have often made a distinction between believers and nonbelievers as being unequal in the eyes of God, and drawn the conclusion that Muslims and non-Muslims are entitled to different sets of civil and political rights in an Islamic state. We strongly disagree with this theory that links spiritual "rank" with equality before the law, and point to the evidence drawn from the Quran, *hadith*, and early Islamic history, all of which affirms the fundamental equality of all human beings and religious communities in matters of conscience and religious belief. Any restriction on either of these by the state transgresses against the right of God as the Supreme Judge, and ultimately, violates the spirit of Islam itself.

Footnotes

1 See also the chapter on freedom of speech.
2 This encompasses both meanings of the word: 1) Truth as synonymous with Religion(Islam); 2) truth as generally distinct from falsehood. In both cases, the obligation to express truth remains paramount.
3 Cited in Kamali, *Freedom of Expression in Islam* (Kuala Lumpur: Berita Publishing, 1994) p. 96. This verse will be referred to again later on in the discussion on the treatment of non-Muslim communities.
4 "People of the Book" is also used to refer to Zoroastrians and Sabeans, of which the latter do not exist today.
5 The Islamic Republic of Iran is one example of such a country. Its constitution makes a distinction between the political rights given to Muslims, to the People of the Book, and to all other remaining citizens.
6 Abdulaziz A. Sachedina, "Jews, Christians and Muslims According to the Qur'an," *Greek Orthodox Theological Review*, 30:1(1986), p. 111.
7 Abdulaziz Sachedina, *The Islamic Roots of Democratic Pluralism* (New York: Oxford University Press, 2001) p. 23.
8 Quoted in Kamali, *Freedom of Expression in Islam*, p.86.
9 Kamali, *Freedom of Expression in Islam*, p. 86.
10 Quoted in Kamali, *Freedom of Expression in Islam*, p. 90.
11 See also chapter on *dhimmi*s for more.
12 See chapter on constitutionalism for complete text and analysis of the Medina Charter.
13 Safi, p.12.
14 Muhammad Hamidullah, *The First Written-Constitution in the World* (Lahore: Sh. Mohammad Ashraf, 1968).
15 Abu Yusuf, Kitab al Kharaj, cited in Afzalur Rahman, *Readings in Political Philosophy*, Vol 1: Liberty, (London : Seerah Foundation Press, 1987), p. 159.
16 Louay M. Safi, "Human Rights and Islamic Legal Reform," p. 6. Available at http://www.wponline.org/vil/Articles/Shariah/human3.pdf.
17 Abu Dawd, quoted in Mohammad Hashim Kamali, *Freedom, Equality and Justice in Islam* (Cambridge,UK: Islamic Texts Society, 2002), p. 83.
18 Quoted in Shaikh Shaukat Hussain, *Human Rights in Islam* (New Delhi: Kitab Bhavan, 1990) p. 59.
19 Kamali, *Freedom, Equality and Justice*, p. 83.
20 Hussain, p. 59.
21 Hussain, p. 60.
22 Hussain, p. 60.
23 Kamali, *Freedom, Equality and Justice in Islam*, p. 83.
24 Hussain, p. 60.
25 Bosworth, p. 46.
26 This assumes that paying *zakat* is not the same as paying income tax. Failure to pay the latter would be subject to legal prosecution in any country.
27 Kamali, *Freedom of Expression in Islam*, p. 91.
28 Noted in Sahih Bukhari, Vol. 4, Book 52, Number 260; Sahih Bukhari, Vol. 9, Book 84, Number 57.
29 Sunan Abu Dawd, Book 39, Number 4487.
30 S.A. Rahman, *The Punishment of Apostasy in Islam* (Lahore: Institute of Islamic Culture, 1978), p.63.
31 Narrated by Ibn Hisham in his *al-Sirah al-Nabawaiah*, quoted and translated into English by Safi, p. 10.
32 Sahih Bukhari, Volume 8, Book 78, Number 647.
33 Quoted in Kamali, *Freedom of Expression in Islam*, p. 94.
34 See also Khalid Abou El Fadl's works, The Place of Tolerance in Islam, and *And God Knows the Soldiers* for more on the negative implications of this kind of restrictive interpretation of Islamic law.
35 Refer also to chapter on freedom of speech.
36 William S. Hatcher and J. Douglas Martin, *The Baha'i Faith: The Emerging Global Religion* (San Francisco: Harper Row, 1985), p. 5.
37 Hatcher and Martin, p. 9.
38 Antonio Gualtieri, *Conscience and Coercion: Ahmadi Muslims and Orthodoxy in Pakistan*. (Montreal: Guernica Editions, 1991), p. 26.

CHAPTER SEVEN

The Status of Women

ome of the traditional Islamic interpretations on women's rights have argued that they are complementary with men's rights in society, rather than being in absolute equality. This line of argument stems from the idea that women's roles are primarily as caregivers and limited to the domestic sphere, and men's are as breadwinners and linked to the public sphere. Thus, biological function is linked to social space in determining gender roles, and the rights and duties of each are derived thereof.

Insisting on absolute equality of opportunity among men and women is difficult. Even if some women can be breadwinners today, men certainly cannot bear children and thereby occupy the same kind of role as caregivers in the family. The argument here is not so much an insistence on absolute equality of rights based on biological function, but on the flexibility and choice that both men and women should have in determining how to live their lives as fellow citizens and members of society. Legal, social and economic rights all come under this category.

Unfortunately, in some Muslim countries, the decision on how Muslim women are to live their lives is often made for them by patriarchal and cultural norms. These are then couched in religious justification of a gender hierarchy that considers women inferior to men. This chapter challenges this perception that assigns all responsibility for the restrictions placed upon Muslim women in some countries on religion, without delving into what exactly Islam sets out as the rights of women.

This discussion will delineate the spiritual, legal and social equality that exists between men and women in Islam, relying mostly on Quranic verses and the circumstances surrounding the Prophet's (pbuh) life and his treatment of his wives. It is later juristic tradition and the compilation of *hadith* in later centuries that have superimposed patriarchal attitudes on gender relations and rendered women as inferior to men in Islamic tradition. We critique this notion by laying out a Quranic argument for the equality of women and their inclusion in all aspects of social and political life. We have endeavored to highlight the key points in this argument. Comprehensive coverage of all the various social issues relating to Muslim women today would be impossible to do in the course of just one chapter.

Equality of All Life

With the revelation of Islam in seventh century Arabia came the insistence that the value of a female life is no less than that of a male life. This was exemplified most prominently in the prohibition on female infanticide. According to societal custom at the time, some female infants were left to die after birth, because they were considered to be a vulnerable liability in a warring tribal society. God expresses strong disapproval of this practice in Surah al Nahl – The Bee, 16:58-59. *"For, whenever any of them is given the glad tiding of [the birth of] a girl, his face darkens, and he is filled with suppressed anger, avoiding all people because of the [alleged] evil of the glad tiding which he has received, [and debating within himself:] Shall he keep this [child] despite the contempt [which he feels for it] – or shall he bury it in the dust? Oh, evil indeed is whatever they decide!"* The verse ends by posing a rhetorical question, since both are evil choices – treating female children with contempt or killing them. The larger evil that is being condemned is the low esteem in which daughters were held in Arab society of that time.

This condemnation is articulated again in Surah al Takwir –

Shrouding in Darkness, 81: 8-9, which refers to Judgment Day, *"and when the girl-child that was buried alive is made to ask for what crime she had been slain"*. The verse refers to the fact that God will hold everyone accountable for their actions on Judgment Day. In this context, it is not the female child who is responsible for her own death. It is the parent who killed his/her daughter who will be held accountable, based on the testimony of the female infant. Thus, parents are strongly enjoined to be God-fearing and to treat their daughters with the same esteem that they do their sons.[1]

A *hadith*, attributed to the Prophet (pbuh), stresses the equality of male and female children. It states "one who has two daughters and no son, and spends his life in their proper upbringing and education will be closest to me in Heaven."[2]

All life is equally honored, and all beings are equal in rights and obligations as the creation of God. The equality of men and women is mentioned in Surah An Nisaa – Women, 4:1, *"O Mankind! Be conscious of your Sustainer, who has created you out of one living entity, and out of it created its mate, and out of the two spread abroad a multitude of men and women. And remain conscious of God, in whose name you demand [your rights] from one another, and of those ties of kinship. Verily, God is ever watchful over you!"* The first part of this verse discusses the fact that human beings all originate from similar circumstances. In a general sense, this implies common descent of the human race from Adam and Eve. But it also refers to the fact that the granting of life is an act of God, and He does not distinguish between men and women. The second part of the verse enjoins people to remember their mutual rights and duties that have been granted to them, as a part of their awareness of God. In particular, this includes respect for women, as mothers and wives, since they are the ones that bear children.

From a more biological perspective, the origins of both men and women are also the same. Surah al Qiyamah, 75:37-39 states, *"Was he not once a [mere] drop of sperm that had been split, and thereafter became a germ-cell – whereupon He created and formed [it] in accordance with what [it] was meant to be, and fashioned out of it the two sexes, the male and the female?"* There is no pre-judgment as to the value of creating a male or a female in the process of conception. Both are equal.

The same theme of unity of origin and subsequent equality of status is echoed in Surah al Hujurat – The Private Apartments, 49:13, *"O men! Behold, We have created you all out of a male and a female, and have made you into nations and tribes, so that you might come to know one another. Verily, the noblest of you in the sight of God is the one who is most deeply conscious of Him. Behold, God is all-knowing, all-aware".* Differences based on gender, race, ethnicity, among others, exist merely to allow for greater cooperation and harmony among individuals. It does not necessarily mean that there is a hierarchy, of Muslims over non-Muslims, or men over women, or vice versa. In addition, this verse highlights the fact that the moral and spiritual standing of all is equal before God. The only valid distinctions arise from the degree of righteousness that an individual achieves, not from any biologically-determined characteristic. Thus, a righteous woman would be more honored in the eyes of God, than a relatively less righteous man. The ultimate judgment is, of course, made by God.

Similarly, all of mankind has been favored by God, and bestowed inherent dignity. *"Now, Indeed, We have conferred dignity on the children of Adam, and borne them over land and sea, and provided for them sustenance out of the good things of life, and favored them far above most of Our creation"* (Surah al Isra – The Night Journey, 17:70). Men are not necessarily more favored than women, or vice versa, in the "provision of good things." The entire human race enjoys that privilege.

Moral/Spiritual Equality

First and foremost, from a theological perspective, Islam clearly disagrees with the stigma of original sin that characterized the conception of women in Christianity, and which originated in Eve's temptation of Adam, and their subsequent expulsion from the Garden of Eden. In contrast, the Quran does not single out Eve for her culpability. Satan tempts both Adam and Eve, and later, God admonishes both for their disobedience to Him. *"And [as for thee], O Adam, dwell thou and they wife in this garden, and eat, both of you, whatever you may wish; but do not approach this one tree, lest you become evildoers!' Thereupon Satan whispered unto the two with a view of making them conscious of their nakedness, of which [hitherto] they had been unaware; and he said: 'Your Sustainer has but forbidden you this tree lest you two become [as] angels, or lest you live forever.' And he swore unto them, 'Verily, I am of those who wish you well indeed! – and thus he led them on with deluding thoughts. But as soon as the two had tasted [the fruit] of the tree, they became conscious of their nakedness; and they began to cover themselves with pieced-together leaves from the garden. And their Sustainer called unto them: ' Did I not forbid that tree unto you and tell you, 'Verily, Satan is your open foe?'"* (Surah al Araf – The Faculty of Discernment, 7:19-22).

Apart from the prophets, women were also singled out as recipients of Divine Revelation, or *wahy*. For example, the mother of Moses was instructed to cast her son in the river, and later was able to nurse him, even though he had been adopted by the Pharoah. *"And so, [when he was born,] We inspired [thus] the mother of Moses: 'Suckle him [for a time], and then, when thou hast cause to fear for him, cast him into the river, and have no fear and do not grieve – for We shall restore him to thee, and shall make him one of Our message – bearers!"* (Surah al Qasas – The Story, 28:7). Mary, the mother of Jesus, was also singled out by God and given the divine message that she was going to bear a son. *"And lo! The angels said: 'O Mary! Behold, God has elected thee and made thee pure, and raised thee above all the women of the world"* (Surah al Imran – The House Of Imran, 3:42). In both cases, women were divinely chosen for a particular task, even as men were chosen to carry out others. God did not specifically exclude women from His favor simply because they were women.

As worshippers, both men and women occupy the same spiritual status before God. They are both commanded to submit to God, to believe in Him and to carry out their religious duties in Surah al Ahzab – The Confederates, 33:35. *"Verily, for all men and women who have surrendered themselves unto God, and all believing men and believing women, and all truly devout men and truly devout women, and all men and women who are true to their word, and all men and women who are patient in adversity, and all men and women who humble themselves [before God], and all men and women who give in charity, and all self-denying men and self-denying women, and all men and women who are mindful of their chastity, and all men and women who remember God unceasingly: for [all of] them has God readied forgiveness of sins and a mighty reward".* The constant refrain distinguishing between men and women specifically in this verse underscores the equality of the sexes in the eyes of God.

Similarly, the principle of *hisba*, the commanding of good and forbidding of evil, is equally relevant to men and women in the Quran. Surah al Tawba – Repentance, 9:71 states, *"And [as for] the believers, both men and women – they are close unto one another: they [all] enjoin the doing of what is right and forbid the doing of what is wrong, and are constant in prayer, and render the purifying dues, and pay heed unto God and His Apostle. It is they upon whom God will bestow His grace: verily, God is almighty, wise!"*

Other verses that reflect similar emphasis on virtuous personal conduct, regardless of sex, are:

"As for anyone – be it man or woman – who does righteous deeds, and is a believer withal – him shall We most certainly cause to live a good life; and most certainly shall We grant unto such as these their reward in accordance with the best that they ever did" (Surah al Nahl – The Bee, 16:97).

"And thus does their Sustainer answer their prayer: 'I shall not lose sight of the labor of any of you who labors [in My way], be it man or

woman: each of you is an issue of the other. Hence, as for those who forsake the domain of evil, and are driven from their homelands, and suffer hurt in My cause, and fight [for it], and are slain – I shall most certainly efface their bad deeds, and shall most certainly bring them into gardens through which running waters flow, as a reward from God: for with God is the most beauteous of rewards" (Surah al Imran – The House of Imran, 3:195).

"Whereas anyone – be it man or woman – who does [whatever he can] of good deeds and is a believer withal, shall enter paradise, and shall not be wronged by as much as [would fill] the groove of a date-stone" (Surah an Nisaa – Women, 4:124).

"On the Day when thou shalt see all believing men and believing women, with their light spreading rapidly before them and on their right, [and with this welcome awaiting them:] 'A glad tiding for you today: gardens through which running waters flow, therein to abide! This, this is the triumph supreme!'" (Surah al Hadid – Iron, 57: 12).

Viewed in conjunction with the verses on the unity of origin and creation of all life discussed in the previous section, these Quranic references to the spiritual and moral equality of men and women further our argument for the equal status and rights granted to women by God. The underlying argument of these verses is that God rewards both men and women on the basis of their individual moral actions and efforts. Thus, the same standard for judgment is used for both, implying a sense of equality of the sexes.

We can extend this basic principle and apply it towards the roles of men and women in society. Since God does not "suffer to be lost the work of any", and He does not restrict either men or women from working to achieve *hisba*, as members of society, it behooves human authority to do the same. Restricting the political, economic and social roles of women on the basis of claims to enforce "Islamic teachings" about gender roles is contrary to the spirit of equality that permeates the Quran's view of men and women as partners. Applying this argument more specifically, we uphold the concept of equal pay for equal work in the economic sphere, right to equal participation and representation for women in the political sphere, and recognition of their autonomy and authority in the legal sphere. The following sections will develop these aspects of our argument in more detail.

Legal Equality

Islamic jurisprudence was the first to view women as legally independent members of society, and not merely the property of their guardians. The Quran granted women inheritance rights, the right to voluntarily enter into or refuse marriage, divorce rights and the right to control their own wealth and income. They were no longer considered property and allowed to be passed on to other male kin as wives after the death of their husbands.[3] In other words, they were treated as legally autonomous beings, with certain economic, social and political rights. The following discussion will outline the relevant Quranic verses pertaining to some of these issues of legal equality.

Economic/Financial Autonomy

Legally, both men and women enjoy equal opportunity to work, and have control over what they earn. *"Hence, do not covet the bounties which God has bestowed more abundantly on some of you than others. Men shall have a benefit from what they earn, and women shall have a benefit from what they earn. Ask, therefore, God [to give you] out of his bounty: behold, God has indeed full knowledge of everything"* (Surah an Nisaa – Women, 4:32). Women have the right to engage in any trade, business or commercial transactions, since they are recognized as having the legal autonomy to do so. Historically, there is also the example of Khadija, the Prophet's (pbuh) first wife, who was a businesswoman and ran her trade independently.

There are different financial obligations on husbands and wives. A wife can legally keep her income, her inheritance and her property for herself if she chooses. Her husband cannot force her to use it to for her own sustenance (food, clothing, housing or other "basics" that it is his responsibility to provide as her husband).[4] However, it does not mean that this particular configuration of financial roles within the family is static. Whatever a particular couple decides as being mutually beneficial is equally permissible, since in many cases, both the husband and the wife contribute financially towards domestic needs. The purpose here is to underline the economic independence and autonomy of women as a Quranically-mandated right.

Inheritance Rights

The Quranic verses relating to inheritance rights for women are based on a concept of equity and are not meant to justify superiority of men over women. There is a proportional share for both, noted in the following. *"Men shall have a share in what parents and kinsfolk leave behind, and women shall have a share in what parents and kinsfolk leave behind, whether it be little or much – a share ordained [by God]"* (Surah an Nisaa – Women, 4:7); *"And unto everyone have We appointed heirs to what he may leave behind: parents, and near kinsfolk, and those to whom you have pledged your troth: give them, therefore, their share. Behold, God is indeed a witness unto everything"* (Surah an Nisaa – Women, 4:33).

The first obligation in the division of wealth is to make sure that the deceased's family is taken care of. The division of property is set out as follows in three verses of Surah an-Nisaa, the chapter that deals with the status of women, among other issues.

"Concerning [the inheritance of] your children, God enjoins [this] upon you: The male shall have the equal of two females' share; but if there are more than two females, they shall have two-thirds of what [their parents] leave behind: and if there is only one, she shall have one-half thereof. And as for the parents [of the deceased], each of them shall have one-sixth of what he leaves behind, in the event of his having [left] a child; but if he has left no child and his parents are his [only] heirs, then his mother shall have one-third; and if he has brothers and sisters, then his mother shall have one-sixth after [the deduction of] any

bequest he may have made, or any debt [he may have incurred]" (Surah an Nisaa – Women, 4:11).

"And you shall inherit one-half of what your wives leave behind, provided they have left no child; wives leave behind, provided they have left no child; but if they have left a child, then you shall have one-quarter of what they leave behind, after [the deduction of] any bequest they may have made, or any debt [they may have incurred]. And your widows shall have one-quarter of what you leave behind, provided you have left no child; but if you have left a child, then they shall have one-eighth of what you leave behind, after [the deduction of] any bequest you may have made, or any debt [you may have incurred]. And if a man or woman has no heir in the direct line, but has a brother or a sister, then each of these two shall inherit one-sixth; but if there are more than two, then they shall share in one-third [of the inheritance], after [the deduction of] any bequest that may have been made, or any debt [that may have been incurred], neither of which having been intended to harm [the heits]. [This is] an injunction from God: and God is all-knowing, forbearing" (Surah an Nisaa – The Women, 4:12).

"They will ask thee to enlighten them. Say: 'God enlightens you [thus] about the laws concerning [inheritance from] those who leave no heir in the direct line: If a man dies childless and has a sister, she shall inherit one-half of what he has left, just as he shall inherit from her if she dies childless. But if there are two sisters, both [together] shall have two-thirds of what he has left; and if there are brothers and sisters, then the male shall have the equal of two females' share.' God makes [all this] clear unto you, lest you go astray; and God knows everything" (Surah an Nisaa – The Women, 4:176).

The Quranic verses on inheritance allow us to make a couple of points. First, women have the right to inherit as separate individuals, a right that has historically been denied in many non-Muslim societies. Second, the estate can set aside a portion for "legacies" which are charitable donations, with division of the remaining assets then occurring. Finally, the Quran does not provide an exhaustive list of claimants and shares, nor does it provide for the full disposal of the estate. Depending on the circumstances, 20-30% estate remains discretionary. According to some opinions, a person can top up the share of her female relatives in the will, to maintain equality. The primary thrust though is that all close relatives are due something, which would prevent certain abuses where family quarrels lead to an unjust division of assets. It would appear that given the method of calculating shares and depending on the number of relatives that are to inherit, no one person is ensured of a fixed amount of inheritance. The common theme, though, in all three of these verses pertaining to inheritance rights, is that proportionally speaking, in the division between male and female relatives, women inherit less than men. Sisters receive only half the portion given to their brothers. Wives are entitled to only a fourth or an eighth, for example.

However, taken in their entirety, these verses emphasize the need to ensure equity among family members, given the circumstances of each person and the degree of benefit they will derive from their share. If a widow has two daughters and a son, but she is being financially supported by her daughter, then it is reasonable to expect that the daughter will have a larger share than the son, given her responsibilities. In addition, Islamic law allows for one third of the deceased's wealth to be bequeathed, without restriction as to the beneficiary and without decreasing the division of the remaining wealth. This one third can be used, legally according to some schools, to supplement the share of female relatives.[5] We argue, therefore, that the broader principle in the division of inheritance is to promote justice and equity. It is part of the purpose of the *sharia* to protect the family, which means to protect it against the inheritance being left entirely to outsiders. The inheritance rights of women need to be viewed within this larger context of achieving justice.

Second, there is a difference in the legally-enforceable economic obligations and opportunities of men and women in society, which also serves as an explanation for why sisters receive a smaller share of an inheritance than brothers. A woman is considered sole owner of any property she receives from her father or husband at the time of her marriage. In addition, she is entitled to her dower, which may be paid at that time or deferred till later.[6] She can legally hold possession of her husband's property until it is paid in full. Despite this financial security, the husband is still responsible for maintaining her throughout her life.[7] If judged from this perspective, the differences in the legal shares do not reflect a lower value being placed on women. Instead, they assume the financial security that women already are entitled to, and that they enjoy, theoretically speaking. A legal inheritance is not meant to change that. While men in some cases inherit more, they are also financially responsible in a legal sense for the women in their family (mother, wives, daughters). Women inherit less, but they are not legally obligated to provide for anyone else.

We should emphasize that this division of gender roles does not always correspond with practical realities in contemporary society. Women are sometimes the sole breadwinners in their families, and therefore provide for both male and female family members. With regard to legal implications, however, this division of financial responsibility can be enforced, so that male relatives can be obliged to support female relatives, unless there are mitigating circumstances. The state can adjudicate if people take the case to court, but its cannot set a rigid formula for inheritance which would be applicable to all citizens equally, since inheritance matters are often complicated within a family. The role of the state in inheritance matters requires a balance between ensuring justice for the family members and their respective needs and circumstances. The Quran and Islamic law does provide some degree of flexibility in the division of inheritance, but not at the expense of the inheritance rights of women.

In conclusion, we should note that the verses on inheritance rights were revealed in a historical context in which many women did not have access to the means for financial or economic self-sufficiency or independence. Thus, they were under the guardianship of their male relatives, and required their protection and material support. In this context, the fact that they could inherit at all, and were not inheritable as property themselves, was a novelty for seventh-century Arabia.[8] The changes in economic access for women in society today call for an interpretation of these verses that is in keeping with the contemporary context and also adheres to the core Quranic principles of equality and justice with regard to the treatment of women. For the complexity of the laws of inheritance and for the changing realities of different modern contexts, we invite the specialized jurists of this branch of law examine these issues in light of the goals of *sharia* as well as contemporary changes.

Marriage and Divorce

We have, thus far, discussed the moral and spiritual equality of both men and women before God, and issues relating to the legal autonomy of women as well. Marriage does not change the concept of "equality of the sexes" to "hierarchy of the sexes."

Marriage is considered to be a co-equal partnership between a husband and wife. *"And among His wonders is this: He creates for you mates out of your own kind, so that you might incline towards them, and He engenders love and tenderness between you: in this, behold, there are messages indeed for people who think!"* (Surah ar Rum – The Byzantines, 30:21). *" The Originator [is He] of the heavens and the earth. He has given you mates of your own kind – just as [He has willed that] among the beasts [there be] mates – to multiply you thereby: [but] there is nothing like unto Him, and He alone is all-hearing, all-seeing"* (Surah Ash Shura – Consultation, 42:11). Both of these verses emphasize the equal nature of a couple's relationship, one that is characterized by love and mercy. They do not indicate a hierarchical notion of gender relations in which wives are inferior to their husbands.

In addition to its religious significance, marriage is also a social, legal and moral contract between a man and a woman. Again, this implies equality of status. Its purpose is to provide equal protection to both parties. Both the man and the woman must be legal adults, of sound mind, who freely enter marriage. The confirmation of the marriage contract is achieved through a declaration and acceptance of the terms by the individuals and two adult witnesses.[9]

Women have the right of veto to any marriage proposal, and cannot be married against their will. Juristic tradition that denies women this freedom is contrary to the fundamental egalitarianism of Islamic teaching.[10] The fact that this misogynistic juristic tradition, for example, citing women as being deficient in intellect, or insisting on absolute wifely obedience to her husband, has arisen in later centuries is noteworthy, since it runs counter to the Quranic message of equality of the sexes with regard to marriage.[11]

The dower (*mahr*) is an element of the marriage contract. It is the amount, or equivalent in property, that man must give to his future wife, either at the time of the marriage or to be deferred, in case of divorce. Once determined, the *mahr* is written into the marriage contract, and the husband cannot unilaterally change the terms. *"And [forbidden to you are] all married women other than those whom you rightfully possess [through wedlock]: this is God's ordinance, binding upon you. But lawful to you are all [women] beyond these, for you to seek out, offering them of your possessions, taking them in honest wedlock, and not in fornication. And unto those with whom you desire to enjoy marriage, you shall give the dowers due to them; but you will incur no sin if, after [having agreed upon] this lawful due, you freely agree with one another upon anything [else]: behold, God is indeed all-knowing, wise"* (Surah an Nisaa – Women, 4:24). The key portion of this verse, allowing the dower amount to be amended, makes it conditional upon the agreement of both the husband and the wife, further supporting our argument for marriage as an equal partnership.[12]

The dower should not be confused with the abhorrent idea of a "bride price", which implies that the husband is paying something to a woman's parents in order to procure a wife. It serves as financial security for the woman in case of divorce, not for her family. The Quran also considers it as a token of respect and consideration, and it is deemed part of the covenant of marriage. Even in the case of the husband's decision to remarry, he is not allowed to take back the dower he promised to his first wife. *"But if you desire to give up a wife and to take another in her stead, do not take away anything of what you have given the first one, however much it may have been. Would you, perchance, take it away by slandering her and thus committing a manifest sin? And how could you take it away after you have given yourselves to one another, and she has received a most solemn pledge from you?"* (Surah an Nisaa – Women, 4:20-21).

Married women have the legal right to be financially provided for by their husbands. This does not justify the view that husbands are superior to their wives on the basis of their role as breadwinners. Verse 34 in Surah an Nisaa deals with this issue, and has been traditionally used to argue that God has favored husbands over wives, and in general, men over women. We disagree with this perspective, and subscribe to the following interpretation of this verse. The first part of the verse reads, *"Men shall take full care of women with the bounties which God has bestowed more abundantly on the former than on the latter, and with what they may spend out of their possessions. And the righteous women are the truly devout ones, who guard the intimacy which God has [ordained to be] guarded. And as for those women whose ill-will you have reason to fear, admonish them [first]; then leave them alone in bed; then beat them lightly; and if thereupon they pay heed, do not seek to harm them. Behold, God is indeed most high, great!"* (Surah an Nisaa – Women, 4:34).[13]

There are two points worth underscoring from this interpretation. One, it does not indicate absolute superiority of all men over all women, as a class. The preference referred to is not unconditional.[14] The social role of men as "protectors and maintainers" is conditional upon their financial and material support of women. Wadud argues that this socioeconomic role of men as providers is in proportion to the role of women as childbearers. Within the family, given that a woman alone is biologically capable of the arduous task of bearing children, it is the husband's responsibility to ensure that she has physical protection and material sustenance so that she is not faced with additional burden.[15] In other words, it refers to a specific, mutually beneficial delineation of roles and responsibilities within the family, and does not justify a hierarchical view of gender relations on the basis of biological differences.[16]

When this interpretation is viewed in juxtaposition with verse 228 of Surah al Baqara, the Quranic view of the egalitarian nature of relations between men and women is clearly evident. *"And the divorced women shall undergo, without remarrying, a waiting-period of three monthly courses: for it is not lawful for them to conceal what God may have created in their wombs, if they believe in God and the Last Day. And during this period their husbands are fully entitled to take them back, if they desire reconciliation; but, in accordance with justice, the rights of the wives [with regard to their husbands] are equal to the [husbands'] rights with regard to them, although men have precedence over them [in this respect]. And God is almighty, wise"* (Surah al Baqara – The Cow, 2:228).

In addition, Surah an Nisaa, 4:34 does not specify that women are prohibited from working and providing for their families, if they so choose and/or if circumstances dictate. Theoretically, a wife has the right to keep her income for herself, and it does not have to be used towards the maintenance of the family; *"To men is allotted what they earn, and to women what they earn"* (Surah an Nisaa, 4:32). However, if she does work and chooses to use her income to support the family, she is entitled to do so. The emphasis here is on the woman's choice, and the fact that becoming a wife does not automatically take away her financial autonomy, even within the context of traditional gender roles.

The traditional gender role of a husband as the primary breadwinner does not mean that he is to exercise dictatorship over his family, although it has been used by some scholars to justify unconditional obedience of wives to their husbands.[17] This interpretation is contrary to the Quranic view of marriage as a partnership between equals. Mutual kindness and respect are key characteristics of marriage, from an Islamic perspective. *"It is lawful for you to go in unto your wives during the night preceding the [day's] fast: they are as a garment for you, and you are as a garment for them"* (Surah al Baqara – The Cow, 2:187). *"O you who have attained to faith! It is not lawful for you to [try to] become heirs to your wives [by holding onto them] against their will; and neither shall you keep them under constraint with a view to taking away anything of what you may have given them, unless it be that they have become guilty, in an obvious manner, or immoral conduct. And consort with your wives in a goodly manner; for if you dislike them, it may well be that you dislike something which God might yet make a source of abundant good"* (Surah an Nisaa – Women, 4:19).

The Prophet's (pbuh) gentle and kind treatment of his wives serves as a role model for marital relations between a husband and wife. Numerous reports indicate that the Prophet (pbuh) was never a dictator in his family, and that he never struck or insulted any of them, even when they argued. Bukhari noted an incident in which Umar's wife, while arguing with Umar told him, "You reproach me for answering you! Well, by God, the wives of the Prophet (pbuh) answer him, and one of them might even desert him from morning until night." In fact, the Prophet (pbuh) frequently sought the counsel of his wives. A'isha, one of his favorite wives, is a trustworthy source of a number of *hadith* concerning the Prophet (pbuh), and is known to have corrected Abu Hurayrah on *hadith* that she knew to contradict the Quran.[18]

Divorce is viewed as a very serious step and is not to be taken lightly. *"O you who have attained to faith! It is not lawful for you to [try to] become heirs to your wives [by holding onto them] against their will; and neither shall you keep them under constraint with a view to taking away anything of what you may have given them, unless it be that they have become guilty, in an obvious manner, or immoral conduct. And consort with your wives in a goodly manner; for if you dislike them, it may well be that you dislike something which God might yet make a source of abundant good"* (Surah an Nisaa – Women, 4:19). All attempts at marital reconciliation should be undertaken first, including arbitration and counseling. *"And if you have reason to fear that a breach might occur between a [married] couple, appoint an arbiter from among his people and an arbiter from among her people; if they both want to set things aright, God may bring about their reconciliation. Behold, God is indeed all-knowing, aware."* (Surah an Nisaa – Women, 4:35).

Only when these steps are exhausted is divorce a viable option. *"And if husband and wife do separate, God shall provide for each of them out of His abundance: for God is indeed infinite, wise"* (Surah an Nisaa – Women, 4:130).

Even then, however, it is to be carried out in as amicable and harmonious a manner as possible. The Quran points out the virtues of self-restraint in the following verse. *"And if a woman has reason to fear ill-treatment from her husband, or that he might turn away from her, it shall not be wrong for the two to set things peacefully to rights between themselves: for peace is best, and selfishness is ever-present in human souls. But if you do good and are conscious of Him – behold, God is indeed aware of all that you do"* (Surah an Nisaa – Women, 4:128).

"O Prophet! When you [intend to] divorce women, divorce them with a view to the waiting-period appointed for them, and reckon the period [carefully], and be conscious of God, your Sustainer. Do not expel them from their homes; and neither shall they [be made to] leave unless they become openly guilty of immoral conduct. These, then, are the bounds set by God – and he who transgresses the bounds set by God does indeed sin against himself: [for, O man, although] thou knowest it not, after the [first breach] God may well cause something new to come about" (Surah al Talaq – Divorce, 65:1). This verse clearly prohibits men from harassing, hurting or injuring their wives, having decided upon divorcing them, at the risk of transgressing the limits set by God and wronging their own soul. The terms could not be more severe, to indicate God's displeasure at such behavior.[19]

The divorce process involves a series of steps.[20] Contrary to popular belief, a husband cannot divorce his wife simply by saying "I divorce you" three times consecutively at one moment. The legal procedure for divorce includes a three month waiting period, known as *iddat*, during which both parties are given time to reflect seriously on the matter. It is also done so that if it turns out the wife is pregnant, the child's paternity is firmly established. If she is pregnant, it extends till the child's birth.

"And the divorced women shall undergo, without remarrying, a waiting-period of three monthly course: for it is not lawful for them to conceal what God may have created in their wombs, if they believe in God and the Last Day. And during this period their husbands are fully entitled to take them back, if they desire reconciliation; but, in accordance with justice, the rights of the wives [with regard to their husbands] are equal to the [husbands'] rights with regard to them, although men have precedence over them [in this respect]. And God is almighty, wise" (Surah al Baqara – The Cow, 2:228).

It is the husband's responsibility to provide financially for his wife during this time period, at the standard of living that they have enjoyed thus far. If the wife chooses not to nurse the child, the father is also responsible for paying for a wet nurse. *"[Hence,] let the women [who are undergoing a waiting-period] live in the same manner as you live yourselves, in accordance with your means; and do not harass them with a view of making their lives a misery. And if they happen to be with child, spend freely on them until they deliver their burden; and if they nurse your offspring [after the divorce has become final], give them their [due] recompense; and take counsel with one another in a fair manner [about the child's future]. And if both of you find it difficult [that the mother should nurse the child], let another woman nurse it on behalf of him [who has begotten it]"* (Surah al Talaq – Divorce, 65:6).

At the end of the period of *iddat*, there is one last chance for reconciliation. If divorce is still agreed upon as the best option, then it is legally finalized. *"And so, when you divorce women and they are about to reach the end of their waiting-term, then either retain them in a fair manner or let them go in a fair manner. But do not retain them against their will in order to hurt [them]: for he who does so sins indeed against himself. And do not take [these] messages of God in a frivolous spirit; and remember the blessings with which God has graced you, and all the revelation and the wisdom which He has bestowed on you from on high in order to admonish you thereby; and remain conscious of God, and know that God has full knowledge of everything"* (Surah al Baqara – The Cow, 2:231). Again, this verse reiterates the emphasis on behaving justly towards one's spouse.

According to the juristic rulings of some schools (Hanafi, Hanbali), the custody of children usually goes to the mother, if the children are below the age of seven.[21] This is not a Quranic requirement, however, and it is necessary to examine the suitability of both parents in determining child custody. The father is legally responsible to pay for child support to the mother as long as the children are living with her. Jurisprudence on divorce does not expressly mention alimony to the ex-wife as part of the divorce settlement, but we can interpret from the verses above the need to make it part of the "equitable terms" and "just and reasonable manner" in which the settlement is made. The following verse also refers to this. *"And the divorced women, too, shall have [a right to] maintenance in a goodly manner: this is a duty for all who are conscious of God"* (Surah al Baqara – The Cow 2:241). Another option is to make alimony and child support part of the terms of the marriage contract, which would come into effect only in case of divorce.[22]

The use of the contract to protect the rights of the wife is also important with regard to the manner in which she may initiate for divorce. In practice in Muslim societies, the husband is allowed to unilaterally divorce his wife, while the wife can only get a divorce through the intervention of a judge.[23] She may seek to circumvent this by including the delegated right to divorce, or *talak-i-tafwid*, in the marriage contract.[24] Another approach, one that we endorse, is that the marriage law include this element in all marriage contracts, and that it can only be waived by express consent on the part of the bride. The nation as a whole can write such a law through legislation as a reflection of its commitment to justice and equity in marital relations.

The wife also has the option of seeking divorce or seeking khul. The difference is that in case of divorce, she is also entitled to payment of the dower, if it hasn't already been paid to her. *Khul* means that she seeks a dissolution of the marriage in return for giving up her mahr. In some cases, this process may be faster if the husband refuses to pay her the mahr and so continues to drag out the divorce. Some Muslim countries have enacted legal reforms to counter this imbalance in the divorce rights of men versus those of women. For example, Malaysian law calls for both the husband and the wife to present their case to the court if either wants to initiate divorce. It therefore prevents the husband from exercising uncontrolled power of repudiation.[25] Egypt recently activated and facilitated the right of *khul*.

In sum, although the Quran does not view divorce favorably, it does not prohibit it either. It should be noted that most of the verses on the subject are addressed to men, and not to women. Given the historical context in which they were revealed, it is men who played the dominant role as part of a patriarchal society, and therefore to whom the admonition to behave justly towards their spouses was necessary. This is also the lens through which we must view the skewed nature of divorce rights between the sexes, given the fact that the text does not specify that women have a unilateral right to repudiation, or that they are entitled to alimony. But, this should not prevent us from interpreting the Quran today to reflect a greater congruence between societal roles for men and women and the general egalitarian principles advocated in the Quran.

This is illustrated nowhere more clearly than it is with regard to the issue of polygamy, which is the subject of the next section.

Polygamy

Polygamy, or co-marriage to multiple wives, is discussed in the Quran as a response to a specific social situation. In the context of war-torn society in seventh-century Arabia, one which left many women widowed and children orphaned, the discussion of polygamy was revealed as part of a directive to treat female orphans justly. It was not advocated as a carte blanche to all Muslim men to allow them to fulfill their sexual desires, as is commonly misinterpreted.

Polygamy should be viewed as a component of justice in the treatment of widows, but is mainly conditioned upon the need to offer fair care to orphans, according to the literal reading of the verse. It served a functional purpose for that time period, in allowing widows and orphans to be taken care of in a society in which women usually did not have independent means of financial support. But the text is clear that polygamy is only permissible if all wives are treated justly. The Quran then goes on to say that it will never be possible for a husband to treat all of his wives fairly. This effectively limits the possibility of polygamy today. A detailed rendering of the relevant verses in Surah an Nisaa follows.

"And if you have reason to fear that you might not act equitably towards orphans, then marry from among [other] women such as are lawful to you – [even] two, or three, or four: but if you have reason to fear that you might not be able to treat them with equal fairness, then [only] one – or [from among] those whom you rightfully possess. This will make it more likely that you will not deviate from the right course" (Surah an Nisaa – Women, 4:3). The first imperative in this verse is to deal justly with orphans, and is directed towards their male guardians who would be managing their property or wealth on their behalf. Marriage to female orphans is only advocated if and when the guardian fears that he will not be able to carry out his duty honestly. The assumption is that marriage to the orphan will give the husband a greater stake in carrying out his financial responsibility towards her. It does not by any means represent a requirement for all male guardians to marry their female wards. Second, the verse emphasizes justice towards the wife/wives as well. In other words, polygamy is only possible if the husband will be able to treat his wives justly. Otherwise, he is to marry only one wife, or even a female

slave.[26] The key theme is to prevent him from doing injustice towards the woman (or women) concerned.[27] *"And it will not be within your power to treat your wives with equal fairness, however much you may desire it; and so, do not allow yourselves to incline towards one to the exclusion of the other, leaving her in a state, as it were, of having and not having a husband. But if you put things to rights and are conscious of Him- behold, God is indeed much-forgiving, a dispenser of grace"* (Surah an Nisaa – Women, 4:129).

Polygamy is treated variably in the legal codes of different Muslim countries. While Tunisian and Moroccan personal status law prohibit polygamy altogether,[28] Syria, Iraq, Pakistan and Malaysia have made polygamy subject to court permission, and only granted when certain conditions are fulfilled. These "include the infertility of the existing wife, attainment of 'a lawful benefit', the just character of the husband and his financial ability to maintain a second wife. Some countries have also stipulated the consent of the existing wife to the proposed mar- riage, which must be given before the court."[29] However, these condi- tions do not have any express Quranic sanction, and are determined through social custom and practice.

In conclusion, we subscribe to monogamy as the preferred norm for marriages today. Polygamy is not necessary or relevant today for two main reasons. One, the specific historical context that legitimized polygamy does not exist today. Women have more choices allowing them to be financially independent, even in cases where they are widowed or orphaned. The second, and more compelling reason, is the imperative to do justice, which prohibits having multiple wives, since, as human beings, men cannot ever be perfectly fair and just among them.

Equality before the Courts

Justice before the courts is the right of all citizens, regardless of sex. However, Surah al Baqara, 2:282 is often used to cite the inferiority of women in a legal capacity because it calls for two female witnesses for every male witness in commercial transactions.

The verse states, *"O you who have attained to faith! Whenever you give or take credit for a stated term, set it down in writing. And let a scribe write it down equitably between you; and no scribe shall refuse to write as God has taught him: thus shall he write. And let him who contracts the debt dictate; and let him be conscious of God, his Sustainer, and not weaken anything of his undertaking. And if he who contracts the debt is weak of mind or body, or is not able to dictate himself, then let him who watches over his interests dictate equitably. And call upon two of your men to act as witnesses; and if two men are not available, then a man and two women from among such as are acceptable to you as witnesses, so that if one of them should make a mistake, the other could remind her. And the witness must not refuse [to give evidence] whenever they are called upon. And be not loath to write down every contractual provision, be it small or great, together with the time at which it falls due; this is more equitable in the sight of God, more reliable as evidence, and more likely to prevent you from having doubts [later]. If, however, [the transaction] concerns ready merchandise which you transfer directly unto one another, you will incur no sin if you do not write it down. And have witnesses whenever you trade with one another, but neither scribe nor witness must suffer harm; for if you do [them harm], behold, it will be sinful conduct on your part. And remain conscious of God, since it is God who teaches you [herewith] – and God has full knowledge of everything"* (Surah al Baqara – The Cow, 2:282).

Generalizing from this verse with regard to women's legal competence is misguided for several reasons. First, the verse deals primarily with the details for setting loans and other financial obligations that are deferred to a future date, and therefore the context for determining the number of witnesses is not that of gender relations. Second, the emphasis is on the importance of documenting faithfully such a transaction, by writing it down and acquiring witnesses to it. As such, it is the value of the documentation that is in question, not the value, or "worth" of the witnesses. This is illustrated in the phrase "so that if one of them errs, the other can remind her." Witnessing is merely a procedural detail, for the purpose of verifying the transaction. Third, illiteracy was common among women during the time period when this verse was revealed. Having two female witnesses who could only give oral testimony, and not written, was therefore necessary for corroboration purposes.[30]

The fact that the number and sex of the witnesses is a procedural detail is supported by a verse on testimony in adultery cases. Four witnesses are called for, regardless of whether they are men or women. Surah an Nur – The Light, (24:4): *"And as for those who accuse chaste women [of adultery], and then are unable to produce four witnesses [in support of their accusation], flog them with eighty stripes; and even after refuse to accept from them any testimony – since it is they, they that are truly depraved!"*. In other words, based solely on this verse, there is no gender requirement among the witnesses, such that it is necessary to have extra female witnesses if male witnesses are not available.[31]

The fact that the same number of witnesses is prescribed, without regard to sex, in divorce cases further supports the argument that Surah al Baqara, 2:282 is not meant to portray the overall inferiority of women. *"And so, when they are about to reach the end of their waiting-term, either retain them in a fair manner or part with them in a fair manner. And let two persons of [known] probity from among your own community witness [what you have decided]; and do yourselves bear true witness before God: thus are admonished all who believe in God and the Last Day. And unto everyone who is conscious of God, He [always] grants a way out [of unhappiness]"* (Surah al Talaq - Divorce, 65:2).

Similarly, taking an oath four times is prescribed for both men and women, if there are no witnesses to support an accusation of adultery by one spouse against another. Surah an Nur, 24:6 states, *"But [as for the wife, all] chastisement shall be averted from her by her calling*

God four times to witness and he is indeed telling a lie" (Surah an Nur – The Light, 24:8). In this instance, both men and women enjoy equality in the legal procedure and their respective roles, without regard to gender.

All of these verses discussing witnesses and testimony should be viewed in the context of the advancement of justice as a Quranic principle. It is the duty of all Muslims to uphold justice under all circumstances. Women are not considered to be less capable than men in pursuing justice, or in behaving in a just manner.

This reasoning also applies to their ability to be judges. While some jurists argue that women can only preside as judges in cases in which women's testimony is admissible based on traditional juristic notions (this would include all cases except *hudood* and retaliation cases), others argue that anyone who fulfills the eligibility requirements for the position can be a judge, citing Surah an Nisaa, 4:58 in support: *"Behold, God bids you to deliver all that you have been entrusted with unto those who are entitled thereto, and whenever you judge between people, to judge with justice. Verily, most excellent is what God exhorts you to do: verily, God is all-hearing, all-seeing!"* The argument hinges on what we consider to be the purpose of a judge's role. Since justice is the key, then anyone who is capable of fulfilling the "trust" that is inherent in the position of judge, and is able to "judge with justice" is eligible for the role. That is the correct interpretation from our standpoint. Egypt recently appointed a female judge in the field of general law.

Social Equality

Dress

Dress, modesty and sexuality are interrelated, because all three relate to the physical appearance of men and women. While modesty and sexuality are concepts that also have internal, psychological and emotional components, their external reflection is in the way a person is dressed and how they carry themselves. This section will detail an argument against a state-determined and state-enforced Islamic dress code for women by citing Quranic evidence indicating why dress is fundamentally an individual choice and cannot be tampered with by the state. This does not exclude having laws that prohibit indecent exposure or public nudity, since those are deemed necessary for maintaining public order.

A disproportionate emphasis on "Islamic dress" for Muslim women, as compared to that for Muslim men, has skewed this relationship. Part of this preoccupation stems from the idea that women's sexuality needs to be controlled more rigorously by enforcing a strict dress code, one that will limit the effect of their "female charms" on men who might otherwise be susceptible to temptation. Secondly, an "Islamic dress code" for women makes the external appearance the absolute, empirical indicator of modesty. In other words, intention and internal motivation have no role to play in defining a woman's moral behavior, as long as she conforms to the dress code in question. Thirdly, the responsibility for policing women's dress has been appropriated by Muslim males, individually and collectively in many Muslim communities, and excludes women altogether. Hence, we see the "morals police" in Iran and Saudi Arabia, enforcing the mandatory "Islamic" dress code for women in public places.

All three of these points are contrary to Quranic teaching on a number of counts. First, the Quran is emphatic about the equal responsibility of men and women, with regards to guarding their modesty. The Quran states, *"Tell the believing men to lower their gaze and to be mindful of their chastity: this will be the most conducive to their purity – [and,] verily, God is aware of all that they do"* (Surah an Nur – The Light, 24:30); and *"And tell the believing women to lower their gaze and to be mindful of their chastity"* This verse ends with *"And let them not display [more of] their charms to any but their husbands, or their fathers, or their husbands' fathers, or their sons, or their husbands' sons, or their brothers, or their brothers' sons, or their sisters' sons, or their womenfolk, or those whom they rightfully possess, or such male attendants as are beyond all sexual desire, or children that are as yet* unaware of women's nakedness; and let them not swing their legs [in walking] so as to draw attention to their hidden charms. And [always], O you believers – all of you – turn unto God in repentance, so that you might attain to a happy state!" (Surah an Nur – The Light, 24:31).[32] Therefore, it is an individual obligation to guard one's modesty, and not that of the state.

Two other verses also address all Muslims on this theme. *"And who are mindful of their chastity, [not giving way to their desires] with any but their spouses – that is, those whom they rightfully possess [through wedlock] - : for then, behold, they are free of all blame"* (Surah al Muminun – The Believers, 23:5-6)

"Verily, for all men and women who have surrendered themselves unto God, and all believing men and believing women, and all truly devout men and truly devout women, and all men and women who are true to their word, and all men and women who are patient in adversity, and all men and women who humble themselves [before God], and all men and women who give in charity, and all self-denying men and self-denying women, and all men and women who are mindful of their chastity, and all men and women who remember God unceasingly: for [all of] them has God readied forgiveness of sins and a mighty reward" (Surah al Ahzab, 33:35).

Modesty is linked to chastity in these verses, and enjoined upon everyone equally, by God. The Quran does not state that women's chastity requires greater vigilance than men's. In addition, the moral implications of modest and chaste behavior are not solely the responsibility of women.

Second, the contention that women are a source of enticement and temptation to men is also erroneous. The Quran does not consider women to be the source of original sin, seduction or temptation. Eve is not responsible for the expulsion of Adam and Eve from the Garden of Eden, as she is in Christian teaching. Both Adam and Eve are equally responsible, and bear equally the punishment given to them by God. It is later juristic tradition that links women to the issues of *'awra*[33] and *fitna*, and requires women to veil in public so as to limit their sexual impact on men. This argument does not have a Quranic basis, and takes away basic moral freedom from women, while absolving men of all moral responsibility for their sexual behavior.

Given that both men and women have equal moral responsibility for their sexual behavior, they are commanded to observe modesty in the context of particular degrees of relationships. Islam does not call for a denial of sexual identity altogether, but imposes limits on the context in which it is appropriate to express it. Clearly, the marital relationship is primary among the relationships within which both partners are free to express their sexual roles. This is mentioned in Surah al Muminun, 23:5-6, noted above. In a more general sense, for women, the injunction to *"not display their charms [in public] beyond what may [decently] be apparent thereof" does not include "their husbands, or their fathers, or their husband's fathers, or their sons, their husbands' sons, or their brothers, or their brothers' sons, or their sisters' sons, or their women-folk, or those whom they rightfully possess, or such male attendants as are beyond all sexual desire, or children that are as yet unaware of women's nakedness"* (Surah an Nur, 24:31).

The exact parameters of modesty are often culturally and socially determined. The discussion in this section so far has emphasized the general equality of men and women in maintaining modest dress and behavior as a matter of individual choice. But specifically, the principle has been interpreted differently with respect to cultural norms in various Muslim countries. While the Saudis consider the full length black *'abaya* to be appropriate dress, Afghani and Iranian women wear the *chador*, and Muslim women in other countries only cover their hair and do not wear a full-length coat or cloak over their clothes when they go out in public. The following verses discuss these varying interpretations more fully.

Referring back to Surah an Nur – The Light, 24:31, the text allows some degree of flexibility in interpretation. It states, *"And tell the believing women to lower their gaze and to be mindful of their chasti-*

ty, and not to display their charms [in public] beyond what may [decent-ly] be apparent thereof". The only exception to this is noted for elderly women, although modesty is still expected to be maintained. *"And [know that] women advanced in years, who no longer feel any sexual desire, incur no sin of they discard their [outer] garments, provided they do not aim at a showy display of [their] charms. But [even so,] it is better for them to abstain [from this]: and God is all-hearing, all-knowing"* (Surah an Nur – The Light, 24:60).

The key to modesty in both of these verses is that sexually explicit display and/or behavior that invites unnecessary attention is not allowed. Even if there are cultural variations in what is ordinarily appar-ent of a woman's beauty, depending on the society one is living in, there is a clear injunction that breasts must always be covered. This supports creating laws prohibiting indecent exposure.

The issue of who should veil and what part of the body should be veiled has been interpreted in various ways. For one thing, dress served to distinguish non-Muslim, slave girls from free, Muslim women in Medinan society, in order to protect the latter from harassment on the streets. Caliph Umar took this a step further and issued a legal injunc-tion that explicitly prohibited slave girls from imitating free women by covering their hair. The overlap between social stratification and a dress code for women demonstrates that multiple factors were at play in determining the latter.[34]

In addition, some jurists also argued that *"beyond what may [decent-ly] be apparent thereof"* (24:31) is what would appear by custom, nature or necessity. Slave women at that time did not have to cover their hair, face or arms because of necessity; the nature of their work required mobility in the public and private spheres. Relating to custom, early reports state that during the Prophet's (pbuh) time, women in Arab society often wore a long headdress that covered their hair, and also wore vests that left their chests exposed. Therefore, these authorities suggest that the Quranic verse in question was in specific response to this custom, when it called for women to "draw their veils over their bosoms."[35]

All of these points support the fact that there is no absolute definition of what part of the body should or should not be clothed, and whether this is a compulsory practice or a matter of choice by individual women, or a social class of women. Our argument is that the actual physical dress is merely an external reflection of internal modesty, which can only be judged by God and which it is the duty of all Muslims to guard. The Quran gives us leeway to interpret what is ordinarily apparent and what must be hidden of women's beauty and ornaments in the context of the society we live in. It is the individual choice of each woman how she chooses to define modest dress. Furthermore, there is no legal precedent for state enforcement of a dress code, either in the Prophet's (pbuh) time or that of the Rightly-Guided Caliphs.

In addition, we should note that the Quran is only addressing Muslims with regard to modest dress, and not non-Muslims. The most strict Islamic dress codes practiced in Saudi Arabia and Iran have no direct Quranic support. They are derived from a *hadith* that alleges that women should only expose their face and hands when in public. This *hadith* is highly problematical on two grounds. First, it is not supported by the Quran itself. Secondly, the chain of transmission does not go back to the Prophet (pbuh) and so must be considered a weak *hadith*. To burden women with such a restrictive dress code on such a poor foundation is not defensible. If a woman accepts the validity of this *hadith*, and wishes to live by it, that choice should be respected. But we disagree with those who would argue that this a clear Quranically-mandated requirement of all Muslim women. On practical grounds, it would be impossible for the state to first determine whether each person is Muslim or not, and then enforce a dress code upon them. As noted in various places throughout this work, it is not the state's responsibility to determine the religious faith of each citizen.

Therefore, a uniform, "Islamic dress code" imposed by men or by the state denies women their moral agency and freedom in making that choice, and is contrary to the autonomy which God has granted them. This does not exclude having laws against indecent exposure in terms of dress, or against public nudity, but these serve as a minimum standard for ensuring a general level of security.

Women's Seclusion

Hand in hand with insistence on strict "Islamic" dress codes for Muslim women, is the idea that women should lead secluded lives, remain primarily at home and avoid taking part in public affairs. If they must go to school and work outside the home, it should be primarily in female-dominated environments. At issue is not so much whether it is preferable for women with young children to stay at home, but whether all women should be forced by law or custom to stay at home. We argue that this choice should not be made for them simply because some think "Islam calls for it." This kind of thinking represents a sharp divergence from the active public lives that Muslim women led during the time of the Prophet (pbuh) and is not a Quranically-sanctioned interpretation of social roles for men and women. In fact there are no Quranic verses that call for the limiting of female social roles.

Quranic revelation on women's seclusion are directed solely to the Prophet's (pbuh) wives, because of their unique status. The Quran distinguishes between the esteemed status of the Prophet's (pbuh) wives and other women in Surah al Ahzab, so much so that any misconduct on their part would make them liable to double the punishment given to others. Note that the punishment is determined by God in the HereAfter; it does not call for a state-enforced temporal punishment. *"O wives of the Prophet! If any of you were to become guilty of manifestly immoral conduct, double [that of other sinners] would be her suffering [in the hereafter]: for that is indeed easy for God"* (Surah al Ahzab – The Confederates, 33:30). *"O wives of the Prophet! You are not like any of the [other] women, provided that you remain [truly] conscious of God. Hence, be not over-soft in your speech, lest any whose heart is diseased should be moved to desire [you]: but, withal, speak in a kindly way"* (Surah al Ahzab – The Confederates, 33:32-33).

The rest of the directive is towards those who came to the Prophet's (pbuh) to seek his counsel. *"O you who have attained to faith! Do not enter the Prophet's dwellings unless you are given leave; [and when invited] to a meal, do not come [so early as] to wait for it to be readied: but whenever you are invited, enter [at the proper time]; and when you have partaken of the meal, disperse without lingering for the sake of mere talk: that, behold, might give offense to the Prophet, and yet he might feel shy of [asking] you [to leave]: but God is not shy of [teaching you] what is right. And [as for the Prophet's wives,] whenever you ask them for anything that you need, ask them from behind a screen: this will but deepen the purity of your hearts and theirs. Moreover, it does not behoove you to give offense to God's Apostle – just as it would not behoove you ever to marry his widows after he has passed away: that, verily, would be an enormity in the sight of God"* (Surah al Ahzab – The Confederates, 33:53). This verse emphasizes the highest esteem that the Prophet's (pbuh) wives were and should be given, both during his lifetime and after his death. The purpose is to prevent their image and dignity from being tarnished by gossip or slander, even by accident. There is no implication in any of this for all Muslim women to follow a similar practice of seclusion.

In fact, these verses from Surah al Ahzab stand in contrast to reports of the active participation of women in public life during the Prophet's (pbuh) lifetime. For example, women participated in public discussions at the mosque, attended prayers and took part in battles in various capacities. They were among the individuals who pledged their allegiance to the Prophet (pbuh) on at least two occasions, known as the First Aqaba and Second Aqaba.[36] Reports also document women who would come up to the Prophet (pbuh) in the street, sit with him and discuss their problems.[37]

As a separate line of argument, we should note that, even assuming the conservative framework giving a primary maternal role for women in society, it is illogical to use this as a basis for permanently excluding women from public life. There are four related points to this argument. First, even if the vast majority of Muslim women were to accept the cultural prescription to marry early and have children, there will remain a small minority for whom this does not happen for any number of reasons. For example, some women never marry (in most societies women slightly outnumber men), some couples are infertile and never have children, some women may lose their children to disease or accident, some women get divorced and custody goes to the father, some women are widowed young and choose not to remarry and so remain childless. If we combine these groups together, then perhaps 5-10% of young women, even in a conservative Muslim society, will not have childrearing responsibilities. Therefore, they have no maternal obligation that prevents them from working, and even conservative Muslims should allow them to fully achieve what they can in the public sphere.

A second point is that women must also discharge the responsibility of enjoining the right and forbidding the wrong, alongside men. This includes both private acts within the family, and the pursuit of good works in society. Women must be free to participate in society in order to accomplish this Quranic imperative. These good works could include being a doctor or nurse, teaching, earning a high salary and donating sums to charity, creating a business that provides employment to other citizens, etc.

A third point is that in the classical time period, most women worked very hard in order to provide for their families. The vast majority of people lived in subsistence agriculture villages, and women did not simply provide moral instruction to their children. They were doing work to provide for their families. Even today if one goes to villages in Muslim countries, farm women do much of the agricultural work. Now that many live in a society in which paid employment has replaced agriculture to a large degree, women should also be able to engage in it, to provide for their family's well-being. The mother herself can best decide if this is truly necessary, not the state.

Finally, constraining women's roles based on the overriding need to provide constant mothering for young children ignores a basic demographic fact of the modern world. Assuming the conservative framework that women get married in their early 20's, have two or three children, and raise them to adulthood, they will have finished raising their children by age 45. At that time, they still have on average 30 more productive years in their lifespan. It is not for the state to say that they cannot pursue good works in public life in their remaining 30 years, when their maternal obligation has been fully discharged. In a modern context, a woman could pursue a career in her 20's, have children in her thirties and take a break to raise them, then return to her career later in life. To deny a woman the right to public life based on the need to be a mother for 25 years out of her life of 75 years is illogical. The overall decision of whether to participate in the labor force or other aspects of public life should be the responsibility of each woman as an individual. Only at that level can they decide what is truly in the best interest of their family.

Political Participation

The right of women to hold public office or to take part in political affairs has been the subject of controversy. Some scholars point to the Quranic text, Surah an Nisaa, 4:34 and Surah al Baqara, 2:228[38] as the basis for male superiority, and link it with the disputed *hadith* that "no nation whose affairs are led by a woman shall succeed"[39] to conclude that women are not allowed to hold public office in the government since they cannot be placed in positions of authority over men.

This reasoning is faulty for a number of reasons. First, the verses mentioned speak to a mutual exchange of rights and responsibilities that allow both men and women to be guardians and protectors of each other. It does not refer to inherent, biological superiority of men over women. The Quran does not advocate gender hierarchy of any sort, as was discussed earlier in this chapter.

Second, the *hadith* quoted above is in reference specifically to a female ruler of Persia and is not indicative of a general assumption. It also stands in contrast to what we know historically of the public role of women during the Prophet's (pbuh) time and that of the Caliphs. For example, when the Companions of the Prophet (pbuh) differed on a matter, on many occasions, they referred the case to A'isha, the

Prophet's (pbuh) wife. A'isha was also the first woman to lead a military campaign against a caliph, Caliph Ali, in 658A.D., to demand punishment for the assassins of Caliph Uthman. The battle is referred to as the Battle of the Camel, in reference to the camel that she rode, as the only woman in the battlefield, leading her troops.[40] In another instance, on the day of the Battle of Hudaybiyah, the Prophet (pbuh) consulted one of his wives, Umm Salamah, on a public issue and acted on her counsel. Caliph Umar also appointed a woman, Shifa' bint 'Abd Allah, to be in charge of market inspection in Medina, which is clearly a position that would place her in authority above men.[41] In another case, a woman publicly corrected Caliph Umar with regard to his proposal to place a quantitative limit on the dower, by citing a Quranic verse. The Caliph agreed with her.[42]

With regard to holding public office, we can point to Surah an Nisaa (4:58), which states *"Behold, God bids you to deliver all that you have been entrusted with unto those who are entitled thereto"*. The verse does not specify that women are not eligible for these trusts. Anyone who fulfills the necessary qualifications is entitled to serve.

Education

The pursuit of knowledge and the right to education, both religious and non-religious, is recognized in Islam for both men and women. A *hadith* that states, "pursuit of knowledge is a duty of every Muslim" supports this contention. Also, historically, we know that A'isha was recognized as a leading scholar among the Companions because of her knowledge of the Quran and the *Sunna*. The Prophet (pbuh) also employed a woman, to teach Hafsah, one of his wives, basic literacy and writing.[43]

The right to education as a basic human right is recognized in the first revelation that the Prophet (pbuh) received, which began with the word *"Iqra!"* or "Read!" Humans are unique in that they have been created with the capacity for speech and communication. *"The Most Gracious has imparted this Quran [unto man]. He has created man: He has imparted unto him articulate thought and speech"* (Surah al

Rahman, 55c:1-4). God teaches both Adam and the angels how to identify "the nature of all things" in Surah al Baqara, 2:31-33, and links teaching and gaining knowledge as desirable characteristics. *"And He imparted unto Adam the names of all things; then He brought them within the ken of the angels and said: 'Declare unto Me the names of these [things], if what you say is true.' They replied: 'Limitless art Thou in Thy glory! No knowledge have we save that which Thou hast imparted unto us. Verily, Thou alone art all-knowing, truly wise. Said He: 'O Adam, convey unto them the names of these [things].' And as soon as [Adam] had conveyed unto them their names, [God] said: 'Did I not say unto you, 'Verily, I alone know the hidden reality of the heavens and the earth, and know all that you bring into the open and all that you would conceal'?"*

Therefore, the opportunity to develop that innate capacity further, through formal education, is a basic right of all human beings, since God has already granted every human being the ability to learn. The state cannot limit anyone, male or female, from access to education and knowledge, and must, in fact, try to facilitate that access to the greatest extent possible.

In sum, seclusion is not mandated by the Quran for Muslim women. It has been culturally and historically interpreted as a mark of elite status, first regarding the Prophet's (pbuh) wives, and later that of the women of the aristocracy and royal families in Muslim-ruled lands. In recent history, however, it has been misguidedly used as a way to limit women's access to educational, political and social opportunities in Muslim countries, under the pretext of religion.

Conclusion

The issue of women's rights has long been used as an indicator of how "liberated" a society is, by Western standards. Particularly in Muslim societies, where the perceived stereotype is of "oppressed" Muslim women, women's rights are considered to be practically non-existent, due to Islam.

While there are Muslim countries, like formerly-Taliban-ruled Afghanistan, Pakistan and Saudi Arabia, which place severe restrictions on their female citizens by treating them as "second-class citizens," these restrictions stem from patriarchal cultural attitudes that are not necessarily also "Islamic." To the extent that their proponents claim to be enforcing an Islamically-mandated blueprint of gender relations, this blueprint represents a harsh, intolerant and misogynistic view of Islam that is contrary to the dignity, respect and freedom that are the rights of Muslim women, as granted to them by God.

Footnotes

1 Asma Barlas, *"Believing Women" in Islam: Unreading Patriarchal Interpretations of the Quran*, (Austin: University of Texas Press, 2002), p. 181.

2 Tahir Mahmood, ed., "The Islamic Law on Human Rights," *Human Rights in Islamic Law* (New Delhi: Institute of Objective Studies, 1993) p. 39.

3 Parveen Shaukat Ali, "Equality as a Basic Human Right in Islam," *Human Rights in Islamic Law*, ed. Tahir Mahmood (New Delhi: Institute of Objective Studies, 1993) p. 142.(118-152).

4 With regard to single or divorced women, it is their fathers or other legal male guardians who are legally responsible to provide materially for them, even if these women have jobs and an income of their own.

5 Amina Wadud, *Quran and Woman* (New York: Oxford University Press, 1999), pp. 87-88.

6 More on the dower in the next section on marriage and divorce.

7 Sheikh Showkat Husain, "Human Rights in Islamic Law: Principles and Precedents," *Human Rights in Islamic Law*, ed. Tahir Mahmood, (New Delhi: Institute of Objective Studies, 1993), p. 109; Jamal Badawi, "Gender Equity in Islam" World Assembly of Muslim Youth Study on Islam series.

8 *"Ye are forbidden to inherit women against their will"* (Surah an Nisaa, 4:19).

9 Shaheen Sardar Ali, *Gender and Human Rights in Islam and International Law*, (The Hague: Kluwer Law International, 2000), p. 153.

10 Shaf'i and Maliki schools allow a father to compel his daughter into marriage, while the Hanafi insist that the woman has final say in the matter. Similarly, the Shaf'i require the consent of the woman's guardian for a marriage to be valid, while Hanafis allow a woman to get married, despite family disapproval. Safi, p. 7. The legal age of majority is generally considered as that reached at puberty, but there is no fixed age that all legal schools agree upon.

11 See also Khaled Abou el Fadl's book, *Speaking in God's Name: Islamic Law, Authority and Women* (Oxford: Oneworld Publications, 2001).

12 Alternately, both the husband and wife can agree to waive the dower and that can be expressly stipulated in the marriage contract as well. This would not undermine the legal validity of the marriage itself.

13 Translation in Wadud, p. 70.

14 For more on the semantics and other implications of the Arabic term *fadala* (preference), see Wadud, pp. 69-74.

15 Wadud, p. 73.

16 Of course there is the possibility that some women may choose not to have children, or that some couples may not be able to have children. The verse should not be read then as absolving husbands of financial responsibility. The broader principle is reciprocity of rights and responsibilities in the marital relationship.

17 This interpretation comes from the second portion of Surah an Nisaa, 4:34. *"So good women are obedient, guarding in secret that which Allah has guarded. As for those from whom you fear [nushuz; disruption of marital harmony], admonish them, banish them to beds apart, and scourge them. Then, if they obey you, seek not a way against them."* Wadud's translation, p. 74. This will be discussed more in the section on violence against women in the chapter on Security of Person.

18 Khalid Abou el Fadl, *Speaking in God's Name: Islamic Law, Authority and Women* (Oxford: Oneworld Publications, 2001), pp. 214-215.

19 Barlas, p. 194.

20 We will examine the differing options for initiating divorce for the husband and wife at the end of this section.

21 Nasir, pp. 187-188. See also discussion of child custody in the chapter on Children's Rights.

22 Cassandra Balchin, ed., *Women, Law and Society, Women and Law,* Pakistan Country Project, (Lahore: WLUML/Shirkat Gah, 1996) p. 123.

23 Wadud, p. 68.

24 Ali, p. 158.

25 Wadud, p. 79.

26 This is specifically relevant to the social structure of Arabian society at the time, since female slaves or concubines were common. It should not be interpreted today as a sanction for slavery.

27 Barlas, pp. 190-191.

28 Tunisian Law of 1957 and the Moroccan Law of 1958, respectively.

29 Kamali, *Freedom, Equality and Justice in Islam,* p. 77.

30 Kamali, *Freedom, Equality and Justice in Islam,* p. 67; Miriam Cooke and Bruce B. Lawrence, "Muslim Women between Human Rights and Islamic Norms," *Religious Diversity and Human Rights,* ed. Bloom et al (New York: Columbia University Press, 1996), p. 325.

31 This is in contrast to juristic rulings which call for witnesses to be male. Our approach in this work is to emphasize the Quran over juristic rulings.

32 Surah an Nur, 24:31, in its entirety, reads *"And say to the believing women that they should lower their gaze and guard their modesty; that they should not display their beauty and ornaments except what (must ordinarily) appear thereof; that they should draw their veils over their bosoms and not display their beauty except to their husbands, their fathers, their husband's fathers, their sons, their husbands' sons, their brothers or their brothers' sons, or their sisters' sons, or their women, or the slaves whom their right hands possess, or male servants free of physical needs, or small children who have no sense of the shame of sex; and that they should not strike their feet in order to draw attention to their hidden ornaments. And O ye Believers! turn ye all together towards Allah, that ye may attain Bliss."* We will discuss it in portions in this section.

33 *'Awra* is defined as the private parts of a human being, for both men and women. Jurists discussed *'awra* primarily in the context of what should be covered during prayer. Its link to *fitna,* defined as moral temptation, enticement that will lead to sin, and in this case seduction, is a juristic tradition, not a Quranic one. The Qu'ran uses the word to refer to non-sexual temptations. Abou El Fadl, *Speaking in God's Name,* p. 233.

34 Abou El Fadl, *Speaking in God's Name,* pp. 240-241.

35 Abou El Fadl, *Speaking in God's Name,* p. 241.

36 There were 73 men and two women who accepted Islam and took the *baya* shortly before the *Hijra.* Al Marzouqi, p. 462; Kamali, *Freedom, Equality and Justice in Islam,* p. 72.

37 Abou El Fadl, *Speaking in God's Name,* p. 239.

38 The relevant part of this verse is *"And women shall have rights similar to the rights against them, according to what is equitable; but men have a degree (of advantage) over them."*

39 Attributed to Bukhari, Kamali, *Freedom, Equality and Justice in Islam,* p. 64.

40 Fatima Mernissi, *The Forgotten Queens of Islam* (Cambridge, UK: Polity Press, 1993), p. 66.

41 Kamali, *Freedom, Equality and Justice in Islam,* p. 72.

42 Hussain, *Human Rights in Islam,* p.50.

43 Kamali, *Freedom, Equality and Justice in Islam,* p. 74.

Non-Muslims

his chapter focuses on the status of non-Muslims within a Muslim-ruled state. The institution of dhimma (the formalized status of non-Muslims in Muslim lands, most prominently Ottoman Turkey) has sometimes been misused to justify the subordinate civil and political status of non-Muslims, in particular, of Jews and Christians. However, this paradigm does not have relevance for our contemporary understanding of citizenship rights of non-Muslims in a Muslim country. All citizens, regardless of religious identity, are entitled to equal respect and equal treatment before the law. This is part of the state's responsibility to uphold justice for all its people.

While the chapters on freedom of religion and citizenship rights elaborate on this line of argument some more, this chapter focuses specifically on the institution of *dhimma*, and the historical treatment of *dhimmi*s under Muslim rule. *Dhimmis* are defined as a "protected people" or "covenanted people", i.e. those (non-Muslims) who live peacefully amongst Muslims. It dates from the Treaty of Khaybar, which signaled the end of a battle at the oasis of Khaybar in 628.[1] The Jewish inhabitants of Khaybar surrendered to the Prophet's (pbuh) forces based on the terms of a treaty, known as the *dhimma*. According to these, they were allowed to continue cultivating their land, but had to give half of their produce to the Muslims as a tribute, known as *kharaj*,[2] and to pay the poll tax, known as *jizya*. On the part of the Prophet (pbuh), he undertook to defend them and to respect their religious practices.[3]

The main argument in this chapter is that the historical implications of the concept of the *dhimma* are limited. In the context of early Islamic history, it was a marker of political and legal status that identified the specific non-Muslims who fought against the Prophet (pbuh) and were defeated then decided to live within the Muslim polity. It did not refer to all non-Muslims for all times. While the Quran does state that the Prophet (pbuh) should fight those who have broken the treaty with the Muslims, it does not make this a general statement valid for all times. On the contrary, the Quran repeatedly emphasizes the equality of all human beings, of all faiths, before God.

However, the course of Islamic history frequently has departed from the nature of Quranic injunctions on the treatment of non-Muslims. Muslim rulers applied a flawed interpretation of the institution of the *dhimma*, to reflect a permanently unequal relationship between all Muslims and non-Muslims. Furthermore, the development of juristic rules affecting the status of non-Muslims added to this negative perspective.[4] Today, this body of jurisprudence has combined non-Muslim religious identity with an inferior political status. It is used to justify the "second class citizenship" given to non-Muslims in some Muslim countries, by denying them rights equal to Muslim citizens. This chapter argues that the institution of *dhimma*, as it was originally conceived of by the Prophet (pbuh) was not based on religious inferiority or superiority. But, in the following centuries, it has turned into a politico-legal institution that has been abused, ostensibly in the name of upholding religious practice. This application signifies an imperfect interpretation of the Quranic verses regarding those who fought the Prophet (pbuh), and which was then given religious legitimacy by jurists in the following centuries.

This chapter has three sections. In the first section, we refute the usual argument given in support of treating non-Muslims as inferior to Muslims. Our contention is that the Quranic injunction on the payment of *jizya* (a form of tax) was limited to a specific set of non-Muslims who were hostile to the Muslims, who had violated a treaty with them, and whom the Muslims were then compelled to fight. They then decided to live with the Muslims. They further decided that military duty would be optional, with those serving earning exemption from paying this tax. It does not denote the inferiority and subjugation of all non-Muslims, by any means; such a stance would contravene the principles of religious freedom and justice noted in the Quran.

The second section, on historical precedent, illustrates the variation in the treatment of non-Muslims, depending on the time period and the ruler. We illustrate the historical innovations that allowed the institution of *dhimma* to become a formalized system of social and legal rights, within a particular social context. History diverged from the Quranic emphasis on respect and equality that is the right of non-Muslims, and in doing so, led to their oppression and persecution. We criticize this behavior as stemming from an intolerant Islamic interpretation that is in contrast to the interpretation we have developed in this work.[5]

The last section on juristic opinions discusses the disagreements among the schools of traditional Islamic jurisprudence on various issues relating to non-Muslims. While there was an increasing historical tendency to deny non-Muslims equality with Muslim citizens as the juristic opinion developed, this does not mean that we must condone it blindly. Juristic opinion does not overturn Quranic emphasis on the equality of all human beings, and the need to do justice by all citizens before the law. We conclude with a reiteration of these principles.

Quran and Sunna on the Treatment of Non-Muslims

Relations between Muslims and non-Muslims are often viewed by some scholars in the context of hostility and constant conflict. This perspective mistakenly views *jihad* as "an institutionalized expression of Islam's hostile attitude towards non-Muslims"[6] and the *dhimma* as "legalized persecution."[7]

Surah at Tawbah – Repentance, 9:29 is cited in support of this perspective: *"[And] fight against those who – despite having been vouch-safed revelation [aforetime] – do not [truly] believe either in God or the Last Day, and do not consider forbidden that which God and His Apostle have forbidden, and do not follow the religion of truth [which God has enjoined upon them], till they [agree to] pay the exemption tax with a willing hand, after having been humbled [in war]."* We should emphasize that this verse was revealed in a historical context, and did not extend to all non-Muslims. This line of argument will be elaborated upon in the following pages.

With regard to the payment of the *jizya*, it was symbolic of the acceptance of Muslim rule by the non-Muslims who had actually fought against the Prophet (pbuh), and it included monetary compensation of some kind. In later times, *jizya* tax was levied on non-Muslims in lieu of providing military service to the state. Despite the fact that it was revealed with regard to specific circumstances, to the extent that it symbolizes acknowledgement of legitimate political authority, we can extend its meaning today to mean a formal public acknowledgement of the legitimate authority of the government by its citizens. It can be in the form of willingness to pay taxes, which all citizens are legally obligated to. Thus, non-Muslims should not be distinguished from Muslims as citizens today in an Islamic state, by being asked to "prove" their obedience through special payments.

Several other verses are also erroneously used to perpetuate an intolerant and hostile attitude towards the People of the Book. They should not be viewed as universal, generalized prescriptions about the relationship of Muslims with non-Muslims, but rather as specific injunctions that were revealed to the Prophet (pbuh) in the context of war.

"Now if the followers of earlier revelation had attained to [this kind of] faith, it would have been for their own good; [but only few] among them are believers, while most of them are iniquitous" (Surah al Imran – The House of Imran, 3:110).

"And fight in God's cause against those who wage war against you,

but do not commit aggression – for, verily, God does not love aggressors" (Surah al Baqara – The Cow, 2:190).

"Hence, fight against them until there is no more oppression and all worship is devoted to God alone; but if they desist, then all hostility shall cease, save against those who [willfully] do wrong" (Surah al Baqara – The Cow, 2:193).

"O you who have attained to faith! Do not take the Jews and Christians for your allies: they are but allies of one another – and whoever of you allies himself with them becomes, verily, one of them; behold, God does not guide such evildoers" (Surah al Maida – The Repast, 5:51). In this verse we take the Arabic word translated in a limited way as "friend" to mean specifically "superior protector" and is meant to signify political and military alliances, at a time of war that was based on religion not social friendship.

All four of these verses refer specifically to the Jews and Christians who actively fought against the Prophet (pbuh) and his army and who were defeated or surrendered voluntarily. They do not refer to all Jews and Christians, since Surah al Imran – The House of Imran, 3:110 also states that some of the People of the Book were in fact believers. Viewed as universal injunctions, these verses have been mistakenly interpreted to constitute a narrow, intolerant understanding of the position of the People of the Book and the institution of *dhimma*. We stress that these verses are only applicable in the specific historical context faced by the Prophet (pbuh) and his attempt to protect his community from non-Muslim tribes who turned against him.

The fallacy of an intolerant interpretation of these verses lies in the fact that it conflates submission to political authority, on the part of non-Muslims, with an imperative for religious submission, i.e. conversion to Islam. This is then used as license to humiliate non-Muslims, while implying that Muslims were being "tolerant" by merely humiliating them and making them paying the *jizya*, instead of just killing them outright. The subtext is a hierarchical understanding of Muslim-non-Muslims relations, one that condemns all non-Muslims to an inferior status on the basis of religious identity.

We strongly disagree with this perspective and challenge it on a number of points. One, we separate religious identity from concepts of power and hierarchy. Political submission does not automatically call for religious submission, and the identity of *dhimmis* derives from their political status, and not their religion. The Quranic prohibition on compulsion in matters of religion (Surah al Baqara – The Cow, 2:256) does not call for non-Muslims to be forced to convert as an aftereffect of war, (or in any other circumstances). Therefore, they are not being "favored" if they are not forced to convert, nor are they to be humiliated because of their religion.

Two, we critique the idea of citizenship in an Islamic state, one which privileges Muslims over non-Muslims in granting civil and political rights. Religious and political membership within the community are not necessarily synonymous. The equality of all human beings and the state's Islamic duty to do justice by all of its citizens compels the equal treatment of all citizens before the law, regardless of religious identity. This is supported by Quranic emphasis on the universal principles of Islam, such as freedom, justice and equality of all humans. It is also noted in the sharia, which protects the life, property, religion, intellect and family of all.

The basis for our argument lies in the spiritual and moral equality of Muslims and non-Muslims, which was discussed in detail in the chapter on Freedom of Religion. It expanded the definition of "faith" to include more than the religious practices of Islam or other revealed religions, but also the idea of achieving virtue through good conduct, which is not limited to any one religious community over another. For example, Surah al Imran – The House of Imran, 3:110, includes some members of the People of the Book among the community of believers.

Furthermore, all Muslims are not necessarily guaranteed salvation simply by virtue of being born Muslim. They are also judged by God on their conduct and moral actions, like everyone else. We will not delve into the details of the entire argument here, since it has already been discussed fully in another chapter. Instead, we reiterate the emphasis on the equality of all human beings as created by God, with the free will to make moral and spiritual choices. This is the starting point for the equal treatment of Muslims and non-Muslims in an Islamic state.

In contrast to the Quranic verses about enmity, we point to verses that stress the similarities and amicable relations between Muslims and People of the Book. For example, Surah al Maida – The Repast, 5:5 states, *"Today, all the good things of life have been made lawful to you. And the food of those who have been vouchsafed revelation aforetime is lawful to you, and your food is lawful to them. And [lawful to you are], in wedlock, women from among those who believe [in this divine writ], and, in wedlock, women from among those who have been vouchsafed revelation before your time – provided that you give them dowers, taking them in honest wedlock, not in fornication, nor as secret love-companions. But as for him who rejects belief [in God] – in vain will be all his works: for in the life to come he shall be among the lost"*

Surah al Mumtahanah – The Examined One, 60:7-9 emphasizes that hostility is to be directed only towards those non-Muslims who actively persecuted the Muslims and drove them out of their homes. It does not preclude all amiable interactions with non-Muslims altogether. *"[But] it may well be that God will bring about [mutual] affection between you [O believers] and some of those whom you [now] face as enemies: for, God is all-powerful – and God is much-forgiving, a dispenser of grace. As for such [of the unbelievers] as do not fight against you on account of [your] faith, and neither drive you forth from your homelands, God does not forbid you to show them kindness and to behave towards them with full equity: for, verily, God loves those who act equitably"* (Surah al Mumtahanah – The Examined One, 60:7-9).

These three verses of Surah al Mumtahanah – The Examined One were revealed in Medina, in the context of a state of war between Muslims and some non-Muslim tribes, in the 7th or 8th year of *Hijra*. This was sometime during the interval between the Treaty of Hudaybiyah and the fall of Mecca.[8] Thus, it speaks to a very specific set of circumstances under which the Muslims needed to be careful about whom they befriended, as they tried to build their own community, socially, politically and spiritually. We cannot generalize these verses as sanctioning the inferior treatment of all Jews and Christians as *dhimmis* for all time periods and contexts, since they clearly state the need to do justice and treat equitably those who have respected the Muslims. The emphasis on justice and equitable treatment is important to note, since it reflects a key theme in the Quran. The principle of justice is treated as the supreme Quranic value, one that does not vary with time, and therefore needs to be upheld uniformly in the treatment of non-Muslims under all circumstances.

The same emphasis on relations with non-Muslims in the context of war is indicated in Surah al Tauba. The first few verses deal with the conditions under which treaties with non-Muslims are valid, and when they are violated. They were revealed in A.H. 9, as the Prophet (pbuh) prepared to launch the campaign of Tabuk, against the Byzantine Empire.[9] The key point is that religious identity is secondary to the fact that some of the non-Muslims are party to a covenant with the Muslims. Hostility against non-Muslims is only permitted if they break the peace treaty with the Muslims. *"Respecting no tie and now protective obligation with regard to believer; and it is they, they who transgress the bounds of what is right!"* (Surah at Tawbah – Repentance, 9:10).

"But if they break their solemn pledges after having concluded a covenant, and revile your religion, then fight against these archetypes of faithlessness who, behold, have no [regard for their own] pledges, so that they might desist [from aggression]" (Surah at Tawbah – Repentance, 9:12-13).

Conversely, those who have maintained peaceful relations with Muslims are not to be considered enemies. *"But excepted shall be – from among those who ascribe divinity to aught beside God – [people] with whom you [O believers] have made a covenant and who thereafter have in no wise failed to fulfill their obligations towards you, and neither have aided anyone against you: observe, then, your covenant with them until the end of the term agreed with them. Verily, God loves those who are conscious of Him"* (Surah at Tawbah – Repentance, 9:4).

"How could they who ascribe divinity to aught beside God be granted a covenant by God and His Apostle, unless it be those [of them] with whom you [O believers] have made a covenant in the vicinity of the Inviolable House of Worship? [As for the latter,] so long as they remain true to you, be true to them: for, verily, God loves those who are conscious of Him" (Surah at Tawbah – Repentance, 9:7).

This brief citation of some verses of Surah at Tawbah - Repentance supports the argument that religious identity is not the main factor in the treatment of non-Muslims. They do not become inferior citizens by virtue of their religion. Rather, they are to be treated the same as Muslim citizens, both of whom profess their obedience to the legitimate political authority. However, even in the case of war today, between an Islamic state and a non-Muslim state, they cannot be used to make blanket generalizations about the treatment of non-Muslims. These verses were revealed to the Prophet (pbuh) in a specific historical circumstance, and their utility today needs to be tempered by an equal and in-depth application of the universal Quranic principles of justice.

The following two *hadith* can be quoted in support of the equal rights and obligations of non-Muslim citizens. "Beware that I myself shall be the opponent, on the Day of Judgment, of anyone who is unjust to a covenanted person, or burdens him with something he cannot bear, or takes something from him, or makes him suffer a loss without his valid consent."[10] According to another *hadith*, the Prophet (pbuh) said "I am the bearer of a trust to impose just retaliation in favor of the *dhimmis*." Having said this, he ordered the execution of a Muslim who had murdered a non-Muslim.[11]

This theme is also reflected in the Medinan document negotiated by the Prophet (pbuh) with the residents soon after his arrival in Medina in 622. Alternately referred to as the Constitution of Medina, or the Medina Charter, it is notable in that it gives us concrete, basic principles for governing the nascent city-state of Yathrib (later known as Medina). It creates the reality of a religiously pluralistic state. It grants moral and religious autonomy to the Jews and other non-Muslims, while stressing the mutual obligations of all of the communities in matters of security.[12] For example, the Charter states, in Article 16, "Whoever of the Jews follows us has the (same) help and support (as the believers), so as long as they are not wronged (by him) and he does not help (others) against them." Article 25 continues "The Jews of Banu' Awf are a community (umma) along with the believers. To the Jews their religion and to the Muslims their religion. (This applies) both to their clients and to themselves, with the exception of anyone who has done wrong or acted treacherously; he brings evil only on himself and on his household."[13]

This document clearly treats the Jews as equals, without insisting on their conversion to Islam as a requirement for signing the treaty. Thus, it serves as a counterexample to the perspective that demands all non-Muslims be treated as subordinates. The Prophet's (pbuh) example in this case stands in contrast to the intolerant and oppressive behavior of Muslim rulers in later centuries. The next section will discuss this historical aspect in more detail.

Historical Precedent

The fact is that the evidence for the inferior treatment of non-Muslims originates in historical precedent not from direct Quranic injunction. This makes it necessary to examine the changes in the political status of non-Muslims over time. We already noted earlier that the Quranic prescription on the imposition of *jizya* is limited to the context of war and hostility that prevailed during the Prophet's (pbuh) time. This section will discuss the historical experience regarding the imposition of *jizya* on non-Muslim peoples.

There have been both benevolent and tyrannical rulers in Islamic history, similar to the history of any other civilization, and their interpretation and application of Islamic laws has also been variable, depending on the time period and the region. Therefore, we cannot make blanket generalizations about the historical treatment of non-Muslims. However, we can identify historical trends and variations. In doing so, our purpose in this section is to demonstrate that the oppressive treatment of non-Muslims, which came to characterize Islamic history from the eighth century onwards, represents a deviance from the Quranic principles regarding the freedom and equality granted to non-Muslims, and the respect with which the Prophet (pbuh) and the Caliphs are reported to have treated them.

Beginning with the early caliphate, the kind and just treatment of non-Muslims is emphasized by Caliphs Abu Bakr, Umar and Ali. For example, under the rule of Abu Bakr, a treaty made by Khalid Bin Waleed on the conquest of Hira stated that if an elderly [non-Muslim] person became incapable of working, or fell sick, or became destitute, such that his co-religionists had to start giving him money, then his *jizya* would be remitted. He and his children would be allowed to receive a maintenance allowance from the public treasury as long as he lived in Muslim country. If he left, then the Muslims would not be under obligation to maintain his family.[14]

Caliph Umar ibn al Khattab advised his successors to fulfill their covenant and be good to non-Muslims, to defend them against aggression and not to cause them hardship.[15] He also lived up to this ideal during his own reign. An ordinance to his army commanders in Iraq stated "Take services from whichever mounted soldiers you feel the need and remit their *jizya*."[16] In one incident, a [non-Muslim] Syrian cultivator claimed that the army had trampled his crops. Caliph Umar ordered the payment of 10,000 dirhams to him as compensation out of the public treasury.[17] In another example similar to the one under Abu Bakr's rule, the Caliph saw an old man begging, in order to pay his jizya. He brought him back to his house, gave him some cash, and sent word to the treasury officer that the elderly, who could not earn their living, should be given stipends from the public treasury. He said, "It is not just that we derive benefit from men while they are young and drive them out when they are old."[18]

The Caliph Ali is similarly noted to have said, concerning non-Muslims, that "they only entered the covenant so that their lives and properties would be [protected] like our lives and properties."[19] This point is important because it highlights the underlying purpose of entering into a treaty with the ruler. The state has the ability to provide protection for its people and both Muslims and non-Muslims enter into a political contract with the state so that they are granted equal protection.

The equality with which all are to be treated before the law is illustrated when the Caliph lost his armor in the battle of Siffin. A few days later, he noticed a Christian wearing that armor. He referred the case to a judge, and both he and the Christian appeared before the judge, each arguing that it was his armor, but the Christian stated that his possession of it was proof of his ownership. Caliph Ali could not produce any witnesses to support his own claim to it. When the judge hesitated in pronouncing a verdict, given the Caliph's status, he exhorted the judge to disregard any such considerations. The judgment was in the Christian's favor, and the Caliph accepted it.[20]

Further evidence of Caliph Ali's just treatment of non-Muslims is apparent in a letter he wrote to Malik al-Ashtar, the governor of Egypt and its provinces, upon his (the latter's) appointment. "Infuse your heart with mercy, love and kindness for your subjects. Be not in face of them a voracious animal, counting them as easy prey, for they are of two kinds: either they are your brothers in religion or your equals in creation. Error catches them unaware, deficiencies overcome them, (evil deeds) are committed by them intentionally and by mistake. So grant them your pardon and your forgiveness to the same extent that you hope God will grant you His pardon and His forgiveness. For you are above them, and he who appointed you is above you, and God is above him who appointed you."[21] A key point in Caliph Ali's instructions is the emphasis on the equality of non-Muslims with Muslims, as "equals in Creation." Thus, there cannot be any justification for treating them as subordinates before the law. He concludes with the admonition to remember that God is watching over everyone, and to act with justice and humility, knowing that he will be ultimately accountable to God.

All of these examples from the rule of various Caliphs demonstrate the importance of justice and equality in the treatment of non-Muslims. They also illustrate the fact that non-Muslims are not inferior to Muslims in essential dignity and rights.

Historically, what distinguished a non-Muslim from a Muslim in socio-political terms? First and foremost, the imposition of the *jizya*, or the poll tax, was unique to non-Muslims, and marked them as a separate group. It can be argued that, in principle, the *jizya* represented a substitute to the *zakat* that was obligatory for Muslims to pay to the state. Since non-Muslim citizens could not be asked to pay the *zakat*, they were supposed to pay the *jizya*, assessed as a similar percentage of their income.[22] It was also used to denote exemption from military service.[23]

In practice, the assessment rate was at the ruler's discretion, and it differed from place to place.[24] In the early Caliphate period (632-661), jizya was often paid in crops or other goods, in addition to money. For example, some of the people of Bahrain paid in dates, while others paid one dinar. In Yemen, every adult male was to pay one dinar in money or its value in cloth. In another instance, the terms of the treaty that the Prophet (pbuh) made with the residents of Najran (a part of Arabia) included, among others,: 1) the payment of 2,000 cloaks of the value of 40 dirhams weight of silver, with deficiencies to be made up in the form of horses, camels, arms or provisions; 2) the supply of 30 horses, 30 camels and 30 coats of mail in the event of war in Yemen; these were to be replaced if destroyed.[25]

It wasn't until the Abbasid era (749-1258) that the *jizya* was formally denoted a head tax, to be paid by individuals in money. The fact that it also denoted an exemption from military service meant that those who were not eligible to fight, such as women, children, the elderly, the destitute and the sick, were excused from paying it. [26]

There is also variation in the manner in which *jizya* was to be paid to the tax collector. Some rulers exacted it as a form of humiliation. In a guide to the duties of a civil servant, the instructions for collecting the poll tax state: "It is to be collected without violence or flogging. [The *dhimmi*] has to stand while paying, and the officer who receives it sits. [He] has to be made to feel that he is an inferior person when he pays, he is not to be treated with honor."[27] Others ordered clemency and justice in the treatment of non-Muslims, as they paid the tax. In a text dating from the rule of Caliph Harun al Rashid (786-809), Abu Yusuf, a classical Muslim jurist, wrote, "In order to collect the payment of the poll tax, one must not beat the taxpayers nor expose them to the sun nor resort to other such methods, of inflict upon them repulsive physical torments. They must be shown gentleness."[28] This variation demonstrates that the treatment of non-Muslims was more the outcome of historical conditions rather than an awareness of Quranic injunctions.

The second marker of non-Muslim status was the imposition of the *kharaj*, or land tax. While the *jizya* has its basis in Quranic injunction, the *kharaj* was introduced by the Prophet (pbuh) as part of the Treaty of Khaybar. In return for continuing to use their lands, the Jews of Khaybar had to pay half their produce as tax.

In general, *kharaj* land was defined either as land conquered by Muslims, land abandoned by inhabitants who had fled, or land whose inhabitants decided to pay a tribute to the Muslims in exchange for retaining ownership. The *kharaj* was distinct from the *jizya* in that it went towards the protection and security of the land, and did not entitle non-Muslims to exemption from military service. It was analogous to the tithe collected from land-owning Muslims. Since it was a tax on arable land that remained in possession of its original owners, female owners were not exempt from it, as they were from the *jizya*. Payment was assessed on the basis of acreage, percentage of actual harvest, amount of the crop, and included a fixed amount as well. It was to be collected once a year.[29]

Both the *jizya* and the *kharaj* were fiscal markers of non-Muslim status which varied over time. This is not to say that Muslims were not taxed by their rulers, or enjoyed a dispensation that non-Muslims did not. In fact, both Muslim and non-Muslims were equally entitled to financial support from the state treasury, by virtue of contributing to it through their taxes. Since the state was obligated to dispense support to all the poor and the needy, without distinction, all citizens in need could benefit from it.[30]

The institution of *dhimma* started as a series of ad hoc, and probably oral, agreements between the Muslims and non-Muslim tribes in Arabia, where the key feature was the payment of the *jizya* and/or *kharaj* in exchange for protection. Other common features of these treaties might also have included the obligation for non-Muslims to provide shelter to Muslim travelers for one to three nights, to supply provisions if required, and to agree not to provide aid or comfort to the Muslims' enemies.[31] In return, non-Muslims were allowed to exercise freedom of conscience, property and religion. Only houses or churches that were abandoned by their owners could be appropriated by Muslims.

But over time, the institution came to be a strict system of formalized social and legal behavior that was designed to perpetuate the inferior status of non-Muslims. This rigorousness was reflected literally in provisions requiring them to wear distinctive badges or dress. In political terms, it meant a significant curtailing of civil liberties.

The Covenant of Umar is one such treaty that codifies this attitude. The historical authenticity of it is doubted.[32] Even if we accept the fact that it was fabricated by later historians, it requires examination, if only to illustrate the degree to which intolerant attitudes towards non-Muslims had taken root by the late 11th and 12th centuries. The covenant is reported to be a response to a request for a peace by the Syrian Christians. Its intention seems to be clearly to humiliate and subjugate the Christians, and represents a wide divergence from earlier Islamic precedent and Quranic principles. The basic points are as follows:

"The Christians undertake not to erect any new churches, monasteries, or monk hermitages, and not to repair those falling in ruin; to give hospitality to Muslim travelers for up to three days; not to shelter spies or harm the Muslims in any way; not to teach the Quran to their children; not to celebrate their religious services publicly; not to prevent any of their kinsfolk from freely embracing Islam; to show respect for the Muslims in various ways, such as rising in their presence; not to imitate the Muslims in matters of dress or hairstyle, to use their manner of language and their patronymics; not to use riding-beasts with saddles, or to bear any arms; not to have seals engraved in Arabic characters; not to sell alcoholic drinks; to shave the front of the hair and to wear the distinctive girdle or *zunnar*; not to parade the emblem of the cross publicly in Muslim quarters and markets, or to beat the *naqus* (wooden clappers used instead of bells to summon the faithful to worship) or to chant loudly; not to conduct public processions on Palm Sunday and at Easter; not to bury their dead in the same neighborhoods as Muslims are interred; not to keep slaves who have been the property of Muslims; and not to build houses which might overlook those of Muslims."[33]

While the conditions noted do not fit what is known historically about the conquest of Syria, which casts serious doubt on its authenticity, it is important to note that this degree of persecution and intolerance is in direct contrast to the freedom of conscience and religious and moral autonomy described in the Quran. Furthermore, it also contradicts the Prophet's (pbuh) treatment of non-Muslims, such that he did not impose any restriction on them in matters of dress or religious practice. Unfortunately, it reflects a period of generally strained Muslim-Christian relations, that began in the 8th century and continued to worsen.

Another historical innovation in the institution of *dhimma* was the inclusion of Hindus, who are not People of the Book, as subject to the jizya. The Moghul rulers had all exacted a tax from their Hindu subjects, until the reign of Akbar (1556-1605), who abolished the *jizya*.[34]

Akbar was also known for his policy of religious tolerance and open-mindedness. He abolished the pilgrimage tax on Hindus, permitted conversions from Islam to other religions, allowed public celebrations of all religious events, Muslim or non-Muslim, allowed construction of places of worship without hindrance, and employed Hindus, Muslims and Christians, without regard to religious considerations, in his government. [35] His two successors, Jahangir and Shah Jehan, continued this general policy of tolerance, if not as actively as Akbar.

However, Aurangzeb, who ruled the Moghul empire from 1658 to 1707, represented a departure from this precedent. He reinstated the *jizya* in 1669, as part of a general policy designed to create an "Islamic state" out of the empire. He was known to be exacting about the manner in which it was to be paid (only in person, and with due humility), and did not allow any exemptions from it (other than those generally granted to women, children, the poor, the elderly and the sick). Aurangzeb used the same method of three different rates of assessment, depending on the wealth/income of the payer, but his version placed a disproportionately greater burden on the poor. [36]

In conclusion, this section has surveyed the historical variation in the treatment of non-Muslims, both positive and negative. The oppression of non-Muslims cannot be justified, as derived from "Islamic tradition", since the "tradition" has differed so much, depending on the ruler. Also, one cannot claim that the behavior of all Muslim rulers is uniformly based on the Quran and/or *Sunna*, without regard to historical context. Nevertheless, we strongly condemn persecution of non-Muslims, on the basis of our Quranic interpretation given in the first section of this chapter, one that enjoins mutual respect and freedom and justice in the treatment of non-Muslims.

Juristic Opinions

While there is general agreement on the essential dignity and equality of all humans and the importance of justice in general among Muslim scholars, there remains dispute over the equality of all people before Islamic law. Although classical Muslim jurists devoted considerable effort to detailing the areas in which non-Muslims living under Muslim rule were granted autonomy, their assumption remained that, as a community, they were governed by separate rules when it came to certain issues, such as criminal justice, inheritance, and personal status laws. We argue that this differential practice of law needs to be examined critically in order to remove discriminatory practices against non-Muslims. "Separate but equal" treatment of non-Muslim minority groups is contrary to the universal command to do justice, as noted in the Quran.

Non-Muslims are entitled to equality in their treatment before the law. The state is responsible for ensuring justice and equity for all its citizens, as derived from their legal rights and duties, and not their religion. This is reflected as an absolute principle in the following verses. Justice is an Islamic duty, indicated in Surah an Nahl – The Bee, 16:90 *"Behold, God enjoins justice, and the doing of good, and generosity towards [one's] fellow-men; and He forbids all that is shameful and all that runs counter to reason, as well as envy; [and] He exhorts you [repeatedly] so that you might bear [all this] in mind."* Furthermore, it applies towards all mankind, without distinction, Surah an Nisaa – Women, 4:135 states, *"O you who have attained to faith! Be ever steadfast in upholding equity, bearing witness to the truth for the sake of God, even though it be against your own selves or your parents and kinsfolk. Whether the person concerned be rich or poor, God's claim takes precedence over [the claims of] either of them. Do not, then, follow your own desires, lest you swerve from justice: for if you distort [the truth], behold, God is indeed aware of all that you do!"* All of these Quranic verses are contrary to juristic restrictions on the treatment of non-Muslim before the law. Therefore, we need to move away from sole reliance on man-made juristic rulings when they depart from the spirit of equality enshrined in the Quran.

While some schools claim that a Muslim cannot be killed for killing a non-Muslim, the Hanafi position is that the "value" of a Muslim's life is no different from that of a non-Muslim's. In other words, human life cannot be valued as a function of the religious identity of the person, and justice applies equally to all who take a life, or commit a crime.[37] As mentioned in Surah al Maida – The Repast, 5:42, *"Hence, if they come to thee [for judgment], thou mayest either judge between them or leave them alone: for, if thou leave them alone, they cannot harm thee in any way. But if thou dost judge, judge between them with equity: verily, God knows those who act equitably"* There is no indication of a lower standard of justice for non-Muslims. We endorse the Hanafi position that all human life is equally valuable, and the state's commitment to justice and providing protection for all citizens demands that all murderers be subject to the same standards of legal punishments.

Another issue that needs to be reexamined today is the rules of inheritance between family members of different religions. As a traditional juristic opinion, non-Muslims were not allowed to inherit from Muslims, and vice versa. This juristic ruling comes out of the historical circumstances under which the Muslims who joined the Prophet (pbuh) in Medina had all left behind their non-Muslim Meccan family members, who were hostile to Islam. Since the Prophet's (pbuh) purpose was to create an *umma* which superseded the ties based on tribe and kinship, inheritance rights were also circumscribed by religious identity. However, one exception to this general ruling is the Hanafi position, which allows the legal admissibility of a bequest in favor of a non-Muslim, to overcome this problem in families where members might be of differing religions.[38] In addition, we can again refer to Surah al Mumtahina, 60:8, which considers justice and kindness to be the primary mode of dealing with non-Muslims who are not hostile to Muslims, and use it to remove the juristic bar on inheritance by non-Muslims from Muslims, and vice versa.

Juristic opinions developed in the centuries following the Prophet's (pbuh) death, and the legal scholars who carried out this difficult task were themselves influenced by the political and social conditions in which they worked. Therefore, there is variation among the rulings given by early Muslim jurists and those developed in later periods. As already noted in the previous section on historical precedent, the treatment of non-Muslims throughout Islamic history has varied considerably, such that it is oftentimes more the outcome of specific historical circumstances, rather than Quranic injunctions.

As an example of this variation, early Muslim jurists appeared to be closer in practice to the spirit behind the Prophet's (pbuh) and the Rightly-Guided Caliphs' treatment of non-Muslims. They granted full legal and moral autonomy to non-Muslims living under Muslim rule. Non-Muslims had the right to own property and businesses, to be employed in the government, and to engage in legal and economic transactions as the partners and associates of fellow Muslim citizens. [39] They enjoyed freedom of residence, worship, cultural and religious autonomy, including the right to collect taxes for their own institutions and provide religious education for their own community.[40] They were free to engage in practices that were otherwise forbidden to Muslims, such as trade in wine and pork in Christian towns.[41]

Their rights to personal safety and security of property stemmed from the Prophet's (pbuh) example at Khaybar. Regarding the Treaty of Khaybar, al-Shaybani writes that "the Prophet's (pbuh) spokesman announced that none of the property of the covenanter is permitted to them [the Muslims]. Also because they [the non-Muslims] have accepted the peace covenant so as they may enjoy their properties and rights on par with Muslims."[42] This is illustrated during the time of Caliph Umar, when a poor non-Muslim refused to sell her house to the local governor, who wanted to appropriate the land in order to enlarge the mosque. She took her complaint to the Caliph, who ordered the house returned to her, and reprimanded the governor for forcing her to give it up.[43] Both of these examples indicate the legal equality granted to non-Muslims by Muslim rulers.

In practice as well, with regard to employment in government positions, non-Muslims were allowed to hold public office, including that of a judge or a minister. For example, many gained influential positions and were employed in large numbers under the Ummayyads and the Abbasids. They also served in ministerial positions, as army commanders and chiefs of religious schools during the time of the Rightly Guided Caliphs.[44]

However, in the later centuries of Islamic rule, jurists developed a notably more restrictive body of jurisprudence regarding the civil and religious rights of non-Muslims, and the example set by the Prophet (pbuh) for co-existence among differing religious communities came to be disregarded. Safi notes that starting in the eighth century, these rules treated non-Muslims living under Islamic political rule as second-class citizens inferior to Muslims in civil, political and social rights. We need to stress that these limitations on the freedom of non-Muslims come out of historical practice, and an intolerant interpretation of Islam, and did not stem from the entire religion itself.

In conclusion, this discussion on juristic opinion is meant to indicate the gap between the spirit of the Quran in treating non-Muslims and Muslims as equals, and the classical interpretations of jurists who singled out non-Muslims as a separate community with separate rights. Separate but equal treatment of non-Muslim minorities does not constitute justice. We have discussed areas which require re-interpretation in order to move away from restrictive juristic opinions, and closer to the Quran as the primary source for determining the legal implications for the treatment of non-Muslims in a contemporary Islamic state.

Conclusion

The institution of *dhimma* has historically been used to justify the subordinate civil and political status of non-Muslims, in particular, of Jews and Christians. However, this paradigm does not have relevance for our contemporary understanding of citizenship rights of non-Muslims in a Muslim country. All citizens, regardless of religious identity, are entitled to equal respect and equal treatment before the law. This is part of the state's responsibility to uphold justice for all its people.

As noted earlier, the original purpose of the treaty between non-Muslims and the Prophet (pbuh) was to guarantee them protection in return for their obedience to his political authority. This ultimately turned into a historically-legitimized sanction for oppression and legal and political discrimination against non-Muslims by Muslim rulers, which is contrary to a tolerant interpretation of the Quran. This change over time need to be kept in mind when re-evaluating the status of non-Muslims in the sharia today.

We have advanced a tolerant, inclusive interpretation of Islam in this chapter, one that calls for the equal treatment of all citizens in an Islamic state with respect, and the preservation of their legal and political rights without regard to religious identity.

The category of *dhimmis* was originally a political category, one that was used to identify a very specific group of hostile opponents to the Prophet (pbuh), and not necessarily all non-Muslims. The fact that it was later fused with ideas of religious inferiority of non-Muslims gave rise to persecution that, unfortunately, has persisted until today and represents a gross misuse of religion to justify discrimination by Muslim states against their non-Muslim citizens. We strongly condemn this behavior that is contrary to the fundamental teachings of the Quran.

Footnotes

1   The battle was against the Jewish tribes who were hostile to the Prophet (pbuh) and the Muslims. It took place after the Treaty of Hudaybiyah was made with the Meccans, ensuring ten years of peace between the two parties.

2   "*Kharaj*," *The Oxford Encyclopedia of the Modern Islamic World*, vol. 2, ed. John Esposito (New York and Oxford: Oxford University Press, 1995) p.417.

3   Ye'or, p. 44.

4   Ann Elizabeth Mayer, *Islam and Human Rights*, 3rd ed. (Boulder: Westview Press, 1999) pp. 134-135.

5   See also chapter on freedom of religion.

6   Kamali, *Freedom, Equality and Justice in Islam*, p. 79.

7   Bat Ye'or, *The Dhimmi: Jews and Christians Under Islam* (London and Toronto: Associated University Press, 1985), p. 48.

8   Abdullah Yusuf Ali, *The Holy Qur'an* (Riyadh: Dar El-Liwaa Publishing,) p. 1530.

9   Yusuf Ali, p. 436.

10 Abu Dawd, quoted in Kamali, *Freedom, Equality and Justice in Islam*, p. 83.

11 Cited in Kamali, *Freedom, Equality and Justice in Islam*, p. 83.

12 See chapter on constitutionalism for a more detailed discussion on this.

13 Muhammad Hamidullah, *The First Written-Constitution in the World* (Lahore: Sh. Mohammad Ashraf, 1968).

14 Quoted in Shaikh Shaukat Hussain, *Human Rights in Islam* (New Delhi: Kitab Bhavan, 1990) p. 59.

15 Kamali, Freedom, *Equality and Justice in Islam*, p. 83.

16 Hussain, p. 59.

17 Hussain, p. 60.

18 Hussain, p. 60.

19 Kamali, *Freedom, Equality and Justice in Islam*, p. 83.

20 Hussain, p. 60.

21 Quoted in Sachedina, *Islamic Roots of Democratic Pluralism*, p. 110.

22 "Jizya," *The Oxford Encyclopedia of the Modern Islamic World*, p. 378.

23 "Jizya," *The Oxford Encyclopedia of the Modern Islamic World*, p. 377.

24 There is juristic disagreement as to what the *jizya* rate should be, whether or not it is a fixed rate or left to the ruler's discretion. In practice, the lack of detailed guidance in the Quran and *hadith* about this issue has resulted in variable application throughout history.

25 A.S. Tritton, *The Caliphs and Their Non-Muslim Subjects* (London: Frank Cass & Co., 1970), pp. 203-204.

26 Ye'or, p. 53.

27 Tritton, p. 227.

28 Abu Yousuf, "Fate of the Annexed Territories and the Conquered Peoples", transl. in Ye'or, p. 168.

29 "Kharaj," *The Oxford Encyclopedia of the Modern Islamic World*, p. 417

30 Kamali, *Freedom, Equality and Justice in Islam*, p. 91.

31 C.E. Bosworth, "The Concept of Dhimma in Early Islam," *Christians and Jews in the Ottoman Empire*, vol. 1, ed. B. Braude and B. Lewis (New York: Holmes and Meieir Publishers, 1982), p. 44-45.

32 Both Bosworth and Tritton, respectively, argue that this Covenant did not really exist, but they note that the intolerant attitude of it is cited in various historical works, the authors of which claim that it originates in an earlier time period.

33 Bosworth, p. 46.

34 Sri Ram Sharma, *The Religious Policy of the Mughul Emperors* (New Delhi: Munshiram Manoharlal Publishers, 1988), p. 19.

35 Sharma, p. 60.

36 Sharma, pp. 153-154.

37 Kamali, *Freedom, Equality and Justice in Islam*, pp. 84-85.

38 Kamali, *Freedom, Equality and Justice in Islam*, p. 89.

39 Kamali, *Freedom, Equality and Justice in Islam*, p. 90.

40 Ye'or, p. 49.

41 Safi, p. 6.

42 Muhammad b. al Hasan al-Shaybani, translated and cited in Louay M. Safi "Human Rights and Islamic Legal Reform" p. 6.

43 Kamali, *Freedom, Equality and Justice in Islam*, p. 89.

44 Kamali, *Freedom, Equality and Justice in Islam*, p. 90.

CHAPTER NINE

Property Rights

"Verily your blood (lives) and your property and your honor are as sacred unto you as sacred is this day of yours, in this month of yours, in this city of yours. Let him who is present convey it to one who is absent."[1] This was part of the Prophet's (pbuh) Farewell Pilgrimage address to the Muslims. This emphasis on the protection of property rights is noted in the Quran and is also a vital component of the normative goals and substance of the *sharia*.

This chapter explores property rights from spiritual, legal and historical perspectives, arguing that the protection of private property rights for all citizens is part of an Islamic vision of a just society. The first section of the chapter discusses the concept of ownership and property rights from the Quran and *hadith*. The second section applies this framework to non-Muslims, illustrating the existence of equal legal protection of property rights of non-Muslims in the early Islamic state. The third part of this chapter delves into the legal aspect of property rights by examining three categories of legal ownership, public, private and state, with an emphasis on private property. Lastly, we situate this topic within the context of a discussion on capitalism, and argue that Islamic principles are compatible with a capitalist framework that upholds, among other issues, private property rights.

Islamic Perspective on Ownership/Property Rights

Human beings are not prohibited from enjoying the fruits of their labor, resulting in the acquisition of wealth and property in the temporal world. But, from an Islamic perspective, material ownership or possession is not an absolute right, since ultimately, everything belongs to God, as part of the bounty that He has bestowed upon human beings. This idea is described as "dual ownership," meaning that, theoretically, man shares with God ownership rights over material property.[2] It is also related to the concept of humans as the vicegerents of God on earth, noted in Surah al Anam – Cattle. *"For, He it is who has made you inherit the earth, and has raised some of you by degrees above others, so that He might try you by means of what He has bestowed upon you. Verily, thy Sustainer is swift in retribution: yet, behold, He is indeed much-forgiving, a dispenser of grace"* (Surah al Anam – Cattle, 6:165). This larger context of man's relationship with God is juxtaposed with a more specific look at property rights, especially with regard to inheritance, in this first section.

A number of verses in the Quran refer to the supreme power of God, and the gifts He has made available to mankind. These include natural resources, food, and other material comforts. Humans share in the ownership of these with God.

"Say: 'Who is there to forbid the beauty which God has brought forth for His creatures, and the good things from among the means of sustenance?'" (Surah al Araf – The Faculty of Discernment, 7:32).

"For among His wonders is this: He send forth [His messages as He sends forth] the winds that bear glad tidings, so that He might give you a taste of His grace [through life-giving rains], and that ships might sail at His behest, and that you might go about in quest of some of His bounties, and that you might have cause to be grateful" (Surah al Rum – The Bynzantines, 30:46).

"Who has made the earth a resting-place for you and the sky a canopy, and has sent down water from the sky and thereby brought forth fruits for your sustenance: do not, then, claim that there is any power that could rival God, when you know [that He is One]" (Surah al Baqara – The Cow, 2:22).

"[And remember that] it is God who has created the heavens and the earth, and who sends down water from the sky and thereby brings

forth [all manner] of fruits for your sustenance; and who has made ships
subservient to you, so that they may sail through the sea at His behest;
and has made the rivers subservient [to His laws, so that they be of use]
to you; and has made the sun and the moon, both of them constant
upon their courses, subservient [to His laws, so that they be of use] to
you; and has made the night and the day subservient [to His laws, so
that they be of use] to you. And [always] does He give you something
out of what you may be asking of Him; and should you try to count
God's blessings, you could never compute them. [And yet,] behold,
man is indeed most persistent in wrongdoing, stubbornly ingrate!"
(Surah al Ibrahim – Abraham, 14:32-34).

"He it is who has made the earth easy to live upon: go about, then,
in all its regions, and partake of the sustenance which He provides: but
[always bear in mind that] unto Him you shall be resurrected" (Surah
Mulk – Dominion, 67:15).

Implicit in all of these verses is the idea of man as the vicegerent of
God on earth, and, as a result, entitled to use the resources available for
his benefit. But, in return for this largesse, God asks humans to remember their faith and to give thanks for what they have. Wealth is a part
of life's moral test, since individuals are asked to spend of their wealth
in charity, as part of their faith. "Do they think that by all the wealth
and offspring with which We provide them We [but want to] make
them vie with one another in doing [what they consider] good works?
Nay, but they do not perceive [their error]! Verily, [only] they who
stand in reverent awe of their Sustainer, and who believe in their
Sustainer's messages, and who do not ascribe divinity to aught but their
Sustainer, and who give whatever they [have to] give with their hearts
trembling at the thought that unto their Sustainer they must return: it
is they who vie with one another in doing good works, and it is they
who outrun [all others] in attaining to them!" (Surah al Muminun –
The Believers, 23:55-61).

God stresses the fact that material luxuries and their acquisition is
not the goal of life. In fact, to get caught up in material acquisition is

to neglect other duties of worship, such as giving charity and doing good work, which are more important in the eyes of God, and ultimately more relevant to one's spiritual well-being. *"Believe in God and His Apostle, and spend on others out of that of which He has made you trustees: for, those of you who have attained to faith and who spend freely [in God's cause] shall have a great reward"* (Surah al Hadid – Iron, 57:7).

The Quran highlights the negative implications for those who are too wedded to their material possessions. The first is in this verse from Surah Tawba. *"Say: 'If your fathers and your sons and your brothers and your spouses and your clan, and the worldly goods which you have acquired, and the commerce whereof you fear a decline, and the dwellings in which you take pleasure – [if all these] are dearer to you than God and His Apostle and the struggle in His cause, then wait until God makes his manifest His will; and [know that] God does not grace iniquitous folk with His guidance'"* (Surah Tawba – Repentance, 9:24). It lists the issues that distract people from their moral and spiritual orientation towards God, including undue attachment to family, wealth, trade, or property.

The example of Qarun,[3] who rose up in rebellion against Moses and Aaron, and whose conceit and arrogance over his wealth led to his eventual downfall also stands as a strong injunction against material greed. *"[Now,] behold, Qarun was one of the people of Moses; but he arrogantly exalted himself above them – simple because We had granted him such riches that his treasure-chests alone would surely have been too heavy a burden for a troop of ten men or even more. When [they perceived his arrogance,] his people said unto him: 'Exult not [in thy wealth], for, verily, God does not love those who exult [in things vain]! Seek instead, by means of what God has granted thee, [the good of] the life to come, without forgetting, withal, thine own [rightful] share in this world; and do good [unto others] as God has done good unto thee; and seek not to spread corruption on earth: for, verily, God does not love the spreaders of corruption!'"* (Surah al Qasas – The Story, 28:76-77).

Lastly, verse 180 of Surah al Imran – The House of Imran warns people of dire consequences on the Day of Judgment, against those who hoard their material wealth and refuse to share God's Bounty with others. *"And they should not think – they who niggardly cling to all that God has granted them out of His bounty – that this is good for them: nay, it is bad for them. That to which they [so] niggardly cling will, on the Day of Resurrection, be hung about their necks: for unto God [alone] belongs the heritage of the heavens and of the earth; and God is aware of all that you do"* (Surah al Imran – The House of Imran, 3:180).

As the discussion has illustrated thus far, faith is an important component of man's role on earth. Although human beings are entitled to enjoy their material comforts and the fruits of their labor, that material ownership is part of the larger spiritual relationship between man and God. The point is that wealth is not evil, but rather a means by which God tests the faith of those who have been granted wealth, in a manner similar to which he tests the faith of those who suffer poverty.

Coming back to property rights in a more temporal sense, ownership of property is viewed as a trust, one that comes with certain responsibilities and obligations. The Quran outlines three main points on this issue. First, a person acquires a private right over property, whether of ownership or priority of use, through his efforts. *"And that nought shall be accounted unto man but what he is striving for; and that in time [the nature of] all his striving will be shown [to him in its true light]"* (Surah al Najm – The Unfolding, 53:39-40). Second, his efforts must be through lawful means, and not through indulging in illegal activities. Once acquired, the property must be used productively, and not wasted or squandered. *"Beautify yourselves for every act of worship, and eat and drink [freely], but do not waste: verily, He does not love the wasteful!"* (Surah al Araf – The Faculty of Discernment, 7:31). Lastly, the individual has to pay any obligatory taxes or zakat on it, as well as fulfill his financial obligations towards his family and community members. *"Believe in God and His Apostle, and spend on others out of that of* which He has made you trustees: for, those of you who have attained to faith and who spend freely [in God's cause] shall have a great reward" (Surah al Hadid – Iron, 57:7). The following verses elaborate further on these three points.

"O you who have attained to faith! Do not devour one another's possessions wrongfully – not even by way of trade based on mutual agreement – and do not destroy one another: for, behold, God is indeed a dispenser of grace unto you!" (Surah al Nisa – Women, 4:29). Acquisition or use of property should not be in deliberately wasteful or frivolous manner. Buying or selling it on mutually acceptable terms, i.e. through trade, is one lawful means of acquisition. Certainly, acquiring property by illegal means is not acceptable. *"And as for him who does this with malicious intent and a will to do wrong – him shall We, in time, cause to endure [suffering through] fire: for this is indeed easy for God"* (Surah al Nisa – Women, 4:30).

God's disapproval of acquiring property through unjust means is outlined in this *hadith*. "There came a person from Hadramaut and another one from Kinda to the Apostle (pbuh). One who had come from Hadramaut said: Messenger of Allah, only this man has appropriated my land which belonged to my father. The one who had came from Kinda contended. This is my land and is in my possession: I cultivate it. There is no right for him in it. The Messenger of Allah said to the Hadramite: Have you any evidence (to support you)? He replied in the negative. He (the Apostle of Allah) said: Then your case is to be decided on his oath. He (the Hadramite) said: Messenger of Allah, he is a liar and cares not what he swears and has no regard for anything. Upon this he (the Messenger of Allah) remarked: For you then there is no other help to it. He (the man from Kinda) set out to take an oath. When he turned his back the Messenger of Allah (pbuh) observed: If he took an oath on his property with a view to usurping it, he would certainly meet his Lord in a state that He would turn away from him."[4]

The same emphasis on upright behavior in ownership and property rights is echoed in Surah al Baqara – The Cow, 2:188. *"And devour not* one another's possessions wrongfully, and neither employ legal artifices with a view to devouring sinfully, and knowingly, anything that by right belongs to others". Again, there is the disapproval of wastefulness or illegal means. But, those illegal means are spelled out more specifically here: engaging in fraud, bribery, corruption or any other unlawful means that may hurt others' interests in order to secure property.

Once acquired, the "just use" of property means that the income derived from it is not solely the absolute right of the owner, but needs to be shared with less fortunate members of society through the payment of *zakat*, for example. *"And [would assign] in all that they possessed a due share unto such as might ask [for help] and such as might suffering privation"* (Surah adh Dhariyat – The Dust Scattering Winds, 51:19). The same sentiment is also noted in Surah al Maarij – The Ways of Ascent, 70:24-25. *"And in whose possessions there is a due share acknowledged [by them], for such as ask [for help] and such as are deprived [of what is good in life]"*

The balance between individual earnings and the distribution of wealth/property is noted in Surah al Nisaa - Women. *"Hence, do not covet the bounties which God has bestowed more abundantly on some of you than on others. Men shall have a benefit from what they earn, and women shall have a benefit from what they earn. Ask, therefore, God [to give you] out of His bounty: behold, God has indeed full knowledge of everything. And unto everyone have We appointed heirs to what he may leave behind: parents, and near kinsfolk, and those to whom you have pledged your troth: give them, therefore, their share. Behold, God is indeed a witness unto everything"* (Surah al Nisaa – Women, 4:32-33).

Turning to the inheritance of property, that division must be conducted fairly and justly. *"Men shall have a share in what parents and kinsfolk leave behind, and women shall have a share in what parents and kinsfolk leave behind, whether it be little or much – a share ordained [by God]"* (Surah al Nisaa – Women, 4:7).

"And when [other] near of kin and orphans and needy persons are

present at the distribution [of inheritance], give them something thereof for their sustenance, and speak unto them in a kindly way. And let them stand in awe [of God], those [legal heirs] – who, if they [themselves] had to leave behind weak offspring, would feel fear on their account – and let them remain conscious of God, and let them speak [to the poor] in a just manner" (Surah al Nisa – Women 4:8-9). Man's duty to deal justly with the income and division of property is linked to his relationship with God, stressed in the injunction to "fear Allah" and to "have the same fear in their minds as they would have for their own if they had left a helpless family behind." This serves to underscore the nature of the obligation, both legal and spiritual, to act with justice in property matters.

Bukhari notes this in a *hadith* emphasizing the importance of fulfilling one's obligations towards one's heirs in the division of property. The Prophet (pbuh) went to visit a dying man in Mecca, who was concerned about the division of his property after his death. "Narrated Sad bin Abu Waqqas: The Prophet came visiting me while I was (sick) in Mecca. I said, 'O Allah's Apostle! May I will all my property (in charity)?' He said, 'No.' I said, 'Then may I will half of it?' He said, 'No.' I said, 'One third?' He said: 'Yes, one third, yet even one third is too much. It is better for you to leave your inheritors wealthy than to leave them poor begging others, and whatever you spend for Allah's sake will be considered as a charitable deed even the handful of food you put in your wife's mouth. Allah may lengthen your age so that some people may benefit by you, and some others be harmed by you." At that time Sad had only one daughter.'⁵ The import of this *hadith* is that obligations to one's family supersede those of charity in the division of property. But, in one's lifetime, giving to charity (from one's wealth and property) is commendable and preferred over waiting to do so as part of the division of the estate after the individual's death. In addition, although Sad was told not to give most of his estate to charity, the reason for this was clearly to prevent destitution on the part of his family. If Sad was an extremely wealthy man, and could have provided adequately for his family out of small part of his estate, then the vast bulk of the estate could have been given to charity and still be in keeping with this *hadith*. We would find it absurd that a billionaire would feel religiously obligated to provide two-thirds of his estate to his immediate family.

The concept of property rights as a trust is demonstrated most clearly in the Quranic passages on administering the property of those unable to do it for themselves: orphan children and the mentally incompetent. Regarding orphans, the Quran states: *"Behold, those who sinfully devour the possessions of orphans but fill their bellies with fire: for [in the life to come] they will have to endure a blazing flame!"* (Surah al Nisaa – Women, 4:10). *"And test the orphans [in your charge] until they reach a marriageable age; then, if you find them to be mature of mind, hand over to them their possessions; and do not consume them by wasteful spending, and in haste, ere they grow up. And let him who is rich abstain entirely [from his ward's property]; and let him who is poor partake thereof in a fair manner. And when you hand over to them possessions, let there be witnesses on their behalf – although none cane take count as God does"* (Surah al Nisaa – Women, 4:6).

These verses primarily address the issue of fiduciary responsibility with respect to the property of orphans. The guardian must act with integrity and oversee the property in a just manner. He is not allowed to waste it, and may draw a small stipend from the estate, if necessary to support himself, while he acts as a trustee. The same responsibility applies to the guardians of those deemed (legally) mentally incompetent to administer their own property. In these cases, the trustee should use the property to support the heirs and make sure their needs are taken care of in a just manner. *"And do not entrust to those who are weak of judgment the possessions which God has placed in your charge for [their] support; but let them have their sustenance therefrom, and clothe them, and speak unto them in a kindly way"* (Surah al Nisa – Women, 4:5).

In conclusion, this section has outlined an Islamic perspective on ownership and property rights. There are two main points worth underlining from this discussion. One, humans are not the absolute owners of material possessions, since ultimately, everything in this world belongs to God. Human beings are reminded of this spiritual aspect to their material lives, even as their individual productivity and hard work are rewarded through the acquisition of property and wealth. Two, the enjoyment of property rights is also linked with fulfilling certain responsibilities and conditions. Property must be acquired through lawful and just means. It must be used productively and not squandered. Lastly, resulting financial obligations from ownership must be discharged faithfully. In short, property matters are viewed as both a legal and spiritual trust.

Equal Protection of Property Rights for All

A recurring theme in this chapter is that of justice towards others, as part of one's responsibility as a property owner. Justice also requires that the property of both Muslims and non-Muslims be given equal legal protection. Transgression of this principle invites God's disapproval, as illustrated in Surah al Imran – The House of Imran, 3:75. *"And among the followers of earlier revelation there is many a one who, if thou entrust him with a treasure, will [faithfully] restore it to thee; and there is among them many a one who, if thou entrust him with a tiny gold coin, will not restore it to thee unless thou keep standing over him – which is an outcome of their assertion, 'No blame can attach to us [for anything that we may do] with regard to these unlettered folk': and [so] they tell a lie about God, being well aware [that it is a lie]."* This verse explicitly condemns those among the Jews and Christians who do not honor their debts in a timely fashion, because they believe that unequal treatment of others (outside their community) is acceptable. However, God sees all and requires that everyone be treated equally in financial matters, regardless of whether they are Muslims or non-Muslims.

Both early Muslim juristic and historical precedent preserved the property rights of non-Muslims. Non-Muslims living under Muslim rule had the right to own property and businesses, to be employed in the government, and to engage in legal and economic transactions as the partners and associates of fellow Muslim citizens.[6] They enjoyed freedom of residence, worship, cultural and religious autonomy, including the right to collect taxes for their own institutions and provide religious education for their own community.[7]

Their rights to personal safety and security of property stemmed from the Prophet's (pbuh) example at Khaybar. Regarding the Treaty of Khaybar, al-Shaybani writes that "the Prophet's (pbuh) spokesman announced that none of the property of the covenantor is permitted to them [the Muslims]. Also because they [the non-Muslims] have accepted the peace covenant so as they may enjoy their properties and rights on par with Muslims."[8] Caliph Ali made a similar statement, such that "they [non-Muslims] only entered the covenant so that their lives and properties would be [protected] like our lives and properties."[9] The Treaty of Khaybar is notable because it established the institution of *kharaj*, or land tax, for land that remained in the possession of their non-Muslim owners. In return for continuing to use their lands, the Jews of Khaybar had to pay half their produce as tax.

In general, kharaj land was defined either as land conquered by Muslims, land abandoned by inhabitants who had fled, or land whose inhabitants decided to pay a tribute to the Muslims in exchange for retaining ownership. The *kharaj* went towards the protection and security of the land, and did not entitle non-Muslims to exemption from military service. It was analogous to the tithe collected from landowning Muslims. Since it was a tax on arable land that remained in possession of its original owners, female owners were not exempt from it, as they were from the *jizya*. Payment was assessed on the basis of acreage, percentage of actual harvest, amount of the crop, and included a fixed amount as well. It was to be collected once a year.[10] The importance of the institution of the *kharaj* is that it reflects Muslim recognition of full, private ownership rights of non-Muslims to their land, even though their territory was under the political rule of Muslims. The tax rates may appear onerous to modern eyes, and we make no claim that the actual rate of taxes is of modern significance.

Historically, Caliph Umar's government scrupulously protected the private property rights of non-Muslims. The state offered monetary compensation to those whose property had been damaged or been appropriated by the state. In one incident, a [non-Muslim] Syrian cultivator claimed that the army had trampled his crops. Caliph Umar ordered the payment of 10,000 dirhams to him as compensation out of the public treasury.[11] In another incident, during the construction of the central mosque of Kufa by the government, the remains of some old forts on land owned by non-Muslims were also used. The amount of compensation that they were entitled to as a result was adjusted into the amount they were supposed to pay as *jizya* to Caliph Umar's government.[12]

In another example, a poor non-Muslim woman's property rights were upheld after she refused to sell her house to the local governor, who wanted to appropriate the land in order to enlarge the mosque. She took her complaint to the Caliph, who ordered the house returned to her, and reprimanded the governor for forcing her to give it up.[13]

All of these examples in this section indicate the legal equality in property rights granted to non-Muslims by Muslim rulers. Although allowing non-Muslims to retain ownership of their agricultural lands might also be construed as a financial benefit to the state, because it could levy a tax on them and therefore be assured of a source of revenue, the legal implications of the practice are still important. More on the treatment of property rights in Islamic law will be outlined in the following section.

Economic Freedom

In simplistic terms, the assumption behind a free-market economic system is that individual self-interest and the profit motive, combined with vigorous competition, are the key driving forces that allow for the growth of employment and the economy. The protection of private property is therefore an important aspect of such a system, as an incentive and a means for individuals to engage in economic activity. The antithesis of this is a system that abolishes private property rights in favor of communally-owned (or state-owned) property rights, with the aim of achieving greater social equality in income distribution.

The Quran does not specify the ideal type of economic system. It merely prescribes the means and the end goal of the use of resources to be that of achieving justice, among other things. God has created the world with certain resources and given humans the capability to decide how to use them most efficiently to achieve their well-being. Any ethical use of resources that achieves this goal is valid.

Nevertheless, we are making an argument for a free market system as being in line with Quranic principles, provided it does not trample the weak and disadvantaged. Islam does not condemn self-interest, the profit motive, private property or a market-driven economic system at face value. Indeed, commerce and productivity are viewed favorably in Surah al Baqara – The Cow, 2:275. *"Those who gorge themselves on usury behave but as he might behave whom Satan has confounded with his touch; for they say, 'Buying and selling is but a kind of usury' – the while God has made buying and selling lawful and usury unlawful. Hence, whoever becomes aware of his Sustainer's admonition, and thereupon desists [from usury], may keep his past gains, and it will be for God to judge him; but as for those who return to it – they are destined for the fire, therein to abide!"* The distinction between legitimate trade and illegitimate usury will be elaborated upon in the following section.

This verse is supported by a *hadith*, which discusses the permissibility of trade during the season of *Hajj* in Mecca. "Ukaz, Majanna and Dhul-Majaz were market-places in the Pre-Islamic period of ignorance. When Islam came, Muslims felt that marketing there might be a sin. So, the Divine Inspiration came: *"[However,] you will be committing no sin if [during the pilgrimage] you seek to obtain any bounty from your Sustainer"* (Surah al Baqara – The Cow, 2:198).[14]

Islamic teaching also encourages individual labor and effort, and the rewards of these actions, described both in the Quran and in *hadith*. These are also integral to the underpinnings of a capitalistic outlook. *"And that nought shall be accounted unto man but what he is striving for; and that in time [the nature of] all his striving will be shown [to him in its true light]"* (Surah al Najm – The Unfolding, 53:39-40). Similarly, a *hadith* recorded by Bukhari elaborates, "Nobody has ever eaten a better meal than that which one has earned by working with one's own hands. The Prophet of God, David used to eat from the earnings of his manual labor."[15] In both examples, the individual remains responsible for his actions and their outcomes. This applies in both moral and economic terms.

The Quran also notes verses on ethical business practice in the marketplace. As a general command for honesty in trade, it states, *"O you who have attained to faith! Intoxicants, and games of chance, and idolatrous practices, and the divining of the future are but a loathsome evil of Satan's doing: shun it, then, so that you might attain to a happy state! By means of intoxicants and games of chance Satan seeks only to sow enmity and hatred among you, and to turn you away from the remembrance of God and from prayer. Will you not, then, desist?"* (Surah al Maida – The Repast, 5:90-91). Referring more specifically to the measurement of goods for sale, it states, "Weigh, therefore, [your deeds] with equity, and cut not the measure short! " (Surah ar Rahman – The Most Gracious, 55:9). God remains aware of who is honest and who is dishonest in trade. *"Woe unto those who give short measure: those who, when they are to receive their due from [other] people, demand that it be given in full – but when they have to measure or weight whatever they owe to others, give less than what is due! Do they not know that they are bound to be raised from the dead [and called to account] on an awesome Day"* (Surah al Mutaffifin – Those Who Give Short Measure, 1-4). All of these verses refer to the moral implications of trading, but nevertheless, they also implicitly support an argument for an ethical, free market system.

A number of *hadith* further the importance of honesty and ethical behavior in transactions and sales. For example: "The seller and the buyer have the right to keep or return goods as long as they have not parted or till they part; and if both the parties spoke the truth and described the defects and qualities (of the goods), then they would be blessed in their transaction, and if they told lies or hid something, then the blessings of their transaction would be lost."[16] Another *hadith* echoes the same; "'He who buys foodstuff should not sell it till he is satisfied with the measure with which he has bought it.'"[17] Both of these seek to regulate trade so that the legitimate interests of both the buyer and seller are adequately protected, and any uncertainty in the terms of transaction are minimized.[18]

A third *hadith* highlights the ethical behavior of the Prophet (pbuh) in trading with non-Muslims, in describing an account where he bought food grains from a Jew on credit and mortgaged his armor to him in exchange.[19] Lastly, the following *hadith* prohibits a practice which prevents the market from working fairly. People would buy goods from the caravan before it reached the city and then go sell them in the marketplace to the urban residents at a higher price.[20] "Narrated Tawus: Ibn 'Abbas said, 'God's Apostle said, 'Do not go to meet the caravans on the way (for buying their goods without letting them know the market price).'" [21]

The discussion above highlights, on the individual level, an argument for ethical trade. We can also extend it, on moral grounds, as support for a free market system, one that lets the market achieve equilibrium on prices without artificial restraints. In addition, an Islamic perspective expands the command for ethical business practices and the idea of individual self-interest to include spiritual self-interest as well. In other words, a person's self interest includes both his material and spiritual well-being. In order to achieve the latter, he must be mindful of his religious duties and social obligations to his family members and the community. Therefore, concern for a spiritual accountability to God tempers the socially destructive effects of materialist self-interest run amok. The emphasis is on "an internal, self-regulating mechanism instilled in the inner consciousness of the individual himself, with its constant emphasis on belief in accountability before God, human brotherhood, and socio-economic justice."[22]

This emphasis also applies when we contrast private property rights with communal rights in a capitalistic system. One of the main criticisms of the communist system (and which eventually led to its collapse) was a lack of efficiency resulting from the abolishment of individual profit motive. The ideal of distributive economic and social justice was not attained in practice, even though the abolition of private property (in addition to other coercive acts) should have done so, in theory. In this aspect, Islam encourages individual effort and does not expect an individual to completely overlook his self-interest in his material, physical and spiritual well-being.[23] The social and financial obligations to give charity (*zakat*), to support one's family members, and to pay taxes are part of the Islamic vision of social justice that tempers pursuit of the profit motive. Within this theoretical framework, private property rights are permissible, and in fact integral, to the success of a capitalist system since they can engender greater economic efficiency.

But, where do we draw the line between individual economic behavior and state financial/economic policy? While the individual capitalist holds significant power in this kind of economic system, the state also carries responsibility for creating suitable conditions for prosperous trade and economic behavior. The state can establish laws for payment of taxes. It can punish illegal financial practices, as part of the general public welfare that it is enjoined to preserve. Fundamentally, the state does not have the power to judge what is moral and immoral behavior, since only God has that authority. But, within the larger context of public good, and *hisba*, it is required to protect the ability of individuals to make choices – in this case, economic choices – as they see fit. This includes punishing theft, which would cover business fraud, and punishing criminal business enterprises, such as those engaged in drug-dealing.

The Role of *Riba* (Usury)

The general concern for ethical behavior in trade forms the back-drop for this section's examination of riba, or usury. A very contro-versial aspect of property rights in Islam is the right to utilize savings (i.e. capital). In all societies, some save a greater share of their income than others. The result is that society as a whole saves some portion of its income, with the rate varying from person to person based on their circumstances and goals. People may save to purchase a desired item, they may save to pay for education or housing, or they may save for retirement.

There are also in every society people who wish to spend more money than they have at the moment. They are willing to borrow in order to purchase something of value now, and in return will pay back the borrowed funds in the future. For example, a newly married couple with young children may borrow funds to buy a house, relying on their income over the next ten or 20 years to pay back the cost of the house. Or a student may borrow funds to go to university. Businesses borrow money to pay for new investment, or to purchase raw materials, or to manage cash flow so they can pay bills while waiting for their customers to fully pay what they owe the business. But without borrowed funds all of these useful activities would not occur or would occur with much less frequency. The net result would be that the economy remains stunted and human misery and poverty are increased.

There have been two great credit crunches in modern industrial eco-nomic history. The first was the Great Depression of the 1930's, whose trail of destruction and havoc led to the rise of Nazi Germany and the Second World War. The second has been the collapse of the Japanese economic miracle in the 1990s. Although Japan has not suffered depres-sion, its industrial output has not grown in 12 years, and its economy remains stagnant. Credit is indispensable to economic activity. It is also useful to note that both credit crunches were associated with very low rates of interest (less than 1% in Japan's case).

Given that there is a pool of savers in a society and a pool of borrowers who wish to put that saving to productive use, how can the two groups be connected? There are essentially two mechanisms, one is through shared ownership (equity financing), and the other is through loans (debt financing). In most advanced economies, there exists a group of intermediary institutions that allow these modes to function. Equity financing can be done on a personal level through partnerships, and on a corporate level through the stock market. For example, if a person has an idea for a business, but no money, she can find someone who has money and make him her partner in exchange for part ownership in her company. He has purchased equity in her company. Conversely, if her company was large enough, she could sell a portion of it to the public by using an investment bank that would conduct a "public offering" of a portion of the shares of her company's stock.

She could also engage in debt financing. In that case she could borrow money from friends, or from a bank, or if she had a large enough company, issue "corporate bonds" to the public through an investment bank. Both equity and debt financing are commercial transactions that represent a choice the owner of the business makes after evaluating his economic situation. It is often the case that one mode is superior to the other, or often only one mode is available while the other is not.

For private individuals, borrowing is mostly done to fund consumption rather than investment. Individuals borrow to purchase durable goods likes cars or refrigerators, or they borrow for education, or to purchase housing, or short-term for material consumption such as clothes, meals, entertainment, or travel. Although debt financing for consumption can be arranged, equity financing does not make much sense. A saver will not give you her savings to become part owner of your clothes or your university books.

It would seem after considering these basic issues, that there is an important role to play for both equity and debt financing in any economy. The presence of these mechanisms allows savers the highest return possible on their savings, while giving borrowers the maximum choice and flexibility in finding a source of funds. The problem from an Islamic perspective is that the Quran forbids "usury".

Two Quranic verses which explicitly rule out usury are: *"O you who have attained to faith! Remain conscious of God, and give up all outstanding gains from usury, if you are [truly] believers"* (Surah al Baqara – The Cow, 2:278).

However, other than making a distinction between trade and usury, such that the former is allowed and encouraged, while the latter is expressly frowned upon, the Quran does not exactly define what constitute riba. *"Those who gorge themselves on usury behave but as he might behave whom Satan has confounded with his touch; for they say, 'Buying and selling is but a kind of usury' – the while God has made buying and selling lawful and usury unlawful. Hence, whoever becomes aware of his Sustainer's admonition, and thereupon desists [from usury], may keep his past gains, and it will be for God to judge him; but as for those who return to it – they are destined for the fire, therein to abide!"* (Surah al Baqara – The Cow, 2:275).

Thus, scholars have turned to the sunna for elaboration. The majority of *ulema* claim that there is an absolute prohibition against transaction involving interest. During the Meccan period it is noted as a strong recommendation against taking interest. During the Medinan period, however, it is articulated as an outright prohibition.[24] But, there are varying degrees of difference among the legal schools as to how this prohibition is put into practice.[25] There is a tendency to conflate all types of interest as being equally forbidden without delving into the details.

Semantically, *riba* means excess or an addition. It refers to an excess stipulated in a contract or an exchange. There are two juristic categories of *riba*: *riba al fadl* and *riba al nasi'ah*. *Riba al fadl* refers to an excess in weight/measure, while *riba al nasi'ah* refers to an excess arising from the benefit of delay.[26] Some Hanbali scholars, including Ibn Qayyim al-Jawziyya, have added a third category, called *riba al jahiliyya*, referring to the *riba* practiced in the pre-Islamic period. According to this practice, the lender increases the interest on debt if borrower has not paid it by the maturity date of the loan. In effect, the rate of increase is so great that it pushes the borrower deeper and deeper into debt, and unable to ever pay it off. This kind of exploitative practice is what the Quran refers to in its discussion of *riba*.[27] The other two types of *riba* have been developed later by jurists by examining the *sunna*.

However, most Islamic scholars over the years have interpreted the prohibition on usury to mean all forms of interest, which essentially means that debt financing is illegal in Islam, at least according to that interpretation. This has led to the creation of so-called "Islamic banking", a banking system that allegedly does not rely on debt financing, but only equity financing. The reality is that "Islamic banking" essentially repackages interest under a different name such as "markup rate" or "profit rate", and reprices goods to include the full interest cost within the loan. For example, if a person bought a new $15,000 car with a conventional 8% loan, he would pay interest and principle until the debt is cleared. An Islamic bank on the other hand would simply calculate the total dollars he would pay back over the loan term with interest, and then charge him that amount for the car to be paid over the same loan term while claiming that there was no interest being levied. It is simply a semantic game being played.

There are a few exceptions in which the Islamic banks do engage only in equity financing, but then they are unable to finance consumption purposes. They do however take part ownership in the ventures of their borrowers. The problem with this is the bank then becomes a high risk investor in a whole series of businesses that its management has neither the time nor the expertise to manage. The end result is that many of the businesses fail unexpectedly and the bank itself then fails leaving its depositors completely wiped out.

We argue that the Quran does not mandate equity over debt

financing, and allows transactions that are mutually beneficial. The usury verse is not the only verse in the Quran on business. Much more prominent in the Quran is the command to engage in honest business, in particular to give "full measure". Specifically, the Quran says, *"Woe unto those who give short measure: those who, when they are to receive their due from [other] people, demand that it be given in full – but when they have to measure or weigh whatever they owe to others, give less than what is due!"* (Surah al Mutaffifin – Those Who Give Short Measure, 83:1-3). This command requires that both parties to any business transaction pay the full and fair value of what they are purchasing. Failure to do so is a profound violation of Quranic commercial principles. Debt financing, when done in accord with this principle is permissible. When the lender gets more than he is entitled to, he commits the sin of usury. When he gets less, he is engaging in charity. But charity is a voluntary act, and not one required in business transactions.

What is the "full measure" in debt financing? It is the value that the borrower gains from the use of the funds and the lender foregoes by giving up control of those funds for the period of the loan. There are three components of the value of the funds. The first is the inflation premium. If a borrower takes money this year, and returns the same amount 10 years later, has he returned what he borrowed? Only if there has been no inflation in those ten years. Inflation shrinks the value of borrowed funds, and this shrinkage must be compensated for if the borrower is to fully return the value of the borrowed funds. Secondly, there is what is called the "opportunity cost". Savers can always engage in equity financing rather than lending money. They can purchase a piece of rental property, or shares of stock of a company, or they can find a partner with an idea and fund his business for a share of ownership. Some of these schemes may yield fantastic profits, while others may go bankrupt, but on average there is a positive return to investment in business. This rate varies over time depending on the economy and business conditions. But let us assume for argument purpose that it averages out to about 5% per year. This notion is often referred to as the "time value of money". If a saver is to lend money, he is giving up the opportunity to earn 5% in equity investments by lending money instead. A borrower must then compensate him for this opportunity loss over the life of the loan, otherwise the borrower is not giving "full measure". Finally, the last component to consider in debt financing is risk. When a saver lends money, she has no guarantee that the borrower will pay the money back. The borrower may lose his job, or his newly bought car might get stolen, or his business may fail. In these circumstances, the lender is unable to get her money back, and takes a loss. This willingness to take risk must be compensated for in the loan. The risk level can be reduced by the borrower offering collateral, but even collateral can lose its value, for example if the price of houses collapse and homeowners stop paying their mortgages due to job losses. Risk can never be eliminated, and in some debt the risk is quite high, such as credit card debt where there is no collateral pledged whatsoever other than the good faith of the borrower.

We argue that lending money at interest is not in all cases a violation of the "usury" verse, when the interest rate is a true reflection of the inflation, opportunity cost, and level of risk in the loan. If that is the case, then both parties are giving "full measure" and are engaging in Islamically sanctioned business practices. It is for Muslim economists to offer a contemporary *ijtihad* on the issue.

Some Muslims criticize interest as inherently exploitative, and believe that it creates an oppressive economic system. This is not necessarily a correct reflection of the nature of modern commercial lending and the activities of the village moneylender, who often was exploitative. Excessive and burdensome interest rates would often lead to a lifetime of debt that was impossible for villagers to escape. Even today this sort of exploitation occurs in villages in the Muslim world. But this paradigm presupposes that the lender is the rich and powerful, while the borrower is the desperate and poor. Modern banking has inverted this equation. Modern banks gather together the modest savings of millions of the poor and middle class, and then make that pool of savings available to big business and large borrowers. The majority of saving is done by the poor and middle classes, while most of the borrowing is done by the powerful. So who is exploiting whom? The purpose of *sharia* is to implement justice. If there is justice, then it is sharia. Where is the injustice in this that would lead debt financing to be banned? In fact, if banks were to be restricted to equity financing, they would be taking unacceptable risk with the modest savings of the poor. The poor cannot tolerate losing their life savings. They need the lower risk of having their savings used for debt financing rather than the much higher risk of equity financing. One of the main purposes of banks is risk management. They have a responsibility to earn a profit so that they can pay interest to the savers, but not risk a loss that wipes them out.

The only real difference between equity and debt financing is the risk to reward ratio. In both systems the lender takes a risk, and hopes to earn a reward. In equity financing, the lender actually becomes a legal part-owner of the investment, and can fully participate in the success of the venture, but also fully risks catastrophic loss if it fails. The debt financer lends the business money at interest, but his profit is limited to the interest payment itself, while his risk is limited by two factors. First, the borrower must pay the lender before he takes home any profit, so the lender has priority over the earnings of the business, and secondly, the lender takes possession of any collateral the business may have offered to secure the loan if the business fails to make its loan payments. The collateral may reduce the loss but often does not fully cover the loss.

A good example of the difference is two investors, one who bought shares of Microsoft Corporation at its initial public offering in 1986, and another who lent Microsoft money at interest by buying a Microsoft corporate bond. The first investor earned much more profit than the second over time, while the second took less risk. In neither case was Microsoft exploited. This is not to say that rapacious credit card companies and other unscrupulous lenders cannot exploit borrowers. But this is an argument for a strong regulatory framework enacted by the state to watch over the activities of lenders so that credit is made available to all at a reasonable price, and that exploitative practices are quashed. It is not the basis of banning debt financing entirely, a goal that no so-called "Islamic banking" system has been able to do in reality anyway. The state should allow "Islamic banking" to exist, and provide a regulatory and legal framework for it, but it may also allow a traditional banking sector to exist in parallel, and let savers and borrowers utilize the system that best suits their needs.

Zakat and Capitalism

Zakat is perhaps the most misunderstood and underestimated of the five pillars of Islam. While the other pillars address issues of personal faith and devotion, *zakat* is actually a carefully constructed system of social justice in a capitalist setting. Fundamentally, zakat is intended to tame capitalism and wealth in general.

In any society, there is always the problem of disparate wealth. Some have plenty while others have little. Some save and invest, while others don't. Some have the advantage of wealthy families or good education or contacts while others lack marketable skills or have illness or handicaps. The homeless in America have a high proportion of severely mentally ill among them, and simply cannot function in society. There are a multitude of reasons for this disparity of wealth. How society handles this issue is a measure of its humanity.

In the United States, income is concentrated in the hands of the upper 10% of society. The lowest 10%, while living comfortable lives by Third World standards, are clearly considered poor or in poverty by American standards. In fact, the reported poverty rate in the United States is about 11% of the population, a fraction that has stayed constant over the last 25 years with only slight ups and downs. A different way to look at the picture is to see what share of personal income goes to each group. The upper 10% of households in the United States earn about 30% of the annual personal income, while the lowest 10% earn less than 2%. The top 20% in the United States earn almost 50% of annual income, while the bottom 20% get by on about 3.5%. So there is a sharp difference in circumstance among various groups in society. This data does not include the cash value of government benefits such as food stamps or Medicaid health insurance, but that would only change the figures slightly.

If even the wealthiest and most productive society on the planet has problems of poverty and social justice, then it stands to reason that this is a universal problem. Over the centuries, nations and societies have grappled with this issue and what it means for how economics should be regulated. Robin Hood robbed from the rich and gave to the poor, and that is one solution. Karl Marx advocated the leveling of society by force, with all personal property outlawed, and the state in control of the economy. In milder forms, left wing and liberal responses to this issue have called for a redistribution of wealth, by force if necessary, from the rich to the poor. The corollary to the left-wing answer is that wealth is evil, the pursuit of wealth is inherently immoral and unjust, and that capitalism is an affront to social justice and God's will. Only tight government control of the economy can prevent terrible social exploitation from occurring.

But capitalism has no inherent moral content. Just as a hammer can be used for construction or destruction, capitalism is a tool that can be used for good or ill. The drug dealer, arms merchant, or loan shark are engaging in capitalism, but their activity is a destructive one. Conversely, the drug company seeking to make a profit investing a billion dollars in research is engaged in a morally useful purpose, even though it is not necessarily motivated by morality. This requires any capitalist economy to be regulated and constrained against illegal or destructive activities. The maintenance of competition is one of the single most important functions of a government in a capitalist system. Without competition the system fails.

Is capitalism then Islamic? Is it appropriate to consider free enterprise the form of economic activity most consistent with the Quran? Muhammad (pbuh) engaged in that quintessential activity, trading. He took goods that were bought cheap in Mecca and led caravans north to trade where they could be sold dear, and then reversed the process. Would any leftist Muslim accuse him of exploitation? By doing the arduous and potentially dangerous task of leading caravans across the Arabian sands, he earned his reward for carrying out this business. The Quran is full of admonishments for Muslims to deal fairly and honestly in business. Implicit in that is the idea that engaging in honest business is very much part of Islam.

So how should the issue of social justice be addressed? If capitalism is desirable because it is so productive, how are its inevitable inequalities to be mitigated without destroying the system itself? Obviously, somehow the poor must be cared for. And this would require an adequate and regular supply of funds. It makes the most sense that those who are the most financially secure should provide these funds. Ideally, the donor should have some control over the disbursement of funds. One could provide a tax on income, as is done by most governments, or one could look at taxing wealth, which differs from income. Everyone who has a job has income, but only those who have saved something and invested perhaps have wealth. The man who spends all his income on providing for his family would have no wealth and therefore may have to pay an income tax but would not be obliged under a wealth tax. The very top of the income ladder on the other hand have wealth that far exceeds their income. Bill Gates, the richest man in the world, has wealth of over $50 billion in his stock holdings in Microsoft, but earns less than a million dollars a year in income as President of Microsoft. A wealth tax could hit him hard while an income tax would mean nothing to him.

There are some religions that practice "tithing" where adherents are supposed to give 10% of their income to charity or the church each year. Tithing seems fair, but it hits low-income people with little wealth much harder than high-income people with great wealth. The tithe hurts lower incomes more because all of their income is needed for life's necessities, while richer people can more easily bear the burden of the tithe. So tithing is a system that causes relatively more pain and hardship to those least able to bear it, which is not the ideal and just way to do things.

Zakat, on the other hand, is a wealth tax. *Zakat* is owed on what you have saved over and above the requirements of life. *Zakat* is not owed on household personal property such as auto, home, furnishings etc. But all investments and savings beyond a minimal threshold are subject to *zakat*. The burden of *zakat* seems light, at only 2.5% of savings. But that is in reality a very heavy tax. The average profit earned on most investments is 5-10% per year, so to give 2.5% to charity amounts to a large fraction of an investor's annual return. Bill Gates would owe over $1 billion per year on his stockholdings in *zakat*.

Because *zakat* is such a heavy tax on wealth, it potentially generates a huge amount of money. Americans are among the most generous people in the world in terms of charity giving. Unlike Europe, much of American social life is not funded by the state, and the welfare system is much smaller, so average citizens have a regular habit of giving to private charities. In 1999, Americans gave $190 billion to charities; 145 billion came from individuals while the rest from corporations, foundations, and wills. $80 billion of that went to fund religious institutions, $27 billion for education, $18 billion for health, $17 billion for services for the poor, and $2.5 billion went to foreign projects and aid. So although Americans give a lot, only a small fraction of their giving is actually assistance to the poor, which is the primary purpose of *zakat*.

What would be the effect if all Americans practiced *zakat*? How much money would be transferred, and to what extent would the excesses of capitalism be softened? We have to first determine how much wealth exists in the United States, and how much of that is subject to *zakat*. Fortunately, those numbers are fairly easy to arrive at. We will illustrate this point using figures from 2001. The total size of the U.S. economy (GDP) was about $11 trillion of production per year. Of that, about $8 trillion shows up as personal income. But *zakat* is not a tax on income, so we need to determine personal wealth. That figure is about 5 times personal income, so about $40 trillion. Not all of that would be subject to zakat. Home and personal property are exempt, as are assets in a company pension plan and the value of a personal business that is one's primary source of income (*zakat* is not owed on the market value of a small business that is your main livelihood, but if you buy a business on the side as an investment, *zakat* is payable on the value of that investment). Removing the exempted wealth still leaves about 20 trillion dollars of personal wealth in the United States.

Twenty trillion dollars of wealth would mean $500 billion in *zakat* per year owed by Americans. Compare that to the $17 billion donated for the American poor and $2.5 billion sent abroad as charity. *Zakat* is in fact a mammoth wealth transfer from the rich to the poor. $500 billion is 6% of U.S. personal income, a figure that exceeds the current personal income share for the lowest 20% of the population. That scale of wealth transfer essentially eliminates the issue of material poverty in an advanced capitalist society. *Zakat* is the Islamic solution to the inequalities and excesses of capitalism.

Even in a poor country like Pakistan, *zakat* would generate a huge amount of money if everyone actually paid the required and full amount. Pakistan's GDP is about $100 billion in 2005, with personal income of about $80 billion and personal wealth of around $400 billion. Assuming half of that is subject to *zakat*, $5 billion would be generated per year, a figure that vastly exceeds the foreign aid that Pakistan receives. It would go a long way to alleviating the most extreme forms of human misery.

Zakat is not a government tax. Muslim governments do not have the right to use *zakat* funds for running the government. It is a charitable tax with a clear list of allowed recipients. In addition, each payer of *zakat* has the right to determine how and where his or her money goes. Some Muslim governments have attempted to enforce and collect *zakat*, which is against the basic principle of charity. If one is forced to observe the pillars of Islam, then they will have lost their meaning. Islam should be practiced out of love for Allah, not fear of jail.

The central role of *zakat* in Islam is made clear by the fact that it is one of the five pillars. The Quran admonishes people repeatedly to pray and pay *zakat*. But *zakat* cannot fulfill its social function if there are few who are subject to it. By definition, a wealth tax requires some to be wealthy enough to pay. The leftist solution of leveling society through force or other means is therefore un-Islamic as it negates the power and purpose of the *zakat* pillar. Doing the opposite, pursuing wealth as long as you pay your *zakat*, is in accordance with the Islamic concept of social justice.

Conclusion

This chapter has outlined various perspectives on property rights in Islam, with a particular focus on the protection of private property rights, legally and historically. In general, Islam upholds one's right to ownership as a trust. Material possession is a permissible right, but it comes with certain obligations and responsibilities that must also be discharged. Namely, property must be acquired and used in productive and legal ways, without hurting others' interests. The wealth or income from one's property must be used in payment of *zakat*, charity and financial support for one's family members. Property rights are viewed in the context of a free market system that allows citizens to engage freely in trade and economic productivity and to reap the rewards of their efforts. A common misperception is that all forms of interest are equally prohibited because the Quran prohibits usury. However, we have argued that excessive and exploitative forms of interest fall within the category of usury, and interest which takes into account the appropriate financial risks involved in the transaction is not necessarily outlawed as well. However, we recommend a new *ijtihad* in this dynamic and changing area. The common underlying theme in this entire chapter is the need to remain mindful of social justice concerns as part of one's orientation towards God and faith.

Footnotes

1 Sahih Muslim, Book 016, Number 4161; also Sahih Bukhari, Vol 1 Book 3 No. 67; and Vol 8, Book 81 No 776.
2 Akhtar A. Awan, *Equality, Efficiency and Property Ownership in the Islamic Economic System* (Lanham: University Press of America, 1983), p. 30.
3 Referred to as Korah, in the Bible. He was of the tribe of Moses and Aaron. Yusuf Ali, p. 1023, n. 3404.
4 Sahih Muslim, Book 1, Number 257.
5 Sahih Bukhari, Volume 4, Book 51, Number 5.
6 See also the chapter on Non-Muslims for more. Kamali, *Freedom, Equality and Justice in Islam*, p. 90.
7 Ye'or, p. 49.
8 Muhammad b. al Hasan al-Shaybani, translated and cited in Louay M. Safi "Human Rights and Islamic Legal Reform" p. 6.
9 Kamali, *Freedom, Equality and Justice in Islam*, p. 83.
10 *"Kharaj,"* *The Oxford Encyclopedia of the Modern Islamic World*, p. 417
11 Shaikh Shaukat Hussain, *Human Rights in Islam* (New Delhi: Kitab Bhavan, 1990) p. 60.
12 Hussain, *Human Rights in Islam*, p. 44.
13 Kamali, *Freedom, Equality and Justice in Islam*, p. 89.
14 Sahih Bukhari, Volume 3, Book 34, Number 266.
15 Sahih Bukhari, Volume 3, Book 34, Number 286.
16 Sahih Bukhari, Volume 3, Book 34, Number 293.
17 Sahih Bukhari, Vol. 3, Book 34, No. 336.
18 S. M. Hasanuz Zaman, *Economic Functions of an Islamic State* (Leicester: The Islamic Foundation, 1991), p.50.
19 Narrated by Aisha, Sahih Bukari, Vol. 3, Book 34, No. 309.
20 Zaman, p. 50.
21 22 Sahih Bukari, Vol. 3, Book 34, No. 367.
23 M. Umer Chapra, *Islam and the Economic Challenge* (Leicester and Herndon: Islamic Foundation and International Institute of Islamic Thought, 1992), p. 221.
24 Chapra, p. 220.
25 Nabil A. Saleh, *Unlawful Gain and Legitimate Profit in Islamic Law: Riba, Gharar and Islamic Banking*, 2nd ed., (London: Graham and Trotman, 1992), p. 13.
26 Saleh, p. 15. For more details on the views of each legal school, both Sunni and Shia, see pp. 24-38.
27 Imran Ahsan Khan Nyazee, *The Concept of Riba and Islamic Banking* (Islamabad: Niazi Publishing House, 1995), p. 21.
28 Saleh, p. 17.

- CHAPTER TEN -

Citizenship

itizenship defines membership of individuals in a territorially-defined, sovereign political community. It is a constructed membership, however, and is granted by the state unilaterally to its members. The state gets to choose who belongs to the community and who does not, and the terms of membership as well.

Citizenship also represents a contract between the state and its people. The responsibility of the state is to protect the divinely-granted human rights of its citizens. In return for this protection, citizens obey the law, pay taxes, and fulfill other requirements that derive from this contract.

Historically, only a particular elite part of society (free, white, male property-owners, in the American case) enjoyed the full legal and political privileges of being citizens. Eventually, the category was expanded to include other groups – women and non-white, minority populations. Citizenship is therefore an evolving concept, with categories of rights that have eventually expanded to be more inclusive over time.

This chapter examines citizenship rights from an Islamic perspective. While there is no parallel concept of citizenship as membership in a territorially defined community in the Quran,[1] there are certain elements that do have roots in Quranic vision of society. We present an argument for an inclusive definition of citizenship, one that treats all members of society as equal before the law, and with equal rights and responsibilities.

The starting point for our argument is a brief overview of citizenship theory. This is then applied to the Islamic context in subsequent sections, by focusing on key themes, such as the idea of individualism, personal autonomy, and pluralism in society, as they are described in the Quran. The basis of citizenship rights is that they are granted to the individual, and are not a hereditary group privilege, assigned to the entire community on the basis of social identity. Islam was revolutionary in seventh-century Arabia precisely for this reason – that it aimed to do away with tribal affiliation and kinship as the primary markers of social identity, and replace it with religion, which recognized the individual and his personal autonomy over inherited group identity. But it did not privilege the rights and duties of Muslims over non-Muslims in the political community, as can be seen by a close reading of the Compact of Medina (discussed in the chapter on Constitutionalism). This idea needs to be applied towards citizenship constructs today, by recognizing individuals of all faiths as having equal rights to membership. The political community founded by the Prophet (pbuh) at Medina offers us one model that illustrates this line of argument.

Citizenship Theory[2]

Liberal concepts of citizenship assume the basic equality of all human beings as the basis for full and equal membership in a community.[3] T.H. Marshall's definition of the three elements of citizenship – civil, political and social – forms an integral part of the modern understanding of citizenship in the Western context.

Marshall defines the civil element as the rights necessary for individual freedom, including liberty of person, freedom of speech, freedom of religion, right to own property, right to make valid contracts, and the right to justice. Implicit in this is the "right to defend and assert all one's rights on terms of equality with others and by due process of law."[4] The political element includes the "right to participate in the exercise of political power," either in terms of voting or running for office. Lastly, the social element encompasses the right to economic welfare and security as well as the right to share in full the social heritage of the community.[5]

The important point to note in the existence of these three elements is the fact that they did not arise simultaneously as components of citizenship. Rather, they came in phases, starting with civil rights in the 18th century, followed by political and social rights in the 19th and 20th centuries, respectively.[6] While there was some overlap between them, nevertheless, the evolution of the modern-day idea of citizenship came about over a significantly long period of time.

Marshall also puts forward the idea of rights and duties as an integral part of citizenship, along with the civil, political and social rights. "Citizenship is a status bestowed on those who are full members of a community. All who possess the status are equal with respect to the rights and duties with which the status is endowed. There is no universal principle that determines what those rights and duties shall be, but societies in which citizenship is a developing institution create an image of an ideal citizenship against which achievement can be measured and towards which aspiration can be directed."[7]

Implicit in this is the concept of a two-way relationship between the individual and the state. The balance between the rights and duties of the individual and the state, determines how the state uses citizenship as an instrument for the social integration of the population. We will come back to the tension between the individual and the community rights in a later section of this chapter.

To the extent that citizenship is defined as membership within the state, then it is useful to examine the modern state as a bounded territory to which access is controlled through membership.[8] Citizenship, then, serves as both a tool and an object of closure. It is a tool because the state uses it to regulate, not only access to the territory, but also to the benefits and privileges that membership within that community provides. Citizenship is also an object of closure because it implies exclusivity by its very nature, and therefore non-citizens, or non-members, are differentiated from citizens of a particular state.[9]

This distinction between citizens and non-citizens can be termed as that between "insiders" and "outsiders." The former are defined "positively, as members of a family, clan, organization or state." In contrast, "outsiders" are defined negatively. In other words, they are defined by what they are not; they are not members of a specific group.[10]

This division between "insiders" and "outsiders", and citizens and non-citizens can be linked to the historical origins of citizenship in the Middle East. In pre-Islamic times, membership within a community was based primarily on tribal affiliation, and anyone who did not belong to the tribe was considered an "alien."[11] With the coming of Islam and spread of the concept of the umma, religious identification became tied to that of membership as well. The Ottomans continued this linkage between these two concepts, until 1869 when the Sultan set forth the first nationality law. This law separated religion and nationality, and instead replaced them with the principles of *jus sanguinis* and *jus soli*. *Jus sanguinis* refers to the fact that citizenship of an individual is determined by citizenship of his/her parents, while *jus soli* states that citizenship is determined by the place of birth.[12]

The salient point in this brief theoretical survey is the constructed and selective nature of citizenship. Marshall's division of citizenship rights into civil, political and social rights highlights the evolutionary aspect of it, as a way of defining membership within the political community and differentiating between those who belong and those who do not. We argue that all three of these components should be included and recognized as equally integral in an Islamic state. Distinctions based on sex, religion, race, among other characteristics, should not define gradations of citizenship rights.

Individualism in the Quran

Citizenship rights are predicated on the concept of the individual as a legal entity. The role of the state is to protect the individual's rights, while also emphasizing the discharge of that individual's responsibilities towards the state. The concept of the individual as an autonomous agent can be found in the Quran and the *sharia*. While the Quran views the individual in moral terms, the sharia recognizes his/her legal independence.

According to the Quran, God has created humans with the ability to reason and to make moral choices. Every individual is responsible for his/her own actions, as a result of these moral choices. Both punishment and reward for these actions are determined on an individual basis by God. Humans are accountable to God on the Day of Judgment, and will be rewarded or punished by Divine Will accordingly, as evidenced in Surah al Isra – The Night Journey, 17:13: *"And every human being's destiny have We tied to his neck; and on the Day of Resurrection We shall bring forth for him a record which he will find wide open."*

This idea is reiterated in several places in the Quran. *"'God does not burden any human being with more than he is well able to bear: in his favor shall be whatever good he does, and against him whatever evil he does"* (Surah al Baqara – The Cow, 2:286).

"And whatever [wrong] any human being commits rests upon himself alone; and no bearer of burdens shall be made to bear another's burden. And, in time, unto your Sustainer you all must return: and then He will make you [truly] understand all that on which you were wont to differ" (Surah al Anam - Cattle, 6:164).

"Whoever chooses to follow the right path, follows it but for his own good; and whoever goes astray, goes but astray to his own hurt; and no bearer of burdens shall be made to beat another's burden" (Surah al Isra – The Night Journey, 17:15).

"And no bearer of burdens shall be made to bear another's burden; and if one weighed down by his load calls upon [another] to help him carry it, nothing thereof may be carried [by that other], even if it be one's near of kin" (Surah Fatir – The Orginator, 35:18).

Similarly, the *sharia* aims to protect individual life, freedom and property, among other goals, quite explicitly.[13] As a general injunction, this is reflected in the Prophet's (pbuh) Farewell Pilgrimage address. "Verily your blood (lives) and your property and your honor are as sacred unto you as sacred is this day of yours, in this month of yours, in this city of yours. Let him who is present convey it to one who is absent."[14]

In addition, the Quran values each individual life so much so that *"if anyone slays a human being – it shall be as though he had slain all mankind; whereas, if anyone saves a life, it shall be as though he had saved the lives of all mankind"* (Surah al Maida – The Repast, 5:32). Life is also valued before the law, so that "just cause" is the only reason for taking a life. *"And do not commit any shameful deeds, be they open or secret; and do not take any human being's life – [the life] which God has declared to be sacred – otherwise than in [the pursuit of] justice: this has He enjoined upon you so that you might use your reason"* (Surah al Anam - Cattle, 6:151).

Individual rights to personal liberty, free speech, freedom of religion, freedom of movement, freedom of association, economic rights, right to political participation, are all recognized in the Quran as derivatives of basic human freedom. It is not the purpose of this chapter to delve into the details of these specific rights, since they have been discussed individually in their own respective chapters. Nevertheless, our aim is to emphasize that all of these rights and freedoms already exist in Islam, and therefore need to be protected by an Islamic state as well through the institution of citizenship rights.

The Equality of all Citizens

Modern citizenship seeks to eliminate hereditary group privilege before the law. It treats all individuals as equals before the law, with the same set of rights and duties, regardless of social identity, religion, sex, race, etc. Islam was revolutionary in seventh-century Arabia precisely for this reason. It aimed to do away with tribal affiliation and kinship as the primary markers of social identity, and replace it with religion, which recognized the individual and his personal autonomy over inherited group identity.

This idea of universal equality as the basis for law is enshrined in the Quran and is integral to our conception of the sharia.

All beings are equal in rights and obligations as the creation of God. *"O mankind! Be conscious of your Sustainer, who has created you out of one living entity, and out of it created its mate, and out of the two spread abroad a multitude of men and women. And remain conscious of God, in whose name you demand [your rights] from one another, and of these ties of kinship. Verily, God is ever watchful over you!"* (Surah an Nisaa - Women, 4:1). Human beings all originate from similar circumstances. In a general sense, this implies common descent of the human race from Adam and Eve. But it also illustrates that men and women are equal in rights and obligations.[15]

"O men! Behold, We have created you all out of a male and a female, and have made you into nations and tribes, so that you might come to know one another. Verily, the nobles of you in the sight of God is the one who is most deeply conscious of Him. Behold, God is all-knowing, all-aware" (Surah al Hujurat – The Private Apartments, 49:13). Differences based on gender, race, or religion, among others, exist merely to allow for greater cooperation and harmony among individuals. It does not necessarily mean that there is a hierarchy, of Muslims over non-Muslims, or men over women, or vice versa.

Continuing with the same theme, all of mankind has been favored by God, and bestowed inherent dignity as human beings. *"Now, indeed, We have conferred dignity on the children of Adam, and borne them over land and sea, and provided for them sustenance out of the good things of life, and favored them far above most of Our creation"* (Surah al Isra – The Night Journey, 17:70).

A horizontal relationship of equality with reference to religious identity among people is also valued in the Quran. Some people mistakenly draw a distinction between Muslims and People of the Book (Jews and Christians primarily) in the Quran, to argue that the latter should be considered spiritually inferior to Muslims. This erroneous interpretation is responsible for the treatment of non-Muslims as second-class citizens in a number of Muslim countries. The justification behind this is that the unequal relationship of these two groups before God allows non-Muslims to be treated unequally before the (temporal) law as well.

We rigorously critique this concept as part of the framework for citizenship rights. While reiterating again that God is the only judge of moral and spiritual matters, we can still make a case for tolerance and religious pluralism as necessary components for the state's relationship with Muslim and non-Muslim communities on earth. This argument is outlined briefly here, and explored in detail in the chapter on religious freedom.

Religious pluralism is predicated on the concept of freedom of belief, which is protected by God as part of individual autonomy. It is available to all mankind, not just to Muslims. *"And [thus it is:] had thy Sustainer so willed, all those who live on earth would surely have attained to faith, all of them: dost thou, then, think that thou couldst compel people to believe"* (Surah Yunus - Jonah, 10:99). Surah al Maida – The Repast, 5:48, introduces the concept of religious pluralism to the idea of human diversity. *"Unto every one of you have We appointed a [different] law and way of life. And if God had so willed, He could surely have made you all one single community: but [He willed it otherwise] in order to test you by means of what He has vouchsafed unto you."*

The universality of God's Message is such that it is not the exclusive spiritual domain of any one religious community. It is not limited to Muslims over Christians or Jews, nor vice versa. Only God knows who has true faith and who does not. Therefore, in order to apply Islamic teaching in an authentic and genuine manner, the state must exercise tolerance and respect for religious diversity, which is a component of God's creation.

The state must treat all of its citizens, Muslims and non-Muslims, as equal before the law. Since the other chapters in this work have already covered this argument in various ways, we are merely emphasizing its main points again here. Equality before the law derives from four inter-related arguments. First, it is based on the equality of all human beings, with their moral freedom and human dignity, as created by God. Second, it is based on the state's duty to ensure justice for all of its citizens, by protecting their human freedom and institutionalizing this protection in citizenship rights. It must discharge this duty without discrimination, in the spirit expressed in the following verse. *"O you who have attained to faith! Be ever steadfast in upholding equity, bearing witness to the truth for the sake of God, even though it be against your own selves or your parents and kinsfolk. Whether the person concerned be rich or poor, God's claim takes precedence over [the claims of] either of them"* (Surah an Nisaa – Women, 4:135).[16] Third, on both practical and moral grounds, the state cannot go about trying to establish the religious faith/belief of every individual citizen. It cannot take on the moral authority, which is God's right, in this respect. Therefore, the state must, as a necessity, treat everyone as equals before the law, regardless of religious identity. Lastly, in order to uphold its commitment to the implementation of the five basic goals of the *sharia* (protection of life, religion, intellect, property and family), the state must make sure that all of its citizens are granted equal protection.

Gender equality and religious equality in society are but two examples which illustrate the broader argument for the inclusion of all individuals in society in the political community, as delineated by citizenship. The law cannot discriminate among social groups in granting citizenship rights, because to do so is to contradict the divinely-granted universal equality of all human beings.

The Individual and the Community

The discussion so far has outlined the role of individual rights and the equality of all citizens as the bases for citizenship rights. A related issue is the balance between the individual and the community, as mediated by the state. While the state grants citizenship rights on an individual basis, it is engaged simultaneously in the construction of community, or national identity. In addition, it is charged with protecting both individual and community rights. How are the two to be resolved?

A conservative Islamic perspective has generalized a monolithic nature of Muslim societies and Islamic law, to claim that the interests of the *umma* (community) are always placed above those of the individual. The fact that most Muslim rulers have historically emphasized maintaining order and security at the expense of individual challenges to political and religious authority has been translated into the perception that this state of affairs is endemic to Islam as a religion.[17]

While there is no doubt that the community is valued in Islamic tradition, in fact, this work has aimed to disprove this monolithic construction, by illustrating that the individual and his/her accompanying freedom and rights are valued and protected, both in the Quran and the sharia. In certain cases, individual legal rights take precedence over state rights, such as in private property matters or private contracts. It is Islamic history, not religion, which has turned citizens into subjects, stressing blind obedience and submission to political and religious authority at the expense of individual freedom of reasoning, thought and action.[18] Part of our argument here for expanding the notion of citizenship rights is to reclaim individual autonomy and individual rights and duties, which it is the state's duty to protect for all of its citizens, and to balance it against the community's interests.

Having argued for an expansive definition of who should be granted citizenship, there remains the issue of the types of citizenship rights that should be conferred. Earlier, we presented three types of rights – civil, political and social – which have gradually become accepted as integral components of citizenship. These need to be implemented within an Islamic state as well, without any social distinctions. In practice, this means, for example, that women must be legally granted the same civil, political and social rights as men, and non-Muslims the same as Muslims. The only distinction is based on law – legal rights of citizens versus those of (non-citizen) permanent residents. Usually, this distinction is on the basis of the right of political participation, i.e. voting and running for office, which is denied to the latter.

However, the process for achieving full citizenship and associated rights needs to be accessible and not inherently discriminatory against particular groups in society. The naturalization process needs to be recognized as a way of attaining citizenship, in addition to the *jus soli* principle (citizenship by birth).

Medinan Model

This chapter has outlined the theoretical basis for an inclusive definition of citizenship in society. But, this theoretical framework for equality was applied by the Prophet (pbuh) himself in the Charter of Medina. The chapter on constitutionalism provides the full text and detailed analysis of the Constitution of Medina, but we will highlight a few salient points from that discussion as a practical application of the ideas surveyed above.

First and foremost, Medina was a distinctly pluralistic polity made up of autonomous social and religious groups. The Constitution of Medina defines the parties involved in its construction and administration as: the emigrant Muslims of the Quraysh, the Muslims of Yathrib, the Jews, and the client tribes (mawla) that are attached to all of these parties through military/political alliances. The mutual co-existence of multiple ummas, or communities, based on religion, kinship and patron-client ties in the city-state of Medina is noted. The political community of Medina subsumes all of the individual religious communities, including the polytheist Arabs, as well as the Jews and Muslims. The document proposes the equal participation of all in the political community, without regard to religious identity. This ideal is worth underscoring precisely for its departure from the notion of citizenship rights based purely on religious identity in a homogeneous Islamic state.

Also noteworthy is the fact that the state does not make Muslim identity a requirement for membership in the polity or the rights granted by the state. The state does regulate the religious communities and individual freedom of religion is left unfettered. Neither is there official recognition of the dominance of one religious group over another, nor pressure for others to convert to Islam. In fact, Article 25 distinctly states, "To the Jews their religion and to the Muslims their religion." The only cause for distinction between believers and nonbelievers is if one party threatens to disrupt the peace or violates the treaty, and is therefore punished or expelled by the community. If a polytheist is to be shunned, it is because he has sided with the Quraysh against the Muslims of Medina (Art. 20).[19]

In addition, other markers are used to refer to the communities, instead of religion. For example, the Jews and Arabs are referred to through their tribal affiliations, and their clients, likewise (Art. 3-10 and 25-35). Since the Jews acceded to the Constitution by clans, and not as one religious community, when one tribe broke the pact, only it was expelled from Medina, and not the entire Jewish community (Art. 16).[20] The Muslims are identified as being either the emigrants from Mecca, or the helpers from Medina (preamble), or in other instances, as simply "believers." All of these details illustrate the fact religious identity is not the primary basis for citizenship rights within the political community of Medina.

Security is the pivotal concern of the Constitution of Medina and what unites the political community. "The security of God is one" (Article 15). The protection granted by God to the community encompasses all of its members. The borders of the city-state of Medina are demarcated and the security of all of the inhabitants is ensured in Article 39: "The valley of Yathrib is sacred for the purpose of this document." All those who threaten this security from outside these borders face the collective military strength of the Medinans (Art. 44). In conjunction with Articles 17 and 18, which deal with equal rights to make peace and compulsory military service for all, respectively, all of these articles point to the regulation of war and peace and the paramount goal of maintaining the security of the political community. Article 22 condemns anyone who has agreed to the terms of the Pact to give protection to a wrongdoer. Therefore, membership in the political community, while all-encompassing with regard to social and religious identity, is severely restrictive against those who threaten its foundational security. Political security, codified in law, takes precedence over any and all individual social and religious concerns. This is the basis for the loyalty granted to the state by the Medinans. The state provides security for all of its citizens, in exchange for obedience to its laws.

The Constitution of Medina highlights the reciprocal nature of rights and duties between the individual and the state. The political authority headed by the Prophet (pbuh) guarantees equality, justice and protection for all those who accede to the terms outlined in the document. For example, there is evidence that Jews asked the Prophet (pbuh) to settle disputes among them as well, and that he ruled according to their biblical law.[21] Religious identity is not a precondition. Non-Muslims were not asked to recognize the Prophet (pbuh) as a prophet, but only as a political leader, and swear allegiance to him accordingly. This demonstrates the basis for citizenship rights as primarily political in nature, and not a religious duty. It also allows the possibility of naturalization as a way of gaining citizenship rights – since the majority of those who lived in Medina voluntarily ascribed to membership in the polity as adults, and were not born there.

The Medinan model represents one way of understanding citizenship rights in the context of Islamic history. But unfortunately, this model was not sustained in the centuries after the Prophet's (pbuh) death. Instead, juristic classification of the legal rights of Muslims vs. non-Muslims in society gained greater influence, and led to the entrenchment of discriminatory, two-tier systems of citizenship on the basis of religious identity in Muslim states. We reiterate our criticism of the historical and legal basis for this model, also noted in the chapters on Non-Muslims and Religious Freedom, respectively.

Conclusion

Citizenship reflects the rule of law as the basis for determining membership within a political community. This chapter has focused on outlining a broad theoretical framework for defining citizenship rights in an Islamic state. The specific contents of these rights – freedom of speech, religious freedom, freedom of movement, right to private property, etc – are detailed in their own chapters and do not need to be reiterated here. What is key in this discussion is that an inclusive conception of citizenship rights is in harmony with an Islamic perspective on the role of the individual as a member of society. Given the rights and freedom that God has granted to all human beings, it is the state's duty to safeguard all of them, for all of its citizens, without regard to religious identity, in exchange for political allegiance and obedience to the state authority. For example, this means excluding religion as an official category in state, official documents. This political compact between the individual and the state derives its moral sanction from the Quran, which upholds equality, freedom and justice as paramount obligations for all, and in particular for those who govern.

Footnotes

1   The closest link between geography and religious identity is that found in classical juristic discourse, dividing the world into *dar al islam* and *dar al harb*. We consider this dichotomy obsolete and irrelevant in modern times. This terminology is not in the Quran nor in the teachings of the Prophet (pbuh).

2   This section is adapted from unpublished paper, Uzma Jamil, "Citizenship Theory in Saudi Arabia and Kuwait."

3   T. H. Marshall, *Citizenship and Social Class* (Cambridge: Cmbridge University Press, 1950), p. 8.

4   Marshall, p. 10.

5   Marshall, p. 11.

6   Marshall, p. 14.

7   Marshall, p. 28.

8   Rogers Brubaker, *Citizenship and Nationhood in France and Germany* (Cambridge: Harvard University Press, 1992), p. 22.

9   Brubaker, p. 23.

10 Brubaker, p. 29.

11 Sharon Stone Russell, "Migration and Political Integration in the Arab World," *The Politics of Arab Integration*, vol. 4, ed. G. Luciani and G. Salame, (London: Croom Helm, 1988), p. 187.

12 Russell, pp. 187-188.

13 See the individual chapters on sanctity of life, property rights and various types of political freedoms for more detailed exploration of these topics.

14 Muslim, Book 016, Number 4161; also Bukhari, Vol 1 Book 3 No. 67; and Vol 8, Book 81 No 776.

15 See chapter on women's rights for more on legal equality between men and women.

16 See chapter on the justice system for more on the primary role of justice as a Quranic principle and the state's role in discharg-

ing it.

17 Nawaf A. Salam, "The Emergence of Citizenship in Islamdom," *Arab Law Quarterly*, 12:2(1997), p. 129.(125-147).

18 See Fatema Mernissi's Islam and Democracy, transl. Mary Jo Lakeland (Cambridge: Perseus Publishing, 2002) for a more detailed criticism of this historical dynamic and its contemporary effects in the Arab world. For example, Abbasid state patronage of thinkers who emphasized a strict interpretation of the sharia led to the marginalization of dissenting Muslim scholars and suppressed an intellectual tradition which had previously thrived on critique, p. 36.

19 Quraysh is the name of the Prophet's (pbuh) tribe. In the earlier portions of the Constitution, the term refers to the Muslims who migrated with the Prophet (pbuh), in contrast to the Medinan Ansar. In later portions, the term is used exclusively to refer to the non-Muslim, Makkan Quraysh who used to torment the Prophet (pbuh) while he was still living in Makkah. They were therefore the enemies of the Muslims who undertook the *hijra*. One of the Prophet's (pbuh) concerns was that the non-Muslims of Medina might collude with Makkan Quraysh against the Emigrant Muslims. Articles 20 and 43 expressly prohibit this.

20 Hamidullah, p. 33.

21 Hamidullah, p. 35. Bulaç, pp. 174-175.

Freedom of Association

reedom of association, or assembly, refers to individuals' right to voluntary membership in any formal or informal organization, association or group, for political or non-political purposes. It also includes the right to peacefully assemble in public, in order to express particular views in relation to the government or government policies. Thus, freedom of association is related to both freedom of speech and freedom of political dissent as legal rights. It is also connected to civil society, such that the existence of freedom of association is integral to the vitality of civil society, which in turn, is important in a democratic system.[1] We propose a conception of freedom of association that allows citizens the greatest possible protection in exercising this right, with minimal state interference.

The Quran does not treat freedom of assembly as a discrete topic, nor is it discussed as such in classical juristic scholarship. Our discussion of it here will draw from general injunctions in the Quran regarding cooperation and participation in community affairs, which is introduced in the first section. The subsequent sections of the chapter offer two distinct, but nevertheless interrelated, arguments supporting freedom of association. The first of these details its relationship with freedom of speech, while the second one focuses on civil society.

Hisba

We situate freedom of association as a right within the context of *hisba*, the Quranic principle of "commanding what is good and forbidding what is evil: *"amr bil-ma'ruf wa nahy 'an al-munkar."* The defini-

tion of "good" (*ma'ruf*) is a relative one, i.e. what is commonly understood to be "good" as "the product of human experience and constructed normative understandings".[2] What is considered "good" may change
over time, such as the acceptability of slavery, although it is bound by
the principles that we rely on in this work. It serves as a universal moral
principle in the Quran, and therefore retains importance for all societies and in all time periods. For our purposes here, freedom of association is necessary in order for Muslims to achieve *hisba* and to work
towards "the good" in public and political life. It is only through the
freedom to engage with diverse viewpoints and groups that individuals
can arrive at this goal.

We begin by examining a few verses regarding the concept of *hisba*
in the Quran. Surah al Araf – The Faculty of Discernment, 7:157 discusses *hisba* as one of the objectives of the Prophet's (pbuh) mission.
*"Those who shall follow the [last] Apostle, the unlettered Prophet whom
they shall find described in the Torah that is with them, and [later on]
in the Gospel: [the Prophet] who will enjoin upon them the doing of
what is right and forbid them the doing of what is wrong, and make
lawful to them the good things of life and forbid them the bad things,
and lift from their burdens and the shackles that were upon them [afore-
time]. Those, therefore, who shall believe in him, and honor him, and
succor him, and follow the light that has been bestowed from on high
through him – it is they that shall attain to a happy state."* What is
"good" is also "lawful" and "just", which adds to the moral weight of
hisba as a core principle. However, God is the only judge of morality;
not human beings. Humans are asked to make moral choices, to choose
the good and lawful over the bad and the unlawful, with the faith that
God will reward or punish them accordingly on the Day of Judgment.
It is part of the Prophet's (pbuh) goal to spread this message, but not to
stand in judgment over the choices that people make.

As part of the message of Islam, enjoining the good and forbidding
the evil is a moral command to all Muslims, and serves to identify them
as Muslims. It is on par with belief in God and the Prophet Muhammad

(pbuh) as His Messenger, the credo of faith in Islam. This theme was mentioned in the previous verse, and is also noted in Surah al Imran – The House of Imran. *"You are indeed the best community that has ever been brought forth for [the good of] mankind: you enjoin the doing of what is right and forbid the doing of what is wrong, and you believe in God"* (Surah al Imran – The House of Imran, 3:110).

The obligatory quality of *hisba* as an individual duty of faith is also illustrated in the following *hadith*. "If any of you sees something evil, he should set it right by his hand; if he is unable to do so, then by his tongue, and if he is unable to do even that, then (let him denounce it) in his heart. But this is the weakest form of faith."[3] This *hadith* stresses action and speech over unvoiced disapproval, as the preferred mode of action in implementing good and standing up against evil. It also demonstrates the spirit in which individuals should relate with each other within a community. This point will be addressed again later on in this section.

This idea of *hisba* as a collective obligation, in addition to an individual duty, is supported in the Quran in several verses. Surah al Imran – The House of Imran, 3:110, quoted above, is one example that refers to Muslims as a community, engaged in *"enjoin the doing of what is right and forbid the doing of what is wrong, and you believe in God."* Verse 104, from the same Surah, also distinguishes the community as moral agents; *"and that there might grow out of you a community [of people] who invite unto all that is good, and enjoin the doing of what is right and forbid the doing of what is wrong: and it is they, they who shall attain to a happy state!"* (Surah al Imran – The House of Imran, 3:104). Other verses include:

"[Well aware of] those who, [even] if We firmly establish them on earth, remain constant in prayer, and give in charity, and enjoin the doing of what is right and forbid the doing of what is wrong; but with God rests the final outcome of all events" (Surah al-Hajj – The Pilgrimage, 22:41).

"But rather help one another in furthering virtue and God-con-

sciousness, and do not help one another in furthering evil and enmity; and remain conscious of God: for, behold, God is severe in retribution!" (Surah al Maida, 5:2).

"And [as for] the believers, both men and women – they are close unto one another: they [all] enjoin the doing of what is right and forbid the doing of what is wrong, and are constant in prayer, and render the purifying dues, and pay heed unto God and His and His Apostle. It is they upon whom God will bestow His grace: verily, God is almighty, wise!" (Surah at Tawba – Repentance, 9:71).

Surah an Nisaa – Women, 4:114 comments on the social aspect of achieving *hisba*. *"No good comes, as a rule, out of secret confabulations – saving such as are devoted to enjoining charity, or equitable dealings, or setting things to rights between people: and unto him who does this out of a longing for God's goodly acceptance We shall in time grant a mighty reward"* (Surah an Nisaa - Women, 4:114). This verse stresses the desirability of publicly shared advice or opinions over secret ones, when carried out with regard to achieving particular goals: charity and reconciliation between people. This can be interpreted literally as sanctioning the existence of social work oriented organizations, or it can be applied in a more general sense towards groups that promote knowledge, education or awareness in all fields.

All of the verses cited above expand the definition of "faith" in Islam to include more than just belief in one God and the Prophet (pbuh) and the duties that constitute the five pillars of Islam. Enjoining the good and forbidding evil is an equally integral constituent of faith. *Hisba* is not limited to individual moral behavior; it is also incumbent upon the community as a blueprint for collective behavior. It is reflected in a spirit of cooperation within the community, which includes positive action and speech in public affairs, as illustrated in the *hadith* mentioned earlier.

The equal importance of *hisba* as a way of organizing both individual and public affairs sheds light on understanding freedom of association as a related principle. Despite the fact that Quranic reference to *hisba* is predominantly in moral terms, we can expand the meaning of it to the socio-political sphere as well. "In bare essence, *hisba* entitles every individual to the moral and political freedom to speak out and to act in pursuit of what he or she considers to be beneficial and good, or to discourage and forbid what he or she considers to be evil."[4] Translating this imperative from the private to the public sphere requires the individual to be an active participant in community affairs, and to have the freedom to shape public policy by organizing and associating with like-minded individuals.[5]

This is not to say that everyone has to agree with a particular individual's opinion or view. We are not claiming that only groups which adhere to a single standard of "the good" be allowed to voice their opinions and exist freely in society. The moral component of hisba does not mean that the state can prohibit the existence of particular types of organizations as "evil", if they adhere to an ideology or perspective that is antithetical to the interpretation of Islam that the state may uphold. (An example would be the Communist Party, on the grounds that it adheres to an atheist outlook and is therefore antithetical to Islam.)

We are arguing, instead, for an expansion of the concept of *hisba* to include the existence of a variety of organizations and groups, political and non-political, all of which work to achieve some degree of benefit for society.[6] It would be presumptuous for any one citizen to limit the interpretation of what constitutes *hisba* for others. Debate and discussion in and of themselves have value and allow the nation to gain insight. In this case, we can define "benefit", or "good" as diversity and pluralism in public political and social affairs, and as an expression of the autonomy and freedom of the individuals that compose a particular society. But, the point here is that the right to air diverse opinions in the public sphere goes hand in hand with the right to freedom of assembly, both of which are components of the duty of *hisba*. The connection between freedom of speech and freedom of association will be elaborated further in the following section of this chapter.

As discussed elsewhere in this work, we propose a sharp limitation on the state's role as an enforcer of moral authority, since God is the ultimate judge of moral behavior. The state's primary concern is to regulate social and political affairs so that the safety and security of individuals in the community are not jeopardized. The lack of safety and security is the only "evil" that can and should be prohibited by the state. Direct threats to safety and security are the only thing that the state can do something about. It is in this context that the broadest protection of freedom of association is necessary. On moral grounds as well, the state cannot limit the autonomy and freedom of individuals, unless it involves a clear and direct threat to public safety.

In conclusion, this section has laid out the theoretical basis for understanding freedom of association as a component of the Islamic duty of enjoining good and forbidding evil, both for the individual and for the community. For society to achieve this goal, there must be ample space for civil society to take root and for groups and organizations to form to advocate on behalf of public issues. It is only through an open process of setting the public agenda, that society can strive to reach what is truly good and to avoid that which is evil. We do not take *hisba* as a license for the state to create a tyrannical system that enforces a narrow interpretation of Islam on the rest of society, and with no method for a change in policy. That is a profound abuse of the concept and must be rejected.

Freedom of Expression

All humans are granted freedom of expression as a right by God, which also includes freedom of inquiry or thought. Detailing the parameters for allowing individuals the right to express their views and opinions in a social and political context is a concern of government. As noted in the chapter on freedom of speech, this is not an absolute right, but one that is tempered by the government's duty to maintain public security.

The same line of argument can apply towards freedom of association as well. Everyone is endowed with the capacity for thought and speech by God. Freedom of thought would be meaningless without equal freedom to associate with others, to communicate with them, and to exchange ideas and perspectives, as part of a larger effort to exercise one's own right to free speech. The freedom to associate with others, to organize meetings or demonstrations, and to form parties, interest groups or other kinds of organizations are all a consequence of freedom of expression. We have argued, in the chapter on freedom of speech, for the protection of free speech as a legal and political right according to Quranic principles. As a related concept, Islamic teaching also upholds freedom of association as part of citizens' political rights. To limit it is to restrict the basic freedom of expression that has been granted to individuals by God, and that they exercise in society.

An example of the overlap between free speech and freedom of assembly dates from the rule of Caliph Ali, the fourth caliph after the death of the Prophet (pbuh). The Kharijites were a religio-political opposition group to Ali. "They used to abuse the Caliph openly and threatened to murder him. Whenever they were arrested for these offenses, [the Caliph] would set them free and tell his officers: 'As long as they do not actually perpetrate offenses against the state, the mere use of abusive language or the threat of the use of force are not such offenses for which they can be imprisoned.'"[7] This incident exemplifies the broad parameters of freedom given to the Kharijites to associate as a group, even when their speech and actions were deemed offensive, and clearly oppositional to the political authority in question. We will refer to this example again in the discussion on civil society.

Caliph Ali's directive also illustrates the fact that the government's ability to pose restrictions on this right is conditioned by its ability to prove that a group is a clear danger to public safety. There must be legal evidence regarding direct involvement by an individual in criminal activity, or as a member of a particular group that is suspected of criminal activities. An individual cannot be subject to legal prosecution on the basis of "guilt by association" alone. This does not mean, however, that criminal activity is to be tolerated. Membership in an organized crime group is not protected by freedom of association.

In sum, freedom of speech is related to freedom of assembly because both are required for citizens to participate in shaping government and performing *hisba*. These rights must therefore be protected by the state. The common root for both is the fact that they represent a basic freedom to think and to communicate those views with others, as given to humans by God. The previous discussion on *hisba* highlighted the moral imperatives behind protection of freedom of association as a discrete topic. This section has focused more on the legal aspects of the issue.

Civil Society

As a separate argument to the one elaborated so far, the existence of a vibrant civil society is linked to the individual right to freedom of association. Both are important for maintaining a pluralistic, democratic society where the ruled have the right to be involved in, to monitor and to critique the ruler and his policies. One method for achieving this kind of political participation is through the institutions of the state; i.e. by voting, or running for office. But, outside the formal state sphere, membership in political parties, lobbies, the press, trade unions, professional associations or other interest groups can also function as a check on government power, and/or influence policy-making in a particular direction. In both cases, freedom of association is important for achieving a civil society that challenges the absolute power of government in a democratic context. The following discussion defines civil society and gives evidence of its prevalence, both within the Quranic worldview and in Islamic political thought and society.

Civil society is defined as the space in which people can associate voluntarily, and is made up of a set of relations networks, formed for the sake of faith, interest, and ideology.[8] The space referred to is the buffer zone between the state and the individual citizen, that allows room for the latter to critique, monitor and assess the state's actions, but remains free from direct state influence. Nevertheless, civil society often exists within the broad legal framework laid down by the state; even if within that framework the members have the freedom to choose their actions. Thus, the idea of civil society refers to "a part of society which has a life of its own, which is distinctly different from the state, and which is largely in autonomy from it."[9]

In addition to the existence of autonomous institutions, civil society also requires "civility" among these groups, implying a willingness to tolerate and engage with disparate, often opposing, social and political views and attitudes that are represented. It also indicates support for the various institutions of civic order, such as political parties, trade unions, a free press and voluntary associations.

In sum, civil society denotes the existence of a variety of autonomous institutions, separate from the state, and composed of groups that engage with each other in a tolerant and "civil" manner. Civil society is integral to the functioning of a representative, democratic system, since it allows for the active participation of citizens in public and political life through debate, discussion and critique.[10]

Civil society is not a uniquely Western concept. It also has roots in Islamic political theory and history. To the extent that it serves as an informal check on state power and seeks to maintain the balances of power between state and societal institutions, there have been and are analogous concerns in Islamic political theory.[11] Part of the purpose of civil society is to check the authoritarian tendencies of the state – a pre-occupation that is also documented in the Quran and *hadith* literature. The Quran condemns tyranny as contrary to the absolute authority of God and because it undermines the freedom given by God to people. It resists the idea of a concentration of political power within one person, or one ruling party, or group of individuals, on the grounds that it leads to arrogance, which is contrary to Islam, or "submission to God's Will."[12] The following Quranic verses support this argument.

The Pharaoh is the most prominent example in the Quran of a tyrannical ruler. He is described in Surah Yunus and Surah al Qasas as an unjust and arrogant ruler because he rules through fear and violence. *"But none save a few of his people declared their faith in Moses, [while others held back] for fear of Pharaoh and their great ones, lest they persecute them: for, verily, Pharaoh was mighty on earth and was, verily, of those who are given to excesses "* (Surah Yunus – Jonah, 10:83). *"Behold, Pharaoh exalted himself in the land and divided its people into castes. One group of them he deemed utterly low; he would slaughter their sons and spare [only] their women: for, behold, he was one of those who spread corruption [on earth]"* (Surah al Qasas – The Story, 28:4). His arrogance is an affront to God, who is the Ultimate Judge of human actions on the Day of Judgment. On that day, the Pharaoh will be judged along with everyone else, but the Pharaoh has lost sight of that eventuality, blinded as he is by the myopia of power. *"Thus arrogantly, without the least good sense, did he and his hosts behave on earth – just as if they thought that they would never have to appear before Us [for judgment]"* (Surah al Qasas – The Story, 28:38). The Pharaoh is condemned here not for his lack of faith in God, but for his tyrannical behavior. This same standard would apply to a tyrannical Muslim government that also behaved "arrogantly."

In another example, an exchange between Abraham (pbuh) and a Babylonian ruler[13] also illustrates the negative attitude towards one who claims to have power equal to that of God. It contrasts the supreme power of God with the arrogance of a ruler who claims to give life and death as well. Ultimately, this verse can be read as an indictment of divine right of kingship, and the absolute power it entails. In this exchange, Abraham cites *"Lo! Abraham said: ' My Sustainer is He who grants life and deals death.' [The king] replied: ' I [too] grant life and deal death!' Said Abraham: 'Verily, God causes the sun to rise in the east; cause it, then, to rise in the west!' Thereupon he who has bent on denying the truth remained dumbfounded: for God does not guide people who [deliberately] do wrong"* (Surah al Baqara – The Cow, 2:258).

Abraham has shown to the ruler that his power is limited, and that he is not the ultimate authority in the universe.

The moral duty to challenge authoritarianism and oppression, which is part of the ethical imperatives of civil society, is illustrated in an encounter between Moses (pbuh) and the Pharaoh in the Quran. Moses (pbuh) speaks up against the tyranny of the ruler, despite the fact that the Pharaoh provided shelter to and raised Moses. *"[But when Moses had delivered his message, Pharaoh] said: 'Did we not bring thee up among us when thou wert a child? And didst thou not spend among us years of thy [later] life? And yet thou didst commit that [heinous] deed of thine, and [hast thus shown that] thou art one of the ingrate! Replied [Moses] : 'I committed it while I was still going astray; and I fled from you because I feared you. But [since] then my Sustainer has endowed me with the ability to judge [between right and wrong], and has made me one of [His] message-bearers. And [as for] that favor of which thou so tauntingly remindest me – [was it not] due to thy having enslaved the children of Israel?'"* (Surah ash Shuara – The Poets, 26:18-22). The Pharaoh has made slaves of his people, but Moses (pbuh) is not deterred from his commitment to speak freely and to challenge that injustice and oppression, even at the expense of a personal relationship. This example demonstrates the evil of tyranny and the need to speak and act against it.

All three of these Quranic examples highlight God's condemnation of concentration of absolute political authority. They point to a moral imperative for the existence of civil society, as a check on all-pervasive state authority. The *hadith* literature on a just ruler, reviewed below, indirectly supports the same argument by stressing the need to resist an oppressive ruler.

Various *hadith* stress the responsibility of the ruler to be just, and to protect his people as a moral duty. "A ruler who, having obtained control over the affairs of the Muslims, does not strive for their betterment and does not serve them sincerely shall not enter Paradise with them."[14] "The worst of guardians is the cruel ruler. Beware of being one of them."[15] A tyrannical ruler who oppresses his people and demands obedience at all costs should be resisted. The Prophet (pbuh) is report-ed to have said, "When you see my community afraid of telling a tyrant, 'O tyrant', then it is not worth belonging to it anymore."[16] All of these *hadith* stress the ideal of a just ruler and the moral duty of cit-izens to criticize him and to counter his tyrannical behavior, if neces-sary by withdrawing political obedience.

Another relevant, Quranic concept is shura, or mutual consulta-tion between the ruler and the ruled. There are two verses that are often cited with regard to shura in the Quran. Surah al Imran – The House of Imran, 3: 159, states *"And take counsel with them in all matters of public concern; then, when thou hast decided upon a course of action, place thy trust in God: for, verily, God loves those who place their trust in Him."* The second verse is Surah ash Shura - Consultation, 42:38: *"And who respond to [the call of] their Sustainer and are constant in prayer; and whose rule [in all matters of common concern] is consultation among themselves; and who spend on others out of what We provide for them as sustenance."* Although *shura* is discussed in more detail as part of the institution-al framework of an Islamic democratic state in the chapter on democ-racy, as a general principle emphasizing cooperation among members of society, it also applies to civil society and the public sphere outside formal state control.

In the context of this chapter, "consultation" with citizens does not necessarily mean direct consultation. It is not possible for the gov-ernment to consult each and every citizen for his/her opinion on a particular policy. However, citizens have the right to express their views through particular associations, lobbies, or interest groups which represent their opinions to the government. Citizens also have the right to exchange opinions among themselves, through their membership in these organizations.[17] Thus, civil society reinforces and is reinforced by freedom of association, as a way to implement the principle of shura.

The Quran and *hadith* give us a moral and theoretical imperative for building a civil society that prevents the state from assuming absolute political power. Turning to Islamic history, there were also various autonomous, non-governmental institutions prevalent in Muslim society and which served (and continue to serve) a similar role as components of civil society. For example, the *awqaf* (plural of waqf), charitable religious endowments, played a role in Muslim societies of the classical time period, by fostering the development of art and science, independent of state authority. Individual citizens could endow foundations that supported schools, scholarships, universities, publications, orphanages, and mosques.[18] This institution was protected from state encroachment as a privately-funded enterprise, but one which potentially fostered associational networks in the public sphere, analogous to the role of civil society today.

During the lifetime of Prophet Muhammad (pbuh), tribal networks formed a segment of society that existed between the individual and the government. Their role is highlighted in the first Islamic political community created by the Prophet (pbuh) at Medina, also described as al *mujtama' al-madani* (civic society). In this case, it refers to the variety of Muslim and non-Muslim tribes, allied on tribal and geographic lines, which made up the polity. The Constitution of Medina reflected this pluralism in society, and institutionalized it to the extent that it gave significant leeway and freedom to the individual tribes to manage their affairs, given that they pledged allegiance to the political authority of the Prophet (pbuh).[19]

Another historical example of civil society is in the rise of diverse political and ideological movements, which eventually solidified into the main schism between the Sunni and Shi'a sects in Islam. The Kharijites, discussed earlier, are an extreme example of political-religious group which challenged the authority and legitimacy of Caliph Ali's government. Although they eventually lost credibility because of their use of violence against the ruler (a Kharijite assassinated Caliph Ali), their initial right to express criticism and opposition and to associate as a group was not contested.[20]

Last, but not least, the *ulema* also functioned as a powerful group in civil society, independent of state authority. The classical jurists organized themselves into various schools of doctrinal and legal thought, and critiqued and expressed their opinions through debate and engagement with other scholars. As legal scholars, they served as a moral check on the legislative and executive authority of the government, but did not hold political authority, and were not necessarily accountable to anyone. For example, Muslim jurists living under Abbasid rule were notable in their insistence on independence from imperial, political authority. Abu Hanifa (d. 767), al Shafi (d. 820) and Ahmad b. Hanbal (d. 855), all of whom were founders of Sunni legal schools, and scholars Abu Yusuf (d. 795) and al-Shaybani (d. 805), are all examples of classical Muslim jurists who resisted attempts of co-optation into the administrative structure of government.[21]

The strength of the *ulema* as actors in civil society is illustrated in a confrontation with the Abbasid caliphs over doctrinal issues. When four successive caliphs (833-848) tried to unilaterally enforce the opinion of the Mutazilites that the Quran was created (as opposed to the view that it always existed), the majority of the other legal schools and jurists were fiercely resistant to the imposition. The rulers eventually had to give way, and the effort was abandoned. This example illustrates the strengthening of the role of the *ulema* as a class of religious/legal scholars with significant informal power in the public sphere, from the third century onwards.[22]

In conclusion, this brief foray into the existence of civil society in an Islamic context has demonstrated an implicit argument for the protection of freedom of assembly as political and legal right. Both issues are intimately linked. While civil society serves to check absolute concentration of power in the state, which is a central moral and political concern for Muslims, freedom of assembly helps to preserve civil society. Both are equally important for maintaining a pluralistic, democratic society where the ruled have the right to be involved in, to monitor and to critique the ruler and his policies.

Conclusion

The doctrine of *hisba* as a duty of faith requires a commitment to uphold the "good" in community affairs as well, through active communication and engagement with other people and groups. It, therefore, sanctions freedom of assembly as a basic right of all individuals. It goes hand in hand with the right to freedom of speech, both of which allow humans to further their potential as individuals created by God. From a political perspective, freedom of association is linked with civil society as a means to achieve a truly diverse, pluralistic, and tolerant democratic state.

But, in practice, the extent to which freedom of association is protected in a particular society is often reflective of the degree to which the government allows political freedom to its people. Too many Muslim countries have used ideological, political, or religious differences with the state, as reasons to discriminate against and suppress any and all potential opposition, especially by banning particular political parties or oppositional organizations and jailing their members. We strongly and firmly condemn this kind of state behavior on the grounds that mere dissent does not constitute sufficient grounds for legal restriction on freedom of expression or freedom of assembly. The existence of dissenting minorities in Islamic history (the Shi'a being a key example) illustrates the ideological freedom that must be given to these groups, and in fact, to all groups in society, regardless of identity, ideology or affiliation.

Footnotes

1   See chapter on Democracy for more on this topic.
2   Khaled Abou El Fadl, *The Place of Tolerance in Islam*, p. 14.
3   Muslim, quoted in Mohammad Hashim Kamali, *Freedom of Expression in Islam* (Kuala Lumpur: Berita Publishing, 1994) p. 33.
4   Mohammad Hashim Kamali, Freedom, *Equality and Justice in Islam* (Cambridge, UK: Islamic Texts Society) p. 25.
5   This can also be construed as an implicit argument for the existence of civil society, which is discussed further on in this chapter.
6   Kamali, *Freedom, Equality and Justice in Islam*, p. 84.
7   A.A. Maududi, *Human Rights in Islam*, p. 30.
8   Farhad Kazemi, "Perspectives on Islam and Civil Society," *Islamic Political Ethics*, ed. Sohail Hashmi (Princeton: Princeton

University Press, 2002),p. 39.

9 Edward Shils, "The Virtue of Civil Society," *Government and Opposition*, 26 (Winter 1991), p.4.

10 Walzer, p. 302.

11 Hasan Hanafi, "Alternative Conceptions of Civil Society: A Reflective Islamic Approach," *Islamic Political Ethics*, ed. Sohail Hashmi (Princeton: Princeton University Press, 2002), p. 58.

12 This theme has been developed more extensively as part of an argument for contract theory in the chapter on Democracy.

13 The text does not name the ruler, but Yusuf Ali's commentary suggests that it might Nimrod, or another Babylonian ruler, equally condemned for his tyrannical ways.

14 Sahih Muslim, Book 20, *Kitab al Imara* (Book of Government), No. 4502.

15 Sahih Muslim, Book 20, No. 4504.

16 Cited in Kamali, *Freedom, Equality and Justice*, p. 24.

17 Kamali, *Freedom of Expression in Islam*, p. 81.

18 Hanafi, p. 60.

19 Ahmad S. Moussali, "Modern Islamic Fundamentalist Discourses on Civil Society, Pluralism and Democracy," *Civil Society in the Middle East*, vol. 1, ed. R.A. Norton (Leiden & New York: E.J. Brill, 1995-96), 83.

20 Moussali, pp. 83-84.

21 Kemal A. Faruki, *The Evolution of Islamic Constitutional Theory and Practice* (Karachi: National Publishing House, 1971), p. 33. For more on the historical development of the Shari'a, see chapter on justice.

22 Dale F. Eickelman and Jon W. Anderson, eds. *New Media in the Muslim World: The Emerging Public Sphere* (Bloomington, IN: Indiana University Press, 1999), p. 2.

CHAPTER TWELVE

Freedom of Movement

reedom of movement refers to the freedom to travel or to migrate within or outside one's country of origin or of citizenship. It includes both voluntary and involuntary migrations. It also reflects freedom to travel within the country, without restriction, and in particular for women to travel without a male guardian.

The chapter opens with a general look at freedom of movement as a basic and accepted human right within the moral context of the Quran. The subsequent sections focus in more detail on the Prophetic tradition of *hijra*, or the migration from Mecca to Medina in 622 A.D. We argue that it is a seminal moment in Islamic history and tradition which sanctions individual freedom of movement and the related right to seek asylum or refuge. The second section of this chapter draws on the Quran to detail the spiritual and social connotations of the *hijra*, as an event during the Prophet's (pbuh) lifetime. After his death, however, there was considerable variation in the interpretation of the *hijra* tradition, in both Islamic history and jurisprudence.

After outlining the spiritual, historical and juristic interpretations of the concept of the *hijra*, the last section present our argument that the *hijra* is the basis for protection of an individual's right to freedom of movement and to migrate in order to seek asylum and refuge. While this individual right is supported by the example of the Muslim emigrants, the generous reception they received at the hands of the Muslim community of Medina highlights the duty of an Islamic state to accept and protect refugees. This moral obligation is supported by the Islamic juristic principle of *aman*. This part of the argument is addressed in the closing section of the chapter, on the issue of refugees and refugees' rights in international law.

Quranic Perspective

The freedom to travel is a mark of the general freedom that human beings are granted by God. God does not place any restrictions on individuals or their ability to move freely over His earth, but only asks that people do so in a way that is mindful of their orientation towards God. This section develops this argument further by focusing on specific Quranic verses on the topic.

Literally and figuratively, man's ability to travel is a blessing from God. He is enjoined to be grateful for the favors that God has bestowed upon him, from the winds that allow ships to sail, to the lightweight and durable skins used to make tents by the Bedouins. *"He it is who enables you to travel on land and sea. And [behold what happens] when you go to sea in ships: [they go to sea in ships,] and they sail on in them in a favorable wind, and they rejoice thereat – until there comes upon them a tempest, and waves surge towards them from all sides, so that they believe themselves to be encompassed [by death; and then] they call unto God, [at that moment] sincere in their faith in Him alone, 'If Thou wilt but save us from this, we shall most certainly be among the grateful!'"* (Surah Yunus - Jonah, 10: 22). *"And God has given you [the ability to build] your houses as places of rest, and has endowed you with [the skills to make] dwellings out of the skins of animals –easy for you to handle when you travel and when you camp – and [to make] furnishings and goods for temporary use of their [rough] wool and their soft, furry wool and their hair"* (Surah an Nahl – The Bee, 16:80). *"Indeed, We have conferred dignity on the children of Adam, and borne them over land and sea and provided for them sustenance out of the good things of life, and favored them far above most of Our creation"* (Al-Isra – The Night Journey, 17:70).

The Quran envisions people to have freedom of travel and movement, without any restrictions. God calls for humans to travel the world, as a way of affirming faith in the power of God. *"Say: 'Go all over the earth and behold how [wondrously] He has created [man] in the first instance: and thus, too, will God bring into being your second life – for, verily, God has the power to will anything!'"* (Surah al Ankabut – The Spider, 29:20). Travel to other lands also serves as a way to illustrate the end of those who have rejected faith, and conversely, to strengthen one's own faith. In other words, we can argue that travel allows individuals to learn about other people and cultures and religions, which is necessary in order for them to understand their own better. For example, Surah al Anam – Cattle, 6:11 states, *"Say: 'Go all over the earth, and behold what happened in the end to those who gave the lie to the truth!'"* and Surah an Nahl – The Bee, 16:36, *"Go, then, about the earth and behold what happened in the end to those who gave the lie to the truth!."* These verses recommend travel throughout the Earth in order to learn a spiritual lesson, but they also imply that it is the correct order of things that such travel be possible.[1]

As a related issue to freedom of movement, a commonly cited juristic opinion is that Muslim women are restricted from travelling freely, and require the permission and escort of their male guardian (*mahram*)[1] in order to do so. The basis for this is drawn from *hadith* sources, and not the Quran. It is noted, with varying conditions, in the following three *hadith*. "A woman should not travel for more than three days except with a *Mahram*."[2] "It is not permissible for a woman who believes in Allah and the Last Day to travel for one day and night except with a *Mahram*."[3] "A woman should not travel except with a *Mahram* and no man may visit her except in the presence of a *Mahram*."[4] This last hadith links travel to another situation where the presence of a woman's *mahram* is required – a social visit. But laying aside this issue and focusing only on the travel restriction element, there are several issues to be noted. First, depending on the *hadith*, the conditions vary as to the type of journey that woman may undertake without her *mahram*, from a journey less than three days to all journeys, regardless of duration. Second, in order to bolster the requirement for a male guardian, one of the *hadith* links belief in God to the travel requirements for women. Third, in general, all of these *hadith* are noted in the context of a discussion on *hajj*, and the requirements surrounding its undertaking.

Without delving into the narrow view of gender relations[5] exhibited in these examples, we can, nevertheless, question the juristic opinion deriving from these *hadith*, which restricts women's independent freedom of movement. First, given that these *hadith* are narrated in the context of *hajj*, to generalize from this to all other situations, is questionable and more reflective of human interpretation than any Divine injunction. Second, there are no conditions attached to belief in (a monotheistic) God in Islam. The only absolute requirement for behavior is observance of the moral standards which the Quran outlines, and which is asked of all Muslims, regardless of gender. Therefore, linking belief in God to the condition of traveling only with a male guardian runs contrary to the Quran. Third, and most importantly, there is no evidence in the Quran restricting freedom of movement for women. In fact, it is directly in contrast to the line of argument regarding the importance of travel for strengthening one's faith, noted in the verses cited above, from Surahs al Ankabut, al Anam and an Nahl, respectively. Nobody is excluded from the opportunity to achieve and strengthen faith, which God has extended to all human beings. In addition, the ability to travel is a mark of God's favor for His vicegerents on earth. Women are not excluded from this Divine favor in any way. We view the issue of *mahram* to be one of physical security only, and if the circumstances of travel are sufficiently safe, then a mahram is not needed. Just as in some locations it is wise for women not to walk alone after dark, the issue is one based on the particular safety of the travel.

In conclusion, these Quranic references reflect a general sanction on freedom of movement as part of human autonomy and independence. But, an important event in Islamic history, the *hijra* serves as a more direct example of freedom of movement and its spiritual and moral implications for understanding this right today. The next section will explore the details of the *hijra*, using the Quran, and link it to a more specific discussion on freedom of movement as part of refugee migration patterns.

The *Hijra* in the Quran

The *Hijra* refers to the Prophet's (pbuh) migration from Mecca to Medina in 622 A.D. He led a small band of Muslims from Mecca, where they were subject to persecution, to Medina, where they were able to settle peacefully and establish the first nascent Islamic state. The band of Meccan Muslims who traveled with the Prophet (pbuh) were known as the Emigrants, or the *Muhajirun.* The Muslims who received them in Medina were known as the Helpers, or the *Ansar.*[6] This migration occupies a central role in the history of Islam, and in the Prophet's (pbuh) struggle to establish the religion in Arabia. This is reflected in the fact that the date was used (retroactively) to mark the starting point of the Islamic lunar calendar.[7]

The ramifications of the *hijra* are not limited to the geographical movement of the first Muslims from one city to another. As a migratory event, it also has spiritual and social connotations, all of which will be examined in detail in this section. Our aim is to link the concept of *hijra* to a more contemporary understanding of migration, and the freedom of movement that it implies, in subsequent parts of this chapter.

As a strategic move, the Prophet's (pbuh) decision to emigrate in the face of gradually increasing hostility from the Meccan was the external manifestation of a spiritual process. Up to that point in time, the response to oppression had been patience and endurance, with an emphasis on the spiritual rewards in the Afterlife. *"That will inherit the paradise; [and] therein shall they abide"* (Surah al Muminun – The Believers, 23:11).

The general command for the *hijra* came from God at approximately the same time as the revelation of a verse allowing Muslims to

wage war against their oppressors as a matter of self-defense.[8]
*"Permission [to fight] is given to those against whom war is being
wrongfully waged – and, verily, God has indeed the power to succor
them -: those who have been driven from their homelands against all
right for no other reason than their saying, 'Our Sustainer is God!' For,
if God had not enabled people to defend themselves against one
another, [all] monasteries and churches and synagogues and mosques –
in [all of] which God's name is abundantly extolled – would surely have
been destroyed [ere now]. And God will most certainly succor him who
succors His cause: for, verily, God is most powerful, almighty"* (Surah
al Hajj – The Pilgrimage, 22:39-40).

The Prophet (pbuh) laid the groundwork for the *hijra* by focusing on preaching to the inhabitants of Medina, in order to make them
hospitable to the community of Muslims coming from Mecca. He also
negotiated two pacts beforehand, in 620 and 621, between the
Muslims of Mecca and Medina. The first pact was called the "pact of
women" because a woman named "Afra" was the first person to swear
allegiance to the Prophet (pbuh). This is noted in Surah al
Mumtahanah – The Examined One, 60:12: *"O Prophet! Whenever
believing women come unto thee to pledge their allegiance to thee,
[pledging] that [henceforth] they would not ascribe divinity, in any
way, to aught but God, and would not steal, and would not commit
adultery, and would not kill their children, and would not indulge in
slander, falsely devising it out of nothingness, and would not disobey
thee in anything [that thou declarest to be] right – then accept their
pledge of allegiance, and pray to God to forgive them their [past] sins:
for, behold, God is much-forgiving, a dispenser of grace."* The second
pact was called the "pact of war" and was meant to ensure protection
in case of war for the community. In both cases, the purpose of these
agreements was to facilitate the social integration between the emigrants and the residents of Medina.[9]

Due to the degree of sacrifice required, the only exceptions made
among the Meccan Muslims were for the "weak" – women, children,

the ill and the poor.[10] Otherwise, the *hijra* was deemed obligatory on all able-bodied Muslims by the Prophet (pbuh).

The difficulties involved in undertaking the *hijra* were also the reason why the spiritual rewards for it were also emphasized in the Quran. The *hijra* came to serve as a proof of faith, linking "those who believe" with "those who emigrate and strive in the way of God." "Belief" refers to placing obedience to God and His Messenger above obedience to one's clan or family. *"O you who have attained to faith! Do not take your fathers and your brothers for allies if a denial of the truth is dearer to them than faith: for those of you who ally themselves with them – it is they, they who are evildoers!"* (Surah at Tawba – Repentance, 9:23). It is also centered around a particular community of Muslims, in this case the *muhajirun* (emigrants), who chose exile and sacrifice in their obedience to God, and the *ansar*, who gave them shelter and refuge. Both of these groups are singled out for spiritual reward on the basis of their efforts in the following verses.

"Verily, they who have attained to faith, and they who have forsaken (their homelands) and are striving hard in God's cause – these it is who may look forward to God's grace: for God is much- forgiving, a dispenser of grace" (Surah al Baqara – The Cow, 2:218).

"And as for those who henceforth come to believe, and who forsake (their homelands) and strive hard [in God's cause] together with you – these [too] shall belong to you; and they who are [thus] closely related have the highest claim on one another in [accordance with] God's decree. Verily, God has full knowledge of everything" (Surah al Anfal – Spoils of War, 8:74-75).

"And yet, behold, thy Sustainer [grants His forgiveness] unto those who forsake (their homelands) after having succumbed to its temptation, and who thenceforth strive hard [in God's cause] and are patient in adversity: behold, after such [repentance] thy Sustainer is indeed much-forgiving, a dispenser of grace!" (Surah an Nahl – The Bee, 16:110)

"And as for the first and foremost of those who have forsaken (their

*homelands) and of those who have sheltered and succored the Faith,
as well as those who follow them in [the way of] righteousness – God
is well-pleased with them, and well-pleased are they with Him. And
for them has He readied gardens through which running waters flow,
therein to abide beyond the count of time: this is the triumph
supreme!"* (Surah at Tawba – Repentance, 9:100).

*"Indeed, God has turned in His mercy unto the Prophet, as well as
unto those who have forsaken (their homelands) and those who have
sheltered and succored the Faith – [all] those who followed him in the
hour of distress, when the hearts of some of the other believers and well-
nigh swerved from faith. And once again: He has turned unto them in
His mercy – for, behold, He is compassionate towards them, a dispenser
of grace"* (Surah at Tawba – Repentance, 9:117).

*"And he who forsakes (their homelands) for the sake of God shall find
on earth many a lonely road, as well as life abundant. And if anyone
leaves his home, fleeing from evil unto God and His Apostle, and then
death overtakes him – his reward is ready with God: for God is indeed
much-forgiving, a dispenser of grace."* (Surah an Nisaa – Women, 4:100).
This verse highlights the spiritual reward of a refugee, one who undertakes a journey of hardship, leaving behind his home in order to be able
to satisfy his commitment to God in a safer place. The underlying theme
is that of movement and change, in a positive direction, but one that also
involves some hardship in its undertaking.

A *hadith* sums up the message of all of these verses, by stressing
the moral implications of the *hijra* and those who undertook it, the
muhajirun. "The reward of deeds depends on the intentions, so
whoever emigrated for the worldly benefits or to marry a woman, his
emigration was for that for which he emigrated, but whoever emigrated for the Sake of God and His Apostle, his emigration is for God and
His Apostle."[11]

The division between the emigrants and non-emigrants is emphasized in Surah al Anfal – Spoils of War, 8:72: *"Behold, as for those
who have attained to faith, and who have forsaken (their homelands)*

and are striving hard, with their possessions and their lives, in God's cause, as well as those who shelter and succor [them] – these are [truly] the friends and protectors of one another. But as for those who have come to believe without having migrated [to your country] – you are in no wise responsible for their protection until such a time as they migrate [to you]. Yet, if they ask you for succor against religious persecution, it is your duty to give [them]this succor – except against a people between whom and yourselves there is a covenant: for God sees all that you do."

In conclusion, we have outlined the spiritual and social connotations of the concept of *hijra*, in the Quran and in Islamic history. The Prophet's (pbuh) *hijra* illustrates two key points. One is that migration is a valid and recommended response to persecution, whether it is permanent or temporary in duration. The second is that it represents freedom of movement to flee from a state of insecurity and disorder, marked in particular by a lack of freedom, towards a more secure place. Thus, the tradition of *hijra* can apply as a model today for asylum-seekers and immigrants, who migrate in search of better circumstances for themselves and their families.

Is the *Hijra* Over?

The Hijra In History

The question posed in the title of this section leads us to consider the role of *hijra* after the death of the Prophet (pbuh), under the Caliphs, the Ummayyads and the Abbasids. The continuation or abolition of *hijra* is disputed in the *hadith* literature. In general, there are two strands of argument on the topic, both of which will be outlined here.

The first holds the position that the *hijra* was a historically-limited religious obligation, and that it came to an end during the lifetime of the Prophet (pbuh), after the conquest of Mecca and the spread of Islam to most parts of Arabia. The *hadith* supporting this argument are narrated mostly by Meccan and Medinan authorities.[12] "God's Apostle said,

'There is no *Hijra* (i.e. migration) (from Mecca to Medina) after the Conquest (of Mecca), but *Jihad* and good intention remain.'"[13] The spiritual aspect of *hijra* remains valid, exemplified in *jihad*, or struggle for the sake of God.[14]

The second, and opposing, line of argument maintains that *hijra* is still a religious duty, as a geographic migration, even after the death of the Prophet (pbuh). Caliph Umar reaffirmed it as a way to convince people to migrate to the newly founded garrison towns in conquered territories. The *hijra* became politicized by later generations, and turned into an institution, a way to recruit soldiers and settle them in newly conquered parts of the Islamic empire in return for a share in the spoils of war, also known as the *fay*.[15] It is important to note that it was still used to sanction movement, even if it was a state-sanctioned population transfer. This is directly in contrast to its symbolic and spiritual meaning, as an act of worship and a testament of faith as a Muslim.

The Ummayyad dynasty, in particular, benefited from the establishment of the *hijra* as a means of maintaining security in the empire and also encouraging people to settle down in urban areas.[16] They are also considered to have officially backed *hadith* that claim that the duty of *hijra* is not over, and that it is especially relevant for advocating migration towards Syria.[17] One states, "There shall be a *hijra* after a *hijra*. The best people on earth will then be those attaching themselves most closely to the abode of emigration of Abraham. The worst of the people will remain in the country."[18] Another prefers Syria as the destination for the *hijra*. "Matters will come to that there will be garrisoned armies, an army in Syria, an army in Yemen, and an army in Iraq...Take Syria for she is God's choice of His land and to her will be drawn His choice among His servants. But if you refuse, then keep your Yemen and draw water from your ponds. For God has vouched to me for Syria and her people."[19] In both cases, we see that the *hijra* is used by the state to further its political goals.

The early Abbasid dynasty terminated the *hijra* as an institution because they did not need the militias of the garrison towns. The

Abbasids relied on their armies of loyalists, who came to occupy the privileged status that the *muhajirun* had previously enjoyed. In particular, the descendants of the *muhajirun* and their families were no longer given pensions drawn from the *fay*. This material privilege had been one of the hallmarks of the settled soldiers in earlier time periods. [20]

Another development during this time period was the dominance of the legal position that the *hijra* was abolished after the conquest of Mecca. However, classical jurists interpreted it as a general obligation on Muslims and converts to migrate from *dar al harb* or *dar al kufr* ("abode of war or disbelief") to *dar al Islam* ("abode of Islam"). We emphasize, however, that these are purely juristic conceptions developed in the centuries after the Prophet's (pbuh) death and are not explicated in the Quran or *hadith*. Nevertheless, this dichotomy warrants deeper examination in the following section because it has survived in juristic discussions over the centuries. It continues to inform some Muslim responses to questions about freedom of movement, and particularly with regard to emigration to and residence in non-Muslim countries today.

To sum up the discussion thus far, this section has outlined historical variation in the interpretations of the concept of *hijra*, from the Caliphate period to the early Abbasids. Even the fact that it was institutionalized for a brief time, as a way of encouraging population movement to specific centers, speaks to the fact that this Prophetic tradition represents freedom of movement. It was only the political authorities who chose to restrict the definition of it, when it suited them, (during the Caliphate and the Ummayyad rule) and to change their interpretation when it was no longer useful (during the early Abbasid time period).

Hijra in Classical Islamic Law: From Dar al Harb to Dar al Islam

Given the acceptance of classical Muslim jurists of the division of the world into the *dar al harb* and the *dar al Islam*,[21] the question remained as to the exact relationship between these two spheres that revived the definition of the *hijra* as an obligatory migration. A general rule was derived that stated that two situations would make migration to dar al Islam obligatory: 1) *dar al Islam* turns into *dar al kufr*; or 2) a resident of a territory outside *dar al Islam* converts to Islam.[22] This raised the issue of how to decide how, when, or if *dar al Islam* transformed into *dar al kufr*, or *dar al harb*, and also, how to determine the legal status of Muslims living in non-Muslim territories. In sum, the main issue centered around defining the legal relationships between Muslims and non-Muslims, as a result of uni-directional movements from one territory to the other. This interpretation restricted the principle of freedom of movement by imposing territorial boundaries on it.

Our purpose in delving into this issue is to demonstrate how classical interpretations of the *hijra* as a concept made it unusually restrictive and indicative of an intolerant attitude towards non-Muslims. This interpretation is NOT in the Quran, but was later superimposed by jurists upon Muslim understandings of the *hijra* as a seminal event in Islamic history.

A brief historical survey of the positions of the various legal schools and their scholars follows. The Shafi'i and Maliki schools hold that Muslims are allowed to live in *dar al harb*, as long as they are free to practice their religion.[23] However, if they cannot do so, all those who have the means to do so must immigrate to a Muslim territory. The only exception is made for those ill or financially unable to undertake the journey.[24]

The general attitude of scholars of classical Islamic law gave preference to emigration as a way of strengthening and consolidating Muslim identity and power, in relation to non-Muslims. Ibn Qudamah, Ibn Hazm, al Qurtubi, Ibn Rushd, all classical jurists, were hostile to the idea of Muslims settling in *dar al harb*, and stressed the undesirability of their aiding non-Muslims in any way, directly or indirectly.[25] There was a general consensus on freedom of religion for Muslims as the criterion for immigration, but Ibn al Arabi added another important one. He directed Muslims to emigrate from a country where they were in danger for their health, life, property and their families, thus highlighting security concerns as a factor.[26]

Security was an especially relevant concern for Muslim communities in Sicily and the Iberian Peninsula in the late eleventh century. In 1085, Toledo (Spain) and in 1091, Sicily, both, were lost to Christian kings. Although many Muslims left, the termination of Muslim rule in these areas raised the question of the legal status of those who remained behind in territories which were now classified as *dar al harb*. The Muslims who stayed in Spain, eventually known as the Moors, did so under terms that allowed them to safeguard their properties and families in return for payment of tribute. But they were viewed suspiciously by their co-religionists who had emigrated from Spain.[27] With the advent of the Spanish Inquisition a few centuries later, under which both Muslims and Jews were tortured and/or expelled, given the choice of expulsion from Spain or conversion to Christianity, many Muslims converted to Christianity but continued to practice Islam secretly.

What was the legal opinion on the situation of these Muslims regarding *hijra*? Citing Malik, Ibn Rushd, and Ibn al Arabi, Al Wansharissi argued in a 1484 *fatwa* that it was obligatory to leave a territory ruled by non-Muslims under all circumstances, especially if the country was in a state of *fitna*, or revolt. A person who lived in a country where he was forced to behave with injustice was in danger of losing his faith. Furthermore, fears of economic difficulties in their new residence in dar al Islam should not deter potential immigrants, who should look at the example of the original muhajirun who gave up everything for the sake of religion and left for Medina.[28]

But a legal ruling dating from 1504 presented a minority opinion. It sanctioned external adherence to Christianity as long as internally, the individual maintained his faith in Islam. The presumption being that the intention of being Muslim was rewarded by God even if it was not manifest in external practice. Implicit in this was permission for Muslims to remain in *dar al harb*, which contrasted with the norm for that time period.[29]

Despite the insistence by the classical Muslim jurists surveyed here on emigration, or *hijra*, as a religious obligation requiring the movement of Muslims towards Muslim-controlled territories and away from non-Muslim countries, the reality was different. History did not respect such neat separation between *dar al Islam* and *dar al harb*. Muslim traders and merchants traveled freely, during the Prophet's (pbuh) lifetime and later, to non-Muslim lands as far east as China and Indonesia. Some married non-Muslim women, and settled down in these lands, without much concern for legal rulings. Merchants were often followed by missionaries, and as a result Islam spread to countries as diverse as the Sudan and Malaysia.[30]

However, as exemplified by the Muslim withdrawal from Spain and Sicily, there were also questions about the legal status of Muslims left behind, which drew variable responses. The common theme among all these legal responses in classical Islamic jurisprudence is a concern for preservation and protection of Muslim identity and community from onslaught by external, "foreign" forces. This concern is also translated into a display of moral superiority over non-Muslims in their discussion.

Contemporary Application of the H ijra

How is this classical legal response relevant to a contemporary understanding of emigration and migration? The *dar al Islam/dar al harb* dichotomy does not apply in practical terms. These are juristic categories, which are not relevant today. The world today is divided into nation-states, each of which holds territorial sovereignty and regulates access to its borders on the basis of law. All individuals who satisfy certain legal requirements are granted visas or residence.[31] While theoretically all Muslims belong to the same *umma*, this principle does not allow them unfettered movement to and from Muslim countries, purely on the basis of religious identity. The only exception to this is the pilgrimage to Mecca, for which the Saudi government only grants visas to Muslims. Even then, visas are required for entry and exit into the country, and allow visitors access only for a specified duration.

Muslim territories are not the only "safe havens" in the world today, contrary to the expectations of classical jurists. In fact, migration has lately tended to be in the opposite direction, away from Muslim countries towards non-Muslim ones, in the 20th century. After the fall of colonialist rule in British India, for example, there was a significant migration of South Asians to Britain in the 1950s and 1960s, mostly for economic and educational opportunities. This theme is also reflected during the Prophet's (pbuh) life, when he sanctioned the *hijra* to Abyssinia, a land which was ruled by a Christian king. In both examples, non-Muslim territories offered greater security and safety to Muslims, although for different reasons.

The criterion of security, instead of religion, as a defining factor is advocated by al Zuhayli, a contemporary Muslim scholar. He states that the traditional division of the world into *dar al Islam/dar al harb* came out of a particular historical context, one in which there was hostility and war between Muslim and non-Muslim lands. Today, most countries, Muslim and non-Muslim, are committed to respecting the territorial boundaries and sovereignty of other nations, by virtue of membership in the international political system. This is most visible in the membership in the United Nations. Hence, only countries that are in a state of war (civil or otherwise) could be categorized as *dar al harb*, and once that war is over, they are *dar 'ahd* (country of treaty).[32] Thus, in the contemporary context, security concerns are more important in defining the lives of Muslims. Though we live in a world where governments are required to provide security for their citizens, in cases where that lapses, individuals have the right to move to other, more secure places.

As al Zuhayli has noted, to the extent that we live in a different historical time period, the Prophet's (pbuh) *hijra* does not apply in the same way to our lives today. However, it is still important as a model for responding to oppressive circumstances in general and not just to religious persecution. It illustrates the principle that every individual has the right to live with dignity and to have security of life, religion, family and property.[33] In order to achieve this, the concept of *hijra* sanctions the right to freedom of movement, to be able to move to another place and live in security and peace there.

While classical jurists have focused on the ability to practice Islam freely as the determining factor in the destination of emigration, we include security as the broader requirement that is necessary to allow for religious freedom for all faiths. For example, religious persecution in their home countries has led religious minorities to seek asylum as refugees in Europe or North America. The Bah'ais, Christians and Jews from Iran and Iraq are just some examples of minority communities that have fled their home countries and settled in the West. In other cases, Muslims enjoy more freedom to practice their religion in some non-Muslim countries than they did in their Muslim countries of origin. For example, Shi'as in Saudi Arabia face significant restrictions on observing their religious rituals, despite the fact that it is a Muslim country.[34]

Refugees

The *hijra* is particularly relevant today as a way of outlining the Islamic state's responsibility to accept and provide for refugees, similar to the example of the Muslims of Medina who adopted and provided for the arriving refugees from Mecca. The *ansar* are singled out as recipients of spiritual reward for their hospitality and generosity with which they treated the refugees. The Quran states in Surah al Anfal – Spoils of War, 8:72 and 8:74, respectively: *"Behold, as for those who have attained to faith, and who have forsaken (their homelands) and are striving hard, with their possessions and their lives, in God's cause, as well as those who shelter and succor [them] – these are [truly] the friends and protectors of one another. But as for those who have come to believe without having migrated [to your country] – you are in no wise responsible for their protection until such a time as they migrate [to you]. Yet, if they ask you for succor against religious persecution, it is your duty to give [them] this succor – except against a people between whom and yourselves there is a covenant: for God sees all that you do;"* and *"And they who have attained to faith, and who have forsaken (their homelands) and are striving hard in God's cause, as well as those who shelter and succor [them] – it is they, they who are truly believers! Forgiveness of sins awaits them, and a most excellent sustenance."*

There are also *hadith* which single out the *ansar* in this manner. "The Prophet said, "Love for the *ansar* is a sign of faith and hatred for the *ansar* is a sign of hypocrisy.""[35] "There is goodness in all the houses of the *ansar*."[36]

The respective roles of the *muhajirun* and the *ansar* illustrate both the individual's right to seek asylum in another country as a result of persecution and oppression in his/her home country, and also the responsibility of the country of refuge to take in and provide protection to the refugee. While the latter can be deemed an ethical and moral obligation to aid and treat refugees without discrimination (as the *hadith* literature stresses), this principle can also be translated into a legal duty on the part of the state.[37]

There are two main principles of refugee law, both of which also have precedents in Islamic tradition. The first is that of asylum, which is described as "discretionary provision by states of formal legal status to refugees, defined as individuals with a well-founded fear of persecution on one of five enumerated grounds."[38] These five enumerated grounds are race, religion, nationality, membership of a particular social group or political opinion, according to the 1951 U.N. Convention on the Status of Refugees, which serves as the primary international legal instrument in refugee law. The second principle is that of non-refoulement, or an "absolute obligation on state parties not to return refugees to countries in which their lives or freedom would be threatened."[39]

Both of these concepts are referred to in Article 1 and Article 33, respectively, of the 1951 Convention. It defines a refugee as a person who "owing to well-founded fear of being persecuted for reasons of race, religion, nationality, membership of a particular social group or political opinion, is outside the country of his nationality and is unable, or owing to such fear, is unwilling to avail himself of the protection of that country; or who, not having a nationality and being outside the country of his former habitual residence as a result of such events, is unable or, owing to such fear, is unwilling to return to it." Article 33 states, "No Contracting State shall expel or return ("refouler" in French) a refugee in any manner whatsoever to the frontiers of territories where his life or freedom would be threatened on account of his race, religion, nationality, membership of a particular social group or political opinion." [40]

The ideas of asylum and non-refoulement are reflected in Islamic tradition and law as well, although they are not explicitly defined as part of refugee law. We have already indicated how the concept of *hijra* serves as a moral paradigm for protecting the rights of asylum-seekers and the recipient community's responsibility to refugees. In legal terms, jurists have developed the institution of *aman*, or "pledge of security," which comes closest to codifying in the *sharia* the recipient country's obligation towards refugees. It refers to the duty of the Muslim community to grant protection to non-Muslims who enter Muslim territories, seeking refuge. The person cannot be refused protection or extradited to his original place of residence, if he has asked for the aid of the Muslim community.

But, there is a contradiction in international refugee law. On one hand, the individual's right to seek asylum, on the basis of certain factors, is enshrined in the Refugee Convention, and is generally accepted. But, the granting of asylum by the state to the refugee is subject to discretion under international law. While the state ought to grant protection, to whom, on what terms, and when is up to the state in question, after ascertaining the validity of the claimant's case. The only legal obligation a state has is that of non-refoulement. [41] So, in practice, a state can legally place refugee claimants in detention indefinitely, until such time as their applications are reviewed and a decision made, because it is still fulfilling its legal duty of not returning asylum-seekers to their original countries of residence.

The juristic concept of *aman* can fill this loophole in international refugee law, regarding the state's duty to accept refugees. It guarantees the legal right of the refugee to seek asylum and the legal duty of the state/community to grant it. This is supplemented by the moral driving force of the precedent set by the *ansar* of Medina.

With respect to the asylum-seeker's integration into the community, *aman* functions primarily as a temporary measure of protection. It grants the individual temporary membership in the political community of Muslims, for a period of up to a year. At that point, the person's membership is reassessed and the status changes. However, the spirit of acceptance and non-discrimination set by the *ansar* towards the Muslims from Mecca can serve as an example of eventual and complete integration of refugees into the political community of an Islamic state. This would include the ability to become naturalized citizens, after fulfilling necessary requirements.

Unfortunately, most Muslim countries today have not acceded to the 1951 Refugee Convention, despite the fact that it is in line with the spirit of the Prophetic *hijra* tradition and that of the *sharia*. Of Middle Eastern Muslim countries, only Egypt, Iran, Tunisia, and Algeria are Parties to the Refugee Convention.[42] This leaves open the door to countries like Kuwait, Saudi Arabia, Syria, and Lebanon who have not signed the Convention, and have a history of inferior treatment of refugees or other displaced persons seeking asylum. Palestinian refugees in particular face severe restrictions in Lebanon and Syria.[43]

Conclusion

This chapter has focused on freedom of movement as a general principle in the Quran as well as its specific manifestation in the Prophet (pbuh) *hijra* from Mecca to Medina in 622. God does not restrict this freedom in any way, or for anyone. In fact, He encourages human beings to explore the world and travel, for trade or leisure, as a way of affirming their orientation towards Him and remaining grateful for the bounty and favors that He has blessed them with. In this context, restricting the freedom of movement for women, or limiting it to certain geographic areas, runs contrary to this God-given right.

Subsequent sections of this chapter have developed the concept of the *hijra* as a basis for protecting freedom of movement as it relates to migration and emigration in Islamic history and law, with the issue of refugees as a contemporary case study. In sum, the Prophetic tradition of hijra reaffirms one's right to live with dignity and security, and a corresponding freedom to migrate, if necessary, in order to achieve that. The example of the *muhajirun* and the *ansar* represent both the right of individuals to seek asylum and the obligation of the Islamic state to accept and protect refugees. The *hijra* illustrates a pro-active spiritual, social and political response to situations of persecution and oppression, one which goes beyond the historical context of seventh-century Arabia.

Footnotes

1 According to legal definitions, if a woman is single, her mahram is her father, or any other male relative whom she would be prohibited from marrying(brother, uncle, grandfather, etc). If married, her mahram is her husband, or any other male relative.

2 Sahih Bukhari, Volume 2, Book 20, Number 192.

3 Sahih Bukhari, Volume 2, Book 20, Number 194.

4 Sahih Bukhari, Volume 3, Book 29, Number 85.

5 For more on gender relations, see the chapter on Women's Rights.

6 Both groups are noted as equal partners, in addition to the non-Muslim, Arab tribes, in the Constitution of Medina, which laid the foundation for the polity founded at Medina. See chapter on Constitutionalism.

7 The Islamic calendar dates from the reign of Caliph Umar. The use of 622 as the starting date demonstrates the importance that the first generation of Muslims gave to this event, as part of the construction of community identity. Daoud S. Casewit, "Hijra as History and Metaphor: A Survey of Qur'anic and *Hadith* Sources," Muslim World, 88:2(April 1998), p. 106.

8 Yusuf Ali, p. 861, n.2816; Casewit, p. 108, n. 11.

9 Masud, p. 31.

10 Masud, p. 30.

11 Sahih Bukhari, Volume 5, Book 58, Number 238.

12 Wilferd Madelung, "Has the Hijra come to an End?" *Revue des Études Islamiques*, 54(1986), p.227.

13 Sahih Bukhari, Volume 4, Book 52, Number 42.

14 "Struggle for the sake of God" does not necessarily imply military struggles.

15 The fay is to be given to the poor muhajirun,(among others) on the basis of Quranic verses in Surah al Hashr – The Gathering, 59: 8. Caliph Umar is reported to have expanded a share of the fay to all Muslims, and not just to soldiers.

16 It is easier to consolidate political rule over a sedentary population rather than a nomadic one. The dichotomy between sedentary people(muhajirun) and nomadic bedouins become more distinct, with the latter considered to be spiritually inferior and excluded from the privilege of a share in the fay.

17 Madelung, p. 227. Damascus was the Ummayyad dynasty's capital.

18 Abu Dawud, cited in Madelung, p. 228.

19 Abu Dawud, cited in Madelung, p. 228.

20 Madelung, p. 235.

21 This is a territorial division based on religion. *Dar al Islam* refers to all territories under Muslim control. *Dar al harb* is non-Muslim controlled territory, in a state of war with the former. These categories are not static, and have been critiqued and reinterpreted by various scholars. Abu Yusuf adds a third category, *dar al ahd*, a country that concludes a treaty of peace with the Muslims. Sami A. Aldeeb Abu-Sahlieh, "The Islamic Concept of Migration," *International Migration Review*, Special Issue: Ethics, Migration and Global Stewardship, 30:1(Spring 1996), p. 39.

22 Masud, p. 34.

23 Masud, p. 37.

24 Abu Sahlieh, p. 43.

25 Abu Sahlieh, pp.43-44.

26 Abu Sahlieh, p. 44.

27 Abu Sahlieh, p. 46.

28 Abu Sahlieh, p. 48.

29 Abu Sahlieh, p. 47.

30 Abu Sahlieh, p. 45.

31 This is not the same as granting citizenship. Religious identity does play an important role in defining citizenship in some countries. This topic is explored in its own chapter.

32 Abu Sahlieh, p. 51.

33 These are also the goals of the Shari'a.

34 In the Saudi case, all non-Wahhabi Muslim sects are equally restricted in their religious practice.

35 Sahih Bukhari, Volume 1, Book 2, Number 16.

36 Sahih Muslim, Book 30, Number 5663.

37 Kamal Kerpat extends this obligation to accept and care for refugees and migrants to pilgrims and travelers, those who are away from their place of residence on a more temporary basis. However, he considers it to be a duty of the Muslim community, and not that of the state. Kamal Kerpat, "Commentary: Muslim Migration: A Response to Aldeeb Abu Sahlieh," *International Migration Review*, Special Issue: Ethics, Migration and Global Stewardship, 30:1(Spring 1996), p. 80.

38 Richard Boswell et al.,ed., *Refugee Law and Policy: Cases and Materials* (Durham: Carolina Academic Press, 1997), p. 5.

39 Boswell et al., p. 5.

40 Convention relating to the Status of Refugees, United Nations Office of High Commissioner for Human Rights, full text, http://www.unhchr.ch/html/menu3/b/o_c_ref.htm.

41 Guy S. Goodwin-Gill, "The Refugee in Internatinal Law," *Refugee Law and Policy: Cases and Materials*, ed. Richard Boswell et al., (Durham: Carolina Academic Press, 1997), pp. 39-40.

42 UN Convention on the Status of Refugees, List of Participants http://www.unhchr.ch/html/menu3/b/treaty2ref.htm

43 World Refugee Survey 2002 from the U.S. Committee for Refugees, "Middle East" http://www.refugees.org/world/articles/wrs02_meast1.cfm

CHAPTER THIRTEEN

Children

ll children are entitled to certain basic human rights. These are the right to life, the right to a name that is not a source of ridicule or embarrassment, the right to knowing their parentage, and the right to maintenance and protection. The right to maintenance encompasses basic necessities such as food, shelter, clothing, education and healthcare, as well as anything required for the child's general welfare. All of these rights stem from the idea that a child is entitled to being a child, and has the right to be taken care of and provided for, until he/she reaches adulthood. This also includes a prohibition of abuse, neglect or exploitation of children in any way. It also means that parents cannot force children into marriage, since that is a matter requiring adult capacity.

Children in the Quran

Children represent the continuity of families and their names, lineage, traditions and customs. They are the heirs, materially and spiritually, of their parents and of the larger community. One *hadith* states, "When a person dies, his period of activity comes to an end except three virtuous deeds, due to which he goes on continues getting the reward from God until eternity. [Among these three are] virtuous children who should continue praying for him."[1] As such, children symbolize God's favor towards His community. *"And God has made for you mates (and companions) of your own nature, and made for you, out of them, sons and daughters and grandchildren, and provided for you sustenance of the best: will they then believe in vain things, and be ungrateful for*

God's favors? And God has given you mates of your own kind and has given you, through your mates, children and children's children, and gas provided for you sustenance out of the good things of life" (Surah an Nahl – The Bee, 16:72).

Children are a blessing. *"And those who pray, "Our Lord! Grant unto us wives and offspring who will be the comfort of our eyes, and give us (the grace) to lead the righteous And who pray: 'O our Sustainer! Grant that our spouses and offspring be a joy to our eyes, and cause us to be foremost among those who are conscious of Thee!'"* (Surah al Furqan – The Standard of True and False, 25:74). The Quran celebrates this blessing in its listing of the prophets and the sons that were granted to them. *"We gave him [Abraham], Isaac and Jacob: all (three) guided: and before him, We guided Noah, and among his progeny, David, Solomon, Job, Joseph, Moses, and Aaron: thus do We reward those who do good, and Zachariah and John, and Jesus and Elias: all in the ranks of the righteous, and Ishmael and Elisha, and Jonas, and Lot: and to all We gave favor above the nations/ (To them) and to their fathers, and progeny and brethren: We chose them, and we guided them to a straight way And We bestowed upon him Isaac and Jacob; and We guided each of them as We had guided Noah aforetime. And out of his offspring, [We bestowed prophethood upon] David, and Solomon, and Job, and Joseph, and Moses, and Aaron: for thus do We reward the doers of good; and [upon] Zachariah, and John, and Jesus, and Elijah: every one of them was of the righteous; and [upon] Ishmael, and Elisha, and Jonah, and Lot. And every one of them did We favor above other people; and [We exalted likewise] some of their forefathers and their offspring and their brethren: We elected them [all], and guided them onto a straight way."* (Surah al Anam – Cattle, 6:84-87).

The Quran also describes prophets who prayed for children, and were finally granted offspring by God. A notable example is that of Zachariah. *"Now I fear (what) my relatives (and colleagues) (will do) after me: but my wife is barren: so give me an heir as from Thyself,*

'(One that) will (truly) represent me, and represent the posterity of Jacob; and make him, O my Lord! one with whom Thou art well-pleased!' (His prayer was answered): 'O Zachariah! We give thee good news of a son: His name shall be Madhya: on none by that name have We conferred distinction before. 'Now, behold, I am afraid of [what] my kinsfolk [will do] after I am gone, for my wife has always been barren. Bestow, then, upon me, out of Thy grace, the gift of a successor who will be my heir as well as an heir [to the dignity] of the House of Jacob; and make him, O my Sustainer, well-pleasing to Thee!' [Thereupon the angels called out unto him:] 'O Zachariah! We bring thee glad tiding of [the birth of] a son whose name shall be John. [And God says,] 'Never have We given this name to anyone before him.''' (Surah Maryam – Mary, 19:5-7). In another verse, *"There did Zachariah pray to his Lord, saying: 'O my Lord! Grant unto me from Thee a progeny that is pure: for Thou art He that heareth prayer!' In that self-same place, Zachariah prayed unto his Sustainer, saying: 'O my Sustainer! Bestow upon me [too], out of Thy grace, the gift of goodly offspring; for Thou, indeed, hearest all prayer'''* (Surah al Imran – The House of Imran, 3:38).

Nevertheless, the Quran cautions against placing too much value in one's children at the expense of one's responsibility towards God. For example, God points out to Noah that his son is not righteous and, therefore, does not merit the spiritual favor that Noah enjoys. *"And Noah called upon his Lord, and said: 'O my Lord! Surely my son is of my family! and Thy promise is true, and Thou art the justest of Judges!' He said: 'O Noah! He is not of thy family: For his conduct is unrighteous. So ask not of Me that of which thou hast no knowledge! I give thee counsel, lest thou act like the ignorant!' And Noah called out to his Sustainer, and said: 'O my Sustainer! Verily, my son was of my family; and, verily, Thy promise always come true, and Thou art the most just of all judges!' [God] answered: 'O Noah, behold, he was not of thy family, for, verily, he was unrighteous in his conduct. And thou shalt not ask of Me anything whereof thou canst not have any knowledge: thus, behold,* do I admonish thee lest thou become one of those who are unaware [of what is right].'" (Surah Hud – Hud, 11:45-46).

If children are a blessing from God, they are also a sort of test in one's life. *"And know ye that your possessions and your progeny are but a trial; and that it is God with Whom lies your highest reward And know that your worldly goods and your children are but a trial and a temptation, and that God there is a tremendous reward"* (Surah al Anfal – Spoils of War, 8: 28). *"Wealth and children are an adornment of this world's life: but good deeds, the fruit whereof endures forever, are of far greater merit in thy Sustainer's sight, and a far better source of hope"* (Surah al Kahf – The Cave, 18:46). *"Say: If it be that your fathers, your sons, your brothers, your mates, or your kindred; the wealth that ye have gained; the commerce in which ye fear a decline: or the dwellings in which ye delight - are dearer to you than God, or His Messenger, or the striving in His cause;- then wait until God brings about His decision: and God guides not the rebellious. Say: 'If your fathers and your sons and your brothers and your spouses and your clan, and the worldly goods which you have acquired, and the commerce whereof you fear a decline, and the dwellings in which you take pleasure – [if all these] are dearer to you than God and His Apostle and the struggle in His cause, then wait until God makes manifest His will; and [know that] God does not grace iniquitous folk with His guidance'"* (Surah al Tawba – Repentance, 9:24).

Despite the bond between parent and child, both still maintain their individual, separate spiritual relationships with God. They will be judged individually on the Day of Judgment. *"Of no profit to you will be your relatives and your children on the Day of Judgment: He will judge between you: for God sees well all that ye do, But [bear in mind that] neither your kinsfolk nor [even] your own children will be of any benefit to you on Resurrection Day, [for then] He will decide between you [on your merit alone]: and God sees all that you do"* (Surah al Mumtahaina – The Examined One, 60:3). *"O mankind! Do your duty to your Lord, and fear (the coming of) a Day when no father can avail aught for his* son, nor a son avail aught for his father. Verily, the promise of God is true: let not then this present life deceive you, nor let the chief Deceiver deceive you about God. O men! Be conscious of your Sustainer, and stand in awe of the Day on which no parent will be of any avail to his child, nor a child will in the least avail his parent! Verily, God's promise [of resurrection] is true indeed: let not, then, the life of this world delude you, and let not [your own] deceptive thoughts about God delude you!" (Surah Luqman – Luqman, 31:33). "It is not your wealth nor your sons, that will bring you nearer to Us in degree: but only those who believe and work righteousness – these are the ones for whom there is a multiplied reward for their deeds, while secure they (reside) in the dwellings on high!" (Surah Saba – Sheba, 34:37).

Children's Rights

In all cases, a child's basic right to live a life of security and with full membership rights in society is paramount. Even if born out of wedlock, the child is not denied maintenance or support or any of its basic human rights. Every individual is guaranteed equal opportunity in life and a minimal claim to basic resources in society. It is up to the state to make these available for all children, especially if the parents either choose not to or are not capable of taking care of their children.[2]

Right to Life

God decides how and when a child is conceived. *"God's alone is the dominion over the heavens and the earth. He creates whatever He will: He bestows the gift of female offspring on whomever He wills, and the gift of male offspring on whomever He wills; or He gives both male and female [to whomever He wills], and causes to be barren whomever He wills: for, verily, He is All-Knowing, infinite in His power"* (Surah ash Shura – Consultation, 42:49-50).

As with all other life, the life of a child is sacred. First and foremost, every child has the right to life after birth. The Quran categorically forbids infanticide, exposure or neglect of infants, for any reason. In particular, female infanticide is singled out as a reprehensible act. *"For,* whenever any of them is given the glad tiding of [the birth of] a girl, his face darkens, and he is filled with suppressed anger, avoiding all people because of the [alleged] evil of the glad tiding which he has received, [and debating with himself:] Shall he keep this [child] despite the contempt [which he feels for it] – or shall he bury it in the dust? Oh, evil indeed is whatever they decide!" (Surah an Nahl – The Bee, 16:58-59). The "evil" is both the father's contempt for the female child and the decision to kill her. The implicit condemnation of this behavior is also noted as a rhetorical question in Surah al Takwir – Shrouding in Darkness, 81:8-9: "When the female (infant), buried alive, is questioned for what crime she was killed. And when the girl-child that was buried alive is made to ask for what crime she had been slain." In fact, her only "crime" was to be female. God grants both male and female children, according to His Will, and both are equal in value. This is stressed by the Prophet (pbuh) in a *hadith* stating that "one who has two daughters and no son, and spends his life in their proper upbringing and education will be closest to me in Heaven."[3] Thus, the preference for male children over females is in contradiction to both the Quran and *hadith* on this subject.

Apart from gender, killing one's children for fear of poverty or of being unable to afford to care for them is also deemed a sin. God reassures parents to have faith and that He will provide the means for them to take care of their children. "Hence, do not kill your children for fear of poverty: it is We who shall provide sustenance for them as well as for you. Verily, killing them is a great sin" (Surah al Isra – The Night Journey, 17:31). "Lost, indeed, are they who, in their weak-minded ignorance, slay their children and declare as forbidden that which God has provided for them sustenance, falsely ascribing [such prohibitions] to God: they have gone astray and have not found the right path" (Surah al Anaam – Cattle, 6:140). The gravity of this issue is also illustrated in Surah al Anaam – Cattle, 6:151, where killing one's children is on par with denying a monotheistic God. "Say: 'Come, let me convey unto you what God has [really] forbidden to you: 'Do not ascribe divinity, in any way, to aught beside Him; and [do not offend against but, rather] do good unto your parents; and do not kill your children for fear of poverty – [for] it is We who shall provide sustenance for you as well as for them; and do not commit any shameful deeds, be they open or secret; and do not take any human being's life – [the life] which God has declared to be sacred – otherwise than in [the pursuit of] justice: this has He enjoined upon you so that you might use your reason.'"

Although these verses speak specifically to killing children, they can also be used to make a general argument that parents who sell their children into slavery or child labor, for fear of future economic difficulties, are "taking the life" of their children. They cannot know the future with enough certainty to justify such a decision.

Right to a Name and Right to Knowledge of Paternity

After the right to life, every child has the right to a name. The name serves as a marker of his/her humanity and human dignity. Usually, it is the parents who choose the child's name. Even if the parents are unknown, however, the child still has the right to a name. A *hadith* on this issue states, "If you send someone [somewhere], see to it that he bears an agreeable name and a pleasant face."[4]

Naming establishes the identity of the child and his/her father in a patrilineal, Muslim society. This is particularly important as an aspect of establishing filiation. Islamic personal status law is expansive on the procedures associated with establishing paternity, and the rights and obligations on the father towards the child. Paternity is important because it is the father's legal responsibility to provide materially for the child.[5] We will discuss the specifics of these in more detail as part of the child's right to maintenance.

Islamic family law links the right to recognition of paternity with the right to legitimacy. Every child must be recognized as having a biological father, and that father must take responsibility for his child.[6] The only legal exception is if the child is born out of wedlock, in which case he/she is identified through the mother and she takes on full responsibility for the child's maintenance.[7] However, we can expand this notion to argue that every child is entitled to know, if possible, who its biological parents are, and if the parents (or the father) is/are unknown, it is not to be discriminated against and still has claim to full membership in society. *"[As for your adopted children,] call them by their [real] fathers' names: this is more equitable in the sight of God; and if you know not who their fathers were, [call them] your brethren in faith and your friends"* (Surah al Ahzab – The Confederates, 33:5).

The legal procedure for determining paternity rights varies. With regard to children born of a legally recognized marriage, jurists have agreed on a time frame to determine that the paternity of the child is that of the husband. The conception-birth span is set at a minimum of six lunar months from the beginning of the period of legal cohabitation,[8] and a maximum of one lunar year after the end of it.[9] A child born outside this time frame is considered illegitimate.

However, he/she can be deemed legitimate if the husband chooses to legally recognize it as his.[10] In such a case, paternity is established by acknowledgement. There are several conditions that apply. First, the child is not known to be the child of another man. Second, the ages of the child and the father are such that they could reasonably be related as father and child. Third, the acknowledgement is done in such a way that indicates that the child is legitimate, and not born of adultery.[11] Fourth, the child can confirm who his/her father is, if he/she is of an age to be able to do so.[12]

If paternity is so important for determining who shall be legally liable for the support and care of the child, what is to be done in cases where the father is unknown: for example, in the case of an abandoned infant? Traditional juristic view was that the baby's finder became the sole guardian, and took on full responsibility for him/her, if no one came forward to claim the child. The guardian is entitled to funds from the public treasury to support the child, unless he voluntarily chooses to forego this assistance and spends his own money on raising him/her. The guardian has the responsibility to educate the child, or to provide the means for it to learn a trade.[13] If, for any reason, the guardian is found unfit to raise the child, the state takes over.[14] We would modify this slightly to note that in the modern context the state can reliably find interested guardians for abandoned or orphaned children. This would mean that the guardian may be someone other than the individual who found the child. The state should find the most appropriate person to be the guardian, whether or not it is the finder. It is the finder's obligation to prove that he is the best person to keep the child. The state may still step in and make an assessment as to whether the person is really capable of fulfilling his responsibilities as legal guardian, through a legal adoption procedure, and to award custody to someone else if that person is found lacking. The main idea, however, is that the child has the right to be supported and taken care by the person most fit to do so – even if that person is not biologically related to him/her.

The use of state funds to support an orphan child is important to emphasize, because it reflects the social and moral obligation of Muslims to take care of children, even when they are not their own biological children. The Prophet (pbuh) admonished Muslims to support all orphans, whether they were biologically related to them or not.[15] Further support for this obligation is in the Quran, which emphasizes generous treatment of orphans and the just management of their property in a number of verses. *"Therefore, treat not the orphan with harshness."* (Surah al Dhuha – The Bright Morning Hours, 93:9). *"Those who unjustly eat up the property of orphans, eat up a Fire into their own bodies: They will soon be enduring a Blazing Fire."* (Surah an Nisaa – Women, 4:10). *"And they will ask thee about [how to deal with] orphans. Say: 'To improve their condition is best.' And if you share their life, [remember that] they are your brethren: for God distinguishes between him who spoils things and him who improves. And had God so willed, He would indeed have imposed on you hardships which you would not have been able to bear: [but,] behold, God is almighty, wise!"* (Surah al Baqara – The Cow, 2:220). *"And do not touch the substance of an orphan, save to improve it, before he comes of age. And be true to every promise – for, verily, [on Judgment Day] you will be called to* account for every promise which you have made!" (Surah al Isra – The Night Journey, 17:34). "Hence, render unto the orphans their possessions, and do not substitute bad things [of your own] for the good things [that belong to them], and do not consume their possessions together with your own: this, verily, is a great crime" (Surah an Nisaa – Women, 4:2). The import of these verses underlines the moral and social duty of Muslims to take care of those unable to take care of themselves, in this case, orphan children. By extension, it also sets a minimum acceptable standard for parental conduct towards their own children, since it cannot be less than what the Quran exhorts guardians to do for their orphan wards.

The purpose of this brief section on how paternity rights are to be established demonstrates the importance of the child's right to maintenance and financial support. The fact that the child is entitled to this is undisputed. The issue is who undertakes this responsibility. In most cases, it is the father's duty. In a situation where the child's origins are obscure, then it falls to the state and the community as a whole, to undertake financial support and maintenance for the child.

Right to Maintenance

In addition to the right to life, right to a name, right to knowledge of paternity, every child has the right to maintenance. We have subsumed several rights within this larger category, those of fosterage, guardianship, maintenance and inheritance, although the law treats them as separate. This section will outline each one briefly.

The right to fosterage refers to nursing. The child has the right to be nursed, and usually it is the mother's responsibility to fulfill this. If she chooses not to do it or is unable to, a wet nurse may be hired, and it is the father's responsibility to pay for her services. "The mothers shall give suck to their offspring for two whole years, if the father desires to complete the term. But he shall bear the cost of their food and clothing on equitable terms... If they both decide on weaning, by mutual consent, and after due consultation, there is no blame on them. If ye decide on a foster-mother for your offspring, there is no blame on you,

provided ye pay (the mother) what ye offered, on equitable terms. But
fear God and know that God sees well what ye do. And the [divorced]
mothers may nurse their children for two whole years, if they wish to
complete the period of nursing; and it is incumbent upon him who has
begotten the child to provide in a fair manner for their sustenance and
clothing. No human being shall be burdened with more than he is well
able to bear: neither shall a mother be made to suffer because of her
child, nor, because of his child, he who has begotten it. And the same
duty rests upon the [father's] heir. And if both [parents] decide, by
mutual consent and counsel, upon separation [of mother and child],
they will incur no sin [thereby]; and if you decide to entrust your chil-
dren to foster-mothers, you will incur no sin provided you ensure, in a
fair manner, the safety of the child which you are handing over. But
remains conscious of God, and know that God sees all that you do"
(Surah al Baqara – The Cow, 2:233). Although this verse occurs in the
context of a discussion on divorce, it upholds the principle that, even
in divorce cases, the child must be taken care of, through nursing and
maintenance, by both parents.

Custody, or guardianship[16], is the child's right from birth. There are
three legal categories of guardianship. The first is guardianship of the
infant, and it falls primarily to women to best look after the baby's needs.
The mother has first claim to custody of an infant, followed by female relatives from the maternal line. The second is guardianship of education,
which refers to the father's ability to provide for the child, including his/her
education, after it has passed infancy. It may or may not coincide with the
child actually living with the father. The third is guardianship of property, which only applies if the child has any property that needs to be
managed until he/she comes of age.[17]

Historically, the issue of guardianship and child support has been
extensively dealt with by Muslim jurists. Each legal school has its own
variation on the intricacies of this matter. We will briefly review some of
these elements as they have been handled in the past.

In order to qualify as a guardian, both men and women have to be adults, mentally competent and free individuals. They have to be able to raise the child, look after its interests and be able to protect it both physically and morally.[18] In general, the father is a minor child's guardian. After him, it is the mother, depending on the age of the child.[19] After her, guardianship falls to the child's paternal grandfather. The line of guardianship is determined a little bit differently by all four legal schools.[20]

The duration of maternal custody of the infant child varies among the four Sunni legal schools. According to the Maliki school, it lasts from birth to puberty for a boy. For a girl, it lasts from birth until she marries. The Hanbali school sets it at age 7 for both sexes. The Shafi'is do not place a time frame, but indicate that it is until the child reaches the age of discretion, when it can choose which parent he/she wants to live with. If the child remains silent on the issue, then by default, he/she stays with the mother. Lastly, the Hanafi school sets it, for boys, from birth until he reaches an age where he can feed and clothe himself, usually at age 7 or 9. For girls, it is from birth until age 9 or 11.[21]

With specific regard to child custody in case of divorce, the infant child goes to the mother first. If she is dead or incapable of taking care of it, then the maternal line is preferred over the paternal in awarding custody. Once the child is past infancy, custody is decided based on the best interests of the child and the capacity of each parent to fulfill the responsibilities of guardianship.[22] Although all of the legal schools assume that maternal custody comes to an end when the child reaches a certain age, in fact, there is no absolute requirement that the child live with the father after that point. He/she can live with the mother or another court-appointed guardian. But the father may still be held responsible for financial support, even if the child does not live with him. This can include maintenance for the mother as part of the divorce settlement, so that she can support herself adequately enough to be an effective mother.[23] All of these are traditional juristic legal opinions however, and are subject to debate. According to our interpretation, both parents are obligated to take care of their children, and custody should go to the parent best suited to fulfill that obligation.

The right to maintenance includes food, shelter, clothing, education, and healthcare. All minors who do not own property have the right to maintenance, from their father if applicable, or from their guardians.[24] While there is the legal obligation to spend on his child's welfare, the father is only obligated to do so within his means. *"[In all these respects,] let him who has ample means spend in accordance with his amplitude; and let him whose means of subsistence are scanty spend in accordance with what God has given him: God does not burden any human being with more than He has given him – [and it amy well be that] God will grant, after hardship, ease"* (Surah al Talaq – Divorce 65:7). This is also noted in a *hadith* according to which, "the Prophet used to sell the dates of the garden of Bani An-Nadir and store for his family so much food as would cover their needs for a whole year."[25] Even if a father refuses to spend money on his children, his wife (and the mother of the children) is entitled to take a reasonable amount to take care of the children's needs without necessarily requiring his permission. In one example, a woman came to the Prophet (pbuh) to complain about her husband's miserly ways. "Narrated 'Aisha: Hind (bint 'Utba) said, 'O God's Apostle! Abu Sufyan is a miser. Is there any harm if I take of his property what will cover me and my children's needs?" The Prophet said, 'Take (according to your needs) in a reasonable manner.'"[26]

If the father is unable to earn a livelihood and therefore to support his children, the responsibility passes to the mother. After her, it passes to the father's father, and on through the paternal line. The maintenance paid is a debt upon the father, which he must repay when he is able to work again. In situations where the father is permanently unable to work, he is released from the obligation of maintenance altogether, and it passes to the nearest relatives.[27]

A male child loses his right to maintenance when he is old enough to earn his own living. The only exception is if he is a student, or if he is unable to work due to illness or handicap. In contrast, a female child has the right to maintenance until she marries, after which the responsibility passes to her husband, regardless of whether she is able to earn her own living or not.[28] A competing line of argument is that since guardianship is for those who are unable to protect their own interests, then a daughter who reaches a point in her education or career where she is able to work and protect her own interests, regardless of whether she is married or not, then also loses her need for guardianship.[29] This would mean that she has the right to maintenance until her education is complete, which may extend well past childhood in those pursuing more advanced education. The main point is that these arguments are juristic opinions and are not drawn directly from Quranic verses. Therefore, there is also a certain degree of discretion as to how and in what circumstances these juristic opinions are applied today. We are arguing for flexibility in their application, given changes in society such that many single, educated Muslim women do have careers and are able to take care of themselves financially and do not require guardianship in the traditional juristic sense of the word.

Maintenance and support also means providing for the general welfare of the child, spiritual, material and psychological. It includes socialization, how to live as a member of society, and teaching him/her moral guidelines for behavior. Though formal education can accomplish this to some degree, the behavior of the parents/guardians, as positive role models, is also important for the child. Religious instruction can also contribute to the general welfare of the child. Parents are enjoined to teach their child, through their own words and deeds, their religion. As an adult, a person may exercise his/her freedom to choose a religion, but the groundwork for it must be laid by the parents in the way they raise their child.[30]

Treating children fairly as possible is another factor in the child's welfare. A *hadith* narrated by Aisha, one of the Prophet's (pbuh) wives, emphasizes the rewards of this. "A lady along with her two daughters came to me asking (for some alms), but she found nothing with me except one date which I gave to her and she divided it between her two daughters, and did not eat anything herself, and then she got up and went away. Then the Prophet came in and I informed him about this story. He said, 'Whoever is put to trial by these daughters and he treats them generously (with benevolence) then these daughters will act as a shield for him from Hell-Fire.'"[31]

Forced Child Marriages

As a separate issue under the category of children's welfare and the role of the guardian, forced child marriages do not uphold the child's best interests. In line with the Quranic argument here for a child to be protected, taken care of and celebrated as a blessing from God, then forced child marriages run contrary to this ideal. This practice is contrary to the argument supporting children's rights developed in this entire chapter.

There are two main reasons for prohibiting forced child marriages. First, a guardian who forces his/her ward into marriage can be held liable legally for failing to fulfill his/her responsibility adequately.[32] The primary basis for determining guardianship is based on the person's ability to provide for and protect the child. Forcing him/her into marriage is not acting in the best interests of the child.

Second, marriage includes a legal contract between two consenting adults, of full legal capacity. A child does not qualify as having full legal capacity, and therefore cannot be forced to make such a decision. In addition, a child does not have the psychological, emotional or mental capabilities to enter into marriage, which is an adult undertaking. The Quran assumes the equality of both partners (as adults) in its description of marriage, and does not conceive of or sanction child marriages in any way. *"And God has given you mates of your own kind and has given you, through your mates, children and children's children, and has provided for you sustenance out of the good things of life. Will men, then, [continue to] believe in things false and vain, and thus blaspheme against God's blessings?"* (Surah an Nahl – The Bee, 16:72). *"And among His Signs is this, that He created for you mates from among yourselves, that ye may dwell in tranquility with them, and He has put love and mercy between your (hearts): verily in that are Signs for those who reflect."* (Surah ar Rum – The Byzantines, 30:21). *"(He is) the Creator of the heavens and the earth: He has made for you pairs from among yourselves"* (Surah ash Shura – Consultation, 42:11).

The age of 'Aisha when she married the Prophet (pbuh) is often brought up as a way to criticize "Islamic sanction" for child marriages. 'Aisha was the second daughter of Abu Bakr, the Prophet's (pbuh) trusted supporter, and the man who later became the first Caliph after the Prophet's (pbuh) death. She was also known to be closest to the Prophet (pbuh) and among his favorites. She served as a source for a number of *hadith* about the Prophet's (pbuh) actions as a result of her proximity to him.

With regard to her marriage, there are several *hadith* which state that 'Aisha was six years old when she was betrothed to the Prophet (pbuh) and nine years old when she went to live at his house. The Prophet (pbuh) was in his fifties at the time. "Khadija died three years before the Prophet departed to Medina. He stayed there for two years or so and then he married 'Aisha when she was a girl of six years of age, and he consummated that marriage when she was nine years old."[33] 'Aisha remained his wife for nine years, until his death.

There is, however, disagreement about her age upon marriage. Although these *hadith* place her as being extremely young, there is stronger evidence that she was in fact older and not a child. First, many of the narratives indicating 'Aisha's extremely young age at marriage are narrated by Hisham ibn Urwah, who reported on the authority of his father. However, although he is considered to be a reliable narrator, what he reported after he moved to Iraq is not considered reliable since his memory was failing at that time. Therefore, his narrative of 'Aisha's marriage and age are subject to uncertainty.[34]

Second, when viewed in terms of the events that happened around the same time, 'Aisha's age has to be older than traditionally surmised at the time of her betrothal and later marriage to the Prophet (pbuh). The first piece of evidence with regard to this is the statement by Tabari that all of Abu Bakr's children, including 'Aisha, were born before 610 AD, the period before the first revelation given to the Prophet (pbuh). If 'Aisha was betrothed in 620 at age 6 or 7, and went to live with the Prophet (pbuh) in 624 at age 9, that would mean she had to have been born in 613 or 614. However, this is three to four years *after* the first revelation and not during the pre-Islamic period. If, however, we accept the statement that she was born before 610, that would put her age as at least 14 when she began to live with the Prophet (pbuh).[35]

Second, the Prophet's (pbuh) daughter Fatima was born five years after the point when the Prophet (pbuh) received his first revelation (610 AD), and she was five years older than Aisha. This puts Aisha at about age ten at the time of her betrothal to the Prophet (pbuh), in 620. Five years elapsed between the betrothal and the marriage, and she would have been fifteen when she came to live in the Prophet's (pbuh) household.[36] In other words, she was still older than nine years.

Third, it is generally accepted by Ibn Kathir and other historians that Asma, 'Aisha's older sister, was 10 years older than her. She died in 73 or 74 AH at the age of 100. This means she would have been 27 or 28 at the time of the *hijra*, in 622, and 'Aisha would have been 17 or 18. If she went to live with the Prophet (pbuh) two years after the *hijra*, she would have been 19 or 20 at the time.[37]

Fourth, there are *hadith* that report that 'Aisha was present at both the battles at Uhud and Badr. She narrates a *hadith* recounting the journey to Badr, therefore indicating that she was there.[38] Regarding Uhud, Bukhari states, "Narrated Anas: On the day (of the battle) of Uhud when (some) people retreated and left the Prophet, I saw 'Aisha bint Abu Bakr and Um Sulaim, with their robes tucked up so that the bangles around their ankles were visible hurrying with their water skins (in another narration it is said, "carrying the water skins on their backs"). Then they would pour the water in the mouths of the people, and return to fill the water skins again and came back again to pour water in the mouths of the people."[39]

It is also narrated by Ibn Umar that the Prophet (pbuh) did not allow him to take part in a battle until he was 15 years old. "God's Apostle called me to present myself in front of him or the eve of the battle of Uhud, while I was fourteen years of age at that time, and he did not allow me to take part in that battle, but he called me in front of him on the eve of the battle of the Trench when I was fifteen years old, and he allowed me (to join the battle)."[40] Putting together all of these narratives, one can conclude that 'Aisha had to have been at least 15 years of age in order to be present at these two battles, which took place within the first few years after the *hijra*.[41]

In sum, there is credible evidence to believe that 'Aisha was not in fact a child of six when she was married to the Prophet (pbuh), and that reports to the contrary need to be viewed with skepticism due to the unreliability and contradictory nature of the sources. 'Aisha was at least 15 when she was married, and at most 18 years old. In other words, she was not a child. In addition, as noted earlier, the Quran requires consent from both parties in order for a marriage to be valid. A child would not have the maturity to be an equal partner in a marriage, and it is unlikely that her father would have been unaware of that fact.

Child Abuse

This entire chapter has outlined the various ways in which taking care of children is a parental, societal and legal obligation. It is the state's responsibility to ensure the welfare of society members, and protecting all of them. Since children are the most helpless and unable to take care of themselves, the state can step in where the parents/guardians demonstrably fail to live up to their responsibilities.

Child abuse or neglect represents an extreme case of parental/guardian failure. It is clearly morally reprehensible and represents behavior that can be punished by law. The Quran clearly states that children are a blessing and need to be honored and nurtured as such. *"And God has made for you mates (and companions) of your own nature, and made for you, out of them, sons and daughters and grandchildren, and provided for you sustenance of the best: will they then believe in vain things, and be ungrateful for God's favors?"* (Surah an

Nahl – The Bee, 16:72).

As an extreme case, infanticide is singled out as an immoral act, *"Lost, indeed, are they who, in their weak-minded ignorance, slay their children"* (Surah al Anaam – Cattle, 6:140). Pulling together these two threads, even lesser offenses than infanticide, such as child abuse, merit punishment.

Furthermore, the description of the body of juristic opinion, setting out details for fosterage, custody, and maintenance of children, makes fulfilling these responsibilities by the guardian a legal issue, and violations of these to be punished by the legal system. In sum, parents have no justification for neglecting or abusing their children, and should be punished if they transgress these Quranic boundaries for the treatment of children.

Conclusion

Equality and non-discrimination are the key principles in formulating a universally applicable code of children's rights. All children, regardless of their birth and parentage, are entitled to basic human rights as human beings. In addition, they require the opportunity to live in security, with full membership rights within the community.

But, the dividing line between childhood and adulthood is, in some sense, arbitrary when it comes to detailing the content of children's rights. Every society in every time period has set it at different ages. Nevertheless, what makes a child distinct from an adult is the latter's ability to take responsibility for his/her actions and choices, morally and legally. Conversely, a child is defined by the lack of judgment and ability in formulating his/her actions and accepting their consequences.

This leaves children in a particularly vulnerable position as members of society. They require protection, by their parents/guardians, by the law and by the state. This chapter has outlined certain basic types of children's rights that should be protected by law under all circumstances. The Quran and the *sharia* provide recognition and protection of these positive rights – the right to life, the right to a name/identity, right to knowledge of parentage, right to maintenance and support, and a right to inheritance. What is equally important, however, is what the child is to be protected from: harm, abuse, neglect, violence, and exploitation of any kind, whether direct or indirect. This includes forced child marriages, child abuse, child labor, child prostitution, child pornography and/or selling children into slavery. Although the primary responsibility to protect and support a child falls to the parents, in cases where the parents cannot live up to this responsibility or the child is an orphan, it falls to the state to step in and bridge the gap.

Footnotes

1   Sahih Muslim, cited in M. Afzal Wani, *The Islamic Law on Maintenance of Women, Children, Parents and other Relatives* (New Delhi: Qazi Publishers, 1995), p. 211.

2   'Abd al 'Ati, p. 193.

3   Tahir Mahmood, ed., "The Islamic Law on Human Rights," *Human Rights in Islamic Law* (New Delhi: Institute of Objective Studies, 1993) p. 39.

4   Cited in Muhammad Abdelkebir Alaoui M'Daghri, "The Code of Children's Rights in Islam," transl. Moncef Lahlou, *Children in the Muslim Middle East*, ed. Elizabeth Warnock Fernea, (Austin: University of Texas Press, 1995), p. 32.

5   And also his/her mother, if she is his wife. If the parents are divorced, then the relevant laws would apply. See the chapter on Women's Rights for more.

6   Hammudah 'Abd al 'Ati, *The Family Structure in Islam* (Lagos: Islamic Publications Bureau, 1982), p. 190.

7   'Abd al 'Ati, p. 191.

8   There is a difference among the Sunni legal schools as to whether the time period starts from the time of a valid marriage contract or that of consummation of the marriage. The ending point may be the result of separation, divorce or widowhood.

9   Jamal J. Nasir, *The Islamic Law of Personal Status*, 2nd ed., (London: Graham and Trotman, 1990), pp.157-158. The maximum time period is subject to juristic disagreement, anywhere from two to five years, depending on the legal school. In practice though, it is usually set at one lunar year.

10   'Abd al 'Ati, p. 191.

11   For example, the husband makes sure that there is no other man who is claiming the child as his.

12   Nasir, p. 163.

13   Nasir, p. 168.

14   'Abd al 'Ati, p. 197.

15   Bukhari, cited in Amira al-Azhary Sonbol, "Adoption in Islamic Society: A Historical Survey," *Children in the Muslim Middle East*, ed. Elizabeth Warnock Fernea, (Austin: University of Texas Press, 1995), p. 55.

16   This does not refer to child custody in case of divorce. It only refers to general custody or guardianship of the infant/child, by the parents, relatives or court-appointed guardians.

17   Nasir, pp. 173-174.

18   Nasir, p. 178.

19   Legally speaking, an infant child is not the same as a minor child. Infancy extends for the first few years after the child's birth, and may go up until ages 7 or 9, depending on the legal school. A minor child refers to the child between the ages of 7 and 9 and the age of majority (which may or may not coincide with the onset of puberty, again depending on the legal school.)

20   Nasir, p. 206. See pp. 173-177 for more on the variations among the legal schools.

21   Nasir, pp.187-188.

22   Nasir, *The Islamic Law of Personal Status*, 3rd edition, (The Hague: Kluwer Law International, 2002) pp. 187-189.

23   See section on marriage and divorce in the chapter on Women's Rights.

24   Nasir, p. 191.

25   Sahih Bukhari Volume 7, Book 64, Number 270.

26 Sahih Bukhari, Volume 7, Book 64, Number 283.

27 Nasir, p. 197.

28 Nasir, p. 194.

29 Nasir, 3rd ed., p. 189. Cited from Abu Zahra, *Guardianship of the Person* (Arabic), pp. 46-67.

30 'Abd al 'Ati, p. 199.

31 Sahih Bukhari, Volume 2, Book 24, Number 499.

32 In general, the guardian of a minor can be held legally liable for not adequately protecting the child's interests and welfare on any issue, not just that of marriage.

33 Khadija was the Prophet's (pbuh) first wife. Sahih Bukhari, Volume 5, Book 58, Number 236. Similar accounts are given in Sahih Bukhari, Volume 5, Book 58, Number 234 and Volume 7, Book 62, Number 88.

34 Tehzib ul- tehzib, ibn Hajar al Asqalani, Dar Ihya al-Turath al-Islami, Vol. II, p. 50, cited in T.O. Shanavas, "Was Ayesha a Six-Year-Old Bride? The Ancient Myth Exposed," *The Minaret*, (March 1999).

35 Tabari, cited in Shanavas.

36 Muhammad Ali, *The Living Thoughts of the Prophet Muhammad* (London: Cassell & Co., 1947), p. 28, n. 1.

37 Al Bidayah wa'l nihaya, ibn Kathir, vol. 8, p. 371-372, *Dar al fikr al arabi*, al-jizah, 1993, cited in Shanavas.

38 Sahih Muslim, Book 19, Number 4472.

39 Sahih Bukhari, Volume 4, Book 52, Number 131.

40 Sahih Bukhari, Volume 3, Book 48, Number 832.

41 Shanavas.

CHAPTER FOURTEEN

Security of Person

he right to security of person involves freedom from cruel punishment, including torture, assault, mutilation or disfigurement to an individual's person, inflicted by the state or by members of society. It is recognized in the Universal Islamic Declaration of Human Rights, which states, "No person shall be subjected to torture in mind or body, or degraded, or threatened with injury either to himself or to anyone related to or held dear by him, or forcibly made to confess to the commission of a crime, or forced to consent to an act which is injurious to his interests."[1] In this chapter, we will discuss both private violence, particularly violence against women, and the state use of torture.

Fundamentally, the security of an individual's body and person is derived from the right to live with dignity, as granted by God. It is the state's responsibility to protect this basic human right as part of its overall duty to treat its citizens with justice. This is noted in law through the *sharia*, since one of its main goals is the preservation of life.

This chapter will focus mostly on acts of violence against individuals, sanctioned explicitly or implicitly, by the state or by members of society in Muslim countries. These include domestic violence, rape and honor killings, all of which specifically target women. They also include the use of torture or other forms of cruel punishment against prisoners or any others detained by the state. All of these are contrary to Quranic prescriptions regarding justice, individual dignity and honor. In addition, on a political level, the use of torture and the mistreatment of prisoners indicate a justice system that lacks integrity and truly seeks to implement justice for all citizens.

Women's Honor and Dignity

Even though all humans are equal in human dignity as bestowed upon them by God, in practice, men and women are treated differently before the law in many Muslim countries. Women have lagged behind in achieving the right to have control over their bodies, and all that this entails, from reproductive rights to the ability to prosecute their rapists before the law.

Part of the reason is due to patriarchal cultural norms and attitudes that emphasize male control over the social and political spaces women have access to. These kind of patriarchal attitudes are also perpetuated through a monopoly on women and their bodies, because women are considered to be the bearers of "family honor", literally and figuratively. Thus, there is an emphasis on women bearing male children, to further the family's name, lineage and honor. Conversely, any hint of sexual/immoral misconduct on a woman's part is deemed to be a transgression against the family's honor. It is in cases such as these that honor killings have occurred. Honor killings are acts of murder carried out to preserve "family honor." They are often carried out by male family members who kill their female family members for the latter's alleged or perceived sexually immoral conduct. Women who have been rape victims are sometimes included in this category.

We firmly and unequivocally condemn honor killings, or any type of violence towards women, as being contrary to Islamic teachings emphasizing the dignity of all human beings. We also reject claims that domestic violence against women is sanctioned in the Quran, as a punishment for disobedience to the husband. This perspective stems from a gender-discriminatory interpretation of verse 34 of Surah al Nisaa. The following section will also focus on a more egalitarian reading of Surah al Nisaa, 4:34 as a means of building a more general Quranic argument for the inherent equality in dignity between women and men. This interpretation was not adopted widely in the past, but that merely reflects how powerfully interpretation is shaped by social and historical circumstances. We inhabit a time where violence against the female half of humanity is unacceptable, and Muslims must find a different, yet legitimate, interpretation of the Quran than what was in the past.

Gender Equality

Islamic teachings prohibit and denounce the treatment of women as property or objects. The Quran has granted them value and dignity equal to that of men in a number of ways. First, with the revelation of Islam in seventh century Arabia, came the insistence that the value of a female life is no less than that of a male life. This was exemplified most prominently in the prohibition on female infanticide. According to societal custom at the time, some female infants were left to die after birth, because they were considered to be sign of shame. God expresses strong disapproval of this practice in Surah an Nahl – The Bee. *"For, whenever any of them is given the glad tiding of [the birth of] a girl, his face darkens, and he is filled with suppressed anger, avoiding all people because of the [alleged] evil of the glad tiding which he has received , [and debating within himself:] Shall he keep this [child] despite the contempt [which he feels for it] – or shall he bury it in the dust? Oh, evil indeed is whatever they decide!"* (Surah an Nahl – The Bee, 16:58-59). The verse ends by posing a rhetorical question, since both are evil choices – treating female children with contempt or killing them. The larger evil that is being condemned is the low esteem in which daughters were held in Arab society of that time.

This condemnation is articulated again in Surah at Takwir - Shrouding in Darkness, 81: 8-9, which refers to Judgment Day, *"And when the girl-child that was buried alive is made to ask for what crime she had been slain."* The verse refers to the fact that God will hold everyone accountable for their actions on Judgment Day. In this context, it is not the female child who is responsible for her own death. It is the parent who killed his/her daughter who will be held accountable, based on the testimony of the female infant. Thus, parents are strongly enjoined to be God-fearing and to treat their daughters with the same esteem that they do their sons.[2]

The Quran also notes that wealth and sons are part of the illusory comforts of this life, and those who place undue importance on these do so at the expense of closeness to God. *"For, it is neither your riches nor your children that bring you nearer to Us: only he who attains to faith and does what is right and just [comes near unto Us]; and it is [such as] these whom multiple recompense awaits for all that they have done; and it is they who shall dwell secure in the mansions [of paradise]"* (Surah Saba – Sheba, 34:37). On the Day of Judgment, *"Neither their worldly possessions nor their offspring will be of the least avail to them against God: it is they who are destined for the fire, therein to abide!"* (Surah al Mujadala – The Pleading, 58:17). A cultural preference for sons is merely a sign of personal vanity. Male children hold no special significance in the eyes of God. The same theme is also noted in Surah ash Shuara – The Poets, 26:88-89: *"The Day on which neither wealth will be of any use, nor children, [and when] only he [will be happy] who comes before God with a heart free of evil!"* A *hadith*, attributed to the Prophet (pbuh), stresses the equality of male and female children states "one who has two daughters and no son, and spends his life in their proper upbringing and education will be closest to me in Heaven."[3] The Prophet (pbuh) himself only had one child, a daughter (Fatima), survive to adulthood.

Second, the Quran clearly honors all life equally and considers all beings equal in rights and obligations, as the creation of God. The equality of men and women is mentioned in Surah an Nisaa – Women, 4:1, *"O mankind! Be conscious of your Sustainer, who has created you out of one living entity, and out of it created its mate, and out of the two spread abroad a multitude of men and women. And remain conscious of God, in whose name you demand [your rights] from one another, and of these ties of kinship. Verily, God is ever watchful over you!"* The first part of this verse discusses the fact that human beings all originate from similar circumstances. In a general sense, this implies common descent of the human race from Adam and Eve. But it also refers to the fact that the granting of life is an act of God, and He does not distinguish between men and women. Unity of origin also implies equal value of both men and women.[4] The second part of the verse enjoins people to remember their mutual rights and duties that have been granted to them, as a part of their awareness of God. In particular, this includes respect for women, as mothers and wives, since they are the ones that bear children.

Similarly, all of mankind has been favored by God, and bestowed inherent dignity. *"Now, indeed, We have conferred dignity on the children of Adam, and borne them over land and sea, and provided for them sustenance out of the good things of life, and favored them far above most of Our creation"* (Surah al Isra – The Night Journey, 17:70). Men are not necessarily more favored than women, or vice versa, in the "provision of good things." The entire human race enjoys that privilege.

The same theme of unity of origin and subsequent equality of status is echoed in Surah al Hujurat – The Private Apartments, 49:13: *"O men! Behold, We have created you all out of a male and female, and have made you into nations and tribes, so that you might come to know one another. Verily, the noblest of you in the sight of God is the one who is most deeply conscious of Him. Behold, God is all-knowing, all-aware."* Differences based on gender, among other qualities, exist merely to allow for greater cooperation and harmony among individuals. It does not necessarily denote a hierarchy of men over women, or vice versa. In addition, this verse highlights the fact that the moral and spiritual standing of all is equal before God. The only valid distinctions arise from the degree of righteousness that an individual achieves, not from any biologically-determined characteristic.

Lastly, Islamic jurisprudence was the first to view women as legally independent members of society, and not merely the property of their guardians. It granted women inheritance rights, the right to voluntarily enter into or refuse marriage, divorce rights and the right to control their own wealth and income. They were no longer considered property, nor allowed to be passed onto other male kin as wives after the death of their husbands.[5] *"O you who have attained to faith! It is not lawful for you to [try to] become heirs to your wives [by holding onto them] against their will; and neither shall you keep them under constraint with a view to taking away anything of what you may have given them, unless it be that they have become guilty, in an obvious manner, of immoral conduct. And consort with your wives in a goodly manner; for if you dislike them, it may well be that you dislike something which God might yet make a source of abundant good"* (Surah an Nisa - Women, 4:19).

Gender Relations in Surah an Nisa – Women, 4:34

The much-debated verse 34 of Surah an Nisa – Women, is translated as, *"Men shall take full care of women with the bounties of God has bestowed more abundantly on the former than on the latter, and with what they may spend out of their possessions. And the righteous women are the truly devout ones, who guard the intimacy which God has [ordained to be] guarded. And as for those women whose ill-will you have reason to fear, admonish them [first]; then leave them alone in bed; then beat them; and if thereupon they pay you heed, do not seek to harm them. Behold, God is indeed most high, great!"*[6]

This verse has been traditionally used to justify the role of men as *qawwamun*, the "protectors and maintainors" of women, and to say that God has favored husbands over wives, and in general, men over women. We disagree with this perspective, and subscribe to the following interpretation of this verse. One, it does not indicate absolute superiority of all men over all women, as a class. The preference referred to is not unconditional.[7] The social role of men as "protectors and maintainors" is conditional upon their financial and material support of women. Dr. Amina Wadud argues that this socio-economic role of men as providers is in proportion to the role of women as childbearers. Within the family, given that a woman alone is biologically capable of the arduous task of bearing children, it is the husband's responsibility to ensure that she has physical protection and material sustenance so that she is not faced with additional burden.[8] In other words, it refers to a specific, mutually beneficial delineation of roles and responsibilities within the family, and does not justify a hierarchical view of gender relations on the basis of biological differences.[9]

Also at issue in this verse are the terms *qanitat*, referring to obedience, *nushuz*, referring to marital discord, and *daraba*, which is often translated as beating, or striking. *Qanitat* means a spirit of humility and obedience towards God, and is not a reference to a wife's obedience to her husband. Absolute obedience is only to be directed towards God, not towards another human being. Even the Prophet (pbuh) did not force his wives to obey him as their husband.[10] Therefore, going back to the verse, "good women" are simply those who obey God, a duty which is required of all Muslims. In the context of the marriage, it refers to fulfilling the rights and obligations that each partner has in relation to the other.

Second, *nushuz* refers to a general state of marital discord, not one that comes specifically out of the wife's disobedience to her husband. The reasons for the disharmony may vary, and some scholars have suggested that it can include everything from a refusal of women to bear children[11] to openly licentious behavior.[12] In both cases, marital disharmony is not linked specifically to gender hierarchy. In addition, the use of *nushuz* in another verse, Surah an Nisa – Women, 4:128, to describe disharmony created by men lends support to the fact that illicit sexual behavior by the wife cannot be the sole meaning of the term *nushuz*. It states, *"And if a woman has reason to fear ill-treatment from her husband, or that he might turn away from her, it shall not be wrong for the two to set things peacefully to rights between themselves: for peace is best, and selfishness is ever-present in human souls. But if you do good and are conscious of Him – behold, God is indeed aware of all that you do"* (Surah an Nisa – Women, 4:128). We take strong note of the fact that God here clearly states a woman has a legitimate claim to seek divorce even if she only "fears" cruelty on the part of her husband. This leads us to conclude that male behavior within marriage that raises even a level of "fear" in females, is unacceptable in a Muslim marriage.

Lastly, the term *daraba* has been translated as sanctioning physical abuse by the husband against the wife. The same term, however, has multiple meanings depending on the context it is used in, such as: to set an example,[13] to travel to get out, to set up, to take away, to condemn, to seal, to cover, and to explain.[14] Thus, there is no reason to believe that physical punishment is the actual meaning of the term in verse 34. One scholar suggests that in the legal context, the meaning of *daraba* as "to hold in confinement", or to leave the person alone at home, is relevant here as well.[15] Again, there is no mention of physical violence. Some Muslim jurists interpret *daraba* as a symbolic physical gesture, striking with a toothbrush, for example, and in a manner that would not cause pain.[16] The rationale is that the first two steps for dispute settlement are more important and should be exhausted first, and therefore the need to engage in any kind of physical chastisement should not arise at all.[17] We reject the notion that this verse is a license for physical violence and note that the Prophet (pbuh) never engaged in violence towards his wives. Expressing his disapproval of the idea in a rhetorical question, he is reported to have said, "Could any of you beat his wife as he would beat a slave, and then lie with her in the evening?"[18] Therefore, there is no *sunna* that supports that interpretation of this verse.

Drawing together all of these meanings, if we examine the verse again, it is clear that it does not sanction domestic abuse in any way. Rather, it is discussing gender roles within a marriage, and within society in general, and offering a way to address potential discord or disharmony that is not a specific consequence of the wife's disobedience towards her husband. The way to deal with marital discord is through a series of steps, starting with verbal discussion, to a temporary separation, and lastly, if these steps do not succeed in resolving the issue, then to set an example by leaving the person to reflect in solitude.

This interpretation is keeping with the Quranic view of marriage as a partnership between equals. Mutual kindness and respect are key characteristics of marriage. *"They are as a garment for you, and you are as a garment for them"* (Surah al Baqara – The Cow, 2:187). *"It is not lawful for you to [try to] become heirs to your wives [by holding onto them] against their will; and neither shall you keep them under constraint with a view to taking away anything of what you may have given them, unless it be that they have become guilty, in an obvious manner, of immoral conduct. And consort with your wives, in a goodly manner"* (Surah an Nisaa – Women, 4:19).

All of these verses demonstrate a Quranic argument for the inherent humanity and dignity that is the right of all women. To violate this is to violate a fundamental principle of Quranic teaching. In the context of the family, the traditional gender role of a husband as the primary breadwinner does not mean that he is superior to his wife or that he is entitled to unconditional and slavish devotion. Most importantly, verse 34 of Surah an Nisa – Women, does not condone domestic abuse of women, in any way. Yet, there is a gap between the spirit of gender equity in the Quran and the subordination and abuse of women in some Muslim societies.

Honor Killings

As noted earlier, honor killings are defined as acts of murder carried out to preserve "family honor." They are often carried out by male family members who kill their female family members for the latter's alleged or perceived sexually immoral conduct. Although rape victims are not the only victims of honor killings, other offenses that may make women liable to be killed are marital infidelity, refusing an arranged marriage proposal or demanding a divorce.[19] In societies where the concept of family honor is closely tied to female chastity and behavior, any perception of "dishonor" stemming from a woman's behavior demands redress from the men of the family.

While many honor killings have occurred in Muslim countries,[20] they do not stem from Islamic teaching in any way. Such murders are not sanctioned by the Quran. Unfortunately, they have become sanctioned by societal attitudes towards women, and also by law in some cases.

A woman has honor in her own right, as a fundamental God-given right. She is not the proxy of the family's honor, and therefore violent crimes against her are not justified in any way. Quran clearly states that no soul may bear the burden of another in the following two verses. *"Say: 'Am I, then, to seek a sustainer other than God, when He is the Sustainer of all things?' And whatever [wrong] any human being commits rests upon himself alone; and no bearer of burdens shall be made to bear another's burden. And, in time, unto your Sustainer you all must return: and then He will make you [truly] understand all that on which you were wont to differ."* (Surah al Anam – Cattle, 6:164).

"And no bearer of burdens shall be made to bear another's burden; and if one weighed down by his load calls upon [another] to help him carry it, nothing thereof may be carried [by that other], even if it be one's near of kin" (Surah al Fatir – The Originator, 35:18).

These verses also highlight the fact that every person has individual responsibility for his/her actions and choices. A woman's moral conduct is not "owned" by anyone else but herself. Her honor belongs to her, and not to her family. It is for God to judge her, and to determine the punishment for any moral indiscretions on her part, not for her family or the society at large to do so.

An aspect of female honor in some Muslim societies (and some non-Muslim societies in Africa), is the practice of female circumcision. This is often referred to as female genital mutilation, as the operation can be extensive and disfiguring, depending on the cultural practice. This practice has no religious basis whatsoever. In Islam, circumcision is restricted to males, and there is no Quranic basis for it. It is of non-Islamic origin, and has maintained itself as a cultural practice. All Muslims should abandon this procedure entirely, and Muslim governments should ban the practice. Attempts by some to grant female circumcision religious legitimacy are misguided and harmful to the lives and health of women.

Nevertheless, the Quran does not dismiss the importance of honor altogether. It is part of the reason why accusations of adultery are to be treated with such seriousness and gravity, precisely for the implications of it for the honor of the accused. However, to negate a woman's individual honor and dignity and to render her life, or organs, expendable in the name of protecting family honor is antithetical to the moral principles of Islam.

Torture in the Legal Context

Thus far, this chapter has focused on violent acts targeted specifically towards women. This section discusses the prohibition on torture more generally, as part of the legal system, and highlights the protection of individual security that is noted in Islamic jurisprudence.

The accused is protected from torture or other cruel and inhuman treatment while under questioning.[21] There are several *hadith* that note the reprehensibility of the use of torture against the accused or prisoners. One states, "God shall torture on the Day of Recompense those who inflict torture on people in life."[22] Umar is also reported to have advised his governors, "Hit not the Muslims, lest they be humiliated."[23] Al Ghazzali recounts an incident in which Umar ibn al Khattab asked Mohammad ibn Kaab al-Qortobi to define justice for him. The latter responded, "Punish every offender in proportion to his offense, and beware of whipping a Muslim out of wrath; otherwise, you will all be in hell."[24] Umar ibn al Aziz's deputies once wrote him a letter, asking for permission to torture those who refused to pay their dues to the public treasury. Umar responded by sending a letter condemning such action: "I wonder at your asking permission from me to torture people as though I am a shelter for you from God's wrath, and as if my satisfaction will save you from God's anger. Upon receiving this letter of mine accept what is given to you or let him give an oath. By God, it is better that they should face God with their offenses than I should have to meet God for torturing them."[25]

Any confession that has been obtained through coercion is

legally invalid and inadmissible as evidence. Caliph Umar is reported to have said, "A man would not be secure from incriminating himself if you made him hungry, frightened him, or confined him."[26] In other incident, Mohammad ibn Ishaq reports that a man accused of theft was arrested and beaten. He confessed to his guilt. The governor of the region sent him to Abdullah ibn Umar, asking what should be done about his punishment. Ibn Umar said not to cut off his hand, since he had confessed after being beaten and therefore his confession was unlawful.[27]

We use all of these examples to develop the theme of transparency and due process in the criminal justice system. This includes everything from a right of notice to the accused, to know what crime he is charged for and the consequences thereof. It also refers to the protection of the individual security of the accused while the case is being investigated or after he is sentenced. It is noted at the end of the jurist Abu Yusuf's directive to the Caliph Harun al Rashid. "Order all of your executors to look into the matter of those who are under arrest pending investigation of a crime each and every day, such that any of whom upon whom there is a punishment should be punished and released and any of whom against which there is no legitimate case should be released immediately. And inform them that they should not be excessive in punishment, and by such excesses step out of the bounds of that which is lawful."[28]

In conclusion, the Islamic criminal justice system guarantees protection of the security of person of the accused. Torture, beatings or other forms of cruel and unusual punishment are unlawful and exceed the boundaries of justice and the law. It is the state's responsibility to ensure justice and uphold the law for all of its citizens, even those who have been accused of or imprisoned for criminal behavior.[29]

Conclusion

Security of person is a fundamental right of human beings. On an individual level, the Quran upholds it as a component of inviolable human dignity and honor, which extends equally to both men and women. In particular, domestic abuse and violence against women, in any form, is not sanctioned by the Quran. We have demonstrated how an erroneous interpretation of Surah al Nisa, 4:34, is used to justify female inferiority and to place less value on women's dignity and honor.

It is the state's responsibility to protect the right of security of person, as basic human right for all of its citizens, as part of its overall duty to treat its citizens with justice. This is noted in law through the *sharia*, since one of its main goals is the preservation of life. In addition, a transparent criminal justice system, which prohibits torture of prisoners, is also a necessity in an Islamic state.

Footnotes

1   Article VII, Universal Islamic Declaration of Human Rights.

2   Asma Barlas, *"Believing Women" in Islam: Unreading Patriarchal Interpretations of the Quran*, (Austin: University of Texas Press, 2002), p. 181.

3   Tahir Mahmood, ed., "The Islamic Law on Human Rights," *Human Rights in Islamic Law* (New Delhi: Institute of Objective Studies, 1993) p. 39.

4   This point is elaborated upon in the chapter on the Status of Women.

5   Parveen Shaukat Ali, "Equality as a Basic Human Right in Islam," *Human Rights in Islamic Law*, ed. Tahir Mahmood (New Delhi: Institute of Objective Studies, 1993) p. 142.(118-152).

6   Wadud's translation, in Amina Wadud, *Quran and Woman* (New York: Oxford University Press, 1999) p. 74..

7   For more on the semantics and other implications of the Arabic term *fadala* (preference), see Wadud, pp. 69-74.

8   Wadud, p. 73.

9   Of course there is the possibility that some women may choose not to have children, or that some couples may not be able to have children. The verse should not be read then as absolving husbands of financial responsibility. The broader principle is reciprocity of rights and responsibilities in the marital relationship.

10 Barlas, p. 187.

11 Riffat Hassan, noted Muslim feminist and scholar, subscribes to this interpretation. Barlas, p. 189.

12 Sa'dullah Khan, "The Verse of Abuse or the Abused Verse," excerpt from *Dimensions of the Qur'an*, vol. 1, http://www.mwlusa.org/publications/essys/abuseverse.htm [August 14, 2003].

13 Wadud, p. 76.

14 Khan, p. 6.

15 Barlas, p. 189.

16 Asad, pp. 109-110, n. 44-45.

17 Khan, p. 7.

18 Muslim and Bukhari, cited by Muhammad Asad in his explanation of this verse, p. 109, n. 45.

19 "Case Study: Honor Killings and Blood Feuds," Gendercide Watch, http://www.gendercide.org/case_honour.thml

20 Honor killings have been reported in Bangladesh, Egypt, India, Pakistan, Jordan, Turkey, Britain, Brazil, Ecuador, Italy, Sweden, Morocco and Uganda. http://www.gendercide.org/case_honour.thml

21 Osman Abd al Malek al-Saleh, "The Right of the Individual to Personal Security in Islam," *The Islamic Criminal Justice*

System, ed. Cherif Bassiouni, (New York: Oceana Publications, 1982) pp. 70-71.

22 Cited in Abd al Malek al-Saleh, p. 72.

23 Abd al Malek al-Saleh, p. 72.

24 Al Ghazzali, cited in Abd al Malek al-Saleh, p. 72.

25 Abu Yusuf, cited in Abd al Malek al-Saleh, p. 72.

26 Abu Yusuf, cited in Abd al Malek al-Saleh, p. 73.

27 Abu Yusuf, cited in Abd al Malek al-Saleh, p. 73.

28 Abu Yusuf, Kitab al Kharaj, cited in Fathi Osman, Huquq, op. cit., p. 8.

29 See also the chapter on the justice system for more on the principles of the Islamic criminal justice.

Slavery

lavery is legitimately banned in the world today, in both Muslim and non-Muslim countries. Article 2 of the Universal Islamic Declaration of Human Rights and Article 4 of the Universal Declaration of Human Rights both condemn slavery unequivocally. Article 2 of the Islamic Declaration states "Man is born free. No inroads shall be made on his right to liberty except under the authority and in due process of the Law." Article 4 of the U.N. Declaration states "No one shall be held in slavery or servitude; slavery and the slave trade shall be prohibited in all their forms."

Despite this international consensus, it took a much longer time for slavery to be abolished legally in Muslim countries than it did in the United States. For example, Saudi Arabia only did so in 1962 and Mauritania in 1980.[1] Furthermore, the illegal practice of slavery continued to the present day in different forms.[2] Also, the exploitation of domestic workers and illegal trafficking of women all over the world continues to be a modern-day manifestation of slavery.

This chapter seeks to address this issue from an Islamic perspective, highlighting the contrast between the Quranic text and the actual, historical practice of slavery by Muslims. From a doctrinal, Islamic perspective, we firmly condemn slavery as an affront to the natural state of freedom in which God created human beings and to the very first pillar of Islam (the declaration of faith) which indicates that no person or power has the right to enslave people. However, there is evidence that in the historical context of early Islam, when the Quran was revealed to the Prophet (pbuh), slavery did exist in Arabian society. The Quran makes reference to slaves and their treatment, and does not expressly outlaw slavery, even if it does implicitly support its abolition through the conditions it sets out. The classical jurists also took slavery for granted, as an institution and elaborated rules for its regulation rather than its prohibition.[3] The Quran never legislated slavery, but legislated abolition.

The issue here is not so much why slavery should be, quite rightly, prohibited today, but the fact that we need to go beyond historical Quranic context as we interpret Islam with regards to contemporary issues and problems. Universal normative principles such as justice and equality and freedom, which have a clear basis in the Quran, are the primary, underlying sources of an Islamic human rights framework. We need not rely exclusively on traditional Islamic jurisprudence, especially with regard to the slavery issue.

This chapter has three sections. The first will survey the historical practice of slavery in the Muslim world, as the backdrop to a Quranic discussion on the issue. The second section outlines the relevant Quranic verses on slaves and slavery, and then uses these to develop an argument for the legal abolition of slavery. In the third part, we apply this interpretation to the modern-day context. We contend that since the same particular historical/social conditions do not exist today, as they did when Islam was revealed, therefore slavery cannot be condoned. Before we begin, however, a brief overview of the practice of slavery in the Muslim world is in order.

Historical Practice of Slavery in the Muslim World

Slavery existed in the ancient Middle East, long before the revelation of Islam. It is mentioned in the records from the Sumerian, Babylonian and ancient Egyptian civilizations, as well as those from the Greek, Roman and Byzantine empires. Both Jewish and Christian texts also recognized and accepted the institution of slavery.[4] By the seventh century, the slave trade in Arabia was well-established, with routes from

Sudan, Somalia and Ethiopia to the markets in Egypt and Arabia.[5] As a social institution, slavery was a normal part of the Arab society that the Prophet (pbuh) lived in.

In the centuries after the Prophet's (pbuh) death (632 AD) as the geographical area conquered by Muslim rulers expanded, so too did the slave trade in the Muslim world, as slaves were recruited from Africa to central Asia and eastern Europe.[6] While in earlier time periods, slaves were recruited from those captured in warfare, these numbers decreased as time went on, and purchase of slaves came to be the most common form of acquisition in the Islamic empire.[7]

The functions of slaves varied. The majority did domestic or agricultural work, although slaves never formed a labor base for the plantation-style agricultural economy that existed in the American South.[8] Others came to serve more specialized functions, in the military or at the royal court. It is these type of slaves that we are most familiar with today, in reference to the Islamic world, and in particular, the Ottoman Empire.

The use of slaves to staff armies was not a new practice, having been common in the Greek and Roman periods. But it was not until the 9th century that slave armies became common in the Islamic empire. In some cases, they were recruited by governors who needed troops that would be loyal to them against any threat from political opponents. In other cases, the caliphs used them to guard their palaces. From palace guards, it was only a short step for slaves to become professional soldiers, and eventually kings, as in the case of the Mamluk dynasty, which ruled in Egypt from the 13th-16th centuries.

The *mamluk* institution, which lasted from the first half of the 9th to the first half of the 19th centuries, formed part of the slave system in Muslim societies. It came to be a very specific category of slaves, however: those who became masters and constituted the uppermost layer of Muslim military society. They were originally drawn from central Asia, and once brought to a Muslim ruler's court, converted to Islam and trained in Islamic studies and military skills. When their studies were completed, they were freed, although they continued to serve in the military. What is notable, however, is the loyal patron-client relationship that characterized the relationship between the master and his former slave, and which was responsible for the cohesiveness and strength of the *mamluk* institution for hundreds of years.[9]

Other slave soldiers were drawn from all regions. In the eastern parts of the Islamic world, they were recruited mainly from the Turkish peoples living in the Eurasian steppes and central Asia. In the west, it was from among the Berbers of North Africa and the Slavs of Eastern Europe.[10] The Ottomans recruited mainly from the Balkans in central Europe.

In addition to the Mamluks, the institutionalized practice regarding the use of slaves as soldiers also existed during Ottoman rule. The system of *devsirme*, through which young Christian boys taken from villages became the property of the sultan, and were trained to serve at the royal court, was established by Sultan Murad II, in the 1420s, and lasted until the 19th century. While some of the men from the *devsirme* eventually served in the cavalry, others could achieve positions as provincial governors. Very few succeeded to the post of vizier, or that of grand vizier. However, it was not an impossible feat. Under Sultan Mehmed II (1444-1481), all of his grand viziers were *devsirme*.[11]

The purpose of the *devsirme* system was to prevent the creation of a hereditary aristocracy that might challenge the sultan's power, by limiting civil servants and military troops to non-Muslims from different regions, who would all be loyal to and dependent on the favor of the sultan, since they were owned by him.[12] From a more practical perspective, the devsirme system provided a constant source of new, loyal soldiers for the military corps known as the Janissaries.

The Janissaries functioned as the standing army loyal to the sultan, and were known for their military prowess. Although it was assumed that these soldiers would have no loyalty other than to the sultan, in fact, they became a tightly knit, cohesive unit with loyalty to their military commanders as well. The fact that the offspring of *devsirme* were not allowed to serve ensured that hereditary loyalties played no role either. The outcome was a remarkably effective military machine. From the 17th century onwards, the Janissaries came to function as a powerful social and political institution as well as a military corps. Around the same time period, the *devsirme* system of conscription was abandoned, and free men were also allowed to join the Janissaries.[13]

The fact that many of the grand viziers and military commanders under the Ottomans were of slave descent, and that even some of the sultans themselves were the sons of slave mothers, illustrates the relative lack of a permanent social stigma attached to being a slave in Muslim society, historically. The possibility of social integration and advancement was also available to slaves who were emancipated by their owners, or those who worked their way to freedom. For example, historical records from 15th century Istanbul indicate former slaves who took up trades or commerce and prospered. Court records show that some of them even took their former masters to court to settle disputes. In one notable case in 1543, a former slave of the sultan, acquired enough wealth to establish a foundation for the construction of a mosque in a downtown quarter that would bear her name.[14]

Some countries took steps to ban the slave trade in the mid-nineteenth century, Tunisia and Turkey being two examples. They formally abolished slavery in 1846 and 1854, respectively. In the Ottoman case, the decision to do so arose more as a result of political pressure from European (notably British) powers, which in the declining state that the empire was experiencing, left it with little choice other than to accept. However, the practical extinction of slavery was a much longer, gradual process, and small numbers of slaves continued to be imported into the Ottoman empire, or its successor states, until the last quarter of the nineteenth century.[15] It was not until 1962 that slavery was abolished in Saudi Arabia, and 1981 in the case of Mauritania.

While political factors are also relevant in explaining the long-standing practice of slavery in the Muslim world, our focus here is on the religious ones. We should distinguish between "Islam" and "Islamic interpretation" as the reasons for the historical existence of slavery. As we will demonstrate in the following section, despite the fact that slavery is contrary to the Quran, the fact that some Muslims did not follow this prohibition in the past does not preclude a Quranic argument for its abolition as an institution.

The Quran and *Hadith* on Slavery

The Quran acknowledges the existence of slaves in seventh-century Arab society, and most often uses the phrase "those whom your right hands possess" to describe them. Its advocacy for the just and humane treatment of slaves, as human beings and not merely property, represented a departure from the social customs of that time period. However, the Quran also foresaw the eventual disappearance of slavery as an institution by limiting the sources of new slaves to the prisoners of war captured in military campaign, and encouraging their manumission as a morally desirable act.

Before delving into the verses relating specifically to slavery, we need to examine the moral backdrop against which they must be assessed. In particular, they should be viewed in light of the normative strength of two Quranic principles – the inherent human freedom and equality of all beings. They lend strength to our interpretation stressing the implicit abolition of slavery in the Quran. Together, these two principles are also components of the concept of justice, as the responsibility of the state.

Freedom is a natural right of all human beings. One *hadith* states, that according to the Prophet (pbuh), "Every child is born in a natural state of freedom."[16] This is affirmed in the juristic position that freedom is the natural human state.[17] It is also supplemented by a statement attributed to Caliph Umar ibn al-Khattab, "Since when did you enslave the people whom their mothers gave birth to as free individuals?"[18] Commenting on the moral reprehensibility of the slave trade as a restriction on natural freedom, a *hadith* states: "There are three categories of people against whom I shall myself be the opponent on the

Day of Judgment. [One of these] is one who enslaves a free man, then sells him and devours the money."[19]

Freedom is inherent in the creation of man by God, and is a component of human dignity. The Quran declares dignity as a natural right in Surah al-Isra, 17:70, *"We bestowed dignity on the progeny of Adam."* There is no evidence that this absolute declaration is qualified anywhere in the Quran, and therefore can be considered to be a normative principle of Islam.[20]

These examples reflect an emphasis on freedom given by God, as part of the human condition, and one that cannot be limited by human beings. From an Islamic perspective, slavery is a socially constructed institution, and not a hereditary one. All children are born free, and the fact that historically, children born of slave parents were also slaves represents a divergence from Quranic teaching.

The second principle is equality. This refers to both the equality of all Muslims, and the equality of all humans before God, and the rights and duties that derive from this human condition. This point is emphasized repeatedly in the Quran and in the example of the Prophet (pbuh), and can be used to support our argument against slavery. All humans are equal in standing in the eyes of God, and are distinguished only by their own good actions. For example, the Prophet (pbuh) has declared in, broad terms, that "People are as equal as the teeth of a comb."[21] This theme is also stressed in the Prophet's sermon on the occasion of the Farewell Pilgrimage: "O People! Your Creator is one, and you are all descendants of the same ancestor. There is no superiority of an Arab over a non-Arab, or of the black over the red, except on the basis of righteous conduct."[22]

An incident surrounding the revelation of Surah al Anam elaborates upon this theme of equality. A group of Qurayshi dignitaries came to visit the Prophet (pbuh), but protested when they saw him in the company of some of his Companions, Bilal al-Habshi, Salman al-Farsi, Suhayb al-Rumi, 'Ammar and others who were former slaves. "How can we sit with you, O Muhammad, while you keep the company of slaves and commoners of [their] type? Exclude them from your company and we will sit with you and listen to your invitation." The Prophet (pbuh) refused to comply, but they insisted on his making a distinction and to 'assign a day for them and one for us.' In response, Surah al Anam, 6:52 was revealed, which rejected all man-made differences and superiorities in those who sought God.[23] *"Send not away those who call on their Lord morning and evening, seeking His face. In naught art thou accountable for them, and in naught are they accountable for thee, that thou shouldst turn them away, and thus be (one) of the unjust"* (Surah al Anam, 6:52).

The Prophet (pbuh) also exemplified the same emphasis on equal treatment for all. Zayd, his adopted son, Bilal, and Salman al-Farsi were all former slaves who enjoyed the Prophet's (pbuh) affection as his supporters. The fact that he wed Zayd to his cousin, Zaynab, illustrates that there was no social stigma attached to freed slaves. In the case of Bilal, as was noted earlier, he was the first person to give the prayer call in Medina. There is also a *hadith* that indicates that a slave named Salim used to lead the prayers. "Narrated Ibn 'Umar: When the earliest emigrants came to Al- 'Usba a place in Quba', before the arrival of the Prophet- Salim, the slave of Abu Hudhaifa, who knew the Quran more than the others used to lead them in prayer."[24] The import of these examples is that neither God and nor the Prophet (pbuh) discriminated against slaves or former slaves, as being any different in status or rank or as people capable of achieving good.

We can also situate the moral argument against slavery within the larger context of the message of Islam, and the Prophet's (pbuh) mission. Surah al Araf, 7:157 outlines the objectives of the Prophet's (pbuh) mission. *"Those who follow the messenger, the unlettered Prophet, whom they find mentioned in their own (scriptures) – in the law and the Gospel – for he commands them what is just and forbids them what is evil; he allows them as lawful what is good (and pure) and prohibits them from what is bad (and impure); He releases them from their heavy burdens and from the yokes that are upon them. So it is those who believe in him, honor him, help him, and follow the light which is sent down with him; it is they who will prosper"* (Surah al Araf, 7:157). Release from "heavy burdens" and "the yokes that are upon them" can be viewed as a reference to an end to any kind of enslavement in the context of allowing what is lawful and prohibiting what is evil (*hisba*) that is part of the larger moral purpose of Islam. Abbas M. Al-Aqqad, a leading modern Islamic philosopher, notes in his writings that Islam brought many laws to liberate slaves, but none to create them.

Challenging the condition of slavery, in any form, is part of the purpose of God's prophets in general, as those who deliver their people from oppression. This is illustrated in the following exchange between Moses and the Pharaoh, before Moses eventually leads the Children of Israel out of Egypt and the Pharaoh's armies, who are in pursuit, are drowned. *"(Pharaoh) said: 'Did we not cherish thee as a child among us, and didst thou not stay in our midst many years of thy life? And thou didst a deed of thine which (thou knowest) thou didst, and thou art an ungrateful (wretch)!'"* (Surah al Shuara, 26:18-19). Moses replies, *"I did it then, when I was in error. So I fled from you (all) when I feared you; but my Lord has (since) invested me with judgment (and wisdom) and appointed me as one of the messengers. And this is the favor with which thou dost reproach me,- that thou hast enslaved the Children of Israel!"* (Surah al Shuara, 26:20-22). Moses defies the Pharaoh's claim to authority, in light of God's omnipotent authority, and in doing so, disputes the idea that any human could have the right to enslave another human.

We can conclude, then, that the inherent equality of all human beings and the state of freedom in which they are born is such that to enslave someone means to deny them a part of their humanity. Both these Quranic principles, of freedom and of equality, in addition to the verses on slavery noted earlier, support our argument prohibiting slavery on moral grounds. The question remains, though, as to how to support the legal abolition of slavery.

In order to answer this question, we must turn to the concept of justice, which it is the state's Islamic duty to uphold. Surah al Nisaa, 4:35, *"O ye who believe! Stand out firmly for justice, as witnesses to God, even as against yourselves, or your parents, or your kin, and whether it be (against) rich or poor: for God can best protect both"* and Surah al Nahl, 16:90, *"Surely God enjoins the doing of justice and the doing of good (to others) and the giving to the kindred, and He forbids indecency and evil and rebellion; He admonishes you that you may be mindful"* both illustrate the paramount importance of upholding justice under all circumstances.

Justice derives from the equality of all human beings, with their moral freedom and human dignity, as created by God, but it is manifested in their equality before the (temporal) law, with equal legal rights and duties. The state must treat all of its citizens, with equity and cannot restrict the freedom of any human being by enslaving them. To do so is to limit the human condition, which is not within the state's prerogative.[25] Furthermore, the state must actively work to eliminate slavery in all its forms, from the use of state funds to free slaves to the enactment of laws that ensure humane treatment of all workers. From a moral perspective as well, the idea of justice demands that the state abolish slavery as a communal act of virtue, as noted in the Quran. The relevant verses on this issue will be discussed in more detail further on.

All three of these Quranic principles form the basis for the following analysis of the specific verses on slavery. For seventh century Arabia, where slavery was socially and globally an accepted institution, the revelation of Islam introduced the idea of just and humane treatment of slaves. It encouraged their manumission in a number of ways, supporting an implicit argument for the eventual abolition of the slave trade.

The Quran refers to slavery being propagated in the context of war, when prisoners of war were taken as slaves. But, Surah al Anfal, 8:67-69 discourages the capture of prisoners and other spoils as the primary purpose of war. They are simply a byproduct of victory. *"It is not fitting for a prophet that he should have prisoners of war until he hath thoroughly subdued the land. Ye look for the temporal goods of this world;*

but God looketh to the Hereafter: And God is Exalted in might, Wise. Had it not been for a previous ordainment from God, a severe penalty would have reached you for the (ransom) that ye took. But (now) enjoy what ye took in war, lawful and good: but fear God: for God is Oft-forgiving, Most Merciful" (Surah al Anfal, 8:67-69).

Once captured, there were two options available for prisoners of war. They could, potentially, either be enslaved or released (with or without ransom).[26] The Quranic recommendation was for the captives to be set free through the generosity of the victor. *"Now when ye meet in battle those who disbelieve, then it is smiting of the necks until, when ye have routed them, then making fast of bonds; and afterward either grace or ransom till the war lay down its burdens. That (is the ordinance)"* (Surah Muhammad, 47:4).

In a more general sense, the Quran views the freeing of slaves as an act of virtue, charity and/or religious penance. Surah al Balad, 90 places this issue in a moral context. It states that God allows people to make moral choices that will bring them closer to God's favor, giving the metaphor of "a steep path" as the way to spiritual achievement. Among the actions that characterize this "steep path" is the manumission of slaves. *"And what will explain to thee the path that is steep? (It is) to free a slave"* (Surah al Balad, 90:12-13). This point is also supported by the following *hadith*. "Bilal said to Abu Bakr, 'If you have bought me for yourself then keep me (for yourself), but if you have bought me for God's Sake, then leave me for God's work.'"[27] In this case, "God's work" requires that he be set free, as an act of virtue. Furthermore, this virtuous act of freeing all slaves is a moral obligation upon both the state and the community.

In another case, the penance for breaking an oath is the freeing of a slave, indicated in Surah al Maida, 5:89, *"God will not call you to account for what is futile in your oaths, but He will call you to account for your deliberate oaths: for expiation, feed ten indigent persons, on a scale of the average for the food of your families; or clothe them; or give a slave his freedom,"* and again in Surah al Mujadila, 58:3, *"Those who put away their wives (by saying they are as their mothers) and afterward would go back on that which they have said, (the penalty) in that case (is) the freeing of a slave before they touch one another."*

In the case of an accidental death of a Muslim by another Muslim, as a legal prescription, it is recommended that the killer set free a Muslim slave and pay compensation to the deceased's family. *"Never should a believer kill a believer; but (If it so happens) by mistake, (Compensation is due): If one (so) kills a believer, it is ordained that he should free a believing slave, and pay compensation to the deceased's family, unless they remit it freely. If the deceased belonged to a people at war with you, and he was a believer, the freeing of a believing slave (Is enough). If he belonged to a people with whom ye have treaty of Mutual alliance, compensation should be paid to his family, and a believing slave be freed. For those who find this beyond their means, (is prescribed) a fast for two months running: by way of repentance to God: for God hath all knowledge and all wisdom"* (Surah al Nisaa, 4:92).

This verse has been interpreted to indicate the importance of and the close ties between life and freedom as Quranic concepts. The gravity of taking a life can only be balanced by giving (back) a life, metaphorically. In this case, this means granting freedom to a slave. It also illustrates the high moral value placed on the manumission of slaves, and conversely, a moral abhorrence of the condition of slavery as a kind of "death".[28]

In practice, there is also the example of Abu Bakr who freed his slave, Bilal. Bilal came to be one of the most favored Companions of the Prophet (pbuh) and was the first to give the prayer call in Medina. The esteem which the Prophet (pbuh) bestowed upon Bilal is illustrated in a *hadith* in which the Prophet (pbuh) said to him, "I heard the sound of your shoes in Paradise just in front of me."[29] The example of Bilal enumerates the desirability of freeing slaves, from an Islamic point of view.

Other avenues for freeing slaves include the establishment of a contract that allows slaves to earn their freedom (*mukataba*). *"And if any of your slaves ask for a deed in writing (to enable them to earn their freedom for a certain sum), give them such a deed if ye know any good in them: yea, give them something yourselves out of the means which God has given to you"* (Surah al Nur, 24:33). This very strong Quranic injunction granting all slaves the right to earn their freedom argues firmly that slavery is an unnatural state from which people should be provided a way out. The ability to enter into this kind of contract indicates that slaves had some kind of a legal identity and, by extension, legal rights, even if they did not enjoy the legal status of a free individual. This was in contrast to the Greek or Roman contexts, for example, where a slave had no rights whatsoever, and little hope of securing his/her own freedom.[30]

Financially, the Quran calls for the ransoming of slaves through private charity (*"Give them something yourselves out of the means which God has given to you,"* Surah al Nur, 24:33) or through *zakat* money deposited in the official treasury. The latter is indicated in the following two verses: Surah al Tawba, 9:60, *"The alms are only for the poor and the needy, and those employed to administer the (funds); for those whose hearts have been (recently) reconciled(to truth); for those in bondage and in debt; in the cause of God; and for the wayfarer;"* and Surah al Baqara, 2:177 *"It is not righteousness that ye turn your faces Towards east or West; but it is righteousness- to believe in God and the Last Day, and the Angels, and the Book, and the Messengers; to spend of your substance, out of love for Him, for your kin, for orphans, for the needy, for the wayfarer, for those who ask, and for the ransom of slaves; to be steadfast in prayer, and practice regular charity; to fulfill the contracts which ye have made; and to be firm and patient, in pain (or suffering) and adversity, and throughout all periods of panic. Such are the people of truth, the God-fearing."* The fact that one of the principle duties of a Muslim (payment of *zakat*) can be discharged by freeing a slave, highlights again how abhorrent slavery is to God. One of the means of achieving salvation is to reduce the number of slaves in this world.

These verses can therefore support the notion that it is the state's political and moral duty to utilize government funds to free all slaves (regardless of whether they are Muslims or non-Muslims) and to abolish slavery as an institution.[31] The Muslim polity, acting as a whole, can abolish slavery and ransom slaves as a collective act of virtue. The individual's moral duty to free slaves as an act of virtue has already been noted in this discussion. Expanding this moral duty to the political sphere of the government does not change the importance of this Quranic obligation. In fact, it becomes a component of the state's socio-political duty, to take care of all of its citizens, as well as its moral duty, to allow the community to do good deeds, as a communal act.

In the historical context of seventh century Arabia, when the Quranic verses regarding slavery were revealed, a number of recommendations were outlined. First and foremost, manumitting slaves was the most desirable course. But, since many chose not to do that, the just and humane treatment of slaves, while they were in custody of their master was also made incumbent upon Muslims. Surah al Nisaa, 4:36 is one such verse that includes slaves among parents and neighbors and others whom Muslims were enjoined to treat well, as an act of worship on par with submission to God. It states *"Serve God, and join not any partners with Him; and do good- to parents, kinsfolk, orphans, those in need, neighbors who are near, neighbors who are strangers, the companion by your side, the wayfarer (ye meet), and what your right hands possess"* (Surah al Nisaa, 4:36).

In practice, this meant treating slaves as human beings and not merely as property. Slaves had the right to be fed, clothed and supported by their masters at the same standard as their masters, who were legally bound to do so. "If a master defaulted on these and other obligations to his slave, a *qadi* (judge) could compel him to fulfill them or else either to sell or to emancipate the slave. The master was forbidden to overwork his slave, and if he did so to the point of cruelty, he was liable to a penalty which was, however, discretionary and not prescribed by law."[32] There is also a *hadith* to this effect, narrated by Bukhari. It was reported that the Prophet (pbuh) said: "Your servants and your slaves are your brothers. Anyone who has slaves should give them from what he eats and wears. He should not charge them with work beyond their capabilities. If you must set them to hard work, in any case, I advise you to help them."[33]

The Quran also prohibited the sex trade of female slaves. Slave women were not to be placed in prostitution, which was also an innovation for the time period.[36] *"And do not compel your slave girls to prostitution, when they desire to keep chaste, in order to seek the frail good of this world's life; and whoever compels them, then surely after their compulsion God is Forgiving, Merciful"* (Surah al Nur, 24:33).

This didn't mean that, in contrast to Quranic injunction, historical practice did not include sexual service to their masters as part of the duties of female slaves. There are several examples of rulers born of slave mothers in the royal harem; al-Mansur, the second Abbasid caliph, and al-Rashid, the sixth one, were both sons of slave girls. Children born of such unions were born free and were legitimate heirs to the father's (master's) property. The slave mother of the child earned the status of *"umm walad"* and could not be sold. Upon the master's death, she became a free woman.[37] This was in contrast to the status of children born of slave marriages, since having a slave father meant that they remained slaves. This practice was, however, contrary to the Quranic emphasis on freedom as a natural right.

In conclusion, this section has outlined our argument for the prohibition of slavery, drawing from Quranic verses and *hadith* literature. The discussion so far has outlined the ways in which the Quran deals with the introduction of slaves into society and their treatment once they are enslaved. The Quran limits the source of new slaves to captives of war, but in doing so, recommends their freedom through ransom or through the generosity of the victor. The revelation of Islam made a difference in the condition of slaves for that historical time period, by advocating kind and humane treatment and the use of private and public funds to realize their eventual emancipation as a virtuous, pious action undertaken both by the state and by individuals. This is not to say that there were no slave owners who were cruel or unjust, or that slavery was not an oppressive institution. Kind treatment of slaves did not mean that they were treated as the equals of free men and women. However, the Quran viewed slavery as a morally undesirable institution, and advocated its eventual abolition altogether. Once abolished, it is prohibited to re-establish the practice again, for all the reasons we have noted here.

In addition, we have also examined the Quranic principles of freedom and equality of all human beings. These should be viewed as normative concepts that prohibit the condition of human enslavement in a broader sense, beyond just the issue of the consequences of the slave trade and the treatment of slaves in a social context. It is this point that needs to be stressed in articulating a legal ban on slavery. The state cannot legally limit human freedom and dignity because it cannot place restrictions on the human condition that has been granted to all by God. Furthermore, it cannot sanction the enslavement of non-Muslims on the grounds that freedom and equality only apply to the condition of Muslims before God. As argued elsewhere,[38] Muslims are not necessarily morally favored over others merely because they are Muslims, and the moral equality of all humans does not allow for inferior treatment of anyone in any way before the law.

Modern-Day Manifestations of Slavery

Despite the normative moral injunctions of the Quran prohibiting slavery, the fact remains that slavery-like conditions have lasted well into the twentieth century in some countries. For example, modern-day manifestations of slavery are apparent in the capture and imprisonment of vulnerable populations in civil war-torn countries, and in the trafficking of women in different parts of the world.

Modern-day slavery-like conditions are also created through the trafficking of women into situations of forced labor or prostitution in various parts of the world. While this is a problem of global magnitude, the oppressive treatment of female domestic workers in the Gulf countries (Saudi Arabia and Kuwait, to name two) is one example. They come primarily from the Philippines, Bangladesh, Sudan, Ethiopia, India, Indonesia, and Sri Lanka to work as domestic servants and nannies. Once they arrive, it is alleged they are forced into situations of coerced labor or slave-like conditions, and in some of those cases they also suffer extreme working conditions and physical and sexual abuse by male employers. Many have their passports withheld so that they cannot escape from their employers. Their contracts are unilaterally altered, and/or they are not paid their salaries. These women have little recourse to help from local authorities. If they manage to escape from their employers, many take refuge in the compounds of their national embassies, while embassy personnel try to negotiate a resolution. But the labor law in these countries provides limited protection to foreign domestic workers.[42] These situations ought to be fully investigated by a neutral body, and if found true, all measures and forms of pressure should be used to bring this shame to an end.

Whatever the cause, we firmly condemn slavery of any kind on moral and Quranic grounds. The dignity of all human beings, as granted by God, must be protected at all times. It is the state's responsibility to make sure that abuse and exploitation of any segment of their populations is prohibited, and appropriately punished. While it is true that economic or political insecurity in their countries of origin often forces many people to seek employment as migrant workers in other countries, this does not justify their abuse or exploitation in any way.

Conclusion

In conclusion, this chapter has argued that slavery is an affront to the Quranic principles of freedom, dignity and equality that are the rights of all individuals, as granted by God. The implicit abolition of slavery is apparent in the Quranic verses on the topic. The Quran limited the source of new slaves to captives of war, but in doing so, recommended their freedom through ransom or through the generosity of the victor. It advocated kind and humane treatment of slaves, such that they are recognized as equals and as human beings. In addition, the use of private and public funds to realize their eventual emancipation was recommended as a virtuous, pious action undertaken both by the state and by individuals.

The emphasis on ethical guidelines for the treatment of slaves as part of the process towards abolition is particularly noteworthy, in contrast to the alternative that the Quran might have advocated: an explicit ban on slavery in one fell swoop. Apart from the practical ramifications that this might have had on Arab society of that time period, it also would not have resolved the issue of integration of former slaves into free society, which, one might argue, was a much more difficult issue to resolve. As a contrast, we can look at the American historical experience with slavery, such that years after it was officially abolished, the African-American struggle for equality before the law and in civil rights continued. Therefore, the fact that society must be ready to believe in and accept the humanity of all of its members, regardless of skin color, is an integral part of the fight against slavery. It is this aspect that the Quran spoke to, and that the Prophet (pbuh) also emphasized in his actions.

The main issue is not so much why slavery should be and is, quite rightly, abolished today, but the fact that we need to go beyond historical interpretations of the Quran as we apply Islam to contemporary issues and problems. Universal principles that have a basis in the Quran, such as justice and equality and freedom, must remain the basis of any contemporary interpretation.

In one sense, this chapter seems superfluous and unnecessary to this book, because even the most conservative Muslim voices have come to the same conclusion about the abolition of slavery. But if one grants that an evolving standard of justice can apply to the issue of slavery, then one must also concede that we can do the same with issues of gender equality or Muslim/non-Muslim relations.

Footnotes

1 Murray Gordon, *Slavery in the Arab World* (New York: New Amsterdam Books, 1989) p. 44.
2 See Amnesty International Report 2002, "Sudan" for details. Available online http://web.amnesty.org/web/ar2002.nsf/afr/sudan!Open
3 Abdullahi Ahmed An-Na'im, *Toward an Islamic Reformation* (Syracuse: Syracuse University Press, 1990) p.174.
4 "Slavery", *The New Encyclopaedia Britannica*, 15th ed.,(Chicago: Encyclopaedia Britannica, Inc, 2002), pp. 288-300.
5 Gordon, p. 18.
6 Seymour Drescher and Stanley L. Engerman, eds., *A Historical Guide to World Slavery* (New York: Oxford University Press, 1998), p. 249.
7 "Slavery", *The New Encyclopaedia Britannica*, p. 292.
8 Gordon, p. 49.
9 David Ayalon, "The Mamluks: The Mainstay of Islam's Military Might," *Slavery in the Islamic Middle East*, ed. Shaun E. Marmon, (Princeton: Markus Wiener Publishers, 1999), pp.90-91.
10 "Slavery," *The New Encyclopaedia Britannica*, pp. 291-292.
11 "Devsirme," *Encyclopedia of the Orient*, 2003. http://i-cias.com/e.o/devsirme.htm [March 3, 2003].
12 "Devsirme," *Encyclopedia of the Orient*, 2003.
13 "Janissaries," *Encyclopedia of the Orient*, 2003, http://i-cias.com/e.o/janissaries.htm [March 3, 2003].
14 Yvonne Seng, "A Liminal State: Slavery in 16th Century Istanbul," *Slavery in the Islamic Middle East*, ed. Shaun E. Marmon, (Princeton: Markus Wiener Publishers, 1999), p. 35.
15 Ehud R. Toledano, *The Ottoman Slave Trade and its Suppression: 1840-1890* (Princeton: Princeton University Press, 1982), pp. 11-13
16 al-Tabrizi, quoted in Kamali, *Freedom, Equality and Justice in Islam*, p. 16.
17 Shaun E. Marmon, ed., *Slavery in the Islamic Middle East*, (Princeton: Markus Wiener Publishers, 1999)p. 2.
18 Kamali, *Freedom, Equality and Justice in Islam*, p. 17.
19 Bukhari, cited in Kamali, *Freedom, Equality and Justice in Islam*, p. 17.
20 Kamali, *Freedom of Expression in Islam*, p. 12.
21 Cited in Kamali, *Freedom, Equality and Justice in Islam*, p. 52.
22 Kamali, *Freedom, Equality and Justice in Islam*, p. 52.
23 Kamali, *Freedom, Equality and Justice in Islam*, p. 54.
24 Sahih Bukhari, Vol. 1, Book 11, No. 661.
25 This is, of course, distinct from punishing people for criminal behavior by putting them in jail. Limiting their freedom in this context comes out of a breach of law on the part of the individual.
26 Ahmad An-Na'im, p. 173.
27 Sahih Bukhari, Vol. 5, Book 57, No. 99
28 Kamali, *Freedom, Equality and Justice in Islam*, p. 26.
29 Sahih Bukhari, Vol. 5, Book 57, No. 97.
30 "Slavery," *The New Encyclopaedia Britannica*, pp. 288-300.
31 Asad, n. 47, p. 540.
32 Marmon, p. 5.
33 Sahih Bukhari, Vol. 1, Book 2, No. 29.
34 Sahih Bukhari Vol. 1, Book 3, No. 97. Also in Sahih Muslim, Book 1, No. 284.
35 See also Muhammad Asad's explanation of these verses, stressing this particular interpretation, p. 106, n. 26 and p. 107, n. 32.
36 Gordon, p.37.
37 Marmon, p. 4.
38 See chapter on religious freedom for more on the legal equality of all citizens, Muslims and non-Muslims.
39 For more on the plight of children captured and enslaved in the Sudan, see "Children in Sudan: Slaves, Street Children and Child Soldiers" Human Rights Watch, Sept. 1995. http://www.hrw.org/reports/1995/Sudan.htm
40 Trafficking in Persons Report 2003, US State Dept, http://www.state.gov/g/tip/rls/tiprpt/2003/ [December 15, 2003].
41 Section III, Articles 49-57 of the Geneva Convention deal with the conditions for utilizing the labor of POWs. Full text is available online. http://www.unhchr.ch/html/menu3/b/91.htm
42 Trafficking in Persons Report 2003, US State Dept, http://www.state.gov/g/tip/rls/tiprpt/2003/ [December 15, 2003].

CHAPTER SIXTEEN

Social Services

e have focused primarily on political rights as human rights in this book. However, we also consider socio-economic rights as basic human rights. This chapter focuses on healthcare, education and social security as part of the basic standard of social services that the state is required to provide for its citizens.

The Quran lays out a moral imperative upon Muslims to ensure basic need fulfillment of their less-privileged fellow members in society, but this is portrayed primarily as a private endeavor, and/or a communal obligation. We are arguing that, as part of the state's responsibility to ensure justice and protect the rights of its citizens, it must also ensure that these basic needs are fulfilled. An Islamic state should provide basic levels of old age security, support for the poor and disabled, basic healthcare and educational services to all of its citizens. The specifics of how much of this obligation is paid for privately and how much by public funds is a balance that each state and society must determine for itself through a democratic process, since it is not the purpose of this chapter to outline highly detailed socio-economic policies. Instead, we offer a general argument for why an Islamic state is responsible for providing basic social services to its citizens.

Helping Others: Individual and Community Obligation

God has granted every human being the right to live with dignity. A state of deprivation – material, physical or spiritual – detracts from this inherent dignity. The Prophet (pbuh) is reported to have said, "Seek God's refuge from poverty, scarcity and ignominy."[1] The individual himself is required to take steps to remedy these problems, to the best of his/her ability.

With regard to financial or material issues, every able-bodied individual, first and foremost, is required to make the effort to earn his own livelihood, to support himself and his family. The Prophet (pbuh) has said: "To earn an honest livelihood is a duty (ranking) next to the chief duty (of offering prayers)."[2] Another *hadith* states, "It is better for anyone of you to take a rope (and cut) and bring a bundle of wood (from the forest) over his back and sell it and God will save his face (from the Hell-Fire) because of that, rather than to ask the people who may give him or not."[3] One should also note that neither of these *hadith* are restricted to males only.

However, as a social response to deprivation, God commands people to help others who are suffering or in need, in a positive spirit of mutual cooperation. This is based on the perspective that everyone in society is connected to each other through their shared humanity, and is therefore required to live in a spirit of cooperation. For example, the Quran states, *"But rather help one another in furthering virtue and God-consciousness, and do not help one another in furthering evil and enmity; and remain conscious of God; for, behold, God is severe in retribution!"* (Surah al Maida – The Repast, 5:2). Another verse *"And [as for] the believers, both men and women – they are close unto one another: they [all] enjoin the doing of what is right and forbid the doing of what is wrong, and are constant in prayer, and render the purifying dues, and pay heed unto God and His Apostle. It is they upon whom God will bestow His grace: verily, God is almighty, wise!"* (Surah al Tawba – Repentance, 9:71).

The spirit of cooperation is reflected in the command to help others by giving in charity. The Quran describes as believers, those *"who believe in [the existence of] that which is beyond the reach of human perception, and are constant in prayer, and spend on others out of what We provide for them as sustenance"* (Surah al Baqara – The Cow, 2:3). It is these people who *"follow the guidance [which comes] from their*

Sustainer; and it is they, they who shall attain to a happy state!" (Surah al Baqara – The Cow, 2:5). There is no restriction to only help others who are Muslims; instead, aid is extended to everyone in society who needs it.

A more specific instance of charity is in the form of *zakat*, which is one of the pillars of Islam and therefore incumbent upon every Muslim. It is both an individual and communal obligation, but not necessarily that of the state as well. *"The offerings given for the sake of God are [meant] only for the poor and the needy, and those who are in charge thereof, and those whose hearts are to be won over, and for the freeing of human beings from bondage, and [for] those who are over-burdened with debts, and [for every struggle] in God's cause, and [for] the way-farer: [this is] an ordinance from God – and God is all-knowing, wise"* (Surah al Tawba - Repentance, 9:60).

Feeding the hungry, the poor, orphans or captives, is another way of helping others. The Quran states, *"And who give food – however great to be their own want of it – unto the needy, and the orphan, and the captive, [saying, in their hearts,] 'We feed you for the sake of God alone: we desire no recompense from you, nor thanks'"* (Surah al Insan – Man, 76:8-9). God stresses that this is done without expecting a material reward or temporal recognition, but simply as a virtuous act. Elaborating on this theme, a *hadith* states, "He is not a true Muslim who eats his fill when his next door neighbor is hungry."[4]

The underlying rationale in the responsibility to help others is that the less fortunate have a share in the wealth of the more privileged, and the latter have a responsibility to help the poor, the sick, and the elderly. It is a mutual relationship of rights and duties. This theme is illustrated in two Quranic verses. *"And [would assign] in all that they possessed a due share unto such as might ask [for help] and such as might suffer privation"* (Surah al Dhariyat – The Dust-Scattering Winds, 51:19). *"And in whose possessions there is a due share, acknowledged [by them], for such as ask [for help] and such as are deprived [of what is good in life]"* (Surah al Maarij – The Ways of Ascent, 70: 24-25).

Wealth is not to be concentrated in a few hands, but must be reasonably distributed throughout society so that it benefits as many people as possible. *"Whatever [spoils taken] from the people of those villages God has turned over to His Apostle – [all of it] belongs to God and the Apostle, and the near of kin [of deceased believers], and the orphans, and the needy, and the wayfarer, so that it may not be [a benefit] going round and round among such of you as may [already] be rich"* (Surah al Hashr – The Gathering, 59:7).

To summarize, the Quran directs the moral obligation to help the less fortunate towards the individual and, in general, towards society. It does not specifically comment on the role of the state. The next section addresses this gap in more detail.

The Role of the State: Guardianship and Distributive Justice

Guardianship

The state carries a moral responsibility to protect its citizens, to preserve their God-given dignity and freedom, and to treat them with justice. It is also the state's legal responsibility to realize the well-being of its citizens by ensuring the protection of faith, life, intellect, property, and family, as the goals of the Islamic law (*sharia*).[5] In particular, the protection of life is possible only if basic survival needs are taken care of.

Juristic literature supports this principle. It identifies three categories of human needs: necessities (*daruriyyat*), conveniences (*hajiyyat*), and refinements (*tahsiniyyat*). Necessities include everything that protects one's physical existence, in addition to that which is necessary for the preservation of the individual's religion, life, intellect, progeny and property. According to jurists, it is the collective responsibility of society to ensure the fulfillment of basic necessities first.[6] We are arguing that this should include access to basic healthcare, education, and social security for the needy, which the state is obligated to provide.[7]

There is also strong tradition noted in the *hadith* and the example of the Caliphs for fulfilling this guardianship role. To give a few examples:

"A locality in which one has to starve a night is deprived of God's protection."[8]

"Protect one who seeks your protection in the name of God and give to him who asks (for something) in the name of God."[9]

"One whom God the mighty, the exalted, puts in charge of some of the affairs of the Muslims and he turns his back on their needs and necessities and poverty God will turn His back on his need and necessities and poverty."[10]

"A ruler who, having obtained control over the affairs of the Muslims, does not strive for their betterment and does not serve them sincerely shall not enter Paradise with them."[11]

"Every one of you is a shepherd and every one is answerable with regard to his flock. The Caliph is a shepherd over the people and shall be questioned about his subjects (as to how he conducted their affairs)."[12]

Although there was no established system for healthcare, education or social security until much later in Islamic history, the moral imperative for the state to provide similar services is demonstrated in the use of the *bayt al mal*, or public treasury. It was seen by the Prophet (pbuh) and the first four Rightly-Guided Caliphs as a trust which they held for the people, to take care of the needy among them. The ruler had the right to draw a fixed stipend from it, enough to cover his and his family's needs, but not more than that.[13] The rest was distributed to the people. The most common way that the Prophet (pbuh) used to do this was whenever the government received anything in cash or kind, everyone would assemble and he would distribute it among them in equal shares.[14] The only exception was camels, which were retained for exclusive distribution among fighters who took part in battles with the Prophet (pbuh).[15]

After the conquests of Iraq and Syria, a greater surplus was available for distribution. The money was distributed in two categories, as part of an institutionalized system of welfare, in the early years of the Caliphate: payments for annual pensions and monthly rations. Caliph Umar is reported to have been the first to institutionalize a scheme for distribution of pensions.[16] Pensions were given twice a year, while rations were distributed every month. If soldiers were mobilized though, they were paid before they left for battle. Sometimes cash was paid in lieu of rations.[17] He fixed the amount of pensions for those who fought in the army and received spoils of war. The rest of the population, including Muslim slaves, was entitled to rations.[18] For example, during a famine, an entire caravan of relief provisions was distributed by Caliph Umar among the countrymen living around Medina.[19]

Pensions were fixed on the understanding that the recipient was obligated to perform military service, or had already done so in the past, if he was not already engaged in service to the state as a civil servant. But it also included others who had demonstrated loyalty to the Prophet (pbuh) and the needy: the Prophet's (pbuh) wives, uncle, grandsons, those who had migrated to Abyssinia, those who migrated to Medina with the Prophet (pbuh), those who had fought battles alongside the Prophet (pbuh), the children of those fighters, orphans, and women.[20] Considerations of high office, courage, bravery, generosity or loyalty were also grounds for being granted a pension. In one instance, a Bedouin's daughter came to Caliph Umar and asked for subsistence, saying that her father had fought with the Prophet (pbuh). The Caliph set a fixed allowance for her.[21]

In addition to pensions, every person was entitled to receive fixed rations of wheat, vinegar and oil. Caliph Umar was the first to set up ration depots in cities. They stored flour, dates, raisins and other provisions for free distribution. These commodities were also available to travelers and guests.[22] Caliph Uthman was known to have supplemented these with clothing as well.[23]

In particular, the Caliphs did not distinguish between Muslims and non-Muslims as recipients of social security from the ruler. Under Caliph Abu Bakr, a treaty made by Khalid bin Waleed on the conquest of Hira stated that if an elderly non-Muslim person became incapable of working, or fell sick, or became destitute, such that his co-religionists had to start giving him money, then his *jizya* would be remitted. He and his children would be allowed to receive a maintenance from the public treasury, as long as he lived in Muslim country. If he left however, the state would not be responsible for maintaining his family.[24] In another example, Caliph Abu Bakr saw an old man begging, in order to have enough money to pay his *jizya*. He brought him back to his house, gave him some cash, and sent word to the treasury officer that the elderly who were unable to earn their living should be given stipends from the public treasury. He is reported to have said, "It is not just that we derive benefit from men while they are young and drive them out when they are old."[25]

The second caliph, Umar, also took his responsibility towards his people very seriously, both Muslims and non-Muslims. He is said to have publicly declared, upon taking office, "I am keen to fulfill a need whenever I see one, as long as we are collectively capable of doing so. When we can no longer afford it, we co-operate in living till everyone is living at the same level of subsistence."[26] He is reported to have included poor Muslims and non-Muslims as beneficiaries of *sadaqa*, and tried to make sure everyone was given equal shares. The excess was left in the central treasury for future use.[27]

These examples demonstrate the general principle of guardianship of the state for all its people. Those who have performed military service, and their heirs, are entitled to pensions. But, more generally, anyone in need – the poor, the sick, the elderly – has a share in the resources allocated by the state.

Justice

Part of the state's role is to uphold justice for all of its citizens. With reference to the topic of this chapter, we include distributive, economic justice within the purview of the state. People who live in a state of poverty and deprivation as a result of socio-economic inequalities are entitled to social support by the state, if they are unable to work and support themselves. Provision of basic social services requires the equitable distribution and allocation of resources in society by the state.[28]

What exactly do we mean by "equitable distribution" and how is the state to determine who qualifies as a recipient?

Distributive justice requires that every individual is guaranteed a standard of living that is humane and in harmony with the regard for the dignity of man as a human being. Beyond that, justice demands that the state should create opportunities for those who are able and willing to work to further themselves.

For example, both the Quran and *hadith* emphasize the importance of individual labor and effort. This principle is also integral to the underpinnings of a free market economy. *"And that nought shall be accounted"* (Surah al Najm – The Unfolding, 53:39-40). Similarly, a *hadith* recorded by Bukhari elaborates, "Nobody has ever eaten a better meal than that which one has earned by working with one's own hands. The Prophet of God, David used to eat from the earnings of his manual labor."[29] In both examples, the first responsibility lies with the individual to work hard to meet his needs.

But, beyond that, when individual efforts are not enough, the state steps in to uphold distributive justice. This does not necessarily mean that the goal of distributive justice is perfect socio-economic equality of outcome among citizens. There will also exist, of necessity, socio-economic inequalities. This differential is accepted and arranged to be so, by God. *"But is it they who distribute thy Sustainer's grace? [Nay, as] it is We who distribute their means of livelihood among them in the life of this world, and raise some of them by degrees above others, to the end that they might avail themselves of one another's help – [so, too, it is We who bestow gifts of the spirit upon whomever We will]: and this thy Sustainer's grace is better than all [the worldly wealth] that they may amass"* (Surah al Zukhruf – Gold, 43:32).

An Islamic perspective on economic and distributive justice requires a balancing of the rights of society as a whole and the individual to see the fruits of his or her labor. The Quran advocates that all people are entitled to what they justly earn, " *[Always] give full measure, and be not among those who [unjustly] cause loss [to others]; and [in all your deal-*

ings] weigh with a true balance, and do not deprive people of what is rightfully theirs; and do not act wickedly on earth by spreading corruption'" (Surah ash Shuara – The Poets, 26:181-183). The goal is to achieve reasonable equity, not perfect equality, of income and wealth in society. Attempts to achieve the latter have resulted in failure, as the fate of communism suggests. While socio-economic inequalities may exist in society, the responsibility of the state is to "manage" these inequalities in such a way that everyone is guaranteed the fulfillment of basic needs to survive.[30] This does not serve as an argument for unlimited, coercive economic state power, but for a limited government that balances the freedom of individuals to pursue economic activity with the socio-economic needs of the poor who are unable to subsist on their own.

Social Services Today

The guardianship and justice components of the state's role are the backdrop against which social services need to be designed and offered to citizens. It is evident that the Prophet (pbuh) and the Caliphs took this responsibility very seriously. But, how do we translate their historical example and the moral imperative behind their actions into a comparable social services system today? Today, we envision an Islamic state as one that is committed to taking care of all of its citizens, from the poorest to the richest. A prosperous state is one that has been blessed by God, and therefore it is morally obligated to provide for the basic needs of the poor. It cannot democratically choose to abandon the underprivileged to their fates, and still be in compliance with Quranic ethics.

We envision a model in which basic healthcare services, universal primary school education, subsidized access to higher education for the poor, social security, disability and retirement payments are included in state provisions. The extent to which these are covered by the state remains at the discretion of the specific polity, given the available resources and the needs of the population.

Every individual has the right to live a healthy and dignified life. It is the responsibility of the state to ensure that this right is protected, by allocating resources into a healthcare system that benefits everyone. Rights to healthcare mean access to basic medical treatment in hospitals and clinics for anyone who is sick and who would be unable to afford them otherwise.

The need for education for all citizens is self-evident. It is part of a larger economic framework that allows people access to opportunities for employment and entrepreneurship, and eventually translates into a better standard of living for all. Education can be seen not as a charitable act, but as an investment that returns a higher standard of living for the entire society over time. While individual initiative and hard work are equally important in this framework, access to education for all is also necessary. It is the state's responsibility to make sure that this is guaranteed, as part of the requirement to ensure justice for all its citizens. In this case, justice is defined as codifying in law the right to an education for all children, and in particular children from underprivileged families. With regard to higher education, the same argument prevails. But, whether it is subsidized by the government only for those who demonstrate financial need, or it is universally subsidized is a decision that depends on the available resources and the needs of the population in question. The underlying principle is the need to facilitate access to education for all.

Lastly, social security payments for the disabled, the elderly and the destitute also fall into the categories of social welfare provisions by the state. The historical precedent set by the Caliphs in this regard has already been enumerated above. It is part of our argument for basic need fulfillment for the underprivileged in society. This should not occur at the expense of individual efforts to find work. As noted earlier, the primary responsibility to take care of one's needs through one's labor and hard work remains with the individual. Social security payments are for those who are unable to work and support themselves, either permanently or temporarily, for any reason. In this case, the disabled, the elderly and the poor are populations that require special assistance. Although voluntary charity can certainly provide valuable assistance to many, it fails to be systematic and does not achieve justice. A system of voluntary charity alone would result in some disabled or indigent individuals receiving generous benefits, while others in the wrong place or condition, may receive little or nothing. Only through a government administered system that catches all those in need can we ensure a real safety net that satisfies the requirements of Quranic ethics.

Conclusion

The moral basis for need fulfillment is noted in the Quran as both an individual and communal obligation. Those who are less fortunate in society are entitled to assistance and social support from their more fortunate neighbors and relatives. We have extended that moral imperative to become part of the mandate of the state, and its responsibility to protect its citizens' dignity and rights, and to do justice by them. This includes the transfer of resources and social assistance among members of society in an equitable manner.

The purpose of social welfare policies are threefold. The first is to maintain life. The second is to reduce suffering as much as possible. The third is to maximize human dignity, or opportunities to build human dignity. To live a healthy, prosperous life of dignity requires physical and economic security. On a basic level, it means food, water, shelter, clothing and basic healthcare services. On a secondary and long-term level, it requires access to educational and employment opportunities so as to prevent people from having to beg or live off of welfare or unemployment. This does not mean that the state needs to give out excessive benefits that reduce the incentive for able-bodied people to seek work on their own. But it does mean that the poor and the needy are not abandoned.

However, the specifics of how this is to be achieved are left to each society to democratically determine for itself, given the resources it has. The balance between individual, private contributions to a universal system of social security and related assistance and state funding is one that is negotiated between the government and its people.

We are also aware that in the juristic tradition there have been arguments made that call for discriminatory treatment of citizens on a variety of criteria. We view these as non-binding opinions. Justice demands an equal distribution of benefits to all citizens and cannot allow discrimination on the basis of religion, race, or gender.

Footnotes

1   Cited in Muhammad Nejatullah Siddiqi, "The Guarantee of a Minimum Level of Living in an Islamic State," *Distributive Justice and Need Fulfillment in an Islamic Economy*, ed. Munawar Iqbal, (Islamabad and Leicester: International Institute of Islamic Economics/The Islamic Foundation, 1988), p. 254.

2   Cited in Siddiqi, p. 254.

3   Bukhari, Volume 2, Book 24, Number 550. Also, Bukahri, Volume 2, Book 24, Number 558: "The Prophet said, 'No doubt, it is better for a person to take a rope and proceed in the morning to the mountains and cut the wood and then sell it, and eat from this income and give alms from it than to ask others for something.'"

4   Bukhari, cited in Ch. Muhammad Hussain, *Development Planning in an Islamic State* (Karachi: Royal Book Company, 1987), p. 30.

5   Siddiqi, p. 258.

6   Ziauddin Ahmad, *Islam, Poverty and Income Distribution* (Leicester, UK: The Islamic Foundation, 1991), p. 19.

7   Umer Chapra, *Islam and the Economic Challenge* (Leicester: The Islamic Foundation, 1992), p. 8.

8   Cited in Siddiqi, p. 255.

9   Cited in Siddiqi, p. 255.

10 Abu Dawd, cited in Siddiqi, pp.256-257.

11 Muslim, Book 20, Number 4502.

12 Muslim, Book 20, Number 4496.

13 S. M. Hasanuz Zaman, *Economic Functions of an Islamic State* (Leicester, UK: The Islamic Foundation, 1991) p. 139.

14 Hasanuz Zaman, p. 144.

15 Hasanuz Zaman, p. 177.

16 Hasanuz Zaman, p. 302.

17 Hasanuz Zaman, p. 306.

18 Hasanuz Zaman, p. 300.

19 Hasanuz Zaman, p. 321, n. 8.

20 Hasanuz Zaman, p. 303. See Table 14, p. 303 for the fixed rates of pensions for these groups.

21 Hasanuz Zaman, p. 321, n. 8.

22 Hasanuz Zaman, p. 319.

23 Hasanuz Zaman, pp. 303-304.

24 Abu Yusuf, Kitab al Kharaj, Cairo, 1382H p. 144, cited in Shaikh Shaukat Hussain, p. 59.

25 Abu Yusuf, Kitab al Kharaj, Cairo, 1382H p. 122, cited in Shaikh Shaukat Hussain, p. 60.

26 Cited in Siddiqi, p. 257.

27 Hasanuz Zaman, p. 187.

28 Chapra, p. 7.

29 Sahih Bukhari, Volume 3, Book 34, Number 286.

30 Iqbal, p. 16.

Conclusion

he Muslim world is in profound flux. The overall theme is the transition from pre-modern to modern societies. This transition is tremendously difficult and leads to intense social instability. Urbanization, industrialization, and globalization are buffeting the Muslim countries. These forces intersect with social change such as the emancipation of women, rise in literacy, and increased demands for citizen participation in decision-making.

Defeatism is rife throughout the Muslim world. The lurid conspiracy theories that explain international and domestic affairs have great currency among Muslim populations, even with educated members of society. But in the larger scheme of things, the Muslim world has been far more successful than is generally recognized, even by Muslims.

A cursory look at infant mortality, literacy, economic growth rates, life expectancy, or population size show a story of growth and development far beyond anything ever experienced by Muslim civilization. Although the statistics are not completely firm, a count of the children on the Earth would show that more are Muslim than any other religion (although Christianity is a very close second). This suggests that by 2050, Islam will be the world's largest religion, with about 2.7 billion adherents. This is a remarkable surge from only 180 million Muslims making up 12% of the global population in 1900. This surging population will have a presence not just in traditional Muslim lands, but will also be felt throughout the world. Already there are close to 15 million Muslims in the European Union countries, and France will likely be over 15% Muslim in a few decades.

Given that the world very much has a Muslim future, how Muslims understand and interpret their religion in the modern context will be critical to ensuring that such a world is peaceful and just and not one characterized by religious confrontation. Muslims living in the West, those who have fully dealt with modernity and its attractions, are strategically placed to confront these issues now. Muslims must deal with the consequences of modernity, but should do so out of their own traditions and intellectual foundations. Only such an approach will be acceptable to the vast majority of Muslims, although to some who are very liberal in their outlook, this approach is seen as unnecessary.

This work has sought to confront these issues head-on. Islam, as this work understands it, is primarily a message of justice. In fact, Islam should be seen as placing justice at the apex of priority. This justice is both Divine, as exercised on the Day of Judgment, and human, as we apply it to our daily lives and our social policies. Human justice should try to apply as much as possible the principles of Divine Justice in its approach.

When it comes to the state, Islam should have a role as the source of principles that guide the constitution of that state. Those principles are developed out of the religion, but are determined through a democratic process of writing and amending a constitution. There is no privileged class of interpreters of the Quran. There is no role for a government by a narrow elite claiming special religious authority. All citizens can participate in this debate, even non-Muslims are certainly free to offer their perspective on basic principles. These basic principles, such as sanctity of life, democracy, freedom of speech and religion, equal treatment regardless of race or sex, the right to basic social services, the main principles of justice including presumption of innocence, punishment that fits the crime, right to counsel, and the overwhelming aspect of mercy in the government's approach to its citizens should be incorporated into the constitution. This book went into extensive detail about many of these principles. By writing a constitution that has these elements in it, the constitution becomes "Islamic", and a path to *sharia*.

In the resulting state, the job of the government is then to abide by the constitution. The legislature must write laws consistent with the constitution, the executive must carry out policy and enforce laws in a way that respects the constitution, and the highest judicial body of the country must assess what laws are inconsistent with the constitution and void them. The particular religious beliefs of any of the state's officers tasked with these matters is irrelevant. As long as they act in accordance with the constitution, the state is "Islamic", even if many of the government officials, including the highest officials in the country are not Muslims.

The interpretation of Islam offered here is put forward on the basis of its intellectual and rational strength. This interpretation may be incorrect, but it was made on the basis of Quranic principles, and on a fair and complete reading of the text. Individual *hadiths*, many of unclear or weak reliability, cannot be the basis of refuting this interpretation. Such an argument is placing too much on too little.

This book must be seen as opening a door for discussion and research. Each individual chapter covered material that deserved a book of its own. There are individual paragraphs that should be covered by their own books. The authors are cognizant that this work has only scratched the surface of many important issues. But we are the first to do so in such a systematic and comprehensive manner. Those that take up this challenge have much to explore.

One critique of this work is that the argument appears to make an Islamic case for a state that closely resembles a liberal Western democracy. As such, it appears that the Islamic tradition is being squeezed into a pre-formed mold that came from John Locke and the American experience.

Although this critique appears to be correct on the surface, it is fundamentally in error. The reason why both the rational system developed over time in the West, and the Islamic system presented here are so similar, is that reason and revelation yield the same result. Islam believes that humans have inherent within them everything they need to be correctly guided through their own reason. Abraham came to God without revelation. The ability to distinguish right from wrong is inherent in all people. As such, when humanity properly exercises its rational faculties, it will come up with an answer to questions that pleases God.

Revelation is a short cut. It is God's way of providing humanity the answers to its questions without having to struggle through centuries of confusion. The gift of revelation is repeatedly described as a "mercy" from God. As such it is something that is actually unnecessary but is sent anyway because God is merciful and offers us his direct message without our having to struggle there on our own.

Many of the founding fathers of the American republic were "deists". They believed in a single God, and in the principles of justice, but did not think that the literal aspects of Christianity were required. They often stood apart from organized religion. Islam is the closest organized religion to deism. The deists believed in "natural law", the concept that certain basic principles are inherent in nature and do not need to be proved to be correct. This is very similar to the Islamic notion of the inherent moral knowledge of all humans. Can we draw any conclusions from this shared philosophical background?

In this work, the Islamic juristic tradition has at times been criticized, and to some readers, not given its due weight. This is not meant to slight the jurists in the least. The juristic tradition is one of the great achievements not just of Muslim civilization but of human civilization. The jurists were intellectual and moral giants of their time and place. What this work argues is that the jurists be seen as part of a living and breathing and growing struggle to achieve *sharia*. *Sharia* is an unattainable ideal. And what constitutes the true *sharia* changes with circumstance, time, and place. The *sharia* as applied by a colony of astronauts on the Moon would be quite different from the *sharia* of the city of Cairo in the 10th century CE. The jurists of the past helped their societies to find the *sharia* as best they could. What the Muslim world needs now is not the return of the old jurists, but a new crop of jurists that seek to move the community forward along the path of *sharia*.

This new jurist, or neo-jurist, could be any Muslim intellectual, male or female, living in a Muslim country, or as a minority in a non-Muslim land. The neo-jurist's job is to put forward the basic arguments about what the essential values of the Quran are. They would have an important role in the debate about constitutional first principles. What the Muslim world needs now is a renaissance of its intellectual heritage. Already there are Muslim thinkers that qualify as neo-jurists. Many of them were cited in this work. Their efforts are indispensable to the true rebirth of Islam.

One of the cardinal features of modernity is the loss of religious belief by the vast majority of people. Among Western nations, this process has been inexorable. Even in the US, where a large segment of society retains a belief in the literal truth of their religious views, it is well known that the more educated the person, the more secular their views become.

This pattern however has not held true in the Muslim countries. Partly perhaps because they are not as modernized as the West, and partly perhaps because of intense social pressure not to openly question the validity of Islam. But there is another factor. All religions have two elements to them. First is their theology, the explanation of the supernatural and man's relationship to it. Second is the social system they support. Islamic theology, being essentially a form of deism with a belief in an afterlife, makes the least demands on the human intellect of any major world religion. The amount that must be taken on faith is minimal; only that a God exists and that he is benevolent and just. But the social system of Islam has up till now been seen as undesirable by most modern Western minds. What this work has shown is that an appealing social system can also be based in Islam in a legitimate manner. If religion is to have a future in human life, it must be appealing on both levels, theologically and socially. Islam has the potential to do both. This inherent strength may shape the future in ways unexpected by both Muslims and non-Muslims.

We have offered a bold but honest interpretation of Islam. As all Muslim thinkers before us also recognized, we know that our view may be wrong. It is in that spirit of humility that we close with the four words Muslim scholars have used to traditionally end their writings: And God Knows Best.

Our Approach to Quran

n our approach to human rights, as in all aspects of thought and study regarding Islam, our foundation, and springboard is the Quran. We bear witness that it is the Divine Word of God revealed to Prophet Muhammad (pbuh) through the angel Gabriel, and that it is the eternal guidance for humanity.

However, Muslims have possessed the Quran for nearly fifteen centuries, which have witnessed great disparities in the condition of Muslims and the Islamic *umma*, from its early zenith to its current nadir. The most salient reason for this decline, in our mind, has been a diminution in the influence of the Quran over the life of the *umma*. Part of this distance from the Quran, certainly, is a general loss of "religiosity" among the Muslims of the last centuries compared to the days of the Prophet (pbuh) and the Companions. Perhaps an even greater source of distance, though, is a loss of our collective ability to properly interpret and apply the Quran – a restriction of the tremendous breadth contained therein, and a loss of touch with its great themes and principles, even in the face of what is commonly called the modern resurgence of Islam.

In the course of this study, we have endeavored to return to two main features characteristics of the Quran:

1) It contains overarching themes and principles, such as God's Oneness, and the necessity of justice as the foundation of human interaction. From these principles, there are specific Quranic laws which represent their embodiment in the various spheres of human

dealings, including the political realm, business relations, family law, penal law, etc.

2) It is tremendous in its breadth and scope. For much of the Quran, there is no unique correct understanding or single interpretation known to humans. To be sure, there are schools of thought or approaches to its understanding which have found following, as well as certain methodologies to steer people clear of whimsical interpretations. Nonetheless, there is a vast realm of possibilities which the Quran offers to its readers and adherents – a flexibility which maintains it as a dynamic ever-living source of guidance through humanity's constant flux of culture and history. This runs directly counter to the rigidity and intellectual authoritarianism often encountered when Muslims discuss the Quran. This rigidity and inflexibility is mistaken as a sign of piety, a protection of the Quran from "compromise" with secularism, or Westernism or any other "ism, etc." Unfortunately, such approaches stifle the flexibility and dynamism of the Quran and defy the vision that its principles can have applications which differ in form depending on circumstances, and that its verses are often open to different interpretations which may be applied in all or some of their forms contingent upon the prevalent needs.

The first of these features will be brought out in discussions of the various human rights topics, where the relevant verses which elucidate the guiding principles of Islam will be discussed. In this section though, we wish to focus upon the second of these features – to establish a certain intellectual and spiritual approach to the study of the Quran, or at least to clarify our vision and our relationship with the Quran: that it is vast and glorious and flexible and dynamic, and above all, that it leaves little room for intellectual authoritarianism. This perspective cannot be genuinely gained by the use of only broad principles, or by hand-waving generalizations. Rather, the Quran must be approached specifically and in a detailed manner, the way a jurist would approach it seeking to educe from it specific rulings. It is in this context that the breadth of the Quran becomes apparent. However, this will require from the reader a genuine resolve to also delve into the details, realizing that they are the brush-strokes of a large and coherent picture.

I. *Muhkam* and *Mutashabih*:

The Quran contains various levels of clarity in its verses, giving rise to different interpretations, with no monopoly on correctness in the hands of any human or school of thought.

The Quran characterizes itself as a book which contains two different types of verse, those with a clear-cut interpretation (*muhkam*), and those capable of more than one interpretation (*mutashabih*): " *He it is who has bestowed upon thee from on high this divine writ, containing messages that are clear in and by themselves – and these are the essence of the divine writ – as well as others that are allegorical. Now those whose hearts are given to swerving from the truth go after that part of the divine writ which has been expressed in allegory, seeking out [what is bound to create] confusion, and seeking [to arrive at] its final meaning [in an arbitrary manner]; but none save God knows its final meaning. Hence, those who are deeply rooted in knowledge say: 'We believe in it; the whole [of the divine write] is from our Sustainer – albeit none takes this to heart save those who are endowed this insight'*" (Surah al-Imran – The House of Imran, 3:7).

The Quran also thus makes it clear that the presence of verses open to interpretation can be a source of trial and discord for the Muslims. One of these trials may be intellectual or spiritual authoritarianism, where one group denies the validity of any interpretations other than their own.

This dichotomy of *muhkam* and *mutashabih*, and the presence of several interpretations of the Quran, is a self-embodying concept – it carries its own proof with it. This can be seen simply by delving into this issue in but a little depth. While in the above verse from Surah al-Imran – The House of Imran, the Quran characterizes itself as composed of both *muhkam* and *mutashabih* verses, we see a different reflection in the verse from Surah Hud – Hud, 11:1, *"Alif Lam*

Ra. (This is) a Book with verses basic or fundamental (of established meaning) [uhkimat ayatuhu, i.e. made muhkam] further explained in detail from One Who is Wise and Well-Acquainted (with all things)." This verse would seem to imply that all of the verses of the Quran are *muhkam.*

Meanwhile, we see that a different reflection yet is present in Surah az Zumar – The Throngs, 39:23. God has brought forth the best of speech, a *mutashabih* repeating Quran; God has revealed the most beautiful message in the form of a Book consistent with itself (*mutashabihan*): *"God bestows from on high the best of all teachings in the shape of a divine writ fully consistent within itself, repeating each statement [of the truth] in manifold forms – [a divine writ] whereat shiver the skins of all who of their Sustainer stand in awe: [but] in the end their skins and their hearts do soften at the remembrance of [the grace of] God…. Such is God's guidance: He guides therewith him that wills [to be guided] – whereas he whom God lets go astray can never find any guide."*

This verse would seem to imply that all of the book is *mutashabih,* but Yusuf Ali translates mutashabih as "consistent", i.e., relying on the primary Arabic meaning of "self-similar".

Rather than posing a contradiction, these verses illustrate the breadth, depth and subtlety of the Quran, as it shows various shades of the meaning of *muhkam* and *mutashabih,* based on context. This issue of the apparent contradiction, yet the true lack thereof, has been discussed at length by our scholars. We may say, for example, that the entire book is *muhkam* in the sense of precision; each verse is well-sealed, fashioned precisely and deliberately and perfectly – one meaning of *muhkam.* We can also say that the verses of the Quran are *mutashabih,* using the primary meaning of this word in Arabic – that of showing similitude; i.e. similar to each other in beauty, perfection and guidance.[1]

Thus, we are immediately forced to confront the issue of the precise meanings of *muhkam* and *mutashabih.* With regard to the

Quran, these terms may have slightly different meanings than the primary linguistic meaning of the words in everyday speech. The famous scholar, Imam al-Shafi'i, said regarding these terms as they apply to the Quran: "The *muhkam* of the Quranic verses are those which do not bear interpretation except for one clear-cut interpretation, while the *mutashabih* of the Quran is that which is capable of multiple interpretations.[2] This opinion is also ascribed to Ibn Jareer, quoting Muhammad ibn Jafar ibn al-Zubayr actions.[3] The scholar Imam ibn Hanbal, however, had a slightly different connotation to the terms: "The *muhkam* is that which stands alone, without need of clarification, while the *mutashabih* is that which needs further clarification."[4] Similar interpretations have been given by many of the major classical scholars, such as Al-Suyuti, Ibn al-Qayim, and Ibn-Taymiyah: that the *muhkam* verses are those which are clear in their meaning and intent, without the potential of confusion or the presence of symbolism, and without any hidden meanings. The *mutashabih* is what does not fit into this category. Interestingly, however, the modern scholar Muhammad Asad understands the term *mutashabih* as meaning "allegorical." Therefore, verses which are allegorical in nature, parables, etc., would be considered mutashabih. Meanwhile, there are classical opinions that the *muhkam* verses are those which came to abrogate others (*nasikh*) while the *mutashabih* are those which were abrogated, an opinion referenced to no less an authority than ibn Abbas. Other opinions are that the *muhkam* verses are those which we may have an actual knowledge of, while the *mutashabih* are those which address matters about which we can have no full knowledge, such as the time of the Day of Judgment or the exact reward for deeds, an opinion mentioned among other opinions by al-Razi in his *tafsir* (interpretation of the Quran). Yet another opinion regarding the mutashabih is that it is "that which is believed in, but not that which is acted upon", i.e., verses concerning beliefs but not mandating specific actions.[5]

Thus, we see a wide spectrum of opinions among our scholars, modern and classical, giving a glimpse of the breadth and flexibility within the Quran, as well as the spirit of intellectual freedom which existed within the Muslim *umma*. Inherent in this lack of a definite meaning for *muhkam* and *mutashabih* is also a lack of specificity as to which verses are which.

We lean toward the opinion advanced by al-Shafi'i , ibn al-Zubayr, and al-Tabari, that the *muhkam* is that which is clear-cut in meaning, while the *mutashabih* is that which is capable of interpretation, and will advance a further refinement in this distinction in what follows, which will have a direct bearing on our approach to the understanding of the Quran as advanced in this work. At this juncture, however, it suffices to underscore that there is significant room for multiple views regarding the *mutashabih* verses.

It is important, by way of illustration, to give some of the classical examples from our literature regarding the *muhkam* and the *mutashabih*, to concretize these concepts.

A. *Examples of Muhkam verses*

"Say: 'He is the One God" (Surah al-Ikhlas – The Declaration of Perfection, 112:1).

"He has forbidden to you only carrion, and blood, and the flesh of swine, and that over which any name other than God's has been invoked; but if one is driven by necessity – neither coveting it nor exceeding his immediate need – no sin shall be upon him: for, behold, God is much-forgiving, a dispenser of Grace" (Surah al-Baqara – The Cow, 2:173).

The first of these verses forms the core of our creed, thus it concerns the belief (*aqeeda*). It is unequivocal in its meaning and is the cornerstone of monotheism. Verses of this import, of course, are required to be *muhkam*, so that there is no discrepancy in their understanding among any reader, whether Muslim or non-Muslim.

The second group of verses concerns itself with some aspects of the law (*sharia*), clarifying the prohibitions in dietary law, once again in an unequivocal fashion with little room for individual opinion or interpretation.

B. Examples of *Mutashabih* verses

"*Alif Lam Mim*" (Surah al-Baqara – The Cow, 2:1).

The beginning disjointed letters, or *muqata-at*, which preface about one quarter of the Surahs of the Quran, are generally regarded to be in this group. There is no evidence that the Prophet (pbuh) ever explained them, or that the Companions ever asked about them.[6] Thus, we have no authoritative guide as to what they mean. Some of the Companions thought that they were abbreviations of certain words or symbolisms for the attributes of God. As Asad relates, a more plausible explanation is that the *muqatta-at* "are meant to illustrate the inimitable wonder of the Quranic revelation, which though originating in a realm beyond the reach of human perception (*al-ghayb*), can be and is conveyed to man by means of ordinary human speech."[7]

"*Behold, all who pledge their allegiance to thee pledge their allegiance to God: the hand of God is over their hands. Hence, he who breaks his oath, breaks it only to his own hurt; whereas he who remains true to what he has pledged unto God, on him will He bestow a reward supreme*" (Surah al-Fath – Victory, 48:10).

It is, of course, entirely unclear what is meant by the "hand of God", as we do not know the nature of God's hand. We can imagine, plausibly, that it implies God's power, or God's support, for example.

II. The Significance of *Muhkam* and *Mutashabih* to Understanding and Applying the Quran:

It seems that many Muslims assume that the Quran is a clear-cut, dogmatic book, with a set of well-defined rules governing faith and action, and that the test for humanity is how well it follows these rules. On one level, we certainly agree with this point of view. As the verse from Surah al-Imran – The House of Imran, above points out, the verses which form the substance and the essence of the Quran, and the core of the message of Islam, are indeed clear. However, there is a second facet – a deeper and perhaps more difficult concept to apprehend – that humanity's test is not just how well we follow the Quran, but also how well we understand it and apply it. Thus, the Quran, in its inimitable way, again combines what may seem to us to be contradictory facets: it is not only the "answer book" to the test, but is also, at the same time, a part of the test.

One key to properly understanding the Quran is a proper appreciation of the role of *muhkam* and *mutashabih* in this regard. Thus, in his commentary on the above verse from Surah al-Imran – The House of Imran, 3:7, Muhammad Asad states the following: "The above passage may be regarded as a key to the understanding of the Quran." Asad, though, departs from the classical definitions given above, and regards *mutashabih* as "allegorical", or as verses expressed in a figurative manner, and considers that many clear, or *muhkam* verses, i.e. not expressed figuratively or allegorically, are still capable of multiple interpretations. This, though, becomes a somewhat semantic definition; the critical aspect is the appreciation of the flexibility of interpretation within the Quran, as this is the key to its dynamic nature.

A refinement to this semantic dilemma is a fuller classification of different subcategories of *mutashabih*. For example, verses may be *mutashabih* because:

a. They are expressed metaphorically or as parables. For example, in talking about the hypocrites, Surah al Baqara – The Cow, gives the following parable in 2:17: *"Their parable is that of a people who kindle a fire: but as soon as it has illuminated all around them, God takes away their light and leaves them in utter darkness, wherein they cannot see."*

b. They discuss matters about which we cannot have any definite knowledge, such as events of the Day of Judgment and the Hereafter, which although expressed in concrete terms, are clearly metaphorical and beyond anything but a vague conceptual understanding. For example, the following verses from Surah al Haqqa – The Laying-Bare of the Truth, 69:13-18:

"Hence, [bethink yourselves of the Last Hour,] when the trumpet [of judgment] shall be sounded with a single blast, and the earth and the mountains shall be lifted up and crushed with a single stroke! And

so, that which must come to pass will on that Day have come to pass; and the sky will be rent asunder – for, frail will it have become on that Day -; and the angels [will appear] at its ends, and, above them, eight will bear aloft on that Day the throne of thy Sustainer's almightiness... On that Day you shall be brought to judgment: not [even] the most hidden of your deeds will remain hidden."

c. They are conceptual in nature. They enunciate a principle quite clearly, but leave the application of that principle open to interpretation, such as the following portion from Surah ash-Shura – Consultation, 42:38:

"And who respond to [the call of] their Sustainer and are constant in prayer; and whose rule [in all matters of common concern] is consultation among themselves; and who spend on others out of what We provide for them as sustenance."

This verse establishes *shura*, or mutual consultation , as the methodology of decision-making among the Muslims with regard to their communal affairs. This principle is clear, and may be considered *muhkam*. Thus Muhammad Asad refers to this verse as follows:

"This *nass* [clear and binding] injunction must be regarded as the fundamental operative clause of all Islamic thought relating to statecraft. It is so comprehensive that it reaches out into almost every department of political life, and it is so self-expressive and unequivocal that no attempt at arbitrary interpretation can change its purport."[8]

However, while the principle is unequivocal and clear (i.e., *muhkam*), the application is left entirely unspecified, and must therefore be considered *mutashabih*, and open to different interpretations. There is, therefore, no support for the opinion that the form of *shura* today must mimic the interpretation it had in the early Islamic state, where a small group gave non-binding advice to the caliph. Rather, it may be more appropriate, for example, to consider the best application today to be in the form of a representative democracy, or a parliamentary system with checks and balances, etc., according to the needs of the *umma*.

As was elucidated in the section on "democracy", this evolution of thought is already taking place among the Muslim intellectuals. Only one example is presented here, from the thought of Dr. Hassan al-Turabi, considered a conservative Islamic thinker and the leader of Sudan's Islamic movement:

"The caliphate began as an elected consultative institution. Later it degenerated into a hereditary, or usurpatory, authoritarian government... The question arises whether the proper Islamic form of government – elective and consultative – amounts to a liberal representative democracy? In a large Islamic state, consultation would have to be indirect and undertaken by representatives of the people. This was practiced in early Islam... It follows that an Islamic of government is essentially a form of representative democracy."[9]

It is this third category of the *mutashabih* that we are interested in emphasizing, and which we consider an essential refinement to the concept of the *mutashabih* expounded previously. This approach once again stresses the unique dichotomy offered by the Quran – that verses can be both *muhkam* and *mutashabih*, rather than having to be *muhkam* or *mutashabih*. The *mukham* portion is offered as a clear principle for the guidance of humanity, while the *mutashabih* portion is the dynamic application of this eternal principle. Thus, the *mutashabih* portion, i.e. the form of application of the eternal *muhkam* principle, can change with circumstances to achieve the best possible application. This is precisely the comment of the great classical scholar Ibn Al-Qayyim Abu Yusuf:

"God All-Mighty and Exalted has sent His messengers, and brought down His messages so that people may establish justice. This is the justice which is the foundation of the heavens and earth. If its signs are evident, and its light shines in any fashion, then that points the way to the law of God and the religion which He has ordained, and His will which He has established, and the path to that which pleases Him."[10]

Wherever there is justice, this is the law of God. In our mind, this particular versus general dichotomy is a more elegant way of resolving the apparent contradiction which faced the classical scholars as they sought to interpret 11:1 and 39:23, as described above. The Quran is thus simultaneously *muhkam* and *mutashabih*, making it both the absolute source of eternal guidance and simultaneously the flexible source of legal injunctions constantly relevant to humanity's changing circumstances, from the age of its revelation until the Day of Judgment.

III. The Flexibility of the Quran as the Main Source of *Sharia*

At this juncture, there will invariably arise the objection that such flexibility of interpretation may have some role in finding a particular application of a general principle, but has no place in the face of the specific rules of *sharia* (Islamic law) revealed in the Quran; i.e., the form of the particular application is already specified.

It is important, though, to realize that there is much greater room for interpretation of the Quran even in what seem to be fairly specific rules. Sheikh Mahmood Shaltut, the former grand rector of Al-Azhar University, provides an excellent discussion of this notion in his well-known and highly respected book, *Al Islam: 'Aqeeda wa Sharia* [Islam: Creed and Law]. The following discussion is based on his relevant chapter, "*Asbab Ikhtilaf al-A'ima fi Fiqh al Quran wal Sunna*" [The Reasons for Differences in Interpretation Among the Imams in the Legal Aspects of the Quran and the Sunna].

I. There are several well-delineated categories where differences in interpretation may arise, based predominantly on the structure of the Arabic language.

A. Differences based on plurality of interpretation of a single term (within a verse)

1. A single term may have two "real" Arabic meanings

a. An example of this multiplicity of interpretations in what seems a very specific law is seen in the following verse from Surah al Baqara – The Cow, 2:228:

"*And the divorced women shall undergo, without remarrying, a waiting-period of three monthly courses: for it is not lawful for them to conceal what God may have created in their wombs, if they believe in God and the Last Day. And during this period their husbands are fully entitled to take them back, if they desire reconciliation; but, in accordance with justice, the rights of the wives [with regard to their husbands] are equal to the [husbands'] rights with regard to them, although men have precedence over them [in this respect]. And God is almighty, wise."*

This verse deals with the *'idda*, or waiting period, which a divorced woman must wait before she may remarry. The verse stipulates that she must wait three *quru'*. However, this word in Arabic may mean either the menstrual period, or the interval of purity between menstrual periods. These two meanings have equal validity and identical authority within the Arabic. To see the practical implications of this difference, assume that a woman is divorced just prior to the start of her period. If the term *quru'* is taken to mean menstrual periods, then the waiting period (*'idda*) becomes that menstrual period, followed by an interval of purity, then a menstrual period, an interval of purity, and the third menstrual period; when she cleanses from that, she may remarry on her first day of ritual purity. If, however, the meaning of *quru'* is taken to be periods of ritual purity, then she would need to wait three full intervals of purity, and after the fourth menstrual period (counting the first), the *'idda* would be complete.

There is no difference among the scholars that the term in question may have either of these two meanings, and that the verse refers to either one or the other, and not both (i.e. they reject the notion of menstrual period, interval of purity, then menstrual period counting as three *quru'*. However, the scholars have differed on which of the two meanings to assign the this term within the verse.

A group of the scholars, among them Imam Malik and Imam al Shafi'i, suggested that the intended meaning is intervals of ritual purity. Another group, among them Imam Abu Hanifa, believe that the intended meaning is menstrual periods.

It is instructive to delve a little into the arguments advanced by each group, to appreciate the depth with which the Quran was, and ought to be, studied.

For example, the group supporting the notion of ritual purity as the intended basis of the waiting period gave the following arguments:

- The word used for "three" in the verse is *thalatha*, rather than *thalath*, cast in the feminine gender. In Arabic grammar, this would indicate that the thing being counted is of the opposite, i.e. masculine, gender. This indicates that what is referred to is *al-tuhr*, or purity, which is a masculine word.

- The plural word used to denote "intervals" (i.e. three intervals) is *quru'*. The singular form, *qir'*, can have the two meanings described above, the menstrual period or the interval of purity. When this word is made plural, it can take two forms: *quru'*, as appears in the Quran, or *aqra'*. The purists in the Arabic language claim that the plural term *quru'* is used when the original meaning referred to is ritual purity, while the other plural form, *aqra'*, is used when the term indicates menstrual period. They support this contention with a tradition ascribed to Prophet Muhammad, when he said to a menstruating woman, "Leave your prayer on the days of menstruation" (in Arabic, "*ayyam aqra' ik*") using the second plural form to refer to menstruation.

The group who supported the meaning of the term as "menstrual period" advanced, among others, the following arguments:

- The *'idda*, or waiting period, is meant to show the lack of pregnancy, and that is proven by menstruation. Therefore, the intention of the verse is to show three menstrual cycles and thereby prove a lack of pregnancy.

- A tradition ascribed to the Prophet regarding the waiting period of the slave (non-free) woman after divorce is "two menstrual periods", using the Arabic word for menstruation (*haidatan*) in the purported *hadith*. This indicates that for the free woman, the count may differ to three, but the essence of the rule is the same, focusing on menstrual periods.

- Verse 4 from Surah al-Talaq – Divorce, 65:4, stipulates that the waiting period for women who no longer have menstrual cycles (using the word for menstruation, *haid*), is three months: *"Now as for such of your women as are beyond the age of monthly courses, as well as for such as do not have any courses, their waiting-period – if you have any doubt [about it] – shall be three [calendar] months; and as for those who are with child, the end of their waiting-term shall come when they deliver their burden. And for everyone who is conscious of God, He makes it easy to obey His commandment."*

This shows that the essence of counting is the menstruation, not the periods of ritual purity.

- Finally, they produced some refutations of the arguments advanced by the first group, showing that the plural form *quru'* can be used to mean both menses or periods of ritual purity, and is not exclusively the plural of ritual purity, and has been used as such in Arabic.

This discourse should provide us with a sense of the possibility of interpretations of the Quran within the confines of the Arabic language, and the sorts of linguistic, analogical and deductive arguments which our scholars have brought forth in their attempts to understand and apply the Quran.

b. A second instance of two possible interpretations of a single legal verse is seen in the following instance, Surah al-Nisaa – Women, 4:22: *"And do not marry women whom your fathers have previously married – although what is past is past: this, verily, is a shameful deed, and a hateful thing, and an evil way."*

The verse states a very clear rule, forbidding men to marry women whom their fathers had previously married. However, the word used to describe the relationship between the fathers and the women is *nakaha*, which has two fully accepted meanings in Arabic: to marry, and to have intercourse with. Therefore, the verse has two different interpretations – the first is as translated above, while the second is "And marry not women whom your fathers have had sexual intercourse with ..." Thus, Abu Hanifa considered the meaning to be that of intercourse, and understood the ruling of the verse to be a prohibition against marrying any woman whom a man's father had had intercourse with, regardless of whether the intercourse was within marriage or as a fornication. However, Al Shafi'i and others understood the term to mean marriage, and thus prohibited marriage by a man to a father's previous wife. However, they did not find it prohibited for a man to marry a woman whom his their father had fornicated with, but not married.

This verse also illustrates to some degree a concept important in Quranic interpretation which will be discussed in more detail below – the so-called historicity of the Quran. In other words, for American Muslim men in the 21st century, this distinction is not nearly as relevant an issue as it was in medieval Arabia. Very few men, we would hazard to guess, would be on the horns of a legal dilemma as to whether Islam allows them to marry a woman whom their father had fornicated with.

2. A single term may have a "real", or literal Arabic meaning, and a figurative or metaphorical meaning

The potential differences in interpretation inherent in this distinction is illustrated by the following verse: *"It is but a just recompense for those who make war on God and His apostle, and endeavor to spread corruption on earth, that they are being slain in great numbers, or crucified in great numbers, or have, in result of their perverseness, their hands and feet cut off in great numbers, or are being [entirely] banished from [the face of] the earth: such is their ignominy in this world. But in the life to come [yet more] awesome suffering awaits them"* (Surah al-Maida – The Repast, 5:33).

This verse brings up several issues, among which are verses which are misused to portray Islam as a violent religion, when this verse is taken *prima facie*. Some of these issues will be discussed below. However, at this juncture, it is used to illustrate the dichotomy between literal and figurative meanings.

The phrase in question here is *aw yunfau min al ard*, referring to the punishment of "exile from the land" as part of the spectrum of punishment for those who wage offensive war against the Prophet. Most of the scholars have taken the meaning at this literal face value, and stipulated exile from the land where the aggression was committed. However, the Hanafi school takes the phrase as a figurative reference to imprisonment. Their justification was along the lines that exile from all of the land could only be achieved by killing, which is legally a different punishment. If the exile refers only to exile from the land of the Muslims, then if a Muslim is the perpetrator of the aggression, this would entail exiling him to the domain of the unbelievers, which is unlawful. Meanwhile, if the exile is only from the local area where the crime was committed, but to another domain within the land of the Muslims, it does not achieve the required ends, as it still provides the perpetrator with the opportunity to spread mischief in the land of the Muslims. Therefore, in the minds of the scholars of this school, the more logical interpretation to adopt is the metaphorical interpretation indicating imprisonment rather than literal exile.

This debate, while highlighting the major theme of this section, that the approach to Quranic interpretation should not be dogmatic, also underscores the ancillary point made above, that the Quran cannot be interpreted in a historical vacuum. While in the Middle Ages, the primary meaning would seem quite sensible, that is because the world was divided along the lines of religion, i.e., Islamdom and otherwise in the minds of Muslims, and Christendom and otherwise in the minds of Christians. Therefore, the routine references in juristic books to the world as divided between *dar al Islam* (the domain of Islam) and *dar al harb* (the domain of war orf hostility). However, history has changed, and the world is now divided along the lines of nations and not empires. Therefore, those citizens who wage war against a country from within, i.e., those guilty of treason or rebellion against lawful authority, etc., are probably no longer extradited or exiled, but rather imprisoned; foreign nationals, however, may be extradited, etc. Therefore, the interpretation which is most reasonable for one historical epoch may give way to another interpretation, also legitimate according to the rules of Arabic and the aims of *sharia*, in another historical epoch.

3. A single term may have a "real" or routine linguistic meaning,

as well as a secondary "legal" meaning.

"Forbidden to you are your mothers, and your daughters, and your sisters, and your aunts paternal and maternal, and a brother's daughters, and a sister's daughters; and your milk-mothers, and your milk-sisters; and the mothers of your wives; and your step-daughters – who are your foster-children born of your wives with whom you have consummated your marriage; but if you have not consummated your marriage, you will incur no sin [by marrying their daughters]; and [forbidden to you are] the spouses of the sons who have sprung from your loins; and [you are forbidden] to have two sisters [as your wives] at one and the same time – but what is past is past: for, behold, God is indeed much-forgiving, a dispenser of Grace" (Surah Al-Nisaa – Women, 4:23).

This verse deals with the category of women to whom marriage is prohibited, and will be cited below to illustrate other examples of issues in interpretation.

In this instance, the issue arises in the first line of the verse, regarding the word *banatukum*, "and your daughters", as one of the categories of women forbidden in marriage. This word (*banatukum*, which means "your daughters") would seem unambiguous. It has a linguistic meaning, i.e. a biological daughter, "created from a man's fluid". This is the meaning assigned the term by Abu Hanifa. However, al Shafi'i restricts the meaning to a biological daughter fathered within marriage, i.e., the "legal" meaning of daughter within Islamic law. The illegitimate daughter, fathered outside marriage, is not legally a daughter in the sense that she does not inherit, and does not regard the father as her *wali* (legal guardian). Therefore, according to this lexicon, the illegitimate daughter is not forbidden in marriage by this verse, because of the restricted meaning assigned to the term in question.

Once again, it is necessary to stress the historicity of the Quran: it was revealed to the medieval Arabs, and therefore had to deal initially with their habits and practices. Today, this issue would not be a subject of debate, where a man would seek to validate a marriage to his illegitimate daughter based on the existence a juristic opinion; very simply, society has changed. This in no way limits the Quran, but is a testimony to its eternal character. In one epoch, a debate about meaning may exist, while in another epoch, this debate fades, and we all coalesce around the understanding advanced by the scholars that the term here is taken in its linguistic sense, and make illegal marriage to biological daughters. Moreover, it is critical to understand that many of these debates and opinions were intellectual exercises, meant to maximize the flexibility within the Quran, rather than opinions necessarily intended for direct application. It is highly doubtful, for example, that marrying one's illegitimate daughter was a common practice in pre-Islamic Arabia, but the issue may have existed.

It is also necessary to understand this historicity in order to defend the Quran from the attacks which it weathers from those who could would use the existence of a medieval legal opinion to portray Islam as a perverse or lecherous religion, as sometimes happens. The Quran was revealed to a people and culture very different from today, and had to, in the first instance, deal with that culture and its practices. Those practices should not reflect on the Quran, and the interpretations offered by medieval scholars in light of that culture should not constrain us in interpreting and applying the Quran to our day and our culture.

B. *Differences in Interpretation Based on the Relationship of Phrases to Each Other Within Arabic Sentences*
1. For the first example in this category, let us return to a verse which we examined above, regarding the punishment of those who wage war against God and His Prophet, as stated in the following verse,

"It is but a just recompense for those who make war on God and His apostle, and endeavor to spread corruption on earth, that they are being slain in great numbers, or crucified in great numbers, or have, in result of their perverseness, their hands and feet cut off in great numbers, or are being [entirely] banished from [the face of] the earth: such is their ignominy in this world. But in the life to come [yet more] awesome suffering awaits them" (Surah al-Maida – The Repast, 5:33).

In the verse, the various possible punishments are phrases linked by the Arabic conjunction *aw*, traditionally translated as "or".

However, in Arabic, this conjunction may be used either to give a choice among a variety of options, in the sense of "this or that", or it may be used to sort and distinguish various categories within a list. Those among the jurists who opted for the second meaning of *aw*, i.e., that its meaning is to sort and distinguish various categories of punishments, understood the verse as sorting the various punishments according to the crimes committed by the enemy. Thus, those who killed civilians would be killed, those who plundered the wealth of the Muslims would suffer amputation, while those who committed lesser crimes would be exiled. This is the majority opinion among the scholars. However, some interpret the meaning of the conjunction *aw* as simply "or", allowing the Muslim authority their discretion in choosing the punishments for war criminals, possibly choosing death for crimes less than the killing of civilians, if the authorities thought that the magnitude of the crimes so warranted. An example of this may be the rape camps seen in the Bosnian genocide.

Both sides educed evidence for their point of view, but that is beside the point at hand. A salient feature of the juristic debates, though, is the tremendous concern in both camps that punishments not be arbitrary or not fitting the crime. While opponents of Islam use this verse to portray Islam as a religion of cruelty and barbarism, whoever troubles themselves himself to read the juristic debates is left with a clear sense that these punishments are meant not for those who simply fought against the Muslims, but for those who are truly criminals of war, guilty of the horrible atrocities which war sometimes brings.

2. A second example in this category regards the consequences to those who slander chaste women with accusations of sexual impropriety without being able to provide the requisite testimony of four witnesses. The Quranic rule in this matter is in Surah an-Nur – The Light, 24:4-5:

"And as for those who accuse chaste women [of adultery], and then

are unable to produce four witnesses [in support of their accusation], flog them with eighty stripes; and ever after refuse to accept from them any testimony – since it is they, they that are truly depraved! – excepting [from his interdict] only those who afterwards repent and made amends: for, behold, God is much-forgiving, a dispenser of grace."

Here, in these two verses, we have two phrases ("reject their testimony", "for such men are wicked transgressors and they indeed are the iniquitous") which are linked to each other, and then followed by the participle *illa* (except), giving an exception to those who "repent thereafter and do righteous deeds end their conduct". In Arabic, this exception may apply only to the last of the two linked phrases ("for such men are wicked transgressors and they indeed are the iniquitous"), or to both phrases, including the one enjoins the rejection of their testimony. In other words, the verses may be understood in two different ways:

a. Those who accuse chaste women without adequate proof are punished by flogging and ineligibility to ever function as witnesses, as their integrity is impugned. Also, they are branded as "wicked transgressors". However, if they repent and do righteous deeds, they are no longer "wicked transgressors" in the sight of God. Clearly, this is the interpretation taken by Yusuf Ali, as can be seen in his translation: "and reject their evidence ever after for such men are wicked transgressors."

b. Those who accuse chaste women without adequate proof are punished by flogging and ineligibility to function as witnesses, as their integrity is impugned. Also, they are branded as "wicked transgressors". However, if they repent and do righteous deeds, they are no longer iniquitous in the sight of God, and their repentance is also accepted with regard to their integrity, and hence they are once again eligible to act as witnesses.

The scholars have differed on the interpretations, with the Hanafi school believing that whoever is flogged in this regarded is considered of questionable integrity, and can no longer function as a witness within the Muslim community. Other schools, though, believe that the repentance clause applies also to the issue of integrity, and their status as eligible witnesses is once again restored.

3. A third example is found in Surah al-Nisaa – Women, 4:23, again dealing with the topic of women who are prohibited in marriage. The full verse and translation are found above. The phrases at issue are the following:

"And the mothers of your wives; and your step-daughters – who are your foster-children – born of your wives with whom you have consummated your marriage; but if you have not consummated your marriage, you will incur no sin [by marrying their daughters]."

A more literal translation of these phrases in Arabic would be something like this:

"And the mothers of your women and your stepdaughters who are in your care from your women, whom you have gone in (i.e. had intercourse with)..."

The verse talks about "your women" (*nisaukum*) twice in this phrase, referring to "the mothers of your women" and "the stepdaughters who are in your care from your women", and then links the prohibition to those women with which a man has had intercourse. The intercourse, functioning as a conditional clause, may refer either to both sets of "your women", or only to the second, and both would be permissible in terms of Arabic grammar.

If it refers to both instances of "your women" (*nisaukum*), then the meaning of the verse is:,

Prohibited unto you are:

1) The mothers of your women with whom you have had intercourse.

2) The stepdaughters from your women with whom you have had intercourse.

In other words, if a marriage has not been consummated with a given woman, then marriage to either her daughter or her mother would be permissible after divorcing that woman. This has been the understanding of a few interpreters.

If it refers only to the latter instance, then the meaning of the verse is, Prohibited unto you are:

1) The mothers of your women (regardless of whether or not you have had intercourse with these women).

2) The stepdaughters from your women with whom you have had intercourse.

In other words, the mothers of wives (after they are divorced), whether or not the marriage had been consummated, are always prohibited in marriage, but the daughters of wives (after they are divorced) become prohibited only after consummation of the marriage. This interpretation is adopted by the majority, and is reflected in the juristic ruling: "the marriage contract with the daughter prohibits marriage to the mother, and consummation of marriage with the mother prohibits marriage to the daughter."

Once again, this example is stated here as an illustration of two principles:

a. Even with what seem to be very specific juristic rules, about which there can be no debate, there is often justified debate.

b. The choice of preferred interpretation can and should change according to the prevailing circumstances. The notion of the historicity of the Quran – that it was revealed to a given group with given norms – must not be ignored when extending the timeless principles overlying the specific rules to other times, other groups, and other social norms. For example, it should be quite clear that at least for American Muslims, this juristic debate, while respected as an effort to understand the Quran and apply it, is not relevant. In this place and time, men do not marry a mother and then her daughter, regardless of the issue of consummation. This notion would be equally distasteful to both men and women of the current era in the West.

C. Differences in Interpretation Based on Different Approaches to the Principles of Jurisprudence

This is a very lengthy topic, which cannot be approached here with any sufficient depth, but rather only by providing a few examples. Among the myriad categories of juristic issues are: how to deal with verses which enjoin actions (compulsory versus laudable), how to deduce specific rules from a general principle or another specific rule, and what is the relationship of *hadith* to this process, or the relationship of *qiyas* (the process of deductive analogy) to this process, and the issue of absolute versus relative in prohibitions, and the relationship of *hadith* in that is process as well.

1. Returning to verse 23 of Surah al-Nisaa – Women, and the women who are prohibited in marriage, we find *"your foster mothers"* among the categories. A more literal translation from the Arabic is *"and your (foster) mothers who have nursed you"*. Therefore, a woman who nurses a man in his infancy becomes a "foster mother", prohibited in marriage because of this nursing. Here, the Quran lays down what seems an absolute prohibition, regardless of the amount of suckling or nursing involved. Thus, a group of the scholars believe that any amount of nursing, whether large or small, prohibits a future marriage. Others, however, view the ruling as relative, although phrased in absolute terms, and that the prohibition applies to significant nursing, not for example, a single feeding. In this group, there are disagreements about the amount of nursing which leads to prohibition of marriage. Some have said three feedings, or five feedings, while others have said ten feedings. This understanding of some relativism in the rule, as well as trying to establish the appropriate limits, comes in general from applying various *hadith* on this topic to the verse. Among the *hadith* quoted by Sheikh Shaltut in his book *Islam: Aqeeda wa Sharia*, are: "one or two suckles does not prohibit". It is a matter of basic philosophy as to whether one will place *hadith*, especially ones narrated through only a single chain, in a position to circumscribe the Quran.

A very interesting point raised by Sheikh Shaltut about this verse is that the entire juristic debate has centered upon whether any nursing is an absolute prohibition, and if not, then precisely how much nursing would make marriage unlawful. However, the verse prohibits *"and your (foster) mothers who have nursed you"*. A very relevant aspect of the prohibition may be the standing of the woman in question as a "mother"; i.e., a man should not marry a woman whom he emotionally considers like a mother. Therefore, psychologically, how much time needs to have been spent in this woman's care until a boy, before he grows to manhood, would look upon her as a second mother? Would there be a difference between a woman who nursed and cared for a boy as a foster mother, so that he viewed her as such, and a woman whom he has never laid eyes upon, but who bottled her milk for his own mother to feed him? The point that Sheikh Shaltut makes is that the issue of "emotional motherhood" in the verse is probably also relevant to the juristic ruling, but has been entirely ignored.

2. A second example has to do with the *'idda*, or waiting period of a pregnant woman who becomes widowed during her pregnancy. The issue at hand is how to reconcile the two Quranic verses, which contain the relevant juristic rules (Surah al-Talaq – Divorce, 65:4; Surah al-Baqara – The Cow, 2:234):

"Now as for such of your women as are beyond the age of monthly courses, as well as for such as do not have any courses, their waiting-period – if you have any doubt [about it] – shall be three [calendar] months; and as for those who are with child, the end of their waiting-term shall come when they deliver their burden. And for everyone who is conscious of God, He makes it easy to obey His commandment" (65:4).

"And if any of you die and leave wives behind, they shall undergo, without remarrying, a waiting-period of four months and ten days; whereupon, when they have reached the end of their waiting-term, there shall be no sin in whatever they may do with their persons in a lawful manner. And God is aware of all that you do" (2:234).

The first verse deals with the pregnant woman, stating that her waiting period (after divorce) is until the end of her pregnancy and delivery of her child. The second verse deals with the widow, stating that her waiting period is four months and ten days. How about if a woman is widowed while pregnant? Which of the rulings takes precedence? If one gives precedence to the first verse, then the waiting period for the pregnant woman is the end of the pregnancy, and this includes the divorced woman or the widow. However, if one gives precedence to the second verse, then the waiting period is four months and ten days, and this includes the pregnant woman or the non-pregnant woman. Most scholars have given precedence to the issue of pregnancy, while Imam Malik's opinion was that the longer of the two waiting periods should apply, or more precisely, that if she delivers before the four months and ten days, she should complete them, but if the four months and ten days expire before delivery, she should wait until the delivery of her child. In this manner, the woman would be fulfilling the conditions stipulated in both verses, since both verses apply to her. Other women, either pregnant only, or widowed only, need to be concerned only about the verse relevant to their situation.

3. A third example, certainly relevant to all circumstances, has to do with the rules of financial maintenance (*nafaqa*) and housing (*sakana*) for the wife following divorce and during the waiting period. If we look at the verse addressing this issue in the Quran (Surah al-Talaq – Divorce, 65:6), we find the following:

"[Hence,] let the women [who are undergoing a waiting-period] live in the same manner as you live yourselves, in accordance with your means; and do not harass them with a view to making their lives a misery. And if they happen to be with child, spend freely on them until they deliver their burden; and if they nurse your offspring [after the divorce has become final], give them their [due] recompense; and take counsel with one another in a fair manner [about the child's future]. And if both of you find it difficult [that the mother should nurse the child], let another woman nurse it on behalf of him [who has begotten it]" (Surah al-Talaq – Divorce, 65:6).

This verse states that the divorced woman should be allowed to stay in the husband's house, and or that her housing is the husband's responsibility. If she is pregnant, that responsibility extends until the end of her pregnancy. Various issues have arisen regarding the practical implementation and the import of this verse:

a. Is the "divorced" woman described here divorced less than thrice, in which case there is an opportunity for reconciliation and resumption of the marriage, or does it apply to the so-called "irrevocably divorced?"

Looking at the first two verses of Surah al-Talaq – Divorce, 65:1-2, we see:

"O Prophet! When you [intend to] divorce women, divorce them with a view to the waiting-period appointed for them, and reckon the period [carefully], and be conscious of God, your Sustainer. Do not expel them from their homes; and neither shall they [be made to] leave unless they become openly guilty of immoral conduct. These, then, are the bounds set by God – and he who transgresses the bounds set by God does indeed sin against himself: [for, O man, although] thou knowest it not, after that [first breach] God may well cause something new to come about."

"And so, when they are about to reach the end of their waiting-term, either retain them in a fair manner or part with them in a fair manner. And let two person of [known] probity from among your own community witness [what you have decided]; and do yourselves bear true witness before God: thus are admonished all who believe in God and the Last Day. And unto everyone who is conscious of God, He [always] grants a way out [of unhappiness]."

Hence, the topic seems to be women divorced less than thrice, as verse 2 talks about *"tak[ing] them back on a goodly manner equitable terms"*.

b. For the purposes of this example, we will discuss the juristic debate about the woman who is not pregnant and irrevocably divorced, without an opportunity of return to her husband (prior to another marriage and divorce, etc.). Under the injunctions of verse 6 above, is she entitled to housing? Is she entitled to financial maintenance as well?

Here again, the main juristic schools have come to different conclusions. The Hanafi school believes that she is entitled to housing and financial maintenance, the school of Imam Ahmad believes that she is entitled to neither, and the Maliki and Shafi'i school that she is entitled to housing but not financial support.

Part of the difference of opinion arises regarding the handling of a relevant *hadith* mentioned by Sheikh Shaltut regarding a woman named Fatima bint Qais, and its apparent contradiction with the above verse. While the verse stipulates at least the entitlement to housing, Fatima relates: "My husband divorced me thrice during the time of the Prophet (pbuh) and so I came to the Prophet, and he did not make for me a right to either housing or financial maintenance." In some narrations, Sheikh Shaltut states, the Prophet is reported to have said, "Housing and financial maintenance are for the one whose husband has the right of return to her," (i.e., not for the irrevocably divorced). The Hanafi school did not accept this *hadith*, and preferred over it both the injunction of housing mentioned in the verse, as well as financial maintenance, as that customarily accompanies the provision of housing. It is stated that Umar ibn Al-Khattab likewise did not accept the authority of this *hadith*, saying, "We will not leave the book of our Lord and the sunna of our Prophet for the word of a woman." Umar apparently intended the above verse, and the what was apparently the Prophet's practice that financial maintenance went hand in hand with housing.

The juristic opinion which denied the right of either housing or financial maintenance relied on this *hadith*, considering it a clarification of the above verse in the case of the irrevocably divorced, thus eliminating any contradiction between the Quran and the *hadith*. The remaining point of view accepted the specific injunction for housing present in the above verse, but denied the obligation of financial maintenance, based in part on the *hadith* as stated above, and on a narration in the Muwatta' of Imam Malik, where the Prophet (pbuh) is reported to have said to Fatima bint Qais, "You have no right of financial maintenance form him." Furthermore, he reportedly told her to spend her waiting period in the house of Um Kalthum (rather than her husband's house). However, he did not directly contravene the right of housing in the general sense. Therefore, this group of scholars did not accept the customary, and some say legal, link between housing and financial maintenance, feeling that housing is obligatory according to the above verse, but that financial maintenance is not, according to the *hadith* as mentioned by Malik.

D. Some Basic Conclusions

From all of these examples, hopefully we can see the flexibility of interpretation of the Quran, even in what might seem at first glance "cut and dry" specific legal injunctions. This flexibility and breadth is even more pronounced in the area of extrapolating specific injunctions from general principles, when only the general principle is provided in the Quran. Inherent in both of these processes of interpretation must be some awareness of the historicity of the Quran: it was revealed as a timeless guidance, but in the context of a very specific cultural-historical epoch. Our challenge is to reapply the Quran constantly and accurately to our own cultural-historical context, in this way staying true to its principles, rather than attempting to freeze our society in time, to maintain a context similar to that in which the Quran was first revealed. This challenge is best undertaken by an accurate process of tafsir, with the hope of God's guidance.

IV. The Rise of Different *Tafsir* (Interpretations of the Quran) and the Need for A Contemporary *Tafsir*

During the lifetime of the Prophet (pbuh), he was the reference point for applying the Quran, as well as adjudicating disputes regarding its interpretation. After his death, the Muslims found themselves in need of interpreting the Quran still, and so gradually sprang up the discipline of *tafsir*. While some authors distinguish between the terms tafsir and tawil, we will not make that distinction for the purposes of this analysis.

Initially, *tafsir* consisted simply of transmitting what the Prophet or the companions had said regarding the Quran. This approach gave rise to one of the main types or styles of *tafsir*, known as *tafsir bi-al-ma'thur*, meaning interpretation of the Quran according to related traditions from the Prophet, companions or successors. The classical examples of such *tafsirs*, written in the classical era but still widely used today, are the *tafsir* by al Tabari (*Jami' al-Bayan 'an Ta'wil Ay al-Quran*) and the tafsir by Ibn Kathir (*Tafsir al Quran al 'Azim*). In this style of *tafsir*, there is little room for personal interpretation, logical deduction, etc., but rather a reliance on what has been said in the past. This approach, however, while very valuable in aims and content, proved to be insufficient for the needs of the Muslims, and other types of *tafsir* evolved.

One main drawback of *tafsir bi-al-ma'thur* was "the realization that much of the *tafsir* based on prophetic traditions is actually based on doubtful, weak, and often spurious *hadith*."[11] This criticism has also been echoed by Shaik Muhammad al-Ghazali, one of our leading modern scholars, who said regarding this school of *tafsir*: "what weakens this school, in my opinion, is that it has tied the *tafsir* of the verses of the Quran to *hadith* the majority of which are weak, so it became a trap which prevented the Quranic ideology from reaching its comprehensive aims within the *tafsir*, and it became a vehicle for disseminating the weak *hadith* upon which the *hadith* transmitters built their Quranic opinions."[12] Understanding that this criticism exists is, in and of itself, a major hurdle to thinking properly about the Quran, as there are often Muslims who feel that if an opinion or tradition is found in al-Tabari or Ibn Kathir, then it is, *ipso facto*, true. This belief helps foster an attitude that no other approach to *tafsir* is necessary or valid. This problem is discussed extensively by al-Ghazali.[13]

Of course, where the *hadith* are strong, we believe in the guidance of the Prophet (pbuh) as the prime interpreter and best embodiment of the aims and rules of the Quran, and there is no contention about this principle.

It is important to briefly reflect on some of the sources of the weakness discussed above. One reason, of course, is that the compilers of these *tafsirs* were, by and large, not *hadith* scholars in the sense which evolved later to provide a rigorous level of scrutiny to *hadith* transmission and narration. A more compelling, reason, however, may be intrinsic to the field: there is simply a lack of sound *hadith* resources by which to fully interpret the Quran. This is felt to be due to the reluctance of many of the Prophet's close companions to relay *hadiths* regarding Quranic interpretation. This may be due in part to an ethos embodied in a Prophetic tradition, related on the authority of Ibn 'Abbas, stating that the Prophet said, "Whoever speaks concerning the Quran according to his own opinion, let him expect his seat in the Fire." This *hadith* is related by al Tabari, and quoted by Professor Ayoub, who adds: "because of this stern warning, relatively few traditions on tafsir have come down to us on the authority of the Prophet's close companions."[14] It is, in fact, related that Abu Bakr, when asked about an interpretation of a Quranic verse, replied "What earth shall carry me, what heaven shall shelter me, if I say concerning the Book of God things of which I have no knowledge."[15] To be sure, some of the companions felt more free to expound on the Quran, prime examples being Ali and Ibn Mas'ud.

However, this ethos was apparently strong enough such that Ibn Hanbal, the great traditionist and scholar, remarked: "Three subjects have no *isnad* [sound chain of transmission] – *tafsir, malahim* [apocalyptic *hadiths*] and *maghazi* [accounts of the early battles of Islam]."[16] However, in his classical textbook, *al-Burhan fi Ulum al-Quran* [The Clear Proof in the Science of Quran], the scholar al-Zarkashi presents the arguments of various scholars against this ethos. Among them is Al-Bayhaqi, who makes the contention that the Prophet's warning about speaking regarding the Quran from one's "opinion", if it is *sahih* (sound), refers to the baseless opinion without support, but the opinion offered with proofs or sound arguments is permissible. Also, al-Imam al Mawardi stated that some overzealous opinions take this *hadith* literally, preventing them from trying to deduce and elucidate (*yastanbitun*) the meaning of the Quran through their own *ijtihad*, which he thinks is permissible, considering the warning related only to baseless opinions.[17]

Aside from the above, a second major reason that a different way of approaching the Quran is needed in addition to *tafsir bi-al-ma'thur* (*tafsir* according to tradition), is that this is necessary to maintain the dynamism of the Quran. Thus, Professor Ayoub states: "Another reason for the acceptance of individual interpretation was the need to make the Quran relevant to every time and situation.[18] Al Ghazali is, as usual, more vigorous in his opinion, saying that there are Muslims who are careful to "stop at the limits of *tafsir bi-al-ma'thur*, not giving the mind a chance to ponder and consider, and this has led to a type of inability to move beyond the limits of the vision of [those who lived in] the age of revelation. And this, while correct for the acts of worship, which do not evolve, cannot be accepted in life's other matters, which are constantly evolving, and which must continue along the guidance of the Quran, imbuing itself from it, throughout the ages, whatever they bring in terms of achievements, for this is the requisite for eternity [eternal relevance of the Quran]. Thus, prohibiting analytical thought by circumscribing reflection and logical contemplation about the Quran, becomes a sort of siege around the continuity [of application] of the Quran and its eternity. And so now people recite the Quran for blessings (baraka) and there have developed barriers between them and active contemplation, a type of passivity in forbidding of *tafsir* based on opinion, and an inability to apprehend a correct opinion."[19] Al Ghazali states, however, that *tafsir bi-al-ma'thur* remains necessary to guard against the folly that *tafsir* based on opinion, rather than tradition, may fall into.

Thus, despite the *hadith* quoted above prohibiting expounding about the Quran based on personal opinion, an entire discipline of opinion-based *tafsir* gradually came into being, known as *tafsir bil ra'y* (*tafsir* based on opinion, implying analytical or deductive reasoning). The dynamism of life, as well as the genuine attachment of the Muslims to the Quran, and their sincere wish to keep applying it to life's changing circumstances, made this evolution necessary. Another facet which encouraged the development of this trend is that many scholars understood the Prophet's prohibition in the manner expressed by al Ghazali, "I believe that the 'opinion' which we are forbidden to use in interpreting the Quran refers to personal whim."[20] Indeed, the famous scholar of *tafsir*, al Zarkashi, expresses the same sentiments regarding the intent of the Prophetic prohibition, quoting a famous traditionist, Abu al-Layth, who argued that the prohibition only referred to the mutashabih of the Quran. Al Zarkashi states quotes what seems a reservation against taking the Prophetic prohibition literally, stating that: "If this *hadith* is sound, then its true exegesis is that whoever speaks about the Quran merely according to his own opinion and without recourse and without anything but his own words, even if he arrives at the truth, would miss the right path ... this is because this would be an opinion without supporting evidence."[21] Professor Ayoub's commentary on this matter is most illuminating: "Zarkashi then quotes a *hadith* of the Prophet in support of individual interpretation: 'The Quran is malleable, capable of many types of interpretation. Interpret it, therefore, according to the best possible type.'"[22]

With this , then, the school of *tafsir bil ra'y* (tafsir based on opinion, implying analytical or deductive reasoning), developed. Prime examples in this school of tafsir are *Tafsir Al-Kash-shaf* by Al-Zamakshari, *al Tafsir al-Kabir* by al Razi, and in the recent era, *Tafsir al Manar* by Muhammad Abduh and Rashid Rida, as well as the commentary on the Quran by Muhammad Asad.

It is this approach to which we are partial, and which we follow in our understanding of the Quran. Of course, the Prophet (pbuh) was the embodiment of the Quran in his society, placing before us a model that serves as an eternal guidance. However, as stated above, there is some reservation about the *hadiths* interpreting the Quran which have come down to us, as well as a need to reflect the embodiment which the Prophet gave to the Quran living in his society to our time and our circumstances. Thus, there is a role for *tafsir b'il ma'thur* in allowing us to try to answer the question, "Were the Prophet (pbuh) here today, how would he have applied this or that verse?" There is invariably a reluctance among Muslims to feel that the interpretation would be any different than it was fifteen centuries ago in nomadic desert Arabia; however, we argue, in light of all that has been said above, that there must be a contemporary *tafsir* which is a product of careful intellectual effort, incorporating the knowledge of Arabic, *sunna*, and current conditions, whether in economics, politics, science, etc. Therefore, the task of the interpreter becomes dually difficult: not only must he or she have knowledge of the classical Quranic sciences, but also a state of the art knowledge of contemporary sciences, such as for example, economics, as applied to contemporary circumstances.

To illustrate this point in a practical fashion, let us take a Quranic example for which an interpretation is purported to have been offered by the Prophet (pbuh):

"Hence, make ready against them whatever force and war mounts you are able to muster, so that you might deter thereby the enemies of God, who are your enemies as well, and others besides them of whom you may be unaware, [but] of whom God is aware; and whatever you may expend in God's cause shall be repaid to you in full, and you shall not be wronged" (Surah al Anfal – Spoils of War, 8:60).

A more literal or precise translation of the first phrase of the verse would be: "And prepare for them the maximum you can of strength". Commenting on this verse, the Prophet is reported to have said: "Verily, strength is archery (*al-rimaya*), verily strength is archery". This *hadith* is reported in Sahih Muslim (quoted in tafsir Ibn-Katheer). In the context of the time of the Prophet (pbuh), the Arabic term *al-rimaya* which appears in the *hadith*, would refer to archery. However, a Muslim nation, attempting to build a national defense strategy, clearly will not consider archery as the epitome of strength. We would envisage that at least the following elements would be required in interpreting this verse:

A sufficient knowledge of the *hadith* sciences to be able to properly apply *hadith* to Quran. Is this *hadith* binding? Is it an eternal guidance, or an example given by the Prophet (pbuh) applicable to his time?.

A sufficient knowledge of Arabic to be able to offer sensible alternative meanings of *al-rimaya*, which can alternatively be translated as the process of shooting or hurling a projectile. Thus, in modern terms, it may correspond to ballistic missiles, for instance.

The verse as a whole talks about the preparation of force and strength possibly in the context of deterrence (to strike fear in the hearts of the enemy). Therefore, there must be some serious assessment about of the current political science theories of deterrence strategies and familiarity with these.

4.   There needs to be some expertise, obviously, in state of the art military sciences to know precisely what "strength" to prepare.

5.   There needs to be some knowledge of economic policy to determine funding for military expenditures within the overall national fiscal policy.

6.   There needs to be sufficient knowledge of the Quran to understand how to juxtapose this verse to a more general rule to which it may be governed by, such as the proclamation in verse 190 of Surah al-Baqara – The Cow, *"And fight those who fight you and do not transgress."*

7.   There needs to be sufficient qualification in *sunna* and *hadith* sciences to assess this verse and associated *hadith* in the context of other *hadith* about the sort of behavior which governs combatants, as these will invariably reflect on the types of weapons which they may use. Thus, what role will the injunctions of the Prophet (pbuh) against the killing of children or those in convents, and Abu Bakr's injunctions, derived from Prophetic guidance, against burning of crops, killing livestock, and involving noncombatants such as women and the elderly, play in determining the sort of military armaments which may be developed? Specifically, we Muslims would need to make a decision regarding the development of weapons of mass destruction, such as nuclear weapons and biological weapons. Their use would seem to clearly contravene the Prophetic guidance regarding behavior in warfare, as well as verse 2:190 quoted above, which seems to restrict military activity only to the combatants (i.e., *"those*

who fight you"). However, how can we fulfill the injunctions of verse 8:60, to prepare what we can of strength to the point that it would be frightful to potential or real enemies, if they have nuclear weapons and the Muslim nations do not? The answers to such questions are partly moral and partly scientific, and would require a high level of scholarship in both "Islamics" as well as military science.

This example alone should be sufficient to confirm the notion that application of the Quran, outside the arena of the creed, is often not clear-cut, and that it is definitely variable, according to the prevalent circumstances. This is not a deficiency in the Quran, but rather its miracle, and breadth, and source of constant relevance. The test and task of Muslims at every age is to accept the challenge of trying to correctly apply the Quran to their circumstances.

The simplistic notion that all one has to do is be willing to accept that God makes the laws, and then open up the Quran and find the answer, must be dispensed with. We all believe that God is the source of law. However, we (the authors) do not believe that the sole test of humanity is to submit to this notion. That is the easy part. Once this submission is achieved, the second portion of the test begins: trying to actually discern and understand what it is that God wishes for us to do, in our time and place, and our circumstances.

Of course, this debate has existed since the beginnings of Islamic history. Two illustrative instance from Islamic history especially relevant to this debate are abstracted from Professor Khaled Abou El Fadl's seminal book, *Speaking in God's Name*.[23] Two instances are especially relevant to the point we wish to make regarding the proper approach to the Quran. They are taken nearly verbatim from Abou El Fadl.

1. During the rule of Caliph Ali ibn Abi Talib, he confronted a secessionist movement known as the Khawarij, who accused him of not ruling according to God's law, and raised their famous slogan, echoed by puritanical groups throughout the ages, "Rule belongs only to God" (*inna al-hukm li Allah*), representing the point of view that all that is required is to submit to this notion, then open the Quran, and get the

answer. In response to the accusation that he was not governing by God's law, Ali gathered the people, and brought out a copy of the Quran. He then ordered the Quran, "O, Quran, speak to the people." (i.e. and inform them of God's judgment). Those in attendance exclaimed , "What! Ali, do you mock us? It is but paper and ink, and it is we (human beings) who speak on its behalf." At this point, Ali stated, "the Quran is written in straight lines between two covers. It does not speak by itself. [In order for the Quran to speak] it needs interpreters, and the interpreters are human beings."

2. A Wazir of the early Islamic era is reported to have criticized the restrictive puritanical approach exemplified by the Khawarij by stating the following:

"As to their claim that the only relevant issue [in legal interpretation] is God's word, that is certainly correct, but I would say 'the real challenge is discerning what God actually said.' As to their claim that sovereignty belongs solely to God (la hukm illa li Allah) that we will not concede. It is a part of God's law that he delegates sovereignty to people in interpreting what God said. That is why the Prophet said, ' If you lay siege to a fortress, do not agree to allow the people in the fortress to surrender according to the terms of the law of God because you [and they] do not know what is the law of God. Have them surrender according to your law [or terms].'"

Stipulating, then, that human beings must interpret the Quran, as an integral part of the process of its application, one final point remains to be made. This point has been more than alluded to, and that is the necessity, in this interpretation process, of taking the Quran from the historical-cultural context in which it was revealed, and applying it to our current historical-cultural context.

In this vein, we quote directly from the writings of our modern scholar and former grand rector of Al Azhar university, Sheikh Shaltut. In his chapter, "The Quran did not Innovate all of its Rules", he states the following:

"There was for the Arab nation, where the Quranic revelation first appeared with the Islamic *sharia* (laws), a set of customs by which they governed and according to which they lived, and there were regulations which they resorted to in their disputes and adjudications... What we wish to confirm is that the Islamic *sharia* came while the Arabs had sets of customs and dealings, and laws and ways of worship, and so the Quran supported much of what they were doing in these matters, and brought discipline to [these rules], and adjustments, and nullified some, and changed others. This does not impugn the Quran in its legislative capacity or independence, because Islam is but a religion intended for the benefit of God's creatures, and the establishment of justice and the securing of the rights of people. It did not come to ablate all of what people had been doing, and establish upon its ruins a new structure which has no connection to human nature or social norms. Rather, it looks at things from the vantage of harms and benefits, and so that which is beneficial, it maintains and supports... and that which is harmful to property, or society or family, it forbids, and that which needs adjustment and discipline, it brings to it that discipline which makes it beneficial for the good of humanity."[24]

Therefore, we may find rules regarding a certain issue, such as *zihar* (a man swearing an oath to be apart from his wife), which was an Arab custom present before the Quran was revealed. The Quran then adjusted this practice, within the cultural context of the Arabs, to remove the inherent injustice toward women in the way it was practiced.[25] This should not be, in any fashion, confused with the notion that the eternal law for humanity incorporates or allows *zihar*. Rather, if there is a society which practices *zihar*, or a similar custom, the way the pre-Islamic Arabs used to practice it, that practice should be adjusted to conform with the more humane rules given in the Quran.

The same critique could, and should, be levied against those who argue that the system of *khilafa* (caliphate) should be the form of Islamic government, because that was how the Arabs after the Prophet chose to conduct their affairs of state. The verses pertinent to governance are known, and are clear in their intent for social justice and against dictatorship, but flexible in their generality to allow application to myriad governmental structures.

The mammoth task before us, as Muslims, is to ask: how do we educe from the Quran, as it was revealed (sometimes with very specific rules and regulations) to the Arabs, with their set of customs and laws, the guiding general principles by which we are supposed to live? How do we then deduce from these guiding principles sets of specific rules and regulations for our present situation? This is a much more fruitful, and we believe faithful, endeavor than attempting to recast our present society in the form of that society to which the Quran was originally revealed, so that we can feel more comfortable in applying its specific precepts, because they would then be directly in their original context. As we have seen, however, even those precepts which seem "specific" are indeed often open to multiple approaches and interpretations. Therefore, we must ask God for the bravery to tackle the task before us in the way it needs to be tackled, and to guide us to the right path in this endeavor, in a fashion such that He will be pleased with us on a day in which there is no light except His Light, and no shade except His Mercy.

Footnotes

1 Fouad Ali Rida, *Min ulum al Quran* [From the Sciences of the Quran] (Dar Iqra Publishers, Beirut, 1982), p. 207)

2 Fouad Ali Rida, p.208)

3   See the discussion in *Tafseer al Manar*, by Muhammad Abduh and Rashid Rida (Dar al Mirifa, Beirut, volume 3, pp. 163-165) as well as to al-Tabari, and Muhammad Asad, *The Message of the Quran* (Dar al-Andalus, Gibraltar, 1993), p. 66.

4 *Tafseer al-manar*, op. cit.

5 See the discussion in *Tafsir al Manar*, by Muhammad Abduh and Rashid Rida (Dar al Mirifa, Beirut, volume 3, pp. 163-165)

6 Asad, op. cit., p. 992)

7 Asad, op. cit., p. 992)

8 Muhammad Asad, *The Principles of State and Government in Islam* (Dar Al Andalus Publishers, Gibraltar, 1980), p. 44.

9 Hasan al-Turabi, "Principles of Governance, Freedom, and Responsibility in Islam", *American Journal of Islamic Social Sciences*, Vol. 4, No. 1, September 1987, p.3-4.

10 Ibn al-Qayyim al-Juzziya, *"I'lam al-Muakeen"*, quoted in Fathi Osman, *Huquq al-Insan* [Human Rights] (Dar-al-Shuruq Publications, Cairo, 1982) p. 6.

11 Mahmoud M. Ayoub, *The Quran and its Interpreters* (State University of New York Press, Albany, NY, 1984, Vol. I), p.23.

12 Muhammad al-Ghazali, Translated from *Kayfa nata'amalu ma'a al Quran* [How we should deal with the Quran] (The International Institute for Islamic Thought, Herendon, Virginia, 1991), p.41.

13 Op cit.

14 Op. cit., p. 22.

15 Tabari, as quoted by Ayoub, op. cit., p. 22.

16 Quoted by Ayoub, op. cit., p.24, from Ibn Taymiyah, Muqaddima fi Usul al-Tafsir [An introduction to the foundations of tafsir].

17 Al-Zarkashi, op. cit., volume 2, p. 179.

18 Ayoub, op. cit., p. 24.

19 Al Ghazali, op. cit., p. 248.

20 Al Ghazali, op. cit., p. 248.

21 Al Zarkashi, *Al Burhan fi Ulum al Quran* [The Clear Evidence in the sciences of the Quran], quoted by Ayoub, op. cit., p. 23.

22 Ayoub, op. cit., p. 23, Zarkashi, op.cit., vol 2, p. 180, stating that the *hadith* is found in the sunan of al-Darqatni.

23 Khaled Abou El Fadl, *Speaking in God's Name: Islamic Law, Authority and Women* (OneWorld Publications, Oxford, England, 2001) p.24.

24 *Al Islam: 'Aqeeda wa Sharia* [Islam: Creed and Law], p. 382.

25 See Shaltut, op. cit., p. 384-385.

Our Approach to Hadith

Introduction: A personal story

f all issues in Islamic discourses, few things are as contentious as the role of and use of *hadith*. While there is no controversy about the revered role of Prophet Muhammad, peace be upon him, and the eagerness of Muslims around the world to follow his guidance, the attempts of Muslims to identify his true example and to correctly apply it are often fraught with difficulties and discord.

A small personal example from one the authors' childhoods, what he considers the formative years of his belief in and love for Prophet Muhammad (pbuh), may help illustrate some of the difficulties alluded to above. He was fifteen years old, and had been in the United States for seven years. Along with several friends from his mosque's youth group, he headed for Islamic Youth Camp, a mountain retreat for Muslim youth from across his state. They woke up at the beginning of *fajr* (pre-dawn) time to say their prayers. They gathered outside on a large lawn in the pitch dark. The temperatures were near freezing, and the wind blew a deep chill into them as they pressed their shoulders together to keep warm. After the recitation of *Surah al-Fatiha*, the imam began to recite some verses. As his recitation continued for many minutes, the boy could hear the teeth of many of the younger boys chattering from the cold. During what seemed an interminable recitation in the first *rak'a* alone, some of the children finally began to cry from the pain the cold had begun to inflict upon them. Their crying was easily audible during the prayer. The imam impassively continued his recitation, and followed the first *rak'a* with a similar long torturous second *rak'a*. At the end of this prayer, the boy angrily approached the imam, and asked, "What in the world are you doing? Didn't you hear the children crying from the cold?" He was met with a sneer, and a now familiar recourse to *hadith* to defend his action or position, "You should learn your religion," he sharply rebuked the boy. "The *fajr* should be a long prayer. It was the Prophet's habit to recite 100 verses during the first *rak'a* of fajr and 60 verses during the second, and that's the way *fajr* will be prayed in this camp." He went on to ask where the boy was from. "Egypt and Los Angeles," he replied. "Well, I am from Mecca al-Mukarrama," he said arrogantly, using this proximity of origin to the Prophet to imply superior knowledge of his *sunna* (example).

An argument ensued between them -- an adult counselor and a fifteen-year-old who refused to believe that this conduct embodied the Prophet's will or example. Ironically, the cold was too bitter for them to stand outside to argue, so they went inside a camp bathroom, with some of the boy's friends listening to the argument. Every time either wanted to quote a verse or a *hadith*, the entire group would leave the bathroom and go outside, quote the verse or *hadith*, and then go back into the bathroom to seek shelter from the cold. This scene of comical insanity was the boy's introduction to the controversies surrounding the use and misuse of *hadith*. At that age, of course, he was ill-equipped in terms of *hadith* knowledge to counter the quotes being hurled at him from the textbook *Fiqh al-Sunna* authored by al Sayyid Sabiq.

As he grew older, and began to read and learn about the Prophet's example, he came to learn that the imam had been right. In the book *Fiqh al-Sunna*, under the heading of "Recitation in the Morning Prayer", it states: "He [the Prophet, pbuh] would read from 60 to 100 verses during the morning prayer."

Seemingly, though, the imam had forgotten to mention what was written on the next line, "sometimes he would recite surah Qaf, ar-Rum, at-Takwir, or az-Zilzal [al Zalzallah] in the last two *rak'a*." For reference, these suras contain 45, 60, 29, and 8 verses respectively. The next line in the discourse continues, "While traveling, he would sometimes read the last two *suras* of the Quran." These *suras, al-Falaq* and *al-Nass*, have only six and five verses respectively. One paragraph above under the heading "Recitation after al-Fatiha", this same reference states: "Here we shall mention what Ibn al-Qayyim learned about the Prophet's recitation following the Fatiha in different prayers. He commented, 'When the Prophet finished al-Fatiha, he would sometimes make a lengthy recitation, and sometimes a short one if he was traveling or similarly engaged.'"

The imam also neglected to tell of a few other relevant *hadith*s and opinions of the companions. These are quoted in Yusuf al-Qaradawi's book, *Al Sahwa al Islamia baina al Juhud wal Tattaruf* (The Islamic Resurgence between Unbelief and Extremism). In a chapter heading titled "The Inherent Defects in Religious Extremism", he states about extremism: "It repels people, and is not tolerated by the ordinary human nature... This is why the Prophet became angry with his honored companion Mu'az when he led the people in prayer and prayed too long with them, until one of them complained to the Prophet (pbuh). The Prophet told him, 'Are you trying to spread dissension among the people, Mu'az'? He repeated it thrice. This incident is quoted in Bukhari. In a similar incident, he [the Prophet] said to the imam, in a state of unparalleled anger, 'Some of you are repulsive... Whoever of you leads the people in prayer, let him shorten, for there may be behind him someone who is elderly, or weak, or with some need.' Quoted in Bukhari... And Umar [ibn al Khattab], may God be pleased with him said, ' Do not make God hateful to his servants, such as when one of you is leading the prayer, and he lengthens the prayer upon the people so that it becomes hateful to them.'"[1]

The *sunna* of the Prophet (pbuh), the boy had learned, could be used or misused, quoted wholly or selectively, depending upon the integrity and knowledge of the speaker. This personal example, although trivial, illustrates much of the difficulty Muslims face when dealing with the Prophetic tradition. On the one hand, we all accept the guidance of the Prophet. On the other, his words are sometimes used not in a search for truth, but in support of one person or group's conception of what the truth should be.

Definition of *Hadith* and *Sunna*

The word *hadith* means narration, communication or story, while the word *sunna* means the path or way of doing something. These words are used frequently in the Quran. The word *hadith*, for example, is used in the Quran 23 times, with various meanings. In some usages, it means the communication of God to His servants (i.e. the Quran itself):

"God hath (now) revealed the fairest of statements (ahsan al hadith), a Scripture consistent, (wherein promises of reward are) paired (with threats of punishment), whereat doth creep the flesh of those who fear their Lord, so that their flesh and their hearts soften to God's reminder. Such is God's guidance, where with He guideth whom He will. And him whom God sendeth astray, for him there is no guide" (Surah az Zumr, 39:23).

In other instances, it refers to a historical narrative: *"Hath there come unto thee the story (hadith) of Moses?"* (Surah Taha, 20:9). Interestingly, it is not used to refer to the corpus of Prophetic sayings or deeds.

Similarly, the root *sunna* has been used in the Quran 16 times, to refer to a mode or way of doing something, whether the way ordained by God, as in *sunnat Allah: "It is the law of God (sunnatu God) which hath taken course aforetime. Thou wilt not find for the law of God aught of power to change"* (Al Fath, 48:23) or in the way which humans had become used to doing things, i.e. *sunatu al-awaleen*. Once again, it did not refer to the actions of the Prophet.

Over the first two centuries after the death of the Prophet, however, the terms have become much more specific, and are now used essentially synonymously to refer "to all that is narrated from the Prophet, his acts, his sayings, and whatever he has tacitly approved, plus all reports which describe his physical attributes and character."[2]

The study of this transition in usage of the terms is an interesting historical study outside the scope of this work, but one which has some relevance to the issue of authority of *hadith*. Certainly, although the terms *hadith* and *sunna* were not used in the Quran in relation to the Prophet, there is extensive evidence of the moral and legislative authority of the Prophet within the Quran. Also, the Prophet himself used the term *sunna* in relation to his teachings and his example:

"When the Prophet, peace be upon him, wanted to send Mu'az ibn Jabal [as an emissary] to Yemen, he said to him, 'How will you judge if something is put before you?' He replied, 'I will judge according to what is in the Book of God.' The Prophet said, 'What if you do not find anything in the Book of God?' Mu'az replied, 'I will judge according to the sunna of the Prophet of God.' The Prophet asked, 'And what if there is nothing in the sunna of the Prophet of God?' Mu'az replied, 'I will do *ijtihad* with my own opinion, and will not swerve [into injustice]'".[3] This *hadith*, while important in establishing the place of *sunna* as the second source of Islamic law, is also critical in establishing the role of *ijtihad* as a source of Islamic jurisprudence, and in answering the claim of those who say that even with regard to specific legislation, the Muslims need not look beyond the Quran and the *sunna*.

Likewise, the Prophet is reported to have said to the Muslims, "I have left with you two things that you will not go astray if you hold steadfastly to - the Book of God and my *sunna*."[4]

By the end of the second century after *hijra* (migration from Mecca to Medina), owing in no small measure to the efforts of Imam al-Shafi'i, the term *sunna* became restricted to the practice of the Prophet.[5]

However, even with the specificity of the term as a reference to Prophetic guidance (rather than, for example, the *sunna* of the Companions, a term also reportedly used by the Prophet himself), a distinction needs to be made between two uses of the term *sunna*:

1) *Sunna* as used by the *ulema* of *usul fiqh* (scholars of the principles of Islamic jurisprudence). In their lexicon, the term *sunna* refers to a source of Islamic law, as derived from the example of the Prophet, and second in primacy only to the Quran itself.

2) *Sunna* as used by the ulema of *fiqh* (the scholars of Islamic law). In this lexicon, *sunna* is used as a category of Islamic legal "value" juxtaposed to the term *fard*, i.e. compulsory. In other words, it is used to indicate a category of actions which are not mandatory, but are recommended. Therefore, we would say that this or that action is not a *fard* (not compulsory), but is a *sunna* (it is recommended). An equivalent definition of this usage is that *sunna* refers to that set of actions which the "human is credited for following, but not punished for leaving."[6]

This chapter will be concerned almost exclusively with the first of these definitions -- the use of *sunna* as a source of Islamic law.

The Response of a Few to the Difficulties of *Hadith*

Because ascertaining what the Prophet said or did, as well as understanding how to apply his *sunna*, is sometimes a difficult process, which has led to differences of opinions among scholars, a few scholars have taken the opinion that the Quran is sufficient for legislation within Islam, and that the *sunna* of the Prophet serves as a particular example of applying Quranic principles, but does not in and of itself stand alone as a source of Islamic law. Most Muslims instinctively, and sometimes angrily, reject this point of view, as do the authors. However, it is worth examining the arguments put forth by those who espouse this point of view, as they may have some relevance in developing principles of *hadith* application. This point of view has been well summarized and well debated by Sheikh Mahmud Shaltut in his respected book Islam *'Aqeeda wa Sharia*, upon which the following description is based.[7]

The argument rests on two main propositions:

1) The Quran describes itself as a complete and self-sufficient source of guidance for humanity: *"This day have I perfected your religion for you and completed My favor unto you, and have chosen for you*

as religion (al-Islam)" (a portion of al Maida verse 3).

In this verse, God states that the religion has been perfected and completed. This would imply, for example, that any Prophetic actions or pronouncements following this revelation would not be part of legislation, as that has already been completed, calling into question the role of the *sunna*. Practically, however, it is important to note that this verse was one of the last revelations, occurring only a few months before the death of the Prophet.

Other verses implying the same thing, that the Quran is complete and self-sufficient are also found: *"And We reveal the Scripture unto thee as an exposition of all things, and a guidance and a mercy and good tidings for those who have surrendered (to God)"* (a portion of Al Nahl 89).

"There is not an animal in the earth, nor a flying creature flying on two wings, but they are peoples like unto you. We have neglected nothing in the Book (of Our decrees). Then unto their Lord they will be gathered" (Al Anam, 6:38).

2) The second objection or reservation raised regarding the role of the *sunna* as a primary source of legislation has to do with the Prophet's reluctance to have his *hadith*s written. If the sunna was a primary source of legislation for the Muslims until the Day of Judgment, the Prophet (pbuh) would know this, and would have ordered it carefully preserved in writing, to avoid loss, differences, or alterations, as he was careful to have the Quran written by his scribes in his lifetime (although it was collected later). However, there are *hadith*s which discourage or forbid the writing of the Prophet's sayings. The strongest of these appears in Sahih Muslim, on the authority of Abu Sa'id al Khudri which states, "Do not write anything from me except the Quran, and whoever has written anything from me other than the Quran should erase it. Narrate from me without hesitation, but whoever lies about me let him await his seat in hellfire."

These two objections will be dealt with in the next section.

The Proper Place of *Hadith* (or Refuting the Few)

The majority of Muslims, the authors among them, accept without question the validity of *hadith* as a primary source of Islamic law. This is based on various evidences, primarily on the authority of the Quran, which will be presented below. Given this acceptance, however, the verification of *hadith*, as well as its proper application are difficult topics, and these tend to be where difficulties arise in Islamic discourse, as will be discussed further on.

The primacy of the authentic *hadith* as a source of law in Islam is found in many Quranic verses which clearly spell out the authority of the Prophet (pbuh) as the interpreter of the Quran, and as the supreme human legislative and judicial authority for the Muslims.

1) The Prophet (pbuh) is the primary expounder and interpreter of the Quran: *"With clear proofs and writings; and We have revealed unto thee the Remembrance that thou mayst explain to mankind that which hath been revealed for them, and that haply they may reflect"* (al Nahl 44).

2) Part of the Prophetic mission is that he has been given a legislative responsibility as lawmaker for society: *"Those who follow the messenger, the Prophet who can neither read nor write, whom they will find described in the Torah and the Gospel (which are) with them. He will enjoin on them that which is right and forbid them that which is wrong. He will make lawful for them all good things and prohibit for them only the foul; and he will relieve them of their burden and the fetters that they used to wear. Then those who believe in him, and honor him and help him, and follow the light which is sent down with him: they are the successful"* (Surah al-Araf, 7:157).

3) The Prophet (pbuh) is also extolled in the Quran as offering an excellent model for the believers to follow in their life: *"Verily in the messenger of God ye have a good example for him who looketh unto God and the last Day, and remembereth God much"* (Surah al Ahzab, 33:21).

4) The above considerations bestow upon the Prophet (pbuh) a

spiritual authority over the Muslims for all time, and make obedience to him a duty among Muslims: *"Say: Obey God and the messenger. But if they turn away, Lo! God loveth not the disbelievers (in His guidance)"* (Surah al Imran, 3:32).

"O ye who believe! Obey God, and obey the messenger and those of you who are in authority; and if ye have a dispute concerning any matter, refer it to God and the messenger if ye are (in truth) believers in God and the Last Day. That is better and more seemly in the end" (Surah al Nisaa, 4:59).

The Earliest Phases of *Hadith* Preservation
The Issue of *Hadith* Recording during the Lifetime of the Prophet

Because of the importance of the Prophet's example, Muslims have been very careful and diligent about its preservation as both a path of guidance and as a source of law. The authentic *hadith* is essentially unanimously considered the second source of Islamic law after the Quran.[8]

Therefore, from very early Islamic times, in the first century after hijra (AH), *hadith* learning and teaching became a focus for Muslims, while from the second century AH, *hadith* writing, and then collection and systemization of these written materials, became a major portion of the scholarship of Muslims. In fact, it became a highly developed science which remains a marvel for western scholars.

The first important issue chronologically (and with important substantive implications for the role of *hadith* in jurisprudence, as we have seen above) is whether *hadith* was written during the lifetime of the Prophet (pbuh). As discussed above, there are several *hadith*s in which the Prophet (pbuh) may have advised against, or forbidden, the writing of his sayings. The conventional wisdom, in fact, is that written recording of *hadith* did not begin until about a century after the death of the Prophet (pbuh). It is said that Umar ibn al-Khattab, the second Caliph, who reigned from 13-24 AH, proposed to collect the *hadith* together to preserve the sayings of the Prophet (pbuh). Apparently, he gave this matter serious consideration, and then abandoned the project, for fear that the Muslims would neglect the Quran.[9] The project had to wait until the reign of Caliph Umar ibn Ab al-Aziz in 99 AH to be initiated. He requested from several of the great scholars of that time, who had devoted themselves to learning the traditions of the Prophet, to begin the collection of these traditions. Among these were Abu Bakr ibn Muhammad ibn Hazm (d. 120 AH) and Ibn Shihab al-Zuhri.

However, this conventional wisdom does not paint a complete picture. While during the lifetime of the Prophet his traditions were not, by and large, saved in written form, neither were they neglected nor simply remembered as an afterthought when some scholars attempted to collect them. Rather, the Prophet would sometimes deliberately teach the Companions, repeating things thrice, and then checking from them what they had learnt. The Companions also made a deliberate effort to memorize the Prophet's teachings, as can be seen in the statement of the Companion Anas ibn Malik, "We sat with the Prophet, maybe sixty persons in number and the Prophet taught them *hadith*. Later on when he went out for any necessity, we used to memorize amongst us, when we departed it was as if cultivated in our hearts."[10]

Also, despite the *hadith* quoted previously prohibiting the writing of Prophetic traditions, several Companions are known to have obtained the Prophet's permission to record his *hadith* in written form. For example, 'Abd God ibn 'Amr ibn al-'As kept a written collection of *hadith* which he referred to as *al-sahifah al-sadiqah* (the truthful document). Other Companions who wrote *hadith* included 'Abd God ibn Mas'ud and Sa'd ibn 'Ubadah. Overall, though, this kind of written recording was done on a limited scale.[11]

Reconciling the practice of writing *hadith* with the previously quoted prohibition against this practice as per the Prophet, is an interesting exercise in *hadith* methodology. Muhammad Azami, in his well-known text, *Studies in Hadith Methodology and Literature*, discusses this matter in some detail, but it is beyond the scope of our introduction. In short, several similar *hadith* prohibiting the writing of Prophetic traditions were transmitted on the authority of several Companions, Abu Sa'id al-Khudri (two different narrations), Abu Hurayra and Zayd ibn Thabit. The chain of narration, or *isnad* (to be discussed later) in Zayd's *hadith* is incomplete, so the *hadith* is weak. Also, one of al-Khudri's *hadiths* and the *hadith* through Abu Hurayra both contain in the chain of transmitters a man named 'Abd al-Rahman ibn Zayd, who is considered by *hadith* scholars to be a weak and untrustworthy narrator. Therefore, most of the *hadiths* might be dismissed as not strong. This leaves only one *hadith* considered sound, which is the second narration through al-Khudri, as narrated above. In reconciling this *hadith* with the practice of writing by some of the Companions, one interpretation is that the Prophet's ban was about writing his *hadith* on the same page as Quran, so that the two would not be confused. Another interpretation is that this prohibition was an early ban until the Quran was firmly established in the hearts of the Believers, and then the ban was lifted.

In conclusion, the following points are made:

1) The practice of writing *hadith* was not the norm for Prophetic traditions, as it was for the preservation of the Quran. That the Prophet did not seek to have his *hadith* specifically preserved as he did the Quran should have some implications the legislative authority of *hadith* vis a vis the Quran as a source of permanent legislation.

2) However, there was definitely some written record of some *hadith* by Companions by special permission from the Prophet, as well as numerous letters written for the Prophet to various individuals, rulers, and so on. Many of these contained detailed religious rulings.[12]

3) There was great care among the Companions to learn the Prophet's *hadith*, and to teach them to each other during the Prophet's lifetime. This deliberate care was the origin of *hadith* literature, since shortly after the Prophet's death, his Companions became very active in preserving and propagating his *sunna*.

The Teaching and Writing of *Hadith* by the Companions after the Prophet's Death

It seems that the *hadiths* of the Prophet came to us in at least two basic ways:

- deliberately preserved and taught by a small group of Companions, who "specialized" in learning and teaching *hadith*, and who passed on a large number of *hadiths* to their students.

- sporadically, by a much larger group of Companions who transmitted only one or a few *hadiths*, which were later collected by scholars.

The definition of a Companion itself is something which is debatable. In general, a Companion is someone who lived at the time of the Prophet, and had some direct contact with him; in other words, Muslims of the first generation. The next generation or two following the Companions are known as the Successors. According to the scholar Ibn al-Jawzi (d. 597), about 1,060 Companions related *hadith*. Five hundred of them related one *hadith* each, 132 related two *hadiths* each, 80 related three *hadiths* each, while 52 related four *hadiths* each. At the other end of the spectrum, a few Companions related numerous *hadiths*:

Abu Hurayra	5374
'Abdallah ibn Umar	2630
Anas ibn Malik	2286
'Aisha	2210
Jabir ibn 'Abdallah	1540
Abu Sa'id al-Khudri	1170

Of the one thousand plus Companions, only 55 related 100 or more *hadith*, while only 11 have passed down more than 500 *hadith*, and only seven of these have passed down 1,000 or more *hadith*. (It must be noted, however, that these are not really the number of individual *hadith*, but the number of channels through which a *hadith* is transmitted, and therefore, Abu Hurayra may have related something on the order of 1,236 individual distinct *hadith*.[13]

It is interesting to note that the Prophet's closest Companion, Abu

Bakr, related only 142 *hadith*, while Umar ibn al-Khattab, 'Ali, and Uthman ibn Affan, the remainder of the first four Caliphs, related 537, 536, and 146 *hadith* respectively.[14]

The two most authoritative Sahih *hadith* books, by Bukhari and Muslim, contain material from 208 and 213 Companions respectively. Of these, 149 are common between the two works. This discrepancy between the two *Sahih* works of about 25% of the narrators is of some concern, as is the fact that most of the *hadith* corpus is related by only a few Companions, with the four Caliphs playing a significantly lesser role than many other Companions. For example. Abu Hurayra, the leading *hadith* transmitter, while clearly devoted to the Prophet and to *hadith* memorization, came to Medina and to Islam in the 7th year after the *Hijra* (thus spending only about three years with the Prophet before the Prophet's death). This is in distinction to Abu Bakr, the Prophet's closest Companion for at least 23 years, who only related 142 *hadith*.

Those of the Companions who "specialized" in *hadith* transmission were also very active in teaching it, and played a significant part in the preservation of the *hadith* corpus. An analysis of the early methods of teaching, and how students were certified by their teachers, reveals that there were probably a significant reliance on written materials (although systematic collections were not yet made) even at the time of the Companions. Either they wrote *hadith*, or the students who learned from them wrote down the *hadith* which they transmitted.[15] For example, there are reports that Abu Hurayra had a written collection of *hadith*, and that at least eight of his students wrote *hadith* from him. Also, it is reported that 16 students of Anas ibn Malik had *hadith* from him in written form, and so forth.[16]

The Crisis of Authenticity and the Issue of *Hadith* Fabrication

Given the importance of the Prophet's example and the prestige attached to knowing and teaching this example, as well as the early rise of political tensions in the young Muslim *umma*, it was not long before people began to fabricate *hadith* for their own ends. In fact, "there is no dispute about the occurrence of extensive forgery in the *hadith* literature. The *'ulema* of *hadith* are unanimous on this..."[17] The exact beginnings of forgery are difficult to ascertain, but probably began in the lifetime of the Prophet himself, escalated during the War of Apostasy during the rule of Abu Bakr, and began to become a serious issue at the time of the *Fitna*, or civil strife, between the fourth Caliph Ali and Mu'awiyah, starting at about the year 40 AH.

The types or motives for forgery have been classified by multiple scholars who have written extensive works on the forged *hadith*, a branch of *hadith* studies called *al-Mawdu'at*.[18] The various motives and categories of fabrication are important to those interested in the proper use of *hadith*.

The motives for forgery have been classified into four main types:

a. The Heretics (*Zanadiqa*): This was a diverse group of people who turned against Islam, and attempted to discredit Islam and the Prophet by fabricating *hadith* which distorted the creed of Islam. For example, one 'Abd al-Karim ibn Abi al-'Awja confessed to fabricating 4000 *hadith* where he had distorted the *haram* (prohibited) and the *halal* (lawful).[19]

b. Sectarian *hadith*: These *hadith* were fabricated for political motives. For example, the supporters of Ali have reported that the Prophet said, "When you see Mu'awiyah on my pulpit, kill him." Meanwhile, the supporters of Mu'awiya fabricated the *hadith*, "The trusted ones are three: I, Gabriel, and Mu'awiya."[20] This practice, unfortunately, was extensive, and rigorous *hadith* scholarship has shown numerous examples, a very few of which are:

- Awana ibn al Hakam who belonged to the Ummayyad party concocted traditions in favor of the Ummayyads.

- Abul 'Ayna, on the other hand, forged *hadith* that supported the Alid party.

- al-Muhallab, a general who fought the Khawarij, confessed that he had forged traditions against them.

- Al-Talqani, a member of the Murji'ite sect, forged *hadith* to support his sect's doctrines.

- Ghiyath ibn Ibrahim, from the court of the Caliph al-Mahdi, made intentional alterations to the *hadith* to please the Caliph.[21]

Because this sort of fabrication was so widespread, "most of the traditions which extol the virtues of certain individuals, tribes, provinces, districts, towns, or a sectarian leader, owe their origin to some of these deliberate forgers, and have been identified by the *hadith* scholars as mere inventions."[22]

c. The Storytellers: These are individuals who found their prestige greatly enhanced by claiming knowledge of some *hadith*, and would often take to telling stories in the mosques after prayers. Thus, "they invented thousands of such amusing anecdotes as might appeal to the masses, attributed them to the Prophet, and related them publicly."[23] One amusing story in this vein is of such a man who related to his audience, after prayer, a *hadith* on the authority of he great scholar Ahmad ibn Hanbal and Yahyia ibn Ma'in, that when a man said "there is no god but God," God created from each letter a bird with a beak of gold and feathers of pearl. Unfortunately for this man, both Ahmad ibn Hanbal and Yahya ibn Ma'in happened to be in the audience, and confronted him with the fact that they had related no such *hadith*.

d. The Pious Misguided: This last category of *hadith* forgers is the most puzzling of all. Often men of knowledge and piety, they began to fabricate *hadiths* "for the service of Islam," so to speak. For example, a man named Nuh ibn Abi Maryam, who studied with well-known theologians, and developed a reputation for great learning, related traditions on the virtues of the Quran. When confronted that these were forged, he admitted that he had forged them "for the sake of God, to attract people to His Book."[24]

Numerous other tragic examples exist in the *hadith* literature, such as Aban ibn Abi 'Ayyash, who was known as one of the most pious people of his day; narrated 1,500 *hadith* on the authority of Anas ibn Malik, which turned out to have no foundation. Similarly, a man named Ahmad ibn Muhammad al-Bahili was known for his piety, but was found to have fabricated 400 *hadith*. He confessed to doing so in order to make the hearts of the people more soft and tender. More disturbing still is that the followers of a religious leader known as al Sijistani argued that it was permissible to forge *hadith* in order to enjoin what is good and forbid what is evil.[25]

These stories are amazing, given that one of the strongest *hadith*s recorded by the scholars of *hadith*, passed through numerous chains of narration involving multiple Companions, is the Prophet's saying: "Whoever intentionally ascribes to me what I have not said then surely let him occupy his seat in Hell-fire." (This version of the *hadith* is narrated on the authority of Salama bin al-Akwa, and is found in Sahih al Bukhari, in the Book of Knowledge. It is probably the only *hadith* known to have been related by more than one hundred Companions.[26])

The Process of *Hadith* Authentication

Given both the importance of *hadith* in both the legal and spiritual life of the Muslims as the Muslim umma began to vastly expand, as well as the presence of widespread *hadith* fabrication, it became important to authenticate the *hadith*. This, in essence, means to make sure that the Prophet actually said what he is reported to have said. This conscientiousness was practiced sporadically by the Companions both in the lifetime of the Prophet as well as shortly after his death. For example, the following incident is reported in the Muwatta of Imam Malik: the Companion Abu Musa al-Ashari went to visit Umar; having knocked three times and received no answer, he turned to leave. Umar came out and asked him where he was going, and Abu Musa replied that the Prophet had said, "When one of you ask permission three times and it is not granted, he should go away." Umar asked him to prove that the Prophet had actually said that, or be punished. Abu Musa than brought a witness to the Prophet's statement. Umar then replied that he did not doubt Abu Musa or the veracity of the *hadith*, but wanted people to be more careful in transmitting the sunna of the Prophet.[27]

a. The development of the *Isnad* system

This sort of sporadic verification eventually produced a very sophisticated systematic science of *hadith* authentication, which relied mainly on the chain of narration from the Prophet to the person purporting that the Prophet made a particular statement. This chain of narration, from the Prophet to the *hadith* transmitter, is known as the *isnad* of the *hadith*. For example, we find in the *hadith* book of Bukhari the following *hadith*:

Bukhari was told by Ubaydallah ibn Musa that he was told by Hanzala ibn Abi Sufyan who learned from Ikrima ibn Khalid who learned from Ibn Umar that the Prophet (pbuh) said: "Islam is built upon five [pillars]: Testifying that there is no God but God and that Muhammad is his Prophet, establishing prayer, giving Zakat, performing Hajj, and fasting the month of Ramadan." (Sahih al Bukhari, the Book of Faith, chapter 2).

The first part of this *hadith*, Bukhari was told by Ubaydallah ibn Musa that he was told by Hanzala ibn Abi Sufyan who learned from Ikrima ibn Khalid who learned from Ibn Umar that the Prophet (pbuh) said, represents the *isnad* of the *hadith*, or its chain of transmission. It provides a way of verifying that this *hadith* is authentic, as will be discussed shortly.

It is not quite clear when *isnads* began to be in routine use. A reasonable opinion, offered after exhaustive study of the early *hadith* literature by Professor Muhammad Azami, Professor of the Science of *Hadith* at Riyadh University, is that it was by late in the first century Hijri.[28] The *hadith* work Sahih Muslim relates in its introduction the pertinent statement by Ibn Sirin: "They did not ask about the *isnad*, but when civil war - *Fitnah* - arose they said 'Name to us your men': those who belong to *ahl al sunna*, their *ahadith* were accepted and those who were innovators, their *ahadith* were neglected."

Once the system of *isnad* began to be used, the teaching and recording of *hadith* began to be performed in a fashion to support the *isnad* system as the main tool for the verification of *hadith* authenticity. Therefore, the early scholars of *hadith*, possibly as early as the late first century, and in the second century after the *hijra*, began to teach mainly through books, which were copied and read under close supervision by their students.

For the sake of historical accuracy, some of these famous first century scholars were names such as Ibn al-Musayib (d. 93) and Urwah ibn al Zubayr (d. 94), to name but a few of many. Slightly later, three famous scholars arose in the Medina region: Zuhri, Yahya ibn Sa'id, and Hisham ibn Urwah. The most famous was Zuhri (d. 124). In Iraq, as well, there were already very famous scholars such as al Hasan al Basri (d. 110) and Ibn Sirin (d. 110). These scholars, in turn, taught many of the famous scholars of the second century. It is important to note that by this time, it became the custom for students of *hadith* to travel throughout the Islamic world to learn from and be certified by the greatest scholars. After these travels, they settled in different regions of the Muslim world and began to have their own students. Some of the most famous of these second century scholars were Sufyan al Thauri of Kufa , Malik ibn Anas of Medina, Al Auzai of Beirut, Al Laith ibn Sa'd of Egypt and al Shafi of Egypt. They, in turn, taught the next generation of famous scholars of the mid second century, among whom were Yahya ibn Ma'in of Baghdad and Ibn Hanbal of Baghdad. As teachers in their own right, they then had among their students such names as al Bukhari, al Razi, and Muslim ibn al Hajjaj al Nisapuri. The *hadith* collections written by Imams al Bukhari and Muslim are now accepted as the two most authoritative collections of *hadith* in the Muslim world.

As said above, the method of teaching *hadith* from one generation of these scholars to the next, paid close attention to the *isnad* system, and utilized the supervised reading from *hadith* books between a student and his teacher to attempt to pass *hadith* knowledge without corruption of the *hadith* corpus. Therefore, the teachers "held that it was advisable for students to write on their copies of a book, after the Name of God (the *basmala*), the names of their teachers... and the names of the teachers of their teachers right back to the author of the book. Above the *basmala*... should be inscribed the names of the other students who read the book in the same class with the owner of the manuscript and the places and dates at which the various parts of it were read."[29]

This gave scholars a method of keeping track of *hadith* dissemination in a fairly close fashion, and thus a way of detecting forged *hadiths*. As an example, we take the following *hadith*:

According to Abu Hurayra, the Prophet said, "The Imam (of prayer) ought to be followed. So recite *takbir* when he recites and bow down when he bows down. And when he says, *Sami Allahu liman hamidah* ('God listens to him who praises Him'), say *Rabbana wa laka alhamd* ('O God, our Lord, to the be praise'). And when he prostrates, you should prostrate. You must not prostrate until he prostrates. When he raises (his head) you should raise yours. You must not raise your head until he raises. If he prays sitting, all of you should pray sitting."

This *hadith* is reported by at least ten Companions, in Medina, Syria and Iraq. Details of the transmission thereafter are available for at least five of the Companions. For example, Abu Hurayra transmitted the *hadith* to fourteen successors (among them, for instance, Thabit, Jabir, and ibn Musayyib). Another Companion, ibn Umar, transmitted it to Salim, while Ali transmitted it to Harith. Ibn Musayyib, who learned it from Abu Hurayra, transmitted it to Zuhri and Salim, who were third-generation authorities. By following the *hadith* in this fashion, we know that it was transmitted by 26 third-generation authorities, and is found at this time, in almost the same words and with the same meaning at ten different locations (Medina, Mecca, Egypt, Basraqh, Hims, Yemen, Kufa, Syria, Wasit and Ta'if). Of course, these chains are not known for all or most *hadiths* with this sort of accuracy, but it gives a window into the immense efforts exerted by *hadith* scholars to insure the authenticity of *hadith*.

Therefore, when a narrator named Abu 'Isma reported various *hadiths* on the excellence of many *suras* of the Quran, on the authority of the Companion Ikrima from the Companion Ibn Abbas, he was challenged by the scholars. He was asked how he had acquired these *hadiths*, when none of the known students of Ikrima reported such a *hadith*. He replied, "I saw that people had turned away from the Quran and occupied themselves with the *Fiqh* of Abu Hanifa and the Maghazi of Muhammad ibn Ishaq, so I forged these *hadiths* seeking reward in the next world."

The Sciences of *Hadith*: An Overview

The assessment of *isnads* of *hadith* gave rise to two extensive branches of *hadith* science: *ilm asma' al-rijal* (the biographies of men) and *ilm al-jarh wal tadeel* (the science of criticism of narrators). The first of these deals with the biographies of narrators, such as who lived when and where, and who learned from whom, etc. Mastery of this science afforded scholars the opportunity to spot forged *isnads*. For example, a purported chain of narration may contain a link between two people, one of whom had died before the other was born; a knowledge of the "biographies of men" would easily detect such unsound chains, and reject them. This branch of learning produced an amazing compendium of biographies. Among the most famous classical works in this area are *al Tarikh* by Bukhari and *al Taqabat* of Ibn Sa'd. The former work is said to have collected the biographies of 42,000 narrators. Numerous other sub-branches of this science developed, such as the knowledge of which fathers passed *hadiths* to their sons, which pupils learned with which teachers, and so on.

The science of "criticism of narrators" is more difficult. It entailed an attempt to grade the reliability and the veracity of each *hadith* narrator, and to assess whether he or she could "be trusted" to accurately convey the message of the Prophet. Through fairly painstaking analysis, the early scholars of *hadith* cross-checked chains of narration, wording of *hadiths*, stories about the life and the character of the narrator, relevant details about their memory, among other variables, to give each narrator a "grade." Based on this, *hadiths* could be classified according to their soundness, as will be discussed shortly.

However, it is instructive to note some of the requirements of various scholars (in terms of the narrators) in accepting a *hadith* as sound. Therefore, in his famous work *al-Risalah*, Imam al Shafi states the following:

"Each reporter should be trustworthy in his religion; he should be known to be truthful in his narrating, to understand what he narrates, to know how a different expression can alter the meaning and to report the wording of the *hadith* verbatim, not only its meaning... Moreover, he should have an excellent memory if he recites *hadith* from memory or he should be a good preserver of of his writings if he happens to report from them. He should agree with the narrations of the leading scholars of *hadith* if he reports something which they also do. He should not be a *mudallis* (someone who narrates from someone he has met, but narrates something they did hear directly from that person). He should not report from the Prophet contrary to what reliable sources have reported from him."[30] A second century scholar named Ibn al Mubarak considered acceptable as such: The narrator does not drink. The narrator prays in congregation. He does not tell a lie, and does not suffer from any mental defect.[31] Other scholars, conversely, were much more exacting, requiring such qualities as excellence in grammar and literary style, as well as excellence of moral character.

Thus, it is evident that the scholars of *hadith* attempted to set up a grading system to gauge the reliability of *hadith* narrators, and hence the authenticity of *hadith*. It is also clear that these criteria, while similar, were subjective and individual. Hence, Bukhari and Muslim, for example, do not agree on the reliability of all narrators, and each accepts some *hadiths* from narrators whom the other does not.

Toward Grading of *hadith*: The *Matn* (Content) of a *Hadith*

Before attempting to integrate some of the above information into an understanding of how *hadith* are graded, it is necessary to return to an issue alluded to earlier: the anatomy of *hadith*. Returning to an example used above:

Bukhari was told by Ubaydallah ibn Musa that he was told by Hanzala ibn Abi Sufyan who learned from Ikrima ibn Khalid who learned from Ibn Umar that the Prophet (pbuh) said:

"Islam is built upon five [pillars]: Testifying that there is no God but God and that Muhammad is his Prophet, establishing prayer, giving Zakat, performing Hajj, and fasting the month of Ramadan."[32]

As stated above, the chain of narration of the *hadith* is known as the isnad. The main part, or content of the *hadith* itself is known as the *matn*. This content, or matn, is also used by the scholars in grading the authenticity of *hadith*. This point is extremely important, and often overlooked by those who quote *hadith* superficially, without studying the sciences of *hadith*. Therefore, for a *hadith* to be judged as sound, it must fulfill two main criteria:

1) Its chain of transmission must be sound.

2) Its content must not contain defects which call into question its authenticity.

In our judgement, there has been a serious lack of recent scholarship regarding the issue of *matn*, or content, and its bearing on the acceptance of *hadiths*. Seemingly, many Muslims are afraid of charges of "heresy", or of lack of respect for the sunna. Such spurious charges form a real dis-incentive to serious analysis and debate by pious Muslims who have deep love and respect for the *sunna*, and understand that part of this love and respect is expressed by a brave analysis of the content of *hadith*, not just an assessment of its chain of transmission. It is critical for modern Muslims to remember, as their classical predecessors knew, that "the mere formal soundness of an isnad is not considered definitive proof of the actual genuineness of the text of the traditions to which they are attached. According to the traditionists, even if the *isnad* is completely without fault, the text should still be analyzed before the genuineness of its attribution can be established."[33]

In calling for a renaissance of this scholarship, it is critical for us to showcase some of what the classical scholars have written in this vein (much of which is ignored or rarely quoted). Overall, a *hadith* may be rejected on the basis of its content for one of two main reasons:

1) It contradicts more authentic *hadiths*. This is known as a *hadith shaz* (irregular).

2) It has an inherent defect or, in Arabic, *a'illa*. Such a *hadith* is known as a *hadith ma'lul* (defective).[34]

The second of these reasons is a very broad category, which as pointed out by Imam al Ghazali, goes beyond the scope of the scholars of *hadith* per se, and includes not only the efforts of the scholars of *fiqh* and Quran, but also the experts in the various worldly disciplines with which the contents of a *hadith* may deal.

As an example of the extremely progressive opinions which are part of our juristic legacy, we return to the scholar Suyuti's statement: "If you encounter a *hadith* contrary to reason or to what has been established as correctly reported, or against the accepted principles, then you should know that it is forged."[35] Also, Abu Bakr ibn al Tayyib is reported to have remarked "that it is a proof of the forged character of a tradition that it be against reason or common experience; or that it conflict with the explicit text of the Quran and the *mutawatir* tradition, or the consensus (*ijma*); or that it contains the report of an important event taking place in the presence of a large number of people (when it is related by a single individual); or that it lays down severe punishment for minor faults, or promises high rewards for insignificant good deeds."[36] Based on statements such as these, Professor Siddiqi, in his *Hadith Literature: Its Origin, Development and Special Features*, compiles a fairly comprehensive list of the classical requirements for a matn to be judged as sound:

a. A tradition must not be contrary to the other traditions which have already been accepted by the authorities on the subject as authentic and reliable. Nor should it contradict the text of the Quran, a *Mutawatir hadith*, the absolute consensus of the community, or the accepted basic principles of Islam.

b. A tradition should not be against the dictates of reason, the laws of nature or common experience.

c. Traditions establishing a disproportionately high reward for insignificant good deeds, or disproportionately severe punishments for ordinary sins, must be rejected.

d. Traditions describing the excellent properties of certain sections of the Quran may not be authentic.

e. Traditions mentioning the superior virtue of persons, tribes and particular places should be generally rejected.

f. Traditions which contain detailed prophecies of future events, equipped with dates, should be rejected.

g. Traditions containing such remarks of the Prophet as may not be a part of his Prophetic vocation, or such expressions as are clearly unsuitable for him, should be rejected.

h. A *matn* should not violate the basic rules of Arabic grammar and style.

Thus, reflecting on these criteria, we can review some examples of their application by scholars.

1. A purported *hadith* indicates that the Prophet stated that someone who is mourned at the time of their death will be punished for the crying of his family over him. This *hadith* is mentioned in several venues, with various transmissions, but is predominantly linked to the the stabbing of Umar ibn al Khattab and his final hours. In one version, according to Anas ibn Malik, Umar forbade Hafsa to cry over him, saying that the Prophet stated that the one who is cried over will be punished because of that. In another venue, Abdullah ibn Umar quotes the Prophet making a similar statement at the funeral of a daughter of Uthman.

When 'Aisha, the Prophet's wife, heard this attribution to the Prophet, she rejected it, stating emphatically that he said no such thing, and stating, "Where are you from the words of God, *'No bearer shall bear the burden of another"* (Surah al Anam, 4:164).

Thus, this *hadith* was rejected by 'Aisha not on the basis of a questionable *isnad*, but on the basis that its content contradicted a clear Quranic statement and a basic principle of Islamic justice, that no one would be punished for the actions of another.

The reflection of *hadith* against Quranic principles should be a critical part of *hadith* analysis, and several examples of this will be elicited later in this chapter. For now, we quote the frustration of Imam al Ghazali regarding the deficiency of this essential part of *hadith* analysis: "I have lost patience with people who are weak in their knowledge and understanding of Quran and overly indulged in looking into *hadith*, thus giving rulings and issuing *fatwas* which but increase the *umma* in its confusion."[37]

2. The *hadith* reported by al Bukhari to the effect that Adam's height was sixty cubits has been criticized by the scholar ibn Hajar on the basis of archaeological measurements of the homesteads of ancient peoples, which show that their inhabitants were not of abnormal height. (Ibn Hajar is the great scholar who wrote an extensive commentary on Sahih al Bukhari known as Fath al Bari, which has ben praised by the scholars to the point that they say, "there is no Hijra after the Fath, giving an accolade to the book by linking it to the great event of the opening or Fath of Mecca.[38])

In this case, a *hadith* is criticized on the basis that it is contrary to reason and common experience. It is noted that the reliance on reason to accept or reject *hadiths*, in the experience of the author, has nearly ceased among Muslims, due to intimidation by those who hold themselves as guardians of the *sunna*. However, we note that our classical scholars have stated clearly that reason is a criteria by which *hadith* can be accepted or rejected. Those who truly love the Prophet, peace be upon him, believe that he does not say things contrary to human reason or established scientific fact. We thus recall the commentary by the scholar Ibn Al Qayyim regarding the purported *hadith*: "he who loves, keeps chaste and dies, dies a martyr." Ibn Al Qayyim declares this *hadith* as forged and baseless, stating that even if the *isnad* of the *hadith* were as bright as the sun, it would not cease to be wrong and fictitious.[39]

While we champion the use of reason, we strongly caution against spurious reasoning, which places the whim of the speaker or writer in place of true reason, thus using whim to reject sound *hadith*. An especially egregious example of this has been the refutation by some of the *hadith* quoted above from Sahih al Bukhari establishing that Islam is built upon five pillars. Their reason for refutation is that the *hadith* mentioned the five pillars, but did not mention *jihad*, and since *jihad* is a critical part of Islam, the *hadith* must be categorized as forged.[40] This spurious reasoning ignores the sound chain of transmission, as well as the strong support of the contents of the *hadith* by the Quran, and the *ijma* or the consensus of opinion. Thus, a reason-based critique of *hadith* must be as such, rather than an exercise in whimsy.

3. A *hadith* is reported, on no less than the authority of Abu Bakr, that at the time of the *adhan*, Muslims used to kiss their thumbs when the name of the Prophet was mentioned. This *hadith*, though, is reported by him alone. However, since this event took place in the presence of a large number of Muslims, five times a day without fail, it should have been reported by a number of narrators. Since it is reported by only one Companion, the *hadith* is rejected."[41]

Hadith Classification

Now that the issue of *matn* (content) has been discussed, we can return to *isnad*, and further explore the intricate classification system developed by scholars to aid them in assessing the isnad of a *hadith*.[42]

Using the *isnad*, *hadiths* may be classified in multiple ways:

a. According to the "final authority" relaying the *hadith*.

Marfu': In other words, does the narration go directly back to the Prophet? If so, the *hadith* is called *marfu'* (elevated).

Mauquf: If it stops with a Companion as the final authority, it is called *mauquf* (stopped).

Maqtu': If, instead, it goes back only to a Successor, it is called *maqtu'* (severed).

It is noted that authoritative books, like the *Muwatta'* of Imam Malik, often contain numerous *hadiths* which are not *marfu*, i.e., do not go back to the Prophet. Of Malik's 1,700 hundred or so *hadith*, only about 600 or so are *marfu*, with the rest being sayings of the Companions or the Successors, which cannot be directly linked to the Prophet.

b. According to the links in the *isnad*

Musnad: This means "supported", and indicates a continuous chain of narration from the Prophet to the final reporter of the *hadith*. Thus, by definition, it is also *marfu*.

Mursal (hurried or sent forth): If the link between a Successor and the Prophet is missing (i.e. a Successor reports that the Prophet said, without mentioning the Companion from which he heard the *hadith*) the *hadith* is called mursal.

Although it does not have a continuous chain of transmission, there has been a surprising amount of debate about this particular category of *hadith*, with some scholars assuming that a Successor would not quote the Prophet without knowing that the Prophet definitely said it; by assumption, he heard it from a Companion. However, the situation is often that the Successor might have omitted two names, that of an elder Successor from which he heard the *hadith*, who in turn heard it from a Companion. Some scholars have adopted the position that if the *hadith* comes through an elder Successor, such as Sa'id al-Musayyab, it should be acceptable, because they have been deemed reliable. Imams Malik and Abu Hanifah, for example, accept *Mursal hadith*.[43] We gravitate toward the more conservative views that before Muslims are obligated to a practice, there needs to be certainty that it was required upon us by the Prophet, and this certainty is not present in *mursal hadith*. The scholar Ibn Hazm, for example, agrees with this view, and rejects the *mursal* outright. Also, Al Hakim is extremely reluctant to accept the *mursal hadith*, while the renowned classical scholar al Khatib al Baghdadi, after examining the various opinions on the issue, concludes: "What we select out of these sayings is that the *mursal* is not to be practiced, nor is it acceptable as proof. We say that *irsal* (being *mursal*) leads to one reporter being ambiguous; if he is ambiguous, to ascertain his reliability is impossible. We have already explained that a narration is only acceptable if it comes through a reporter known for reliability. Hence, the *mursal* should not be accepted at all."[44] Our point of view, however, does not deny that the *mursal* can and should be used as a guide to the practice and opinions of the early Muslims (as argued by Imam Malik), which is itself a valuable resource.

Munqati' (broken): If a link is missing anywhere after the Successor (closer to the final narrator of the *hadith*), it is called *munqati'*.

Mu'dal (perplexing): If the number of consecutive missing reporters exceeds one, the *hadith* is called *mu'dal*.

Mu'allaq (hanging): If the entire chain of transmission is omitted, the *hadith* is called *mu'allaq*. For example, Imam Malik sometimes states in his *Muwatta'*, "It reached me that the Prophet said..."[45]

c. According to the Number of Links in the Transmission:

This is one of the most critical facets of *hadith* classification, as it assesses how widely known and well-reported a *hadith* is. *Hadith* can be divided into two main categories:[46]

Mutawatir

The *hadith* is reported at every generation after the Prophet by such a large number of people such that their "agreement upon a lie is inconceivable." This is the strongest kind of *hadith*, and is felt to represent unambiguous evidence of the Prophet's will, or to lead to "knowledge with certainty" in the words of the *hadith* scholars. There has been some debate about whether there exists a substantive number of *mutawatir hadith* (i.e., do many *hadiths* reach this degree of certainty)? Some scholars say there are many such *hadiths*, while others, such as Ibn Salah, say, "the *mutawatir* can barely be found."[47]

However, even in the most liberal of opinions regarding the *mutawatir*, all of the following conditions need to be met:[48]

- The *hadith* must exist in all of the major *hadith* collections

- The chains of transmission must be so numerous as to preclude collusion or falsehood.

- The large number of narrators must be clearly present at every stage in the narration.

If a *hadith* is not present in one of the major books, or is present but all of them quote a single chain or a few chains of transmission, or at some stage of transmission, the chain ceases to be numerous, then the *hadith* does not satisfy the criteria.

Thus, the *hadith* quoted previously regarding lying about the Prophet "whoever lies about me deliberately…", which was narrated separately by over 60 Companions, or *hadiths* that the number of prayers is five, or the number of *rakats* in each prayer, would fall into this category. In the view of the majority of scholars, "the authority of a *mutawatir hadith* is equivalent to that of the Quran."[49]

2. *Ahad* (solitary): *Hadiths* reported by a single person, or a very few individuals from the Prophet (pbuh). In other words, *hadiths* which cannot meet the criteria for *mutawatir*. This category is further subdivided below, but the following point must be emphasized first:

- As opposed to the text of the Quran, which has come to us as *mutawatir*, "the *sunna* has for the most part been narrated and transmitted in the form of solitary or *ahad* reports. Only a small portion of the *sunna* has been transmitted in the form of *mutawatir*."[50]

- For most *hadith* scholars, an *ahad hadith* "does not impart positive knowledge on its own unless supported by extraneous or circumstantial evidence."[51] This critical issue will be revisited when we discuss the authority, rather than the authenticity, of *hadith*.

The *ahad hadiths* have been further subdivided into the following categories:

Mashhur (famous): The *hadith* is transmitted by three or more transmitters at every stage. (It is noted that the Hanafi school considered *mashhur hadiths* a category separate from the *ahad*, intermediate between *ahad* and *mutawatir*. However, this is a minority opinion, and most scholars consider the *mashhur* as a subcategory of *ahad hadith*. This issue will again become pertinent when we discuss the authority of *hadith*, since for the Hanafi school, " the *mashhur hadith* imparts positive knowledge, albeit of a lesser degree of certainty than *mutawatir*"[52]

Aziz (rare, strong): The *hadith* has been transmitted by at least two narrators at every generation.

Gharib (strange): If the *hadith* is transmitted by a single narrator throughout its *isnad* after the Companion, or a single narrator in any stage, it is called *gharib.*

d. Grading of Transmitters: A second look

At this stage, we are ready to return to the issue of grading of narrators, and then using the classifications above, understand the grading if *hadiths* themselves. Classical scholars, as has been briefly discussed, tended to grade *hadith* transmitters into four or six grades, such as:

- Imam or *Hafiz* (preserver), highest grade
- Reliable, trustworthy
- Makes mistakes
- Weak
- Abandoned
- Liar, used to fabricate *hadith*

Slightly later scholars expanded the classification. For example, Ibn Hajar, one of the most famous medieval *hadith* scholars, has twelve grades, in descending order of strength and reliability. This scheme has been followed by many later scholars.

Grading of *Hadith*

Using this scheme, and the numerous categories of information discussed above, we finally arrive at the grading of *hadiths* themselves.

At the most basic level, *hadiths* will be divided into one of two main groups:

1) Accepted or *Maqbul*
2) Rejected or *Mardud*

The Accepted or *maqbul* category is further subdivided into two grades:

a. *Sahih* (authentic)
b. *Hasan* (agreeable)

Each of these groups can be further subdivided into whether it is authentic or agreeable inherently or because of external support (e.g. *sahih li thatihi, sahih li ghairihi,* etc.).

Accepted Hadith

Sahih Hadith:

For a *hadith* to be *sahih*, it must possess the following criteria:[53]

- The chain of transmission must be continuous and unbroken back to the Prophet (according to our view on *mursal hadith* expressed above).

- Each of the narrators must be trustworthy. For example, using Ibn Hajar's criteria, they must be in the top three grades. If a single narrator in the chain is weak, the entire *hadith* then becomes unsound.

- The *hadith* should not be *shadh* (isolated). In other words, as described above, it cannot be contradicted by other accepted *hadith*s by authorities of the same grade but more in number, or *hadith*s narrated by stronger authorities.

- The *hadith* should not be rejected on the basis of its content, or *matn*.

Hassan Hadith

All of the same conditions apply as for the *sahih*, except that one or all of the narrators may be of grade four (using Ibn Hajar's twelve grades). If the transmitters are of grade five or six, but other *hadith*s through different chains which are sound support the *hadith*, it can then move to a grade of *hasan li ghairihi* (*hasan* due to extrinsic support).

It should be remembered that the classical scholars used stringent rules to qualify the authenticity of *hadith*, so that "if a chain of *isnad* consists of ten authorities, and nine out of them belong to second grade and only one of them belongs to grade 8, then the *hadith* would be rejected. The overall acceptability is based on the weakest authority. Thus a single weak narrator would result in weakening of the *hadith*."[54]

Rejected *Hadith*

This category has been divided in numerous ways by the scholars, based on the degree of weakness, as well as the reason for weakness. Broadly, rejected *hadith* may be classified as *da'if* (weak) or *maudu* (fabricated). Neither of these categories has authority in matters of law or of faith.

Looking at the reasons for classified a *hadith* as rejected (whether *da'if* or *maudu*) are instructive. A *hadith* may be rejected due to one of three main reasons:

- Rejection owing to a defect in the narrator

According to Ibn Hajar's grading, any narrator of grade six or lower would cause weakness in the *hadith*. The weakness, of course, could be of various degrees. If the *hadith* is transmitted by a narrator of grade 12, it is classified as forged (*maudu*). If he was of grade 11, it would be called *batil* (defective and rejected). If the narrator is of grade 10, it would be called *munkar* (distrusted and rejected). If the narrator is of grade six to eight, the *hadith* is simply *da'if* (weak). Some scholars also have a grading of very weak (*da'if jiddan*).

- Rejection owing to discontinuity in the chain

In this category are all *hadiths* mentioned above with a broken chain of one type or another (i.e. anything other than *musnad*). This includes the *mursal*, *munqati'*, *mu'dal*, as well as the categories of *mauquf* (saying of a Companion) or *maqtu'* (saying of a Successor). These latter two, of course, do not intend to have the Prophet as the final authority, and so are not "*hadith*" by the standard definition. They are included explicitly because some well known and highly respected books contain *hadiths* of these types, and the non-careful reader may not distinguish one from the other. Therefore, the *Muwatta'* of Imam Malik, which contains about 1,700 *hadith* has the following breakdown: 600 *marfu'* (the Prophet is the final authority), 613 *mauquf*, 285 *maqtu'*, and 228 *mursal*.

- Weakness owing to other reasons

In this category are various other types of weakness in *isnad*, such as mistakes and reversal in names of narrators, or other *'illa* (defect). Presumably, this category also includes defects in the *matn*, or content, which make a *hadith* unacceptable according to the canons of *matn* criticism described above.

It is once again noted that there is a general reluctance, especially among more modern scholars, to declare a *hadith* as rejected due to its content if its chain of transmission, or *isnad*, is sound. However, this should remain a critical facet of *hadith* analysis, and modern *hadith* scholars need to have the bravery needed to return to *matn* analysis. Thus, the classical scholar al Hakim was not afraid to collect *hadiths* which were classified as forged or weak, although they had sound *isnads*. Likewise, al Suyuti remarks that such *hadiths* are encountered frequently.[55] In modern scholarship, this issue has been discussed passionately by Shaikh Muhammad al Ghazali, who has clearly stated, "What good is a *hadith* with a sound *isnad* but a defective *matn* (content)?"[56]

The Canonical *Hadith* Collections

Thus, following these criteria, various pious and scholarly men devoted their lives to the collection, authentication and compilation of the Prophet's *sunna*. From their efforts, there emerged several *hadith* collections which are generally accepted as authoritative by Muslims, and serve as the main source of the *hadith* corpus.

In the first category are the two *Sahih* collections of Bukhari (d. 256 H) and Muslim (d. 261 H). Most authorities consider Bukhari to be slightly more authoritative, but both works are held in very high esteem, and are considered the soundest of the *hadith* books. Bukhari examined about 600,000 *hadiths*, and out of these, he accepted only 7,275 as genuine or *sahih*, and these form his book. Almost immediately, the books of Bukhari and Muslim were accepted as sound by the scholars of their day.

In the second category, there are the so-called four *Sunan* books. Together with the two *Sahihs*, they form the Six Canonical *Hadith* Books. The first two to be accepted were the *Sunan* books of Abu Daud and al Nisa'i. This occurred at about the mid-fourth century Hijri. After some time, the *Jami* of Al Tirmidhi also became accepted by the scholars, and along with the Bukhari, Muslim, Abu Daud and al Nisa'I, these became the Five Books (*al Kutub al Khamsa*). Finally, the work of Ibn Maja, which was initially not considered "canonical" gained acceptance toward the beginning of the seventh century. However, some scholars, such as Ibn Salah and al Nawawi did not accept the work of Ibn Maja as canonical. Nonetheless, these six books are now considered the canonical six books of *hadith* among Sunnis."

Hadith Collection: A Human Endeavor

The Quran, of course, is sacred to Muslims. Likewise, the Prophet (pbuh) and his mission are sacred and revered. However, it must be recognized that the collection and classification of *hadith*, which is our link to the Prophet, was a human endeavor. It involved numerous classifications, subjective judgements, differences of opinion among various scholars, and as such, also some mistakes.

For example, Al Hakim reported from Muhammad ibn Mus'ab from al Auza'I from Shaddad Abu 'Ammar that Umm al Fadl said to the Prophet: "I have seen in a vision last night as if a part of your body was cut out and placed in my lap." He said: "You have seen something good. God willing, Fatima will give birth to a child who will be in your lap." The narration continues with the birth of al Husain, and Umm al Fadl placing al Husain in the Prophet's lap, whose eyes then welled with tears, and he said, "Jibril came to me and told me that my umma will kill this son of mine, and he brought me some of the reddish dust of that place (where he will be killed)."

Al Hakim said, "This is a *sahih hadith* according to the condition of the two Shaikhs (Bukhari and Muslim) but they did not collect it." However, al Dhahabi, in his commentary on al Hakim's work says, "No, the *hadith* is *munqati'* and *daif*, because Shaddad never met Umm al Fadl, and Muhammad ibn Mus'ab is weak (a weak narrator)."[57]

For such an obviously human endeavor, the author has been repeatedly surprised by the dogmatism of Muslims regarding the *hadith* collections, even to the point of accusing other Muslims of blasphemy for questioning the possible correctness of a specific *hadith* in al Bukhari. This, of course, is unacceptable on two counts. First, it goes against the dictates of reason that Bukhari, who examined 600,000 *hadiths* and kept only about 7,000 would have been correct in every single case, either in inclusion or exclusion. That would require a type of infallibility vouchsafed only to Prophets in matters of faith. Secondly, such an attitude implies a complete ignorance of our intellectual tradition as Muslims. While al Bukhari was greatly respected for his piety, dedication and scholarship, he was not considered above criticism by his fellow scholars, since their interest was in safeguarding something more precious than the reputation of al Bukhari (which of course remains quite souns). It is therefore critically important for the intellectual vitality of those Muslims who approach *hadith* literature to understand the statement of Professor Siddiqi in this vein:

"It would be a mistake, however, to suppose that the *Sahih* (of al Bukhari) is free of defects, or that the Muslim scholars have failed to criticize it in certain aspects. Thus it is generally accepted that like other traditionalists, al Bukhari confines his criticism to the narrators of traditions, and their reliability, and pays little attention to the probability or possibility of the truth of the actual material reported by them."[58] This critical quote goes to the heart of what has been described earlier as a deficiency in the analysis of hadith and rejection of *hadith* according to *matn* (content), especially using the criteria of reason, as has been discussed before.

This same quote started above continues without interruption as follows:

"In estimating the reliability of narrators, his judgment has in certain cases been erroneous, and the Muslim traditionists have not failed to point this out. Al Draqutni (306-385 AH) tried to show the weakness of some two hundred traditions contained in the book in his *al Istidrak wa'l tatabbu'*, which has been summarized by al Jaza'iri in his *Tawjih al*

Nazar. Abu Masu'd of Damascus, and Abu 'Ali al-Ghassani have also criticized the Sahih, while al-'Ayni in his celebrated commentary has shown the defects in some of its contents.

Despite this, all the Muslim traditionalists, including those who have criticized the Sahih, have paid unanimous tribute to the general accuracy, scrupulous care, and exactitude of the book's author."[59]

This approach shows the balance between intellectual vitality and engagement on the one hand, and a respect for our classical scholarship on the other, and is the approach which we attempt to adopt.

The Authority of *Hadith*

All of the foregoing has addressed one basic theme: establishing the authenticity of a *hadith*. Once this authenticity is established, to the best of our human ability, and God knows best, many people consider the task complete and the issue at hand decided. After all, since we all believe in the authority of the Prophet (pbuh), once we are comfortable that he has made a statement, the matter is settled, the argument usually goes. For good measure, there may also be recourse to the verse, *"Whenever God and His Messenger have decided a matter, it is not for a believing man or woman to follow another course of his or her own choice"* (Surah Al Ahzab, 33:36).

However, once the authenticity of a *hadith* is established, this is not the end, but rather the beginning of the process of deciding on an issue. Now, the *hadith* has been deemed admissible evidence, so to speak, and must be weighed along with other relevant factors. We term this establishing the authority of the *hadith*; i.e., to what extent will the text of the authentic *hadith* have authority in deciding an issue. This sort of approach, while seemingly radical to many Muslims, is to a great extent the classical approach as well. In the remainder of this chapter, we shall, Godwilling, discuss some of the various issues relating to the authority of a *hadith*, and stress that these must be carefully considered in such matters as the issuance of fatwas or religious opinions which may have impact on others.

a. Back to the Authenticity of a Hadith

While this issue has been covered, and should seemingly be self-evident, a major problem in the use of *hadith* within Islamic dialogues is the use of weak or inauthentic *hadiths*, with either incomplete information or incomplete disclosure on the part of the speaker using the *hadith* to support his or her position.

The examples of this are numerous, but only two will be provided here for the sake of illustration

- The following *hadith* has been reportedly used in *khutbas* (sermons) in various Muslim countries.

On the authority of Fatima, the daughter of the Prophet, she said: "The woman should not see anyone, nor should anyone see her." The Prophet concurred with her, and hugged her, and said, "a lineage one from another" (i.e., the equivalent of 'like father, like daughter').

Another narration of this *hadith* is that the Prophet asked his daughter Fatima, "What is best for a woman?" She replied, "That she not see anyone, nor anyone see her." The Prophet kissed her and said, "a lineage one from another."

Although this *hadith* is widely quoted, Shaikh Muhammad al Ghazali has said regarding it to a man who quoted it: "You are quoting a *munkar* (rejected) *hadith*, not mentioned in any respectable *hadith* book. You quote a *hadith* which contradicts what is known with certainty from the Quran and the *mutawatir hadiths*, and the *seera* of the Prophet and the Caliphs. Shaikh Yusuf al Qaradawi commented similarly on this *hadith* a statement to the effect that it is not worth the ink spent to write the isnad concocted for it.[60]

- On the authority of the Companion Anas, transmitted through Ibrahim ibn Hudba, the Prophet said, "Whenever a woman leaves her house without the order of her husband, she will merit God's anger until she returns to her house or until He forgives her."

This *hadith* is classified as outrightly fabricated by the *hadith* scholars. The narrator ibn Hudba has been called a liar and a fabricator by numerous *hadith* scholars. (Discussed by the outstanding modern authority on *hadith* scholarship, Muhammad al Albani, in his book *Silsilat al Ahadith al Da'ifa wal Mauduwa wa Atharaha al Siy' fi al Umma* [A Collection of Weak and Fabricated *Hadith* and their Detrimental Effect on the Umma] Maktab al Ma'arif Publishers, Saudi Arabia, 1988, hadith 1020. This is an outstandingly thorough analysis of weak and fabricated *hadiths*, many of which are widely quoted, with a four volume collection of 2,000 *hadiths*).

In the regard of weak *hadiths*, there may be issues which would not be suspected by the general Muslim, or non-specialist in the *hadith* sciences. For example, even in Sahih al Bukhari, it "is important to note, however, that he used less exacting criteria for the traditions which he used as headings for some of his chapters, and as corrobaratives for the principal ones. In such cases, he often omits all or part of the *isnad*, and in certain cases relies on weak authorities. The number of suspended (*mu'allaq*) and corroborative traditions in the book amounts to 1,725.[61] Therefore, one needs to be aware which traditions are being quoted, and how closely they are supported by the sahih *hadiths* in the main text.

Secondly, many ignore the clear opinion of the majority of scholars that a "weak or *da'if hadith* does not constitute a *shari* proof (*hujjah*) and is generally rejected."[62] The reasons for this are complex. Sometimes, they are simply ignorance about *hadith* classification. More problematic, however, are those who argue, following the opinion and practice of some scholars, that weak *hadiths* are admissible as juristic proof. This is probably secondary to a confusion about the real opinion of such scholars. The scholars of the *umma* are in agreement that weak *hadiths* cannot be used for law-making in Islam.[63] However, *hadiths* in the realm of manners, *hadiths* which enjoin good deeds, etc., but which are not in the realm of legal injunctions per se, have sometimes been used and quoted by the *ulema*. However, this allowance for those specific types of *hadiths* does not extend to other weak *hadiths*, and "has its place and its conditions. However many have misused this [approach] and have thus moved away from the right path, and sullied Islam's pure spring."[64] Also, some ignore the fact that in the first two centuries, there were essentially only two classes of *hadith* - strong and weak - without the intermediate grade of *hasan* (acceptable) *hadith*. Thus, some may say that Imam Ahmad ibn Hanbal accepts *da'if hadith*. However, Imam Ahmad classified *hadith* into *sahih* and *da'if* only, rather than *sahih*, *hasan* and *da'if*. Hence, "the category *da'if* in his view applied to *ahadith* which were relatively close to being *sahih*, and included many *ahadith* which were classified as *hasan* by other scholars. Overlooking this facet has caused misunderstanding about Imam Ahmad's view on the place of *da'if ahadith* in rulings of *Fiqh...*"[65]

b. Eliciting all Hadiths Relevant to a Topic:

In the personal example which opened this lengthy chapter, we provided an example of a less than thorough reference to the corpus of the sunna. When an issue is encountered, and *hadith* is used to support an opinion or obtain a ruling, it is necessary to refer to the entire set of hadiths on the issue, and attempt a process of compromise or arbitration or decision-making between them.

c. Proper Use of *Qiyas* (Analogical Deduction) Regarding *Hadith*

Often, a *hadith* is not precisely on point regarding an issue at hand, and an analogy between the issue and a potentially applicable *hadith* must be drawn. This process should be subject to various rules, and not done in a careless fashion. In his first major work, *The Authoritative and the Authoritarian in Islamic Discourse*, Professor Abou El Fadl provides an excellent illustration of this general point using a particular case study from the American Muslim experience.

d. The Flexibility of the *Sunna*

There are several instances in the *sunna* of the Prophet (pbuh) that strongly suggest that there is a great deal of flexibility in the approach which the Prophet took in the interpretation and promulgation of religious law, always with a focus on the intent and spirit of an action rather than on the letter of the law. Two examples are presented:

- It is recorded by al Bukhari that on the occasion of the Battle of Bani Qurayzah, he sent a delegation to the Bani Qurayzah, and instructed them: "No one shall perform the [*salah* of] *asr* except in Bani Qurayzah." As the sun neared setting while the delegation traveled, a difference of opinion arose among them. Some took the Prophet's instruction literally, that they should not pray *asr* until they reached Bani Qurayzah, even if this was to be after sunset, and hence prayed the asr after its time. Others, meanwhile, understood the Prophet's instruction to mean that that they should should travel quickly, so that they reach Bani Qurayzah before sunset, and pray asr there. Thus, they tried to travel quickly, but prayed *asr* at its time while still on the road. Later, when the Prophet learned of the matter, he concurred with both courses of action.

- There is a report that two Companions went on a journey. When they failed to find water for *wudu* (ablution), they performed their prayers after doing *tayamum* (wiping the hands and face with clean sand). Later, when they found water, one of them performed the ablutions and repeated his prayers; the other did not. Upon their return, they related the experience to the Prophet, who is reported to have approved both courses of action.[66] This became an example of *sunna taqririya* (*sunna* of the Prophet because of his approval of an action).

The critical importance of this *hadith* is the hypothetical which must be posed: what if only one of the men had been on the journey? He would presumably have returned, reported his action to the Prophet (for example, repeating the prayer after water is available, in the case of the first man), and obtained the Prophet's approval. From that time on, it would have been reported that the religious rule is that when a prayer is done with *tayamum*, it should be repeated with *wudu* when water is available. This, obviously, would be a distortion of the Prophet's *sunna*, and the tremendous flexibility which he displayed.

e. The Issue of *Ahad Hadith*

As stated above, most of the corpus of *hadith* comes to us through *ahad* (solitary) rather than *mutawatir* (consecutive, i.e. certain) transmissions. This is a different issue than whether a *hadith* is *sahih*. The chain of transmission may be sound, but the *hadith* comes through a solitary chain. The scholars of *hadith* have discussed the status of *ahad* at length. To make rules binding upon all Muslims, and speak with the authority of the Prophet, we would like to be certain that indeed the Prophet has enjoined or forbidden a particular thing. However, the view of the majority (except Imam Ahmad ibn Hanbal) is that *ahad hadiths* do not impart positive knowledge on their own, unless supported by external or circumstantial evidence.[67] Some *ulema* "have rejected it on the basis of an analogy they have drawn with a provision of the law of evidence, namely that the testimony of one witness falls short of legal proof."[68] There has been a great deal written by the various scholars and juristic schools on the conditions which an *ahad hadith* has to meet before it becomes obligatory. If the *hadith* meets these conditions, "the majority of the *ulema* of the four Sunni schools [consider that] acting upon *ahad* is obligatory even if ahad fails to engender positive knowledge. Thus, in practical legal matters, a preferable *zann* (conjecture, probable opinion) is sufficient as a basis for obligation."[69] We, however, disagree with that view, and stand with the view that speculative knowledge is not a sufficient basis for obligation, a view also held by many *ulema*.[70] We agree with a slightly different expression of the issue, also agreed upon by the majority of the *ulema*:

"The majority of jurists, however, agree that ahad may establish a rule of law provided that it is related by a reliable narrator and the contents of the report are not repugnant to reason."[71]

Therefore, since the *ahad* engender only speculative knowledge, such *hadiths* need to be subject to the test of reason before becoming a basis of legal injunctions. This is similar to the requirement of the Hanafi school that unless the narrator of the *ahad hadith* is himself a scholar, then *qiyas* (analogical deduction) is given preference over *ahad hadith*. Imam Malik, on the other hand, preferred the practice of the people of Medina over ahad *hadith* as a legal proof, since "he considered the standard practice of the people of Medina to be more representative of the conduct of the Prophet than the isolated report of of one or two individuals."[72] This point of view, of course, represents an application of reason to check *ahad hadith*, with using the actions of the people of Medina representing a "reasonable" reflection of the Prophet's practice.

A few examples of such checks are provided, to illustrate that this process is a practical one.

1. There is a reported *hadith*, narrated through 'Aisha to the effect that the Prophet said "marriage of a woman is invalid without the permission of her guardian." (This *hadith* is quoted, without reference, in Kamali, op. cit., p. 101. A slightly different wording, "Any woman who got married without the permission of her guardian, her marriage would be null and void" is related, without reference, in Abdur Rahman Doi, *Shariah: The Islamic Law*, op. cit., p. 141).

As part of a "reasonableness" test applied to ahad *hadith*, the Hanafi school considers a *hadith* invalid if the narrator of the *hadith* acts contrary to the *hadith*, after having narrated it. Therefore, the Hanafi school does not accept this *hadith* because 'Aisha "acted to the contrary when she contracted the *nika* (marriage) of her niece, the daughter of Abd al-Rahman, while he was absent in Syria."[73]

2. Another application of reason to *hadith* has been discussed in the section on *matn* (content) criticism: if a solitary report exists about a practice which should have been widely known and widely reported and practiced by Muslims, it is not held authentic.

Therefore, with regard to the reported *hadith* of the Prophet, "Anyone who touches his sexual organ should make a fresh ablution," the Hanafi school once again does not accept this *hadith*.[74] The Hanafis reasoned that if this *hadith* were authentic, the situation it addresses is common enough such that the *hadith* would have been well known and widely acted upon by all Muslims, which is no the case.

3. There is a reported *hadith* of the Prophet which states, "Whoever cultivates barren land becomes its owner" (reported in the Sunan of Abu Dawud). According to this *hadith*, if there is unclaimed land, it becomes the lawful property of whoever would cultivate it. During the time of the Prophet (pbuh), this was a sensible policy. It

gave incentive to a small population, living in a vast arid desert, to cultivate the land, and represented a socially positive policy. This is especially so in that, with regard to cultivation, most people would be relatively equal in means, as the cultivation depended solely on manpower. It is easy to see that in today's world, this *hadith* could not be reasonably applied. The legal disputes over land ownership would be endless. Also, business tycoons, for instance, could quickly arrange to cultivate millions of acres of unclaimed land using the latest agricultural technology in terms of large machines, genetically engineered crops, pesticides, and armies of hired cheap labor; then, they would claim ownership of the land. The chances for poor peasants, meanwhile, to compete for land ownership would be minimal. Clearly, such a policy today fails the reason test which should check the application of ahad *hadith*, and should be used against whoever would claim land as their Islamic right based on this *hadith*. This particular *hadith* will be returned to later in another venue.

Before leaving this topic, it must be stressed that the foregoing discussion about the place of ahad *hadith* relates only to the issue of sharia. In terms of *aqeeda*, or the core beliefs of Islam, there is no disagreement that ahad *hadiths* do not form a basis for *aqeeda*. As stated, ahad *hadiths* do not engender positive knowledge; there is always room for doubt that the Prophet did not make the purported statement. Since there is an absence of certainty, *ahad hadiths* do not form a basis of aqeeda.[75]

f. The Quran and *Hadith*

A significant branch of inquiry about the proper understanding and application of *hadith* concerns the relationship between the Quran and *hadith*. While it is clearly accepted that *hadith* is the second source of *sharia* (Islamic law), there should be a clear distinction in priority between Quran and *hadith*. This is due to multiple factors, among them the following are taken from Kamali's *Principles of Islamic Jurisprudence*:[76]

1. "The Quran consists wholly of manifest revelation (*wahy zahir*)

whereas the Sunna consists mainly of internal revelation (*wahy batin*)."

2. "The authenticity of the Quran is not open to doubt. It is, in other words, *qat'i*, or decisive, in respect of authenticity and must therefore take priority over the *sunna*, or at least that part of the *sunna* that is speculative (*zanni*) in respect of authenticity."

3. "The entire text of the Quran has come down to us through continuous testimony (*tawatur*) whereas the *sunna* has for the most part been narrated and transmitted in the form of solitary, or *ahad*, reports. Only a small portion of the *sunna* has been transmitted in the form of *mutawatir*."

4. "The Quran in none of its parts consists of conceptual transmission, that is, transmission in the words of the narrator himself. Both the concepts and the words of the Quran have been recorded and transmitted as the Prophet received them. The *sunna* on the other hand consists, in the most part, of the transmission of concepts in words and sentences that belong to the narrators. This is why one often finds that different versions of the one and the same *hadith* are reported by people whose understanding of a particular *hadith* are not identical." This point is extremely under-appreciated among Muslims. The Quran, we believe, is the direct word of God. The *sunna*, on the other hand, is often not the direct word of the Prophet, but rather a paraphrasing of the meaning he conveyed undertaken by the narrator of the *hadith*. The number of *mutawatir hadith* transmitted verbatim in the words of the Prophet (pbuh) is extremely small.

5. "The [next] point in favor of establishing an order of priority between the Quran and the *sunna* is that the latter is explanatory of the former. Explanation or commentary should naturally occupy a secondary place in relationship to the source." This point gets to the heart of an extensive debate as to whether the *sunna*, in fact, constitutes an independent source of law, or whether it is wholly an extension of the Quran. This issue has been discussed in some length by the classical scholars, and Imam al Shafi'i sums up the debate as follows:

"I do not know anyone among the *ulema* to oppose [the doctrine] that the *Sunna* of the Prophet is of three types: first is the *sunna* which prescribes the like of what God has revealed in His Book; next is the sunna which explains the general principles of the Quran and clarifies the will of God; and last is the *sunna* where the Messenger of God has ruled on matters on which nothing can be found in the Book of God. The first two varieties are integral to the Quran, but the ulema have differed as to the third."[77]

We subscribe to the majority view of the *ulema* that the *sunna* as a whole must be viewed as integral to the Quran, rather than an independent source. This is summed up by Professor Kamali as follows: "According to the majority of the *ulema*, however, the *sunna*, in all its parts, even when it enacts original legislation, is explanatory and integral to the Quran."[78]

One of the main problems in the misuse of *hadith* is the lack of reflection of its contents vis a vis the Quran by those who lack appropriate scholarship, and do not fully comprehend how integral the *hadith* must be to the general aims and themes of the Quran. This notion, of course, is a significant theme in Muhammad al Ghazali's book, *Al Sunna Al Nabawiyah bain Ahl al Fiqh wa Ahl al Hadith* [The Prophetic Sunna between the Scholars of *Fiqh* and the Scholars of *Hadith*], where several examples of pitfalls in the misunderstanding of *hadith* are given. It is also in respect of this order of priority that the Hanafi school gives priority to the manifest or apparent meaning of the Quran over the *ahad hadith*.[79]

An important example of the proper interpretation of *hadith* (and one with significant implications to the Islamic concept of justice) relates to the following *hadith*:

"The Muslim is not killed for a *kafir* (unbeliever)." This *hadith* is reported in the collections of Ahmad and Abu Dawood and al Nisai, and is reported to be *sahih* in terms of its chain of transmission.[80] It relates to the punishment for murder, and specifically in the case where a Muslim murders a non-Muslim. In Islam, the punishment for murder is either the death penalty (*qisas*) or the payment of *diya* (usually translated as "blood money", but we prefer the term compensatory damages).

Based on the above *hadith*, and some similar transmissions, most classical schools of jurisprudence do not allow capital punishment in the case where a Muslim murders a non-Muslim. The Hanafi school, however, rejects this *hadith* since it contravenes the Quranic teaching prescribed on all People of the Book, that "*wa katabna 'alaihim fihah anna al nafs bil nafs*" ["Thus we have prescribed upon them in that a life for a life…"] (Surah al Maida, 5: 45). The Quran, both in spirit as well as in specific text, lays down that the value of a human soul is intrinsic, and that capital punishment is not dependent upon the professed faith of the victim or the perpetrator in a murder case. A *hadith* which contradicts this basic principle of Quranic justice is therefore not accepted, "despite its sound chain of transmission, because its matn [content] is defective due to disagreeing with a Quranic nass [explicit edict]."[81]

Our potion, both in this specific instance, as well as in general approach, mirrors that espoused by Shaikh al Ghazali in his commentary on this particular issue, "Upon reflection, we see that the Hanafi *fiqh* is closer to justice and to the principles of human rights, and to the respect of human life irrespective of whiteness or blackness, freedom or enslavement, or faith or unbelief."[82]

This same view is espoused by other modern scholars in Islamic law, who find the above *hadith* untenable in view of the spirit of the Quran. Therefore, Muhammad S. El Awa says in his work, *Punishment in Islamic Law: A Comparative Study*, "to limit the infliction of qisas [capital punishment] only to cases involving the killing of a Muslim is contradictory to the principle of the law of qisas itself, as was stated before. This law was made in order to protect human life, and if one imposes such a limitation on it, it is a clear contradiction of its purpose."[83] Furthermore, most modern scholars now agree with the Hanafi point of view over that of the "majority" of classical scholars[84], showing clearly that the interpretation and application of *hadith* can shift over time.

g. Understanding *Hadith* in light of different social conditions

In his book, *How We Should Deal with the Prophetic Sunna*, the modern scholar Yusuf al Qaradawi has a section entitled, "Explicit rulings based on conditions which have changed." In this section, he discusses the need to assess the precise circumstances in which a Prophetic ruling was revealed, and the intent of the ruling, rather than the letter of the rule, should be the guiding principle in juristic rule-making. He offers an example of the limits which the Prophet set on the eligibility to pay *zakat* (i.e., the degree of wealth needed to make someone responsible for paying *zakat*, and the poverty line below which the obligation of *zakat* drops). The Prophet (pbuh) had specified that this should either be either 200 dirham of silver or twenty dinars of gold. At that time, the conversion rate was 10 dirham silver per dinar of gold. Since then, silver has diminished in value vis a vis gold, and so what was a consistent standard as set by the Prophet would no longer be consistent today. Al Qaradawi, therefore, advocates that the standard be made uniform, despite an explicit Prophetic pronouncement detailing the limits for *zakat*. This is because Sheikh al Qaradawi understands that there is nothing sacred about the amount 200 dirham. What is sacred, rather, is that there is a system of social welfare wherein those who have been blessed with more help those who are blessed with less. Hence, al Qaradawi states, "And I have shown in my book *Fiqh al Zakat* that the Prophet (pbuh) did not mean to put two discrepant standards for *zakat*, but rather it is one standard, whomever possesses it is considered wealthy such that *zakat* is incumbent upon him. It was assessed by two monetary standards which were customarily used in the age of Prophet hood, and so the explicit rule came based upon this existing custom, and set the standard according to equivalent monetary units in both systems. So, if the situation has changed in our time and the value of silver has drastically diminished vis a vis the value o gold, we cannot [continue to use the same standard and thus] set a system which is markedly discrepant in the two monetary units."[85]

Therefore, we must recognize that the application of *hadiths* which were based directly upon standards which have changed must also change as well to preserve the intent of the *hadith*.

h. Understanding *hadith* in terms of considerations of social welfare

Of course, whatever pronouncements the Prophet (pbuh) made were directed at enhancing either the welfare of the individual or of the community. Therefore, considerations of social welfare must enter into the interpretation and application of *hadith* if the circumstances under which the Prophet made his pronouncement have changed. This concept was clearly understood by the Prophet's companions, who did not feel that they were violating a *hadith* when they altered its application due to considerations of social welfare. As Yusuf al Qaradawi described, the Companions sometimes "stopped applying the explicit meaning of some *hadiths*, when it became apparent to them that they treated a specific circumstance in the age of the Prophet, but that circumstances had since changed from what they were."[86]

An example is presented for illustration. It concerns the disposition of land which the Muslims acquired during the early expansion of the *umma*. The Prophet set a clear precedent by dividing the lands of Khaybar among the military who conquered it. However, during the age of Caliph Umar, he did not divide a portion of Iraq among the Muslims who entered it, keeping it instead with its owners, who paid the *umma* a tax. This change in policy, although the was a precedent set by the Prophet in a matter of significant importance to the Muslim military, was dictated by considerations of social welfare. The classical commentator Ibn Qudama stated, "the Prophet's division of Khaybar was in the early days of Islam and in a time of great need, and this decision was where society's welfare lay. Thereafter, social welfare lay in not dividing the land, and so such became the requirement."[87]

Similar considerations prompted Caliphs Uthman and Ali to alter the Prophet's directive regarding stray cattle. It is recorded that the Prophet had given instructions that if a stray animal was found, that it was to be left alone and allowed to graze, until its owner retrieved it.

However, in the years following the Prophet's death, social mores deteriorated such that these stray animals were often taken by whoever found them and added to their herds - in effect, stolen. Therefore, in the interest of social welfare, both Uthman and Ali devised different policies which involved the government either housing the cattle, or selling the cattle and earmarking the money for the owner, if they returned to claim their animals. Neither Caliph, apparently, felt hesitation in departing from the Prophet's directive. Apparently, they realized that leaving cattle to graze free, or housing them, or selling them, were not issues of sin or virtue. Rather, whatever policy secures the rights of the owner with regard to his stray cattle is the essence of the Prophet's sunna.[88]

i. Understanding *Hadith* in terms of the original purpose behind the law

This is similar to the above considerations of social welfare, but is an even more broad consideration. It entails attempting to educe the original reasons behind a *hadith*. If these reasons are social or administrative rather than spiritual, then the *hadith* is open to reconsideration in terms of application. Such notions seem to always make Muslims anxious, as there is a feeling that the sunna or the Prophet (pbuh) are not being given their due. However, it is important to realize that this sort of analysis process has been, and continues to be, a legitimate part of Islamic jurisprudence. Once again, an illustrative and important example is provided from Sheikh al Qaradawi's important work in this area, the already cited *Kaif Nata'mal ma'a al-sunna al nabawiyya -- m'alim wa zawabit* (How to deal with the Prophetic Sunna -- Standards and Regulations)] .

We take the well-known *hadith*: "The woman should not travel except in the company of a *mahram* [husband or first degree male relative]." This *hadith* is found in both Sahih Muslim and Sahih al Bukhari, according to al Qaradawi. Despite its sound chain of transmission and its clear meaning, al Qaradawi does not shy away from looking at its intent, rather than insisting that its sound chain and clear meaning imply a permanent juristic rule. As he states, if we imagine travel conditions at that time, through an uncharted desert peopled by marauding tribes, without paved roads, lights, etc., it is easy to see that a woman traveling alone may come to physical harm, whereas a woman traveling through many nights in the company of a man who is not a mahram may come to harm in her reputation. He then goes on to say, "however, if the situation has changed - such as in our day - and travel is now via a plane which carries one hundred people or more or via a train which carries hundreds of travelers, and there is no longer fear for a woman if she travels alone, then there is no onus in terms of sharia upon her if she does this [i.e. there is no problem if she travels alone], and this does not count as contradicting the *hadith*."[89]

Clearly, *hadiths* such as this, when not examined on the basis of intent, can form a corpus of rules which lead, for example, to the oppression of women. Therefore, those who are using *hadith* need to be very cognizant of the critical need for a full analysis -- one which goes well beyond the traditional questions as to whether a *hadith* is *sahih* or not. Once again, Sheikh al Qaradawi, perhaps the leading Islamic scholar of the modern age, expresses these sentiments clearly and succinctly in his brief chapter, *Al sunna bain al-lafz wal rawh aw bain al-zawahir wal maqasid* (The Sunna between its letter and its spirit or between the explicit meaning and the intent): "rigidly holding on to the letter of the sunna is sometimes not an implementation of the spirit of the sunna or its intent but rather a contradiction of it, even if on the surface it is an apparent adherence to it."[90] The reader should also honestly examine what his or her attitude may be to such statements if they came from an "average" Muslim, rather than a renowned scholar. It is safe to say that unfortunately such statements would probably be deemed heresy by many, and would not even merit serious consideration, despite their essential place in *hadith* scholarship.

Different types of *hadith*

Perhaps the most important consideration of all which has been said so far is considered in this section. It overlaps the preceding sections to some degree, but stands independently above them as well, as it outlines the notion that there are many different types of *sunna* (and hadith), many of which are not of a religious nature, and therefore not binding upon the Muslim. This, of course, is another of those heretical notions open to immediate rejection by the many who consider themselves the guardians of the Prophet's legacy from the ignorant or the impious. Therefore, we state at the outset that this discussion is abstracted directly from the already cited textbook, Al Islam: 'Aqeeda wa Shar'ia, by Sheik Mahmud Shaltut, the former grand rector of al Azhar University.[91] A very similar analysis of the different types of *sunna* and *hadith* is found in the already cited textbook, "Principles of Islamic Jurisprudence," by M ohammad Kamali, Professor of Law at the International Islamic University in Malaysia.[92]

According to these sources, the sunna can be divided into two broad types: non-legal *sunna* and legal *sunna*.

A. The non-legal *sunna* (*Sunna ghayr tashri'iyyah*) comprises the actions and sayings of the Prophet which were not part of his role as a Prophet, but rather a simple necessity of his humanness. This large branch of the recorded *sunna*, in fact, does not constitute binding legislation upon the Muslims. It is divided into at least three subtypes.

1. The natural human activities of the Prophet, "such as the manner in which he ate, slept, dressed... Activities of this nature are not of primary importance to the Prophetic mission and therefore do not constitute legal norms. According to the majority of 'ulema, the Prophet's preferences in these areas, such as his favorite colors, or the fact that he slept on his right side in the first place, etc., only indicate the permissibility (*ibahah*) of the acts in question."[93]

2. What relates to empiric knowledge, or personal or social habit or custom. In this category, Sheikh Shaltut places such things as advice in matters of agriculture or medicine and habits of personal dress such as the length or shortness of the Prophet's dress. On this category, Kamali states, "*Sunna* relating to specialized or technical knowledge,

such as medicine, commerce and agriculture, is once again held to be peripheral to the main function of the Prophetic mission and is therefore not part of the *sharia*."[94] We would qualify here, however, that the *hadiths* of the Prophet which lay down general principles on the conduct of business and commerce constitute part of Islamic business ethics, and in the opinion of the authors, should be considered part of the legislative *sunna*.

3. Actions relating to specific circumstances not of a general nature. Such areas would include particular strategies of war, timings of attack or withdrawal, etc., since "these too are considered to be situational and not part of the *sharia*."[95]

To aid the reader in accepting this classification, i.e., that there are issues personal to and specific to the Prophet which do not constitute general legislation for the Muslims, we recollect that there are even portions of his *sunna* which are different than the general legislation for the Muslims, such as "polygamy above the limit of four, marriage without a dower, prohibition of remarriage for the widows of the Prophet [and] connected fasting…"[96]

B. The legal sunna (*Sunna tashri'iyyah*): This is the branch of *sunna* which is meant to establish law. This is further subdivided into two broad categories -- general legislation (i.e. meant for the Muslims until the Day of Judgment) and specific legislation, having to do with specific issues of the *umma* during the Prophet's lifetime. Sheikh Shaltut distinguishes these two broad categories by breaking the legislative *sunna* into three subtypes:

1. The *sunna* arising from the Prophet strictly as a Prophet. The rules which the Prophet lays down in his capacity as Messenger of God, such as rules explaining or complementing the Quran, are general guidance to the Believers valid and honored until the Day of Judgement. Thus, "[w]hatever the Prophet has authorized pertaining to the principles of religion, especially in the areas of devotional matters (*'ibadat* [acts of worship]) and rules expounding the lawful and the unlawful, that is the *halal* and *haram*, constitutes general legislation (*tashri' 'amm*)

whose validity is not restricted by the limitations of time and circumstance. All commands and prohibitions that are imposed by the Sunna are binding on every Muslim regardless of individual circumstances, social status, or political office. In acting upon these laws, the individual normally does not need any prior authorization by a religious leader or the government."[97]

2. The *sunna* arising from the Prophet in his capacity as the governor or Imam of the Muslims. Examples of this are sending the military into battle, spending the state's revenue, dividing the spoils of war, signing treaties, appointing judges and officials, "and such other things having to do with governance and public administration for the welfare of the community."[98] Such *sunna* does not constitute general legislation, but rather defines the sphere of things which should be decided by the government. In the opinion of many scholars, therefore, the individual Muslim is not allowed to follow such decisions without the express permission of the Imam (i.e. without legal authorization) on the pretext that the Prophet did or said a similar thing.[99]

It is important to clarify that this sort of distinction, between the different roles which the Prophet played, and therefore, the correspondingly different types of *sunna* arising from each, is not an invention of modern scholars, but is a long-held classical doctrine. Therefore, al-Qarafi wrote in his work *Kitab al Furuq* regarding the sunna coming from the Prophet in his role as Messenger of God that whatever he stipulated in this sphere "becomes a general rule for everyone to whom it is addressed until the day of resurrection, and everyone must act directly, be it an obligation, a prohibition or even an *ibada*. But everything the Prophet has authorized in his capacity as Imam, it is not permissible for anyone to act upon it without obtaining a prior authorization of the Imam, because the Prophet himself acted in that capacity and it would be in keeping with his example to follow the same."[100]

To see the importance of this distinction, we return to the previously quoted *hadith*, "Whoever cultivates barren land becomes its owner."[101] This decision is not a moral or spiritual decision taken by the Prophet as Messenger of God, but rather an administrative policy decision taken by the Prophet in his capacity as the political leader and Imam of the Muslims. Therefore, it would not be lawful for a Muslim to cultivate barren land and then claim ownership of it by "squatter's rights" on the basis of this *hadith*, as the *hadith* was not expounded in the capacity of general legislative *sunna*. Rather, what can be taken from this *hadith* is that the issue of disposition of uninhabited land is a legislative decision which needs to be made by the ruling political authority.

However, this analysis hinges on the classification of the *hadith*. If it classified as a law of God revealed through the Prophet as God's Messenger, then of course it is binding in general, and any Muslim who cultivates barren land may claim it as his own, without or even against, the permission of the ruling authority. However, if the *hadith* is classified, as we have done, as a decision of the Prophet arising as Imam rather than Messenger, then the disposition of the issue if as we have stated above. It is interesting to note that in the classical books of *fiqh*, most of the juristic schools have favored the former opinion, while only Abu Hanifa has taken the latter position, i.e., that this is an administrative decision. We believe that the change of circumstances, as discussed previously regarding this *hadith*, indicate that the Hanafi position is the stronger of the two.

In any case, regardless of the disposition of this particular issue, it is clear that the distinction between the two types of legislative *sunna* is a genuine and well-recognized one. The first of these (classified under category I above) is general and binding, while the second (classified under category II above) does not constitute general legislation.

3. The *sunna* arising from the Prophet as Judge. This is yet a third type of legislative *sunna*, connected with the Prophet's role as the judicial authority of the Muslim *umma*. Like the previous category, "this does not constitute general legislation."[102] Thus, as Sheikh Shaltut explains, when the Prophet (pbuh) adjudicated a case, the specific judg-

ment which he rendered does not constitute general legislation binding upon the Muslims in its specific form. That is because the specific ruling may have to do with the specific details of the case, and may not translate directly to all times and places. Rather, when the Prophet adjudicated an issue, this is taken as an indication that such an issue needs to go before the court in its settlement (i.e., is justiciable and should be adjudicated), and that a Muslim cannot decide on his or her own to settle the issue outside the scope of the judicial system.

Once again, a specific example is examined to clarify the issue. A case came before the Prophet regarding a woman named Hind, who was the wife of Abu Sufyan. Hind complained to the Prophet that her husband was stingy and that despite his wealth, he did not provide sufficiently for her and her child. The Prophet instructed her, "take [of your husband's possessions] what is sufficient for yourself and your child according to customary standards." (this *hadith* is quoted by both Shaltut and Kamali in the sections cited above). There has been some debate by the *ulema* as to whether the Prophet, via this *hadith* was enacting a general rule of law, "or whether he was acting in the capacity of a judge. Were it admitted that the *hadith* consists of a judgement addressing a particular case, then it would only authorize the judge to issue a corresponding order. Thus it would be unlawful for a creditor to take his entitlement from the the property of his debtor without a judicial order. If it were established, on the other hand, that the *hadith* lays down a general rule of law, then no adjudication would be required to entitle the wife or the creditor to the property of the defaulting debtor, as the *hadith* itself would provide the necessary authority."[103]

Clearly, the ramifications of the classification of this *hadith* are enormous both in business law as well as in family law. Since the issue itself is outside the scope of this chapter, we note only that it underscores that judicial *sunna* exists and is not considered a source of general legislation, and that the distinction between a judicial *sunna* and a legislative *sunna* often has enormous implications. For this issue itself, we note only that "the *ulema* have generally considered the *hadith* under consideration to consist of a judicial decision of the Prophet, and as such it only authorizes the judge to adjudicate the wife's complaint and to specify the quantity of maintenance and the method of its payment."[104]

C. Some Preliminary Conclusions

Sheikh Shaltut underscores the importance of understanding that there are different types of *sunna* as follows: "Therefore it is extremely useful to know in what capacity an action [i.e. a Prophetic *sunna*] arises, and this is often hidden in what is transmitted from the Prophet (pbuh). [The action] is looked at only in terms that the Prophet did it, or said it, or countenanced it. And from this we find that much of what is transmitted from the Prophet (pbuh) is portrayed as *sharia* or religion, and *sunna* or commendable acts, when it reality it was not originally propounded by way of rule-making (*tashri'*). And this has become so in many of the actions emanating from him (pbuh) by virtue of his humanness or from habit or empiric knowledge. And we find also that some of which came as part of political leadership or judicial authority, may [instead] be taken as general legislation, and from this there is distortion of rulings and confusion of directions."[105]

Thus, we see that of all of the different classifications of *sunna*, only one is meant to offer general binding legislation upon the Muslims, as described in section B (I) above. Sheikh Shaltut further subclassifies this type of general legislative *sunna*, meant to be a permanent guidance to the Muslims into the different areas with which it deals. The only part of this distinction we wish to stress is that much of the Prophet's guidance as Messenger of God had to do with manners (*al akhlaq or al adab*) rather than laws, and there should also not be confusion between *hadiths* of law and *hadiths* of manners.[106] Professor Abou El Fadl elucidates the importance of this distinction stating that "[a] specific system of analysis pertains to each category and one must be very careful not to jump from one category to the other without clear and persuasive evidence. For example, a *sunna* relating to *adab* cannot be used, by itself, to support an imperative ruling on *'ibadat* [acts of worship] or mu'amalat [dealings]."[107]

As an example, let us consider the *hadith* reported in the collection of Abu Dawood, reporting that the Prophet said, "Any woman who asks her husband for a divorce without suffering hardship will not enter heaven." This *hadith*, if interpreted as a legal injunction, would have very serious social implications regarding a woman's right to divorce. If she has not suffered significantly, a judge would not grant her a divorce. Thus, such an interpretation "would seem to negate the Islamic legal procedure of *khul'* in which a wife returns her dowry or abandons financial claims in return for a no cause divorce."[108] There is strong evidence to suggest that this *hadith* is, in fact, a manners *hadith*, advising women not to take marriage lightly or rush hastily into a decision of divorce. The evidence for this is the *hadith* in Sahih al Bukhari establishing the right of *khul'* as described above. As narrated by Ibn Abbas, the wife of Thabit ibn Qais came to the Prophet (pbuh) and said, "O God's Messenger, I do not accuse Thabit of any defects in his character or his religion, but I would dislike to behave in an un-Islamic manner (if I remain with him). On hearing that, the Prophet said to her, "Will you give back the garden which he has given you (as dowry)?" She said, "Yes." The Prophet said, "O Thabit, accept your garden and divorce her once." (Sahih al Bukhari, *the Book of Khul'*). In this case, the wife of Thabit simply disliked him, and was granted a divorce on those grounds alone, although she had stipulated that she could not fault him in his manners or religion, indicating no significant suffering at his hands. This *hadith* is found in a stronger *hadith* book, and is accepted as a legal injunction establishing for women the right of *Khul'*.

Conclusion

Authenticating, analyzing and properly applying *hadith* is a vast field of Islamic scholarship. We have hoped to show that the question, "Is this *hadith* sahih?", if answered in the affirmative, should be the beginning and not the end of the inquiry on how to understand and apply the *hadith*. Far too many pious scholars, who love the Prophet (pbuh) and revere his legacy, have expended their lives in the study of his *sunna* for these efforts to be trivialized by a superficial approach to *hadith*. Those who wield *hadith* like a club to bludgeon their opponents in Islamic discourses have missed the wisdom and richness of the Prophet's example, and have dishonored the sincere efforts of those who have attempted to understand his path and follow in his footsteps (pbuh) among so many of the generations past.

For those who seek a serious understanding of the sunna, we close with the words of Sheikh Yusuf al Qaradawi in his epilogue to his book on the Prophetic sunna, "The *sunna* is in need of new explanatory works to bring forth its truths and clarify what is unclear and to correct the collective understanding and to rebut the falsehoods, written in their current language and the paradigm of this age. The Quran has garnered in our age, as is its right, the [attention of] great scholars, who have devoted themselves to its *tafsir* (interpretation) and the bringing forth of its gems and essence, addressing the modern mind, with what has been made available to them of [new] facts and knowledge, allowing them to enter the minds and the hearts from the widest of doors. We have seen this in the tafsirs of Muhammad Rashid Rida, Jamal al Din al Qasimi, Al Tahir ibn 'Ashur, Abi al'Ala Al Maududi, Sayyid Qutb and Mahmud Shaltut and others. The books of *sunna*, and particularly the two Sahihs, have not had explanatory works from the likes of these giants who combine authenticity and modernization... and hopefully God will inspire some of the great expositors to write works of commentary and explanation of the Sahihs of the two shaikhs Bukhari and Muslim, a contemporary scholarly explanation. In this way, Islamic scholarship will be served a great service. And the last of our supplications is All Praise be to God, the Lord of the Worlds."

Footnotes

1 Yusuf al-Qaradawi, *Al Sahwa al Islamia baina al Juhud wal Tattaruf* (The Islamic Resurgence between Unbelief and Extremism),

Umma Books, pp. 29-30.

2   Mohammad Kamali, *Principles of Islamic Jurisprudence, The Islamic Texts Society Publishers*, Cambridge, UK, 2003, p. 58.

3   Quoted in the *hadith* collection, Sunan of Abu Dawood, hadith no. 3585.

4   Ibn al Qayyim al Juziyyah, *I'lam al-Muwaqqi'in, 'an Rabb al-'Alamain*. Ed. Muhammad Munir al-Dimashqi. Cairo, n.d., I, 222.

5   Kamali, op.cit., p. 60.

6   Mahmud Shaltut, *Islam 'Aqeeda wa Sharia*, Dar al Shuruq press, Cairo, n.d., p. 494.

7   Shaltut, op. cit., p. 495-496

8   'Abdur Rahman Doi, *Shariah: The Islamic Law*. Ta Ha publishers, United Kingdom,1997; see chapter 3, "The Sunna: Second Primary Source of Shari'ah".

9   Muhammad Sidiqqi, *Hadith Literature: Its Origin, Development and Special Features*. The Islamic Texts Society, Cambridge, 1993, p.6.

10   Muhammad Azami, *Studies in Hadith Methodology and Literature*, American Trust Publications, Plainfield, Indiana, 1992, p. 13.

11   Kamali, op. cit., p. 77; Badran Abu al'Aynayn Badran, *Usul al Fiqh al Islami*, Mu'assasah Shabab al Jami'ah, Alexandria, Egypt, pp. 83-84.

12   Azami, op. cit., p. 29.

13   Azami, op. cit., p. 26.

14   (These numbers are taken from ibn Al-Jawzi's *Talqih Fuhum Ahl al-Athar*, and quoted in Muhammad Zubayr Siddiqi, *Hadith Literature: Its Origin, Development and Special Features*, Islamic Texts Society, Cambridge, 1993, p. 15-19.

15   (This issue is explored at length by Professor Muhammad Azami in his book, *Studies in Early Hadith Literature*, American Trust Publications, Indianapolis, Indiana, 1978, "Writings of the Companions", pp. 34-60. It is noted that this book is distinct from his shorter work, *Studies in Hadith Methodology and Literature*.

16   Azami, *Studies in Hadith Methodology and Literature*, op. cit., p.26.

17   Kamali, op. cit., p. 87; see also Siddiqi, op. cit., p. 31, "All the Islamic authorities agree that an enormous amount of forgery was committed in the hadith literature".

18   (One of the best known of these works is by the scholar al Shaukani, *al-Fawai'd al-Majmu'ah Fi al-Ahadith al Maudu'ah*.

19   Kamali, p. 89.

20   Kamali, op. cit., p. 88.

21   Siddiqi, op. cit., p. 33; a classical source which gives many of these examples is Ibn Hajar al 'Asqalani, Lisan al-Mizan.

22   Siddiqi, op. cit., p. 33. See also Ibn al-Jawzi, *al-Mawdu'at*; ed. 'Abd al Rahman Uthman, Medina, pp. 1386-1389.

23   Siddiqi, op. cit., p. 34.

24   Siddiqi, op. cit., p. 35.

25   Siddiqi, op. cit., p. 36.

26   See Mahmud Shaltut, *Al Islam: 'Aqeeda wa Sharia*, in his chapter heading, "The Rarity of the Mutawatir".

27   Azami, *Studies in Hadith Methodology*, op. cit., p. 54.

28   See *Studies in Early Hadith Literature*.

29   Suyuti, Jalal al Din, *Tdrib al-Rawi [The Training of the Hadith Transmitter]*, a quoted in Siddiqi, op. cit., p. 83.

30   Siddiqi, op. cit., p. 109.

31   Azami, *Studies in Hadith Methodology*, op. cit. p. 58.

32   Sahih al Bukhari, *The Book of Faith*, chapter 2.

33   Siddiqi, op. cit., p. 113.

34   Al Ghazali, op. cit., p. 19.

35   Suyuti, *Tadrib al Rawi, The Training of the Hadith Narrator*, op. cit., quoted in Siddiqi, op. cit., p. 113.

36   Siddiqi, op. cit., p. 113.

37   Al Ghazali, op. cit., p. 29.

38   This objection is quoted in Siddiqi, op. cit., p. 115.

39   Siddiqi, op. cit., p. 115.

40   This is discussed in Yusuf al Qaradawi, *Kaif Nat'amal ma' al Sunna al Nabawiya [How We Should Deal With the Prophetic Sunna]*, published by al Ma'had al 'Alami lil Fikr al Islami, n.d., p. 42.

41   Abdur Rahman Doi, *Shari'ah: The Islamic Law*, Ta Ha Publishers, London, 1197, p.55.

42   The reader is referred to an excellent article, "An introduction to the Science of Hadith", found on the Internet at IslamicAwakenings.com.

43   For an excellent discussion of the various opinions, see "An Introduction to the Science of Hadith",

IslamicAwakenings.com, op. cit.

44 Al Khatib al Baghdadi, *Al-Kifayah fi Ilm al Riwayah [The Sufficient in the Science of Narration].*

45 "An Introduction to the Sciences of Hadith", op. cit.

46 Azami, *Studies in hadith Methodology,* op. cit., p. 43.

47 Shaltut, *al Islam: Aqeeda was Shari'a,* p. 61.

48 Shaltut, op. cit., p. 62.

49 Kamali, *Principles of Islamic Jurisprudence,* op. cit., p. 94.

50 Kamali, op. cit., p. 78.

51 Kamali, op. cit., p. 96.

52 Kamali, op. cit., p. 95.

53 Discussion based on material in Azami, *Studies in Hadith Methodology,* op. cit., p. 62.

54 Azami, op. cit., p. 63.

55 Al Hakim, *Ma'rifa 'Ulum al Hadith;* Suyuti, Tadrib al rawi; quoted in Siddiqi, op. cit., p. 113.

56 *Al Sunna al Nabawyia bain Ahl al Fiqh wa Ahl al Hadith [The Prophetic Sunna between Scholars of Fiqh and the Scholars of Hadith],* Dar al Shuruq, Cairo, p. 21.

57 Quoted from "An introduction to the Sciences of Hadith", op. cit., who quote from Al Dhahabi, *Talkhis al Mustadrak* [a commentary on the Mustadrak of al Hakim].

58 Siddiqi, op. cit., p. 58.

59 Siddiqi, op. cit., p. 58. Siddiqi gives the relevant footnotes in his text.

60 The hadith and these commentaries are found in 'Abd al Haleem Abu Shakka, *Tahrir al Mar'a fi 'Asr al Risalah [Emancipation of Women in the Age of the Prophethood],* Dar al Qalam Publishers, Kuwait, 1990, pp. 5-25.

61 Qastallani, Ahmad, *Irshad al Sari ila Sahih al Bukhari [Guiding the Seeker of Sahih al Bukhari],* and Suyuti, Tadrib al Rawi, op. cit.; quoted in Siddiqi, op. cit., p. 57.

62 Kamali, op. cit., p. 111.

63 Al Qaradawi, op. cit., p. 34.

64 Al Qaradawi, op. cit., p. 35.

65 "An Introduction to the Science of Hadith", IslamicAwakenings.com, op. cit.

66 Reported in Muhammad al Tabrizi, *Mishkat al Masabih,* hadith 533.

67 Kamali, op. cit., p. 96.

68 Kamali, op. cit., p. 97.

69 Kamali, op. cit., p. 98.

70 Kamali, op. cit., p. 97.

71 Kamali, op. cit., p. 97; Sayf al Din al Amidi, *al Ihkam fi Usul al Ahkam,* Al Maktab al Islami, Beirut, 1982, I, p. 161.

72 Kamali, op. cit., p. 103; see also Al Ghazali, op. cit., p. 25.

73 Kamali, op. cit., p. 102.

74 Tabrizi, *Mishkat al Masabih,* op. cit., hadith 319.

75 Shaltut, op. cit., p. 60; Kamali, op. cit., p. 98.

76 See the sections entitled, "The Quran and the Sunna Distinguished", and "The Priority of the Quran over the sunna" in Kamali, *Principles of Islamic Jurisprudence,* op. cit., pp. 77-87.

77 Al Shafi'is Al-Risalah, quoted by Muhammad Abu Zahrah, *Usul al-Fiqh [The Principles of Islamic Jurisprudence],*

Dar al Fikr al Arabi Publishers, Cairo, , 1958, p. 82.

78 This view is expressed by al Shatibi in the *Muwaffaqat,* and cited by Kamail, op. cit., p. 85.

79 Al Ghazali, op. cit., p. 25.

80 Quoted in *Fiqh al Sunna,* by Al Sayyid Sabbiq, Dar al Kitab al Arabi Publishers, Beirut, 1973; volume 2, p. 445.

81 Al Ghazali, op. cit., p. 24-25.

82 Al Ghazali, op. cit., p. 25.

83 Muhammad S. El-Awa, *Punishment in Islamic Law: A Comparative Study,* American trust Publications, Indianapolis, Indiana, 1993; p. 79.

84 El-Awa, op. cit., p. 80.

85 Al Qaradawi, op. cit., p. 133.

86 Al Qaradawi, op. cit. p. 130.

87 Cited by al Qaradawi, op. cit., p. 131.

88 See al Qaradawi, op. cit., p. 131.

89 Al Qaradawi, op. cit., p. 129.

90 Al Qaradawi, op. cit., p. 135.

91 See Shaltut, op. cit., p. 499-505.

92 See Kamali, op. cit., pp. 65-77.

93 Kamali, op. cit., p. 67.

94 Kamali, op. cit., p. 67.

95 Kamali, op. cit., p. 67.

96 Kamaili, op. cit., p. 68.

97 Kamali, op. cit., p. 69.

98 Shaltut, op. cit., p. 500.

99 Shaltut, op. cit., p. 500.

100 Shihab al-Din al-Qarafi, *Kitab al Furuq.* Dar al Kutub al 'Arabiyyah, 1346 AH, Cairo, I, pp. 205-209).

101 Reported in the Sunan of Abu Dawud.

102 Shaltut, op. cit., p. 501.

103 Kamali, op. cit., p. 74.

104 Kamali, op. cit., p. 75.

105 Shaltut, op. cit., p. 501.

106 Shaltut, op. cit., p. 504.

107 Khaled Abou El Fadl, *The Authoritative and Authoritarian in Islamic Discourses: A Case Study of a Contemporary Fatwa;*
MVI Publishers, Los Angeles, First Edition, 1997, p. 39.

108 Abou El Fadl, *The Authoritative and Authoritarian in Islamic Discourses: A Case Study of a Contemporary Fatwa; ,* op. cit., p. 58.

Index

Satan
112, 118, 157, 165, 237-238, 243

Saudi Arabia
xvi, 187, 191, 198, 301, 305, 343, 347, 359, 457

Shafi'i
6, 48, 120, 284, 438, 441

Sharia (Islamic law)
23-25, 27, 29, 32, 43, 44, 46-47, 49, 52, 57, 65, 72-73, 89, 107, 122-123, 127, 146, 157, 171, 173, 206, 222, 247, 259, 261, 263-264, 303-305, 325, 329, 341, 366, 377-379, 386, 391, 396, 402, 417, 426, 463, 469, 471

Shi'a
xiii-xiv, xxiii

Shura (Mutual consultation)
56, 78, 80, 82, 282, 389

Sin
5, 8, 13, 73, 75, 87-89, 95, 103-104, 112, 122, 127, 13, 157, 164, 174-175, 178, 184, 188, 190, 237, 245, 312, 317, 386, 397, 404, 406, 468

Slavery
xii, 199, 272, 313, 326, 343-360

Social services
363-376

Solomon
12, 21, 22, 308

Suicide
85-86, 103-108

Sunna (Prophetic example)
xxiii, 26, 120, 133, 196, 203, 217, 243, 244, 336, 391, 407, 413, 414, 422-427, 431, 436-437, 442, 445, 449, 453, 459, 460, 463-466, 469-477

Sunni
xiii-xv, 48, 61, 64-65, 73, 120, 159, 283-284, 318, 461

Syria
ix, xiii, xv, 79, 124, 183, 216, 296, 305, 367, 439, 462

Taliban
xvi, 61, 198

Tolerance
133, 139, 142, 144, 146, 147, 151, 160, 217, 262, 285

Torture
329, 339

Treaty of Khaybar
201, 214, 220, 235, 468

Tunisia
304, 347

Turkey
201, 341, 347

Ulema
243, 284, 426, 434, 458, 460, 461, 464, 471, 475

Umar ibn al Khattab
xiii, 8, 11, 13, 15, 25, 47, 64-65, 76, 79-80, 124-125, 48-51, 177, 190, 196, 211, 215, 220, 236, 295, 323, 339, 340, 348, 350, 367-369, 407, 423, 429-433, 436-437, 442, 444, 468

Umma (Community)
34, 36, 38, 45, 63, 64, 112, 127, 129, 142, 148, 157, 210, 219, 258, 264, 300, 378, 386, 389, 433, 436, 445, 454, 457, 458, 468, 472, 474

Usury (*Riba*)
19, 237, 241, 243-246, 253

Uthman
64, 76, 198, 368, 433, 444, 468

Voting
31, 44, 256, 265, 278

Wealth
ix, 20, 23, 118, 168, 169, 171, 182, 217, 225, 227-229, 231-232, 234, 248-253, 310-311, 332, 334, 347, 365-366, 370-371, 399, 466, 474

Women
x, xix, 10, 15, 32, 50, 74, 75, 77, 94, 123, 161-198, 207, 213, 217, 231, 261, 274, 280, 287, 290, 299, 317, 329, 334-341, 343, 357-359, 364, 368, 375, 391, 394, 397, 399, 400-406, 414, 417, 470, 476-477

Yathrib
xi, 33, 34, 37-39, 210, 265-266

Yusuf al-Qaradawi
457, 466-470, 477

Zakat (Almsgiving)
18, 152, 213, 229, 231, 240, 248, 251-253, 355, 365, 437, 442, 466-467

About MPAC

he Muslim Public Affairs Council is a public service agency working for the civil rights of American Muslims, for the integration of Islam into American pluralism, and for a positive, constructive relationship between American Muslims and their representatives. Since 1988, MPAC has worked diligently to promote a vibrant American Muslim community and enrich American society through exemplifying the Islamic values of Mercy, Justice, Peace, Human Dignity, Freedom, and Equality for all. Over the years, MPAC has built a reputation as a consistent and reliable resource for government and media, and is trusted by American Muslims as an authentic, experienced voice.

The Mission of MPAC encompasses promoting an American Muslim identity, fostering an effective grassroots organization, and training a future generation of men and women to share our vision. MPAC also works to promote an accurate portrayal of Islam and Muslims in mass media and popular culture, educating the American public (both Muslim and non-Muslim) about Islam, building alliances with diverse communities and cultivating relationships with opinion- and decision-makers.

The Washington D.C. office of the Muslim Public Affairs Council aims to establish a reputation for partnership with public officials and their staff to offer intelligent and nuanced analysis of domestic and foreign policy issues that affect American Muslims. MPAC also works with government to attempt to solve systemic complications facing

American Muslims which have been exacerbated in a 9/11 context. MPAC believes that the investment of resources to dispelling myths about Islam and Muslims is most needed for those who serve our country in government.

MPAC provides expertise and access to opinion leaders to national news media through briefings with reporters and meetings with editors. MPAC's work is regularly featured in national broadcast and print media, including the New York Times, the Washington Post, Associated Press, Los Angeles Times, CNN, MSNBC, and ABC World News Tonight.

Throughout the country, MPAC leaders also train activists in interacting with the media, public speaking, defending Islam against attacks, and engaging with government officials and law enforcement. MPAC believes that empowering the community means equipping individuals with the skills and knowledge necessary to be effective representatives of Islam and American Muslims.

In all its actions, MPAC works diligently to offer the public a portrayal that goes beyond stereotypes in order to elucidate that Muslims worship God, abhor global terrorism, stand against oppression, and are part of a vibrant American pluralism. MPAC operates on the core belief that change in U.S. policy requires more from our community than attending meetings. It requires organized, sustained efforts in coalition with like-minded groups both at the grassroots and national levels. It requires a strong voice in the media, thoughtful analysis and authentic dialogue.

About the Author

aher Hathout is a retired physician best known for his tireless commitment to public service for the American Muslim community. An internationally recognized voice on Islam, Dr. Hathout offers a unique and valuable perspective on national and international issues involving Muslims. In addition to serving at the Senior Advisor to the Muslim Public Affairs Council, he is also a Charter Member of the Pacific Council on International Policy — the western partner of the Council on Foreign Relations — and sits on the Board of Directors of the Interfaith Alliance.

Dr. Hathout has been invited to Capitol Hill and the State Department several times to address a variety of topics such as "Islam and U.S. Policy," "Islamic Democracy," "Emerging Trends in Islamic Movements," and "the Future of the Middle East." He has traveled to Australia, Egypt, Kuwait, Malaysia, Pakistan, and South Africa to lecture on Islam and Muslims. He has written extensively on Islam, human rights, democracy, Middle East politics, and Bosnia. His articles and interviews have appeared in such prominent newspapers as *The Los Angeles Times, The New York Times, The Wall Street Journal* and *The Christian Science Monitor*. He also appears frequently on national television and radio talk shows.